NEW DIRECTIONS IN GERMAN STUDIES
Vol. 3

Series Editor:
Imke Meyer

Editorial Board:

Katherine Arens, Roswitha Burwick Richard Eldridge, Erika Fischer-Lichte, Catriona MacLeod, Jens Rieckmann, Stephan Schindler, Heidi Schlipphacke, Ulrich Schönherr, James A. Schultz, Silke-Maria Weineck, David Wellbery, Sabine Wilke, John Zilcosky.

New Directions in German Studies

Volumes in the series:

Improvisation as Art: Conceptual Challenges, Historical Perspectives
by Edgar Landgraf

The German Pícaro and Modernity: Between Underdog and Shape-Shifter
by Bernhard Malkmus

Citation and Precedent: Conjunctions and Disjunctions of German Law and Literature
by Thomas O. Beebee

Beyond Discontent: 'Sublimation' from Goethe to Lacan
by Eckart Goebel

From Kafka to Sebald: Modernism and Narrative Form
edited by Sabine Wilke

Image in Outline: Reading Lou Andreas-Salomé
by Gisela Brinker-Gabler

Out of Place: German Realism, Displacement, and Modernity
by John B. Lyon

Thomas Mann in English: A Study in Literary Translation
by David Horton

Vienna's Dreams of Europe: Culture and Identity beyond the Nation-State
by Katherine Arens

Citation and Precedent

Conjunctions and Disjunctions of German Law and Literature

Thomas O. Beebee

BLOOMSBURY
NEW YORK • LONDON • NEW DELHI • SYDNEY

Bloomsbury Academic
An imprint of Bloomsbury Publishing Inc

1385 Broadway	50 Bedford Square
New York	London
NY 10018	WC1B 3DP
USA	UK

www.bloomsbury.com

Bloomsbury is a registered trade mark of Bloomsbury Publishing Plc

First published 2011 by Continuum International Publishing Group
Paperback edition first published 2014

© Thomas O. Beebee, 2011, 2014

All rights reserved. No part of this publication may be reproduced or transmitted in any form or by any means, electronic or mechanical, including photocopying, recording, or any information storage or retrieval system, without prior permission in writing from the publishers.

No responsibility for loss caused to any individual or organization acting on or refraining from action as a result of the material in this publication can be accepted by Bloomsbury or the author.

Library of Congress Cataloging-in-Publication Data
A catalog record for this book is available from the Library of Congress.

ISBN: HB: 978-1-4411-1790-8
PB: 978-1-6289-2124-3
ePub: 978-1-4411-6937-2
ePDF: 978-1-4411-5580-1

Typeset by Fakenham Prepress Solutions, Fakenham, Norfolk NR21 8NN

Contents

	Acknowledgments	vii
1.1	Introduction: Citation and Precedent, Conjunction and Disjunction	1
1.2	Subsystem or Public Sphere?	22
2.1	In Search of the Invisible Precedent: Grimm Writes to Savigny	44
2.2	Kant, Codification, and Goethe's *Elective Affinities*	64
3.1	A Recursive Process: Kafka's Law – and Ours	86
3.2	Citing the Weimar Constitution	110
3.3	From Schiller to *Schund*: *Zensur* and the Canonization of Literature	138
3.4	German Literature Fights for its Rights: A Thick Description of an Incident of Weimar Literary Culture	162
4.1	Carl Schmitt and/as Benito Cereno	191
4.2	Citation as Second-Order Observation: Peter Weiss's *The Investigation*	216
	Conclusion	242
	Works Cited	249
	Index	267

Acknowledgments

Numerous colleagues and other friends and neighbours contributed to the making of this book, the contents and ideas of which go back several decades. This study is dedicated to the memory of Roberta Kevelson, semiotician and legal scholar extraordinaire, whose boundless energy, goodwill, sharp insights and hard work created many meetings of the minds at various roundtables on Law and Semiotics, where I learned to live on coffee alone, and presented preliminary versions of some of the work included here. The provocations, suggestions and encouragement of participants at those roundtables, most especially of William Pencak, Philip Mosley, Peter Goodrich and Bernard Jackson, are fondly remembered and greatly appreciated.

Some of the basic ideas of this book when it was at an advanced stage were presented at the Law and Humanities Conference hosted by the John Jay College of Criminal Justice in Manhattan. I appreciate Andrew Majeske's tireless, professional and yet always cheerful efforts in organizing that conference, and in shepherding the subsequent special issue of the journal *Law and Literature* into print, where I took a few ideas of Luhmann for a test run.

Thanks to Sinkwan Cheng, Jay Mootz, David Pan, William Rasch and Jessica Silbey for their interest, suggestions and support on numerous occasions and in a variety of contexts.

The resources of two German institutions were especially important to the completion of this book. The holdings of the Max-Planck Institute for European Legal History (Max-Planck Institut für Europäische Rechtsgeschichte) were invaluable to my research, and I express here my gratitude for the hospitality and generosity of the directory and staff, and beyond that especially to the Institute director Michael Stolleis and to Heinz Mohnhaupt for their generous sharing of scholarly ideas. Another Frankfurt am Main institution that was of great help in my research was the Fritz Bauer Institute, named in memory of the late attorney-general of the state of Hessen who was the driving force behind the Frankfurt Auschwitz trials, and dedicated to the investigation of the history and impact of the Holocaust. My thanks here to the staff and directorate of that archive, and especially to Werner Renz.

This study benefited greatly from the observations and suggestions of a knowledgeable reader: Andreas Gailus of the University of Michigan; I am grateful to him for making this a much better book. Thanks as well to Imke Meyer for editing the *New Directions in German Studies* book series in which this work appears, and for welcoming me onto its list.

Finally, Ariane Audet and Michael DiRaimo were of great help in the preparation of the manuscript for publication, and Haaris Naqvi, acquisitions editor at Bloomsbury, remained helpful, patient and interested through the long process of review and rewriting.

Portions of Chapters 1.1 and 1.2 appeared in the article 'Can Law and Humanities Survive Systems Theory?', *Law and Literature* 22.2 (Summer 2010), 244–68; portions of Chapter 3.1 appeared in the essay 'Kafka's Law: A Recursive Definition' in the *Kennesaw Review* 2.1 (Fall 1989), 39–54; portions of Chapter 4.1 appeared in the essay 'Carl Schmitt and the Myth of Benito Cereno' in *seminar* 42.2 (May 2006), 114–35. Permission to reproduce material from these journals is gratefully acknowledged.

1.1
Introduction: Citation and Precedent, Conjunction and Disjunction

A sort of stain marks someone who leaves one field of study for the other, as with a religious conversion.
[Eine Art von Makel liegt auf dem, der von einer Wissenschaft ab, zu einer andern übertritt, wie bei einer Religionsveränderung.]
Jacob Grimm, Letter to Friedrich Carl von Savigny, 9 March 1807

But since history affords an idea of the fundamental *citability* of its object, this object must present itself, in its ultimate form, as a moment of humanity.
[Indem die Geschichte aber von der grundsätzlichen Zitierbarkeit ihres Gegenstandes einen Begriff gibt, muss derselbe in seiner höchsten Fassung sich als ein Augenblick der Menschheit darbieten.]
Walter Benjamin, Paralipomena to 'On the Concept of History'
(emphasis added)

The conjunctions and disjunctions between German law and German literature occur on at least two levels. One is seen in the personal and apologetic farewell Jacob Grimm bids to his law teacher, Friedrich Carl von Savigny, as Grimm goes off to seek a paying position, one that will allow him enough latitude to continue his studies in literature and philology that will result in the famous *Hausmärchen* (fairy tale) collection and in the great dictionary and grammar of the German language. The other disjunction occurs on the impersonal level of system – literature and law have trouble 'talking' to each other, analogous to the way German and English languages do. I invoke the 'disjunction' between German and English in particular because of the common roots of the two languages. Just as one has imagined a single, originary language trunk from which the branches of German and English emerge, so too one might invoke – as Giambattista Vico, Friedrich Schiller, Karl Marx, Ferdinand Tönnies and Max Weber all were intent on doing – a primal community ('Gemeinschaft') where to be a poet was also to be a lawyer and a legislator. (Indeed, Jacob Grimm will conjoin his literary studies with the law once more when he publishes in 1828 the *Deutsche Rechtsaltertümer*, a collection of citations from medieval legal texts that invoke a world where law was poetry, before the disciplinary divisions invoked in the epigraph.)

Perhaps such non-specialized cultures actually exist or formerly existed, or perhaps they are merely, as Benjamin suggests in the second epigraph, citations of a perceived moment of humanity. The long list of instances where German literature cites law, or vice versa, or where German law serves literature as a precedent, signal the dream of German culture for a unity of interests and objectives between spheres of activity and for a mutual influence on each other of autonomous subsystems of society. Yet in dialectical fashion, the very vitality of this dream stems from real historical and social processes that increasingly and respectively autonomize the two social subsystems and separate them from each other.

Few Western cultures have had more of their leading literary figures trained in the law than have the German-speaking countries: the list includes Johann Wolfgang von Goethe, Jacob and Wilhelm Grimm, E. T. A. Hoffmann, Heinrich von Kleist, Franz Kafka and Bernhard Schlink. Several of these 'Dichterjuristen' (poet-lawyers) are treated in the pages that follow. It is important to understand as well, however, the activities of people of another kind: of writers not trained as lawyers who cite legal texts, as Peter Weiss did in his drama *Die Ermittlung* (The Investigation); of the German politicians who attempt to save *belles lettres* from the tidal wave of *Schund* (pulp fiction) in the early twentieth century; or of the audience members who sue theatres over the improper production of classics in the early twenty-first. In such efforts we see the opposite of Grimm's farewell to law, a vigorous effort at conjunction and a utopian belief that it can be brought about.

One technical name for the conjunction of law and literature is a 'structural coupling'. According to system theory (hereinafter 'ST'), which will provide much of the theoretical framework for the literary analyses to follow, structural coupling occurs when a system considers something normally belonging to its environment (i.e. 'outside' of itself) as subject to its operations, or conversely as an 'irritant' that provokes a response. Law normally does not take literature into account in its operations, but may do so in cases of censorship or copyright protection, in which case the law necessarily makes use of literary or aesthetic concepts for its decisions. A familiar example is the invocation of a work's aesthetic qualities in deciding whether it is obscene. Literature, on the other hand, has the capacity for structural coupling with almost anything in its environment, for example through the mimetic process. Literature's structural couplings with law are quite varied, ranging from the incorporation of the agonistic structure of trials as dramaturgy to the exact citation of legal discourse. Structural couplings envision the topic of law and literature in a way that differs from the two approaches most often seen in previous 'law and literature' scholarship: the first of these locates legal cases and themes in literary works, while the second, the critical approach, uses the weighing of values and ethics that occurs in literature and in literary theory to examine the rhetorical strategies, narrative emplotments and other aspects that appear in legal discourse. Differently from either of these, I accept as foundational the viewpoint of Max Weber, Niklas Luhmann, Pierre Bourdieu and others that the differentiation of complex societies definitively separates the spheres of law and literature in ways that must be accounted for in discussions that explore apparently common themes and even common authorship between them. A recognition of the fundamental disjunction between law and literature should guide our search for moments of structural coupling. These two subsystems, for example, may cite each other, incorporating such citations into their respectively autonomous discursive systems.[1] Unpacking such moments may reveal more about the relationship of law and literature than would analyses of reflection or theories of shared intepretability.

This book adduces a number of study-examples of such structural couplings between law and literature, drawn from the literature and philosophy of the German-speaking countries. My readings fall into three distinct historical periods: (1) the turn of the nineteenth century and the crisis of German law and culture due to French invasion and the possibility of enforced codification; (2) the Weimar Republic and the crisis of German culture due to political and economic instability;

---

1 The difference between a 'system' and a 'subsystem' is not always clear, and is mostly relative, for obvious reasons. My understanding is that the word 'system' in the strict sense should be reserved for society as a system of communications, for example, which is composed of subsystems such as law, literature, politics, and so forth. Other systems include psychic systems, organisms and machines. I mostly adhere to this distinction; however, since maintaining the terminology at every point would be tedious, at times I use 'system' when 'subsystem' would be more precise.

4   Citation and Precedent

and (3) the post-war period and the crisis of German culture due to post-national concepts of state and of law. In the rest of this introductory chapter I will insert my approach within the more general context of law-and-literature scholarship, and explain more fully my deployment of the title keywords 'citation' and 'precedent,' particularly in light of ST.

Law and Literature

Since the 1980s, the movement known as 'law and humanities' has gained much currency in the United States. Attention to what literature, philosophy and literary theory had to say about society and culture by legal scholars became an important part of the so-called 'critical legal studies' movement. Associated above all with the writings of Allan Hutchinson, critical legal studies sought to replace the incremental development of the legal tradition with a more self-conscious, theoretical approach. Literary treatments of law could provide the critical perspective and ethical dimension that is difficult to achieve from within the profession. Overall, the attempt at conjoining law with literature – including literary theory – has counted with such noted figures as Richard Posner, whose *Law and Literature* is now in its third edition, and, at the other end of the political spectrum, Catharine MacKinnon, perhaps the best-known feminist legal scholar. Special issues of law journals have been devoted to the philosophy of Jacques Derrida, and the literary critic Stanley Fish was given an appointment in the Duke Law School, not to mention that his book on law and interpretation, *Doing What Comes Naturally*, is cited as often in law reviews as in literary criticism.

Literary critics entering the law-and-literature field, on the other hand, found a literary theme, an interesting field for the play of literary theory, and an apt outlet for literature as cultural critique. The field now possesses its own journals, such as the *Cardozo Studies in Law and Literature*, *Law and Literature*, and *Law, Culture, and the Humanities*. In the United States, it has focused mainly on Anglo-American literature and jurisprudence, with some comparative explorations. Posner treats Homer and Kafka, for example, while Peter Brooks brings Rousseau, Dostoevsky and Freud into conjunction with American legal cases in his *Troubling Confessions*.[2]

---

[2] The early twenty-first century saw a rather different approach to legal issues, focusing on human rights, frequently from an international or global perspective. To give one example, Joseph Slaughter's *Human Rights, Inc.* traces the connection between international law and a regime of human rights that transcends national boundaries and narrative form, arguing that

Inasmuch as it is a form of cultural critique, literary criticism can hardly avoid acquiring a nomological dimension, since, as Robert Weisberg and Guyora Binder claim, 'legal forms and legal processes play a compositional role in modern culture – that cultural criticism must attend to the legal dimension of culture or remain superficial' (Weisberg and Binder, *Literary Criticisms of Law*, 464). German culture provides one of the most prominent and analyzable examples of this composition, and one whose authors have long practised criticism and literary analysis as a form of critique. Perhaps because of the potential relevance of this field of literary analysis to current jurisprudence as pointed out by Weisberg and Binder, few, if any, monographs written in English venture into German literature at any length. The studies by William Pencak, Vickie Ziegler and Theodore Ziolkowski are exceptions, but only the last-named deals with modern literature and law.

There are similar interdisciplinary interests among German scholars, although, due either to the historical relationship between law and literature or the institutional configurations of German academia, there has been less of a tendency towards considering law and literature as an interdisciplinary undertaking. Criticism tends to be biographical or case-oriented, and the theoretical justification for bringing law and literature into conjunction is rarely given prominence. Peter Schneider has outlined three reasons why lawyers should read literature: for intellectual history; for insight into lay perceptions of law; and for pedagogical insights into how to make law teachable (Schneider, '*Ein einzig Volk von Brüdern*', 20). One of the earliest publications in the area, Hans Fehr's *Das Recht in der Dichtung*, moves from the Middle Ages to the Weimar Republic, and summarizes the themes and ideas (e.g. revenge) as these develop throughout the ages in a systematic treatment at the end of the book (Fehr, 519–62). Some scholars emphasize the influence of law on literature, through prosecution and censorship (Kogel, *Schriftsteller vor Gericht*), or through personal contact between lawyers and writers, including the fact that, as in the celebrated case of E. T. A. Hoffmann, they are sometimes a single, amphibious creature called a 'poet-lawyer' (Dichterjurist) (cf. Wohlhäupter, *Dichterjuristen*).[3]

---

the world novel, whose discourse is not bound by jurisdictional boundaries, naturalizes conceptions of human freedom and dignity in a way that the administrative structures of world justice cannot. Slaughter thus presents an argument in favour of a strong structural coupling between law and literature at the level of international law.

3 Hoffmann (1776–1822) was a judge by profession, active in the cities of Posen, Plozk and Berlin. It is remarkable how infrequently legal themes occur in his work.

Others study the treatment of legal themes in literature (Friedländer, *Rechtsanwälte und Anwaltsprobleme in der schönen Literatur*; Kästner, *Literatur und Wandel im Rechtsdenken*, 609–15; Mölk, *Literatur und Recht*). Despite its title, Heinz Müller-Dietz's *Border Crossings* (*Grenzüberschreitungen*) belongs in the latter category, as does the similarly sounding title *Border Infringements* (*Grenzfrevel*, by Koch et al.), as does also the *Figures of Law* collection edited by Gert Hofmann that examines the 'Interference of Law and Literature'. For the purposes of explaining the work done by law-and-literature scholars, and on the basis of relatively strong ties between the *Germanistik* practised in the US and that practised in Germany, I will move freely between English-language and German-language studies of both law and literature. Beyond scholarship, the two legal systems themselves are certainly comparable, though naturally the more closely one examines them the more differences one perceives, and the more important these differences become.

Writing in 1989, for the first issue of the *Yale Journal of Law and the Humanities*, Robert Weisberg noted that the various approaches adumbrated above can be assimilated into one of two camps:

> Very crudely divided, the [law-literature] enterprise has two parts. [...] The first part is law-in-literature. This, of course, involves the appearance of legal themes or the depiction of legal actors or processes in fiction or drama. The other, somewhat more amorphous, part is law-as-literature. This involves the parsing of such legal texts as statutes, constitutions, judicial opinions, and certain classic scholarly treatises as if they were literary works. (Weisberg, 'The Law-Literature Enterprise', 1)

The title of Weisberg and Binder's own book-length study makes it clear which camp he belongs to. *Literary Criticisms of Law* encouraged 'a legal scholarship that explores and enhances the expressive and compositional power of legal thought and practice in the specific political and economic worlds in which they operate. Such a scholarship recognizes the literary as a constitutive dimension of law rather than as a redemptive supplement' (Weisberg and Binder, *Literary Criticisms of Law*, 19).

In a later, elegiac (i.e. 'what-*was*-law-and-literature') summation, Julie Peters delineates three stages in the evolution of approaches to the topic, which she labels the humanist, the hermeneutic and the narratological. The humanist stage held out hope that literature could supply the central core of humane values supposedly lacking in scientific, technical and formalist approaches to law. The hermeneutic stage, influenced by literary post-structuralism, was based on the fact that law and literature were both grounded in textual interpretation. Of course, such 'grounding' meant for some a destabilization of concepts of truth and normativity without which modern law cannot function. Similarly, the narrative stage, represented by titles such as Peter Brooks's and Paul Gewirtz's *Law's Stories*, focused on the shared capacity of literature and law to tell stories – stories that matter. (Hence, we note a shift in emphasis, from legislation and legal texts to actual investigative and trial procedures.) Oppressed groups, for example, from Holocaust survivors to women, made use of narrative in both legal and literary fora to redress the 'master narratives' formulated by the victors. In all three stages, Peters notes, the marriage of law and literature derived from what each discipline felt was lacking in itself, and hence hoped to find in the other:

> [L]aw and literature might be seen as having symptomatized each discipline's secret interior wound: literature's wounded sense of its insignificance, its inability to achieve some ever-imagined but ever-receding praxis; law's wounded sense of estrangement from a kind of critical humanism that might stand up to the bureaucratic state apparatus, its fear that to do law is always already to be complicit, its alienation from alienation itself. Each in some way fantasized its union with the other: law would give literature praxis; literature would give law humanity and critical edge. (Peters, 'Law, Literature, and the Vanishing Real', 448)

This analysis implicitly upholds an intensional notion of discipline. Disciplines do not so much explain facts and phenomena as create them, through the mechanisms of citation and precedent.

Citation and Precedent

> If there were no art, then there would exist no possibility for the creation of artworks. There is a relationship of citation, artists have a positive or negative attitude towards precedent art, art discusses art with itself, and autonomy is exactly this concept, that one recognizes something as art only in reference to other artworks.[4]
>
> [Wenn es keine Kunst gäbe, gäbe es auch keine Möglichkeit, Kunstwerke zu schaffen. Es gibt eine Zitierbeziehung, es gibt

---

4 Translations not credited to another source are by the author of this study.

eine positive oder negative Einstellung zur Vorgängerkunst, es gibt ein Selbstgespräch innerhalb der Kunst, und Autonomie ist eben genau dies, dass man sie ohne Referenz auf andere Kunstwerke gar nicht als Kunst sehen würde]

Luhmann, 'Ausdifferenzierung der Kunst', 143

The passage tells us that a single artwork does not exist. The system called 'art' exists, and a corpus of tones, colors, lines or verbiage can be referred by those who experience it to that system – or not. Luhmann thus neatly summarizes the role of citation and precedent both in the creation of art as a subsystem, and in the belonging of any particular work to this system. Authors such as Thomas Mann have made citation into a generative machine for the creation of 'new' works – *Doktor Faustus* (1947) is a citation of both the *Faustbuch* and Nietzsche's biography, Mann's *Lotte in Weimar* (1939) a citation of Goethe's works and diaries, and so forth. But even outside of these more radical examples, criticism of a literary work frequently hinges on determination of precedent work, whether this be from a single author, as when W. G. Sebald uses Franz Kafka as a character and directly names the latter's short story 'Der Jäger Gracchus' in his own novel, *Vertigo* (1990; *Schwindel Gefühle*), or from the generic rules established through an interplay of the literary system. Precedent may operate as a foundational text, such as *Lazarillo de Tormes* for the picaresque or Petrarch for the sonnet sequence, or as a set of texts out of whose matrix a genre comes into existence, in relation to which the text-to-be-created projects its own use-value.

From the perspective of the legal subsystem as well, citation and precedent are to be seen as processes of observation that draw a distinction first of all between that which belongs to the law and that which does not. The previous sentence contains a semantic pair that pertains to the technical vocabulary of ST, namely 'to observe' and 'to draw a distinction', which must be understood in conjunction with each other. Both involve deciding which data can be subject to the operations of system, and which cannot. What is outside of a system is called the system's 'environment'. In many places in the world, corporal punishment of children at home or in a school belongs to the environment of law – that is, to what is outside the legal subsystem – whereas other legal subsystems draw the distinction so as to include them as actionable within those systems.

It might be objected that citation and precedent are far more important in the construction of the legal subsystem in common-law traditions than in civil-law ones. In the latter, cases are to be decided through application of a legislated or decreed code rather than by fitting them to the nearest precedent by means of citation. Precisely the increase in complexity of the modern period, however, makes the absolute distinction between these two approaches harder to make. Codification requires legislative action, which in democracies is cumbersome and takes so long that it is unable to keep pace with the developing complexities of commerce, communication, and even social organization. Without a code to go by, courts in such situations are forced to rely on a chain of precedents no less than they do in a common-law system.[5]

At the same time, citation in particular can also provide a point of structural coupling between law and other subsystems. From the perspective of the literary subsystem, legal cases can serve as precedents, i.e. as the object of mimesis and/or of citation. A distinctive feature of literary prose is its ability to cite from or even mimic a variety of non-literary genres and subsystems. Furthermore, the modern period knows no distinctively 'literary' discourse. Rather, a variety of sociolects and jargons can be found in literary texts, many of them imported more or less directly from other discursive contexts. Citations from the law rarely, if ever, appear verbatim as within the system-internal citations of law. Rather, legal discourse tends to be distorted, though this can vary from the stenographic urges of Weiss's *Investigation* to the oddly echoing cross-meanings of the word *Recht* ('law', 'right', 'justice') in Goethe's *Elective Affinities*.

Moving to the other side, how do citation and precedent function to bring about the autopoiesis of the legal subsystem, in which the range of citability is much narrower? Grant Lamond ('Precedents', 2–3) cites four generally accepted theses regarding precedent in Anglo-American jurisprudence (but applicable to any common-law system): (1) precedents lay down rules that are binding in later cases; (2) while only some later courts have the power to overrule precedents, all of them have the power to *distinguish* between precedent and non-precedent; (3) data for this distinction are provided by the precedent court's justification(s) for the rule; and (4) the function of the doctrine of precedent is to create new legal rules to settle uncertainty in the law. The image conjured up by the last tenet is one of laws having broad and generalizable meanings that become more granulated as they get applied to specific cases by the courts. Lamond's article aims at countering the first tenet, arguing that precedents furnish reasons rather than rules. This argument is in line with ST, since it makes precedent a communication to a later court, an input that is used to create a somewhat different output, rather than either a fixed monument or an abstraction the later court makes

---

5   The points made in the preceding paragraph are largely drawn from Angelo Sereni, 'The Code Law and the Case Law'.

of the first case. Emphasis is placed on the citability of precedent. The choosing of relevant precedents is a fundamental observation that a judge makes.

Moving now to the other term of my title, contemporary German law makes use of three main types of citations, according to Angelika Nussberger: internal (systemintern); external (systemextern); and foreign (systemfremd). (It is difficult to translate the second and third terms into English in an idiomatic manner that would point to their difference.) In the first, internal category, judges must provide at least two types of citation: the law relevant to the case; and previous *Rechtsprechungspraxis*, i.e. precedent cases or judicial opinions that cited the same law in a relevant fashion. In this area we see the recursive capacity of the law – using its own previous outputs as inputs – referenced by ST. More than just efficiency is involved in this recycling of the discourse of previous decisions: 'when judges refer to a certain decision, they can avoid a long train of argumentation. They can also make use of the authority [Autorität] accorded to the cited court' (Nussberger, 'Wer zitiert wen?', 763). The autopoietic intensionality of such citations are at times counterbalanced, however, by citations of scholarly literature, which may at times be considered more compelling than case law – citation trumps precedent (Nussberger, 764). The German Constitutional Court that Nussberger studied has a very real external system to take account of: European law. It tends to cite such law when a concrete case has already been decided, and then only in the first relevant decision, which becomes a precedent within German law for citation by future judges. Most interesting in the context of this book are the 'foreign' citations, meaning those from legal systems of other historical periods or cultures, or from discourse previously lacking the force of legal communication. Nussberger notes that in special votes of the court, dissenting opinions frequently make use of such citations, including of 'literary-political' ones. She gives the example of a judge citing the French fabulist Jean de La Fontaine to express the shock produced by procedural failures in a trial. In (probably unintended) alliance with ST, Nussberger considers such citations as incapable of being processed into the system of law itself. Instead, they become indigestible political statements lodged within the language of legal decision.[6]

Trials of authors or of books, as long as they are based on principles of evidence, provide another, circumscribed example of the need for

---

6 Nussberger's database is restricted to the German Constitutional Court; other kinds of court will differ somewhat in the relative amount of citation and in the porousness of their respective systems to foreign citation.

law to cite literature. As the collection edited by Jörg-Dieter Kogel demonstrates, German history has seen many such trials, from that of Quirinus Kuhlmann in the late seventeenth century to Günter Grass's in the late twentieth. They have been of many kinds, from ones where the state carries out censorship through the deterrence of legal prosecution, to libel suits against the utterances in books, to lawsuits for the protection of personality as an inviolable piece of property subject to diminishment through novelistic portrayal, to authors suing each other for plagiarism. In all such cases, citation provides essential evidence for the case.[7]

This book is concerned with *inter*systemic citations, where law cites literature, or vice versa. For example, Judge Stephen Reinhardt of the US Court of Appeals for the Ninth Circuit in Los Angeles cited the song 'Strange Fruit', by Abel Meeropol and made famous by Billie Holiday, in a dissenting opinion he wrote in 1994 (Campbell v. Wood 18 F.3d 662, 701 [1994]). Reinhardt used the song's anti-lynching message to argue against execution by hanging. He gave the entire text of the song in a footnote. As David Margolitch muses, 'How many songs make such appearances? That footnote reminds us of the power of words in the law, and how, on occasion, the law must reach outside itself to convey its message most forcefully' (Margolitch, 'Performance as Force for Change', 108). Here, then, not only has a coupling occurred but, according to Margolitch, the law feels compelled to cite literature in order to accomplish the basic task of communication. Orit Kamir's study of the film *Rashomon* provides another interesting example of this phenomenon. Her article analyzes two US legal cases (from 1990 and 1993) that cite *Rashomon*. In this film, based on two short stories by the Japanese author Ryunosuke Akutagawa, four different versions of a murder are told by four different witnesses whose accounts differ considerably, leaving the viewer with a puzzle to solve that resembles the jury's or judge's dilemma in hard cases. The citations show that '[t]he film's title has become a "legal-cultural" expression, used by the public and legal profession alike in reference, among other things, to the nature of law' (Kamir, 'Judgment by Film', 40–41). Furthermore, Kamir finds that the ultimate reconciliatory thread between the

---

7 Trials of authors can also rest on non-literary evidence, such as that of Georg Kaiser for embezzlement in 1929, and that of Arno Schmidt for non-payment of rent in 1950. Such cases hold interest as peculiarities, but represent the weakest of structural couplings, if any. Nevertheless, literary critics may observe the law's operation on their object of study and communicate something about the writer's work on that basis.

different accounts is that they agree on the woman's guilt – the guilt of a rape victim, whose 'crime' ranges from not committing suicide as she ought to and thus forcing her husband to kill her, to actively encouraging the duel between her husband and her rapist so that one of them will die and her shame remain unknown. In watching this film, argues Kamir, we the jury are being given the blinders, filters and prejudices necessary to form judgments within the ideological space of culture. Kieran Dolan opens his *Critical Introduction to Law and Literature* (1–10) by drawing our attention to the competing interpretations by US Supreme Court justices of the meaning of Robert Frost's poem 'Mending Wall' in *Plaut v. Spendthrift Farm Inc.* in 1995. Finally, a fourth example is provided by the use of the term 'Kafkaesque' or its equivalent by judges and lawyers in the US courts. In an afterword to the publication of the English translation of Franz Kafka's *Office Writings* (2009), the American legal scholar Jack Greenberg gives a statistic that Kafka has been cited in 245 legal cases (Greenberg, 'Wraparound', 355). The language of many of those cases makes it clear that calling a process 'Kafkaesque' functions as a condensed argument in favor of judicial relief or remandment – American law is not supposed to put people in Kafkaesque situations. The legal system has observed Kafka's writings and made self-adjustments to try to avoid resembling them in reality.

These examples show that legal systems, while largely autonomous in ways that I will make use of ST to define, can nevertheless cite and take as precedents the ajudications provided by literature, history and other discursive formations. I will not attempt to prove in this book a much-repeated insight of sociology and history, that in the distant past such intersystemic citations were more frequent, which amounts to saying that subsystems were less autonomous, or – what amounts to the same thing – less differentiated from each other. It is a truism that the functions of a modern society cannot be carried out without the differentiation, i.e. the *Ausdifferenzierung*, of various systems to handle complex tasks. I will be using the German term for this phenomenon (the growing more autonomous and closed of society's various subsystems) since it is more precise than the English, indicating with the prefix 'aus-' (literally, 'out of') the ongoing, processual nature of systemic differentiation. Indeed, the mechanism of *Ausdifferenzierung* replaces the simpler Marxist notion of the superstructure growing out of the base to explain modern societies with a more biological/evolutionary concept of mutations moving in all directions at once and interacting with each other.

Examining citation and precedent, then, can show the double face of conjunction and disjunction between law and other subsystems.

On the one hand, they are important parts of the law's autonomy and of its autopoietic process. In law, 'a present communication links recursively to past communications and establishes fresh possibilities for future communications. For example, when a court communicates a judicial decision, it typically relies on past legal communications, such as prior decisions, and in so doing it creates connective possibilities for future legal communications' (Baxter, 'Autopoiesis and the "Relative Autonomy" of Law', 2006). On the other hand, citations provide an opportunity for 'coupling' between systems, as we have seen above.

As in the cases of 'Strange Fruit,' *Rashomon* and the Kafkaesque, culture as a whole can be seen as an immense supersystem of self-citation. Legal themes are 'cited' back and forth as they circulate between law, philosophy, literature and other cultural forms. The direction and intensity of the 'flow' of citation is influenced by the changing historical configurations of culture.[8] In his book on German law and literature, *The Mirror of Justice*, Theodore Ziolkowski argues that literary portrayals of justice in German literature are stimulated by crisis points in legal history. In positing a sort of 'natural law' of legal influence on literature – the more crisis in the legal system, the more it influences literature in reaction – Ziolkowski's approach provides an important dynamic for the study of law and literature that moves us beyond the simple collection of examples. The further steps I hope to accomplish in this study are: (1) to supplement the 'mirror' metaphor of literature as a reflection of the law with one of citation and intertextuality; and (2) with the help of concepts like 'habitus', 'public sphere', 'state of exception', 'system' and 'thick description', to elaborate more fully the systemic interactions – including the constraints thereon – between the legal and other cultural subsystems.

To put it another way that will be explained more fully though examples in the course of this book, the legal subsystem perpetually finds itself in a 'state of exception'; that is, in a state of being without an ultimate ground – since there can be no law that legislates the existence of law. Citation and precedent are vital substitutes for the law's lack of ultimate origin and self-justification outside of its own operations. In Glyn Daly's formulation,

---

8   One could analogize the monist position of Stanley Fish, who in critiquing Ronald Dworkin points out that 'interpretation is a *structure* of constraints, a structure which [...] renders unavailable the independent or uninterpreted text and renders unimaginable the independent and freely interpreting reader' (*Doing What Comes Naturally*, 98). As in ST, the idea of mind disappears, leaving only system or, in Fish's terminology, structure.

> The system of law [...] no longer appears arbitrary [only] because of numerous layers (sedimentations) of case study, constitutional interpretation, protocol, preceding judgements and so on; all of which help to reinforce coherence and patterning. At the same time, such layers serve to repress the fact that there exists no clear point of origin – autopoietic routinization is precisely the illusion of foundation – and that the legal system cannot be based on any absolutist conception of Law.
>
> A system of law requires, in the first place, a basic code for distinguishing what is lawful and what is not. But this immediately presents a paradox because the legal/illegal distinction is not something that can be determined outside the system of law. (Daly, 'Radical(ly) Political Economy', 10)

Citation serves as one aspect of routinization. Citation, however, is also one of the mechanisms by which language escapes closure and finality, as shown by Jacques Derrida in his essay 'Signature, Event, Context', which is essentially a critique of the speech-act theory of J. L. Austin. While Austin wished to take a radically new approach to language meaning, by dividing utterances according to whether they perform actions, merely make statements about the world, and so forth, Derrida notes that the old philosophical notions of truth reappear in Austin's distinction between original and citational uses of language, such as, for example, if a trial transcript were to be read in a stage play. (We will encounter the example of Peter Weiss's writing a play on exactly this basis in Chapter 4.2.) While for Austin fictionality minimizes the ability of language to be a speech-act in the sense of such an act's capacity for changing reality, Derrida notes that it is precisely the citationality and iterability of language that allows it to function in both contexts, whether 'real' or 'fictional'. In a sense, the possibility of fictional performativity is precisely what allows true performatives (e.g. verbs that carry out what they express, such as 'I promise') to work in language. Hence, asks Derrida, 'is not what Austin excludes as anomalous, exceptional, 'non-serious', that is, citation (on the stage, in a poem, or in a soliloquy), the determined modification of a general citationality – or rather, a general iterability – without which there would not even be a "successful" performative?' (Derrida, 'Signature', 103). A truly radical (and, for Derrida, radically true) theory of language 'would be concerned with different types of marks or chains of iterable marks, and not with an opposition between citational statements on the one hand, and singular and original statement-events on the other' (Derrida, 104–5).

Post-structural theories of reading and interpretation in general, which showed themselves well suited to the reading of literary texts, also had an impact on legal thinking, emphasizing 'the linguistic turn away from positivist sociology of law, the dissolution of social and legal realities into discursivity, fragmentation and closure of multiple discourses, the non-foundational character of legal reasoning, the decentring of the legal subject, the eclectic exploitation of diverse traditions in legal thought, the preference for difference, *différance*, and *différends* over unity, and most important, the foundation of law on paradoxes, antinomies and tautologies' (Gunther Teubner, 'Breaking Frames', 154). ST belongs generally to this post-structural trend. Luhmann's assessment of the role of the legal subsystem, for example, is counter-intuitive and controversial. For Luhmann, the function of the legal system is not the regulation of conduct or resolution of conflicts, but the 'stabilization of normative expectations. [...] Law makes it possible to know which expectations will meet with social approval and which not. [...] One can afford a higher degree of uncertain confidence or even of mistrust as long as one has confidence in law' (Luhmann, *Law as a Social System*, 148). Confidence in a system replaces confidence in individuals that is more typical of traditional societies. Furthermore, law 'produces and maintains counter-factual expectations in spite of disappointments. The communication of this intention to maintain one's own expectations even if they are not fulfilled (that is, to refuse to learn from facts) uses the symbols of normativity, for example, the word "should"' (Luhmann, 'Operational Closure', 1426). The word 'should' and the concept of law as comprised of norms may remind the reader of the legal positivism of Hans Kelsen (or even perhaps of Immanuel Kant's deontological philosophy of law). At the same time, however, this positivist language is denied by being inserted within an ironizing context. Not norms, but the 'symbolism of normativity' comprises the mystical origins of law. People do not, in fact, behave as they 'should', but society proceeds on the contrafactual basis of belief that there are behavioural norms embodied in the law and capable of being fulfilled. The definition is problematic for a number of reasons, among them the lack of exclusivity to law – could not the role of religion be defined in the same way, for example? One suspects Luhmann of irony or of directly attacking legal positivism with this theory, for example. However, even Luhmann's great opponent Jürgen Habermas, whose model of communicative action has been received far more favourably by the legal community than has ST, admits that his concept of communicative reason depends for its functioning on individuals committing themselves to 'pragmatic presuppositions of a counterfactual sort', such as assuming that their addressees are accountable (Habermas, *Between Facts and Norms*, 4). We will explore the Luhmann-Habermas debate in greater depth in the next chapter.

Law and Literature: the German Perspective

Having introduced the concept of structural coupling and elaborated citation as a mechanism for such, let me now outline some of the historical couplings between law and literature in the language and cultures of Germany and Austria. As mentioned earlier, the structural couplings between law, literature and philosophy are stronger in German-speaking countries than in any other national literature that I am aware of. Not only have German *literati* ventured into legal themes, but legal theorists and historians such as Friedrich Carl von Savigny have achieved the status of cultural icons. There are several reasons for this relative strength in the law-literature coupling in Germany, but I wish to rehearse at length the phenomenon known as 'the Reception', since this event also helps characterize the uniqueness of German law in general. What was 'received' in roughly the Renaissance era in German-speaking countries was Roman law. Before that time, German courts had for the most part operated on the basis of customary, feudal, or canon law, depending on the jurisdiction and the particular case at hand. With some notable exceptions such as the compilation *Sachsenspiegel* (ca. 1220), most legal rules and precedents had been orally preserved and transmitted. The discovery of additional sources of Roman law by Italian scholars in the early Renaissance spread northward. In 1495, the Imperial Court or *Reichskammergericht* was instituted as the highest court body in the Holy Roman Empire of the German Nation, and its rulings (mostly appellate) were based in Roman law. This event occurred not long after the first chairs of Roman law were established at Basel in 1460 and Tübingen in 1477. Though the *Reichskammergericht*, at which J. W. von Goethe would eventually serve a stint in Wetzlar as a newly minted law Ph.D., was slow and not very effective due to a number of factors, it nevertheless became a model imitated by German electors and princes, who also introduced Roman law into their courts. In principalities with well-established legal codes, such as Saxony, hybrid blendings of Roman with common law ensued. Most importantly, local courts (comprised mostly of amateurs) reacted to the imposition of Roman law by outsourcing their decisions to law faculties (the professionals) at universities, resulting frequently in a *de facto* abdication of jurisdiction. The universities thus became much more powerful and instrumental in the development of law in Germany than in any other country of Europe.

The concept of a university, however, is of a public sphere where scholars of a variety of disciplines and perspectives meet and converse with each other, thus setting the stage for interactions first between law and theology, and later law and philosophy. Related to this development was the rise of the legal dissertation. In the nineteenth century Germany became 'the land of "scholarly positivism", of "professional law", the only region in the West to build its law on academic treatises. Professors succeeded in commanding the confidence of powerful politicians (Whitman, *The Legacy of Roman Law*, xiii–xiv). Beginning in the late eighteenth century, this reliance of courts and politicians on the university increasingly became coupled with the idea of Germany as a 'Kulturnation': since Germany could not be united under a single legal system, the presence of 'German law' was relegated to philosophy and literature.

So great is the presence of law in German literature, and so broad the definitions of the two terms in the structural coupling, that one's approach to the topic almost necessarily involves a choice between numerous alternatives, none of which by itself can hope to encompass the whole topic of law and literature. Law can be divided into public and private, criminal and civil, trial-court and administrative, to name just a few such distinctions. There is also law as legislated, law as enforced, law as received, and law as theorized and philosophized. The traditional approach to the topic, as mentioned above, has been to use literature as a 'mirror of justice' by looking for images of judges, lawyers and politicians as they appear in German literature, as in studies by Ziolkowski, Hildegard Emmel and others. Michael Kilian (*Dichter*, 14–15) argues that a single type emerging from such literary treatments has largely predominated in the public eye: that of the bloodless craftsman, the legal functionary who is amoral because he works unreflectively. Aside from the question of whether the image of lawyers in English literature (of Tulkinghorn in Charles Dickens's novel *Bleak House*, for example) is very different, Kilian's statement reveals a central paradox in the relationship between law and literature in Germany: the constant and consistent depictions of the law in German literature have formed in the educated public's mind an image of the disjunction of law from nearly every other social sphere: the 'ideal type' of the German jurist is of a 'craftsman' who carries out his unreflective work in an ivory tower, as far removed as possible from the scene of the social and political conflicts that will ultimately influence the legal texts upon which he operates. In creating this image, of course, German literature has at the same time been deconstructing it. The very prevalence of these images in

German literature means that the wished-for privacy and isolation of the legal technician has been shattered all the more noticeably by the activity of writers. However, the promulgation by literature and media of an image of the law or of lawyers is a relatively weak structural coupling, and the present study will not provide a mirror of justice.

Some systems – frequently those of societies without writing – focus on designating the right judge in terms of knowledge of scripture, tribal lore, proverbs, and so on, and then allow him or her great freedom in arriving at decisions and compromises among the parties involved. A counter-example is provided by the Prussian General Code (*Allgemeines Landrecht Preussens*) promulgated in 1794, which is 20,000 paragraphs long, a length that allows for immense detail. For example, it requires parents to provide instruction to their daughters, from the age of fourteen, in the signs of pregnancy and the proper care during and after birth. The ideology of such completeness is that 'laws should rule; judges should not become legislators; any uncertainty regarding the legal basis for their decisions should be removed through the norming provided by the manifold instructions of laws and ordinances' (Klaus Kästner, *Literatur und Wandel im Rechtsdenken*, 16). If German judges are condemned to working on the chain gang of citation and precedent, perhaps this restriction has produced literature that engages in counterfactual portraits,

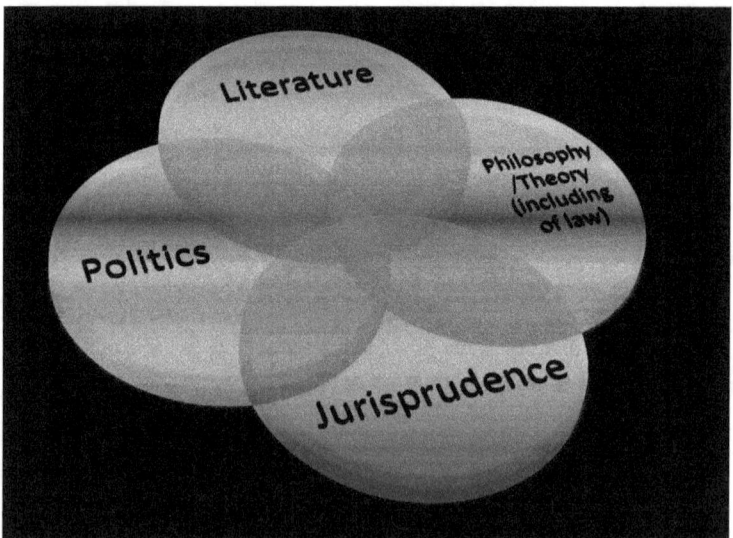

Figure 1: Structural coupling between four social subsystems

showing an extraordinary degree of arbitrariness and humanity (with both the positive and negative implications of both terms) in its legal actors. The most famous of these is Heinrich von Kleist's justice of the peace (Dorfrichter), Adam, in the play *The Broken Jug* (1808; *Der Zerbrochene Krug*), who uses his position to impose himself on women. But returning to the larger issue, can we point to a conjunction of German law and literature beyond mimesis and reflection?

From ST to Systems Criticism

Let us imagine four subsystems in German culture: Literature; Philosophy; Politics; and Law. It is relatively easy to perceive the autopoietic processes of each of these – in other words, their disjunction from one another: convictions in literature send no one to prison, while published verdicts attract few buyers in the bookstores. Evident too, however, are their structural couplings. Political formations lead to new legislation. As noted above, historically German jurisprudence has taken some account of academic views of law, including those of philosophers (e.g. Hans Kelsen was asked to draft the Austrian Constitution in 1920). My thesis is that citation and precedent are more precise terms than 'mutual observations' for understanding how these subsystems interact with each other. In Figure One below, I give a Venn diagram schematizing the couplings that will be in play during the course of this book.

I have chosen for my study examples of literary works, trials and individuals that can be situated in the darker areas of the diagram that represent overlap of jurisdiction or, in the language of ST, structural couplings. A telling drawback of ST – related to the power it derives from abstraction – is its reluctance to provide extensive detail and examples. It is unclear how one draws the boundaries of supposedly autonomous systems, for example, without being told what belongs and doesn't belong to a particular system as a normative example. One literary scholar who has tried to give a detailed account of literature using the concepts of ST is Siegfried Schmidt, in the appropriately titled *Self-Organization of the Social System 'Literature' in the Eighteenth Century* (*Selbstorganisation des Sozialsystems Literatur im 18. Jahrhundert*). The heart of Schmidt's methodology is to look for the emergence of newly functional actors as parts of the system. Schmidt discusses four of these:

1 *Literaturproduzenten*, also known as authors, are not newly functional, but become increasingly professionalized and self-conceiving (as in the concept of genius) in the course of the century.

2 *Literaturvermittler,* also known as publishers and booksellers, and the main new development for the century, periodicals.
3 *Literaturrezipienten,* also known as readers, who increase greatly in numbers and become increasingly more anonymous and unpredictable.
4 *Literaturverarbeiter,* also known as critics and scholars, who (like periodical involvement in promulgating literature) are a new phenomenon in the eighteenth century.

Interestingly, Schmidt also discusses law at length (*Selbstorganisation,* 168–80), but does not bring it into relation with literature.

Evidence for the couplings between systems in the early modern period of Europe is given in another study by Robert Mitchell, who argues in *Sympathy and the State* that 'Romantic theories of sympathy and identification emerged as responses to [...] perceptions of the contingency of the system of state finance, for these theories were attempts to understand the foundations and operations of social systems in ways that would explain, but also contain, the disruptive effects of finance' (Mitchell, 5). Mitchell succeeds more in explaining the role of financial crisis in generating new subsystems than in demonstrating the claim quoted above. Nevertheless, he does locate the idea of sympathy in the 'dark' area of my diagram where a number of the subsystem disks overlap.[9]

According to its title, we would expect Dietrich Schwanitz's *System Theory and Literature (Systemtheorie und Literatur)* to bear some similarity to the approaches of Schmidt and Mitchell, but in fact Schwanitz does not attempt a sociology of literary systems. Instead, he first of all attempts to explain ST in a creative, literary fashion through the construction of imaginary dialogues, for example between Sherlock Holmes and Watson, and between Ulrich and Stumm from Robert Musil's *Man Without Qualities* (1930–32; *Der Mann ohne Eigenschaften*). Schwanitz focuses on ideas of contingency, paradox, and the unity and difference of hetero- and self-reference (Schwanitz, 85 ff.). His one detailed example from literary history involves the conversion of libertine narratives and romances into the modern novel in the works of Samuel Richardson and others, based on the distinction introduced between narration and narrated

---

9 To perhaps overemphasize a point for clarity, 'overlap' is shorthand here for the complex ways that systems may bear a relation to each other. A central insight of ST, to be discussed further later, is that subsystems do not directly influence each other – legislators do not send letters to judges instructing them on the latest changes to the codes, for example – but rather observe each other's operations and make their own autopoietic adjustments.

world, as well as the increased role of contingency as the basis of love interest: applying the loves/does-not-love binary to the main male and female characters of a typical novel, for example, yields four possibilities, ranging from mutual love to mutual indifference, and the reader's interest is largely focused on the question of which outcome will reveal itself. (This is, for example, the standard formula for a Jane Austen novel.)

Critical responses to ST have been intense. Most objections are based on the problem of law as a functionalist, closed system, impervious to moral and ethical ideas. My own concerns lie less with a philosophical refutation of ST than with a desire to test its more concrete applications. The implicit evaluation of ST undertaken through study examples in this book remains secondary to the elucidation of those examples, and bringing them into constellations of meaning and influence. There is something to Theodore Ziolkowski's argument that German literature responds to legal crises – not to patent crises, in my opinion, but to the perpetual 'state of emergency' caused by *Ausdifferenzierung*, the dwindling of extralegal norms of validation (e.g. religious values), and the unbridgeable gap created between social subsystems. The elaboration of this theory of anomie will be given in chapter 2.1 through the relationship between Jacob Grimm and Carl Friedrich von Savigny, and in 3.2, through Walter Benjamin's reading of J. W. von Goethe with the help of the legal philosophies of Immanuel Kant and Carl Schmitt. Besides being an important political theorist, Carl Schmitt (1888–1985) was also a would-be *littérateur* who believed in the power of myth to explain legal complexity; I read this project through the lens of Schmitt's use of a single novella, Herman Melville's *Benito Cereno*, in chapter 4.2. Chapter 3.1, on the literary work of Franz Kafka, argues that at least one of his works, *The Trial* (1924; *Der Prozess*), is conceived as a citation of the recursive bureaucratic procedures the author lived with every working day of his short life. The final chapter takes us well beyond the end of World War II, to the reconstruction of legal and political life in the Federal Republic of Germany through a judicial accounting of the Holocaust and a verdict on the culpability of actors in what became the most infamous of its many death camps, Auschwitz. Peter Weiss's drama, *The Investigation* (1965; *Die Ermittlung*), takes as its subject matter not the Holocaust, but the trial, the testimony given, and the behavior of judges, attorneys and witnesses. It cites rather than represents, and through citation resists that relentless march of disjunction called *Ausdifferenzierung*. Before adducing examples, however, I will explore in greater depth the basic concepts of ST by comparing the approaches to law and cultural expression of Niklas Luhmann and Jürgen Habermas.

1.2
Subsystem or Public Sphere?

> Like the routes of domination, the routes of autonomy are complex, if not impenetrable.
>
> Pierre Bourdieu, *The Rules of Art*, 52

If one were asked to identify a 'system' approach to literary criticism, the difficulty would not be in finding one, but rather in finding an opposite to contrast it with.[1] Or, conversely and from the other end of the spectrum, in Slavoj Žižek's formulation, 'All academic powers have entered into a holy alliance to exorcize the spectre [of the Cartesian subject]: [...] the postmodern deconstructionist (for whom the Cartesian subject is a discursive fiction, an effect of decentred textual mechanisms); and the Habermasian theorist of communication (who insists on a shift from Cartesian monological subjectivity to discursive intersubjectivity)' (Žižek, *The Ticklish Subject*, 1). We may add, I think, both the Luhmanian systems theorist and the Bourdieuvian sociologist who examines how art is created in a field according to rules.[2]

While Žižek does not mention literary criticism *per se*, a contemporary approach to literature that ignores or minimizes systemic cultural contexts in order to defend the genius of the

---

1   The Library of Congress heading uses the singular, 'system theory', and I will conform to this model. I have not emended citations, which may use the form 'systems theory'.
2   To a question as to what differentiates a field from a system, Bourdieu responded: 'An essential difference: struggles, and thus historicity! [...] In a field, agents and institutions constantly struggle, according to the regularities and the rules constitutive of this space of play (and, in given conjunctures, over those rules themselves), with various degrees of strength and therefore diverse probabilities of success, to appropriate the specific products at stake in the game' (Bourdieu, Wacquant, *Invitation*, 102).

author or the unique expressive qualities of the text is hard to find – which is perhaps why the term 'system' is missing from the lexica of most anthologies and encyclopediae of literary criticism. Rather than a binary opposition, we find more of a continuum stretching from those approaches that still accord some degree of autonomy and creativity to the author and ask what texts mean, to the rigidly systematic ones that ask only what texts do within the context of social relations. Examples of the former might be Franco Moretti's world-ST of literary texts in *The Modern Epic: The World-System from Goethe to García Márquez* (1996), which calls for literary scholars to use 'distanced reading' and statistics to understand the effects of spatial movement on literary form. Nevertheless, within such an approach there is both room and necessity for the appreciation of individual accomplishment – in the analysis of how a particularly influential translation rewrites its original, for example. An example of the rigidly monist position might be Stanley Fish's *Is There a Text in This Class?* (1980), which denies the independence of texts apart from their ideational appropriation by 'interpretive communities', without doing the historical or sociological spadework of determining how such communities form and are transformed.

It is not an easy task to define or summarize ST. The view of societal evolution as a process of differentiation has been with us since the British political economists and the idea of division of labour. German thinkers such as Karl Marx, Max Weber, Wolfgang Schlucter, Jürgen Habermas, Niklas Luhmann and Gunther Teubner have made significant contributions to the idea. Luhmann, whose version of ST was influenced principally by Spencer Brown's *Laws of Form* (1969) and by the biological theories of Humberto Maturana, has had much to say about literature and art. There is also a great deal of German literary criticism that either is based on their ideas, or that shows an orientation towards system that is compatible with them. Nevertheless, Luhmann's debate with Habermas concerns the degree to which rational human agency can play a role in the shaping of law, government and politics. Interestingly, the divide between the two sociologists over this issue can itself be viewed from a systems perspective, as a question of whether the Habermasian public sphere exists as a medium for overcoming the autonomy and autopoiesis of social subsystems – hence the title of this chapter.

Luhmann

Luhmann has described the differentiation processes of both the system of art and that of law, and his writing has had much influence on sociologists, philosophers and legal scholars.[3] More of his work has been translated into English than that of other system theorists. I will therefore be basing much of my methodology on his arguments.

The first point to keep in mind is that for system theorists, societies do not consist of persons, but rather of communications. While the term 'communication' seems intuitive, if also indefinable, Luhmann ascribes some features to it that are specific to his theory. The emphasis, of course, is on the utterance rather than the utterer. Only utterances that change the system count as communication. Communications are events, rather than objects. Thus, Luhmann, who makes paradox the basis of this theory, points out that system maintenance involves destruction of small parts of the system. It follows that texts and artworks cannot be communications, because they are frozen. They appear more as records, the self-memory of the system. Nevertheless, Luhmann gives us a choice: we may think of artworks either as 'a compact communication or as a program for innumerable communications about the work of art' (Luhmann, 'Work of Art', 194).

Communications within a functional system are carried out by means of a code, which Luhmann posits as being the drawing of a distinction. Contrary to expectations, evolution causes systems to narrow the range of choices rather than to expand them. Luhmann cites a sentence from Goethe's *Elective Affinities* (1809; *Die Wahlverwandschaften*) in explanation of this rule: 'Every word spoken produces its opposite' (*Gesellschaft*, 1:226; 'Jedes ausgesprochene Wort erregt den Gegensinn'). Given the foundational character of language for the communications that form social systems, Luhmann chooses to emphasize its agonistic character, and the fundamental choice of accepting an utterance or not accepting it. Thus, difference is more fundamental to communication than is consensus. (Here lies one of the main bones of contention between Luhmann and Habermas, as I shall examine below.) In the case of law, the primary binary decision of the excluded middle is *Recht/Unrecht*. The literal meanings of these terms, which we will encounter again and again in the works under consideration in this book, are 'right' and 'un-right.' This terminology is ambiguous, since 'Unrecht' can refer to at least three different things, namely: (1) ending up on the wrong side of a judicial decision (being found guilty or liable); (2) being outside the system of law altogether (being illegal); and (3) simply being in error about something. The choice of legal/illegal by the translator

---

3   Udo di Fabio ('Luhmann im Recht') points out that Luhmann's early pieces on procedure were well received and influential among legal scholars, while his fully elaborated theory has had limited resonance.

of one of Luhmann's major works, *Law as a Social System*, makes for some awkward or misleading sentences, for example: 'All that a case can be is either legal or illegal' (Luhmann, *Law as Social System*, 189). In English, this is not true; a case can be liable vs. non-liable, an individual guilty or not guilty, and so forth. But German *Recht/ Unrecht* covers all such uses. However, more fundamental than the specific communication of guilt or innocence is the one that distinguishes between events and behaviours over which the law has jurisdiction, and those that belong instead to its environment. As in English, German has expanded 'right' from its original directional sense, and the idea of social conformity in the use of the right hand, to include an idea of legal justification. But German 'Recht' is broader than English 'right', being in fact the word not only for rights, but for law in general, and beyond law for the concept of justice (more usually in the form 'Gerechtigkeit'). In terms of the binary decision Luhmann explains below, both 'legal/illegal' or 'proven/not proven' could substitute, depending on the circumstance:

> In jurisprudence, after a long preliminary period of evolutionary development, a precise, binary structure has established itself in this sense, that one from a certain perspective can act either legally [im Recht] or illegally [im Unrechten], but not both at once. Relevant to this structure is the fact that one can decide justice [Recht] by identifying it as the negation of injustice [Unrecht], and decide injustice by identifying it as the negation of justice, as well as the fact that attempts at fleeing from this alternative into vagueness or into other discursive fields [Sinnbereiche] such as love or belief or power or art are blocked whenever possible. (Luhmann, *Ausdifferenzierung des Rechts*, 57)

In the generally accepted English terminology of ST, a decision made by a system is called an 'observation', and the line drawn by the decision is called a 'distinction'. In the arts, by the way, the distinctive binary is *stimmig/nicht stimmig* (i.e. aesthetically pleasing or not so).

The concept of societies as sets of communications both narrows our field of focus, noticeably excluding individuals with their intentions and aspirations, and also widens it beyond concrete institutions to the whole field of communications surrounding social subsystems. Persons, subjects and psyches exist as the environment of the social system, which is defined as a set of communications. But persons or psychic systems do not enter into communication, which responds only to prior communication. When Luhmann points out that 'The legal system is not limited to its organs, any more than the religious system is identical to the church, the political system to the government, the educational system to the primary, secondary, and post-secondary schools, or the economic system to the organization of production' (*Ausdifferenzierung*, 36), he means that law (in this case) is not a set of objects or even relationships that can be objectively fixed, but rather the set of all communications pertaining to law.

The largest system of all, we might say, is a society. However, this system is not really one whole, but a nexus of autonomous subsystems that communicate with each other. The premise, basically unchanged since its formulation by Marx and Engels, is that 'society is a functionally differentiated system' (Luhmann, *Art as a Social System*, 134) and that human history can be seen as the continual process of *Ausdifferenzierung* of society's increasingly autonomous functional subsystems. That is, pre-modern societies do not draw strict boundaries between religion, law, government and art; nor do they have words for these institutions. What moderns consider artworks are not considered by traditional societies in isolation, apart from the social function they are created in order to fulfil. Religious art provides a readily comprehensible example of this imbrication. Only with the Renaissance does European art acquire a distinctly autonomous social function. Similarly, ethnographies of law in traditional societies, for example Llewellyn and Hoebel's *Cheyenne Way*, are frequently forced to use alternative terms for their topic, such as 'conflict management' or 'enforceable norms'.

The autonomy of a system is not to be equated with its independence. In fact, the more interdependent social subsystems become on each other, the greater autonomy they develop. Autonomy does mean, however, that a functional system sets its own limits on the degree to which it may be influenced by other systems through 'observations' of those other systems, and that each system recodes any information coming from elsewhere in its own terms. Natural languages are one example of this. Anything coming from 'outside' a language must be recoded in the grammar, vocabulary and phonology of the receptor language. Probably most readers of this study will be familiar with the second example, of academic disciplines and methodologies. The natural sciences draw a distinction that excludes social and psychic systems from its communications, while the social sciences and humanities symmetrically banish 'natural' processes to their environment. Within the humanities, the same event – the career of Jacob Grimm, for example – could be observed by history, literary criticism and sociology, but the resulting discourses might well be mutually unintelligible.

Literature and other subsystems of art provide an example of the dialectic between autonomy and dependence. The development of a market (including galleries and museums) for art products goes hand in hand with the invention of concepts of artistic genius, of 'art for art's sake', and of the profession or calling of 'artist' or 'writer', with the result that art is more dependent on economics than ever before. At the same time, the reduction of art to publication, exhibition, sales and teaching at universities allows for a more focused and autonomous discourse of art and literature than in any previous historical epoch. A separate subsystem of artistic communications is formed, consisting of the *troc* of *salons* or other artist groups in dialogue, art criticism, negotiations with dealers and galleries, and so forth.

ST thus would deny the classical Marxist notion that art or law are epiphenomena of the economic base (i.e. that they are directly and unilaterally influenced by the 'relations of production'), as it would as well the approaches of Legal Realism.[4] Unnervingly, though, what replaces the base as justification of the super-structure is self-legitimation. As William Rasch puts it, subsystems 'stand under the injunction to legitimate themselves, even if self-legitimation must take the form of "originary" paradox. They do not receive their legitimation from "above" or "outside"' (Rasch, *Sovereignty*, 42).

Taken together, autonomy and autopoiesis remove the possibility of mirroring, both in literature and in law. 'The effect of Luhmann's account is to dismiss, as incapable of realization, the early Legal-Realist dream of mirroring, in law, the world beyond law' (Baxter, 'Autopoiesis and the "Relative Autonomy" of Law', 2033). Luhmann's model also contradicts attempts at connecting law and literature through a *tertium comparationis*, as seen in claims such as Paul Heald's which I find typical of law-and-literature approaches: 'The essential connection of law to the question of how we should live, even when legal discourse obscures the connection, makes the study of literature relevant to law. Why? Because fiction is an undeniably rich collection of studies in the appropriateness of human action' (Heald, 'Literature and Legal Problem Solving', 4). Heald's connection between law and literature goes through a third, general term of 'human action'. Human action (the 'humans in action' of Aristotle's *Poetics*) may indeed provide the material for the operations of both law and literature, just as water provides material necessary to life. But it is not clear that this shared basis provides

---

4   Legal Realism, which arose in the late nineteenth century, is an approach to law that emphasizes contingency and the social construction of jurisprudence. In Oliver Wendell Holmes's famous dictum, law is not logic, but experience.

the 'essential connection' between the two autonomous subsystems Heald desires, since they seem to deal with human action in radically different ways, according to the autopoietic rules of their respective operations.

As noted briefly above, the notion of 'observation' replaces that of 'influence' or 'intervention' in this theory. For ST, to observe is to make a distinction (Luhmann, *Theories of Distinction*, 179). Distinctions always divide the observed universe into two parts, one of which belongs to the system, and the other of which does not and which is thus unavailable to further operations of the system. Rather than mirroring, law 'observes' the world beyond into its own, self-referential system. Conversely, literature and mass media observe the observations of the legal system. In William Rasch's view, 'any observation of the observations of the legal system only relativizes that system – that is, observes it from sets of distinctions other than its own. [...] And as these systems interact and continuously observe each other, patterns develop, patterns that we call rational' (Rasch, *Sovereignty*, 27). Yet these rational patterns have no hope of ever becoming operational. Just as we critique irrationality from the rational, the unconscious from the conscious, the unnameable (in the form of the sublime or of the 'first' as in the philosophy of Charles S. Pierce) from the communicable, so too we critique the legal from the philosophical, religious, or moral side of the distinctive divide. We 'translate' the terms of one subsystem into those of another, to use James Boyd White's term.[5]

One measure of a functioning system's autonomy is its capacity for autopoiesis, the capacity for producing its own elements. 'Systems have to use their operations to be able to continue to use their operations to be able, et cetera' (Luhmann, *Theories of Distinction*, 103). Dieter Schwanitz gives an interesting if perhaps trivial example of autopoiesis. It is the following sentence:

> T is the firsT, elevenTh, eighteenTh [...] letter in this sentence.
> E ist dEr ErstE, sEchstE, achtE, zwölftE, viErzEhntE [...] Buchstabe in diesem Satz.
> (Schwanitz, *Systemtheorie und Literatur*, 32)

---

5 White's title is *Justice as Translation*, but in fact the book references law far more frequently than it does justice. White's thesis is that judicial decisions, for example, should be seen as texts responding to other texts the way a translation responds to its original, rather than as attempts to apply a rule of action or to reconstitute the original intentions of the framers of a statute. This model corresponds roughly to the ST idea of communication.

The 'E's – and, in my translation, the 'T's – have been capitalized for clarity. The trick depends upon the morphology of German case endings for adjectives, which dictates that every ordinal in the series ends in 'e.' Hence, each declaration as to the place of some previous 'e' will add at least one more 'e' to the sequence. (The letter 'T' shows a similar inevitability in English ordinals, so I substituted that letter in my translation.) The word indicating the sixth letter, for example, the second of the series, adds to 'e's in the fourteenth and nineteenth places, and so forth. The series is always trying to catch up with itself by citing itself and, since such catching up is impossible, is theoretically endless. More important, perhaps, is the self-reflexive nature of the system that is identical with its own rule. There is no other communication at work in this sequence than the simple one of placing 'e's within the utterance that says where the 'e's should go. The sentence grows by citing itself.

Luhmann recognizes three categories of autopoietic systems: biological or living; psychic; and social. Again, as he notes, autonomy does not equate to independence. Life depends on water, which however is not a living substance, and which remains separate from life itself, because it does not play a role in the distinctions biological systems must draw:

> Autopoietic systems [...] are sovereign with respect to the constitution of identities and differences. They, of course, do not create a material world of their own. They presuppose other levels of reality, as for example human life presupposes the small span of temperature in which water is liquid. But whatever they use as identities and differences is of their own making. In other words, they cannot import identities and differences from the outer world; these are forms about which they have to decide themselves. (Luhmann, 'Autopoiesis', 3)

An important feature that distinguishes the autopoiesis of social subsystems from those of organisms is that while the latter may negate material, the former negate only data; the reduction of complexity achieved is called *Sinn* (meaning, sense, direction). Negated data, however, are not destroyed as material might be; they are deferred, relegated to the environment, and may be converted into *Sinn* when the system changes to allow this. This obligation of the system to make its own decisions gives it autonomy: 'Autonomy implies that, within its boundaries, autopoiesis functions unconditionally, the only alternative being that the system ceases to exist. Autonomy allows for no half-measures or gradation; there are no relative states, no more or less autonomous systems. Either the system produces its elements or it does not' (Luhmann, *Essays*, 157). Within the arts, it is perhaps easiest to understand autopoiesis in the case of music, and hardest to understand it in the case of literature, where, as Plato pointed out at the dawn of Western criticism, every element seems to have received its initial shape from another system. Thus, while aesthetic autonomy was one of the very first systems ideas to be fully theorized, in the aesthetics of the eighteenth century for which Immanuel Kant's *Critique of Judgment* (1790; *Kritik der Urteilskraft*) became the capstone, Kant's did so by banishing the content of works to art's environment. The *stimmig/unstimmig* distinction drawn by aesthetic judgment is based on form alone.

Autopoiesis is closely related to the idea of self-reference. However, any system must contain both heteroreference and self-reference – neither term is meaningful without the other. Judicial citations of 'Strange Fruit' and of *Rashomon* are heteroreferences; so, too, would be references to 'common sense', 'morality', or other concepts not specifically produced by the legal system itself. Citation of relevant laws and precedent cases, on the other hand, constitute autopoietic aspects of these decisions. Willem Witteveen gives an example of the difference that the principle of autopoiesis can make to our understanding of social events:

> Imagine two autopoietic systems, the law and the economy. Through a legislative measure a price-freeze is imposed on the economy. Is this a direct intervention of law into the economic system, which after all will now presumably change its functioning in accordance with a legal norm? Autopoietic theory denies this common-sense insight altogether. What is at stake is an act of observation. 'The law observes the economy through a legal ruling on price control [...] What was an ambitious piece of external regulation becomes mere self-observation' [Teubner, *Law as an Autopoietic System*, 77]. At the same time, the economic system also performs an act of self-observation, seeing the input from law in its own terms. (Witteveen, 'The Hidden Truth of Autopoiesis', 650–51)

Here the empirical facts do bear out the truth of autopoiesis: lawyers and legislators do not actually 'freeze' the prices – which after all never include lawyers' fees or politicians' compensation. Rather, those more directly involved in the economy, such as merchants, do the freezing (or not), having 'observed' a change in the legal system. From another point of view, however, the notion of systemic autonomy seems to contradict the interactions that take place between lawyers, legislators, economists and businesspeople.

Literary studies should have fewer problems with system theory than some other disciplines, since literature has been viewed in precisely ST terms, as an autopoietic system operating under its own rules, something like that of the endlessly self-elongating sentence given above, and without direct influence on other subsystems. The gradual development of the notion of 'literature' provides a particularly recognizable example of *Ausdifferenzierung*.[6]

Mind cannot interact directly with society, but only through the formulation of a communication, which unites intention, utterance and understanding. Similarly, societal communications can be profoundly deformed by the autopoietic mechanisms of mind. 'Though it would appear that society is inhabited by minds, they are merely the environment for a society that consists of communications. But though a social system cannot think; a psychological system cannot communicate' (Luhmann, *Theories of Distinction*, 165). The structural coupling here depends, it would seem, mainly on illusion and nostalgia, for 'consciousness has grown accustomed to loving certain words, telling certain stories, and thus partially identifies itself with communication' (op. cit., 179). There is more here than Luhmann lets on, since he himself defines communication as uniting intention, utterance and understanding, two of which terms can belong to psychic systems. In any case, however, notions of citation and precedent align themselves well with the autonomy of communication, since they provide empirically verifiable markers of the point at which authors or judges leave their individual psychic systems behind to enter the 'intertext' of the communicative system, be it of literature, of law, or of society in general. In citing a proverb, to give a most basic example (and one frequently used in traditional systems of law), the speaker brackets whatever individual psychic disturbance a particular case has made, and speaks instead a ready-made communication that society has prepared for dealing with the situation. The psyche of the speaker still has a role to play, in choosing from a repertoire of proverbs, for example, but the actual utterance acquires a social facticity that the psyche can never obtain.

Our scepticism vis à vis ST might be aroused by the picture given so far of society as a nexus of subsystems that have no method for mutually influencing each other. The point is not that such mutual influence never happens, but that the channels through which it happens are highly restricted. 'Coupling' is the method by which

---

6 A classic brief review of the narrowing of literature in English from literacy in general to works of high culture is given by Raymond Williams in *Keywords* (183–8).

autonomous systems interact with each other.⁷ According to Bernd Hornung, structural coupling

> makes cooperation and co-evolution possible between systems, thus permitting the system to construct its own internal information and to make sense of what is going on. [... A] kind of communication becomes possible, analogous to when two humans, who do not understand each other's language, start to act, to interact, to develop regular patterns of interaction – even of linguistic interaction, albeit at a rudimentary level. [...] Autopoiesis theory nonetheless insists that in structural coupling there is no information exchange, just irritations or perturbations. (Hornung, 'Luhmann's Legal and Political Sociology', 204–5)

There are certain forms or media for doing this, while others are interdicted. For example, property and contract are the principal forms of structural coupling between economy and law, to the extent that the chapter on structural couplings in Luhmann's *Law as a Social System* (*Das Recht der Gesellschaft*) is mostly devoted to a discussion of the development of these concepts in Western society (Luhmann, 381–422). On the other hand, censorship and copyright are two of the most readily identifiable forms for structural coupling between literature and law, and so I have taken them as the subject of chapter 3.3.

Having put forward the ST concept of autonomy and autopoiesis of social subsystems, let us now test it against the alternative idea of a so-called 'public sphere'.

Is There a Public Sphere?

In 1971 a curious book appeared with Suhrkamp Verlag. Carrying the provocative title *Theory of Society, or Social Technology: What Does System Analysis Accomplish?* (Theorie der Gesellschaft oder Sozialtechnologie – Was leistet die Systemforschung?), it was co-authored by Niklas Luhmann and Jürgen Habermas. More accurately, it contained brief exposés by the two sociologists of their respective theories of society, a 150-page polemic by Habermas against Luhmann, and a somewhat shorter defence by Luhmann. The book began with two essays by Luhmann that lay out important elements of ST as a sociological theory. Habermas then responded with an outline of

---

7   The term seems to be a relatively late addition to the vocabulary of ST. Luhmann's most general work, *Sozialsysteme*, uses instead the related idea of 'interpenetration', where one system makes its complexity available for the construction of others.

Subsystem or Public Sphere? 33

his theory of communicative action. These position-takings were followed by the two polemics. The energy that Habermas saw fit to expend on attacking ST showed how seriously Luhmann's work was being taken in Germany at the time. In 1971, the extra-parliamentary opposition was still in full swing, and East-West tensions were even more in the spotlight due to Willy Brandt's controversial *Ostpolitik*. A theory of society that did not portray itself as interventionist or critical seemed to play into the hands of the political conservatives who had governed Germany until very recently. Habermas asks whether ST does not 'take over the functions of legitimating domination previously accomplished by a positivistic collective consciousness' (Habermas, *Theorie der Gesellschaft*, 144; 'die herrschaftslegitimierenden Funktionen zu übernehmen, die bisher von einem positivistischen Gemeinsbewusstsein erfüllt worden sind'). Yet Habermas insisted that his critique of Luhmann was not ideological, but scientific, based as it is on analysis of ST's grounding in one big false thesis: that of making functionalism the basis of society, thereby ignoring a social lifeworld that enables discursive reason as a force for critique and change.

In directly confronting ST, Habermas voices numerous objections. Firstly, he notes the return of the philosophy of the subject (rather than of intersubjectivity). Where German Idealists such as Johann Gottlob Fichte or Friedrich Wilhelm Schelling might speak of Self and Other, ST translates this into System and Environment, and so forth. 'Luhmann's ST carries out a transformation of thought [*Denkbewegung*] from metaphysics to metabiology' (Habermas, *Der philosophische Diskurs*, 430). And just as Kant's critiques fragmented the Self into relatively autonomous mental faculties, so too Luhmann's subsystems deny the possibility of the construction of a rational society: 'If functionally differentiated societies have no identity, [then] they cannot construct a rational identity' (Habermas, 434). Luhmann would readily agree with both these points, starting with the latter, given 'there is no position outside of society from which one could observe the difference between rationality and irrationality and then use it in order to make a global judgment. Furthermore, the focus on identity as such fails to recognize that society exists only as contingent difference' (Paul Harrison, 'Luhmann and the Theory of Social Systems', 88). Secondly, Habermas observes that systems, whose purpose is supposedly to reduce complexity, in fact create more of it. Thirdly, he notes that the *Sinn* created by systems is value-neutral. ST thus seems to provide an apologia for any existing subsystem, and it is not clear how critique can ever emerge from its modeling activities. Finally, and perhaps most importantly, Habermas disagrees with the apparent monologism of an 'observation'. The world is indeed constructed, but as much through dialogue as through systematic observation and drawing of distinctions. He deploys *Öffentlichkeit*, a concept translated into English as 'public sphere', as the alternative to operatively closed systems: 'Public spheres can be conceived as intersubjectivities to a higher degree. In public spheres, identity-forming collectives can articulate their attributes' (Habermas, *Der philosophische Diskurs*, 435). The functionalism of Luhmanian ST denies this possibility: 'The central and [...] false hypothesis that is decisive for Luhmann's theory is namely, that functional analysis provides the only admissable path for the rationalization of decision-making' (Habermas and Luhmann, *Theorie der Gesellschaft*, 144).

Habermas, like Luhmann, has developed a complex and totalizing theory of social communication that explains and, to a certain extent, defends the managerial aspects of modern politics and law. Despite his vigorous attempt to differentiate his theory from Luhmann's, in the eyes of some onlookers the two are not that different. For Andrew Fraser, for example, 'In providing a philosophical rationale for the managerial revolution, Habermas has begun a new chapter in the intellectual history of enlightened despotism' (Fraser, 'Marx for Managerial', 382). In what follows I concentrate on Habermas's concept of the public sphere, first used extensively in his second book, *Structural Transformations of the Public Sphere* (1962; *Strukturwandel der Öffentlichkeit*, hereinafter *SdÖ*). I argue that the debate between Habermas and Luhmann can best be understood as to whether a public sphere (*Öffentlichkeit*), in the sense developed by Habermas of participatory rational discourse tied to the formulation of policy, can be said to exist to the extent that it would overcome the autonomy of distinct social subsystems. Between 1981 and 1994 Habermas was cited 440 times in American law reviews, more than Jacques Derrida and Niklas Luhmann put together. Arthur Jacobson, who compiled the statistics, believes that legal scholars who embraced Habermasian theory reduced it to the single concept of 'deliberative democracy' (Jacobson, 'Habermas and Luhmann', 5), but there would seem to be a less contingent preference for theories that give law a constitutive role to play in the construction of the social good.[8] In particular, Habermas's notion of the public sphere as a forum for discursive reason provides the most powerful and consistent alternative to Luhmann's picture of social subsystems that are operatively closed on themselves (as well as to the post-structuralist political theories of Jacques Derrida,

---

8   A citation check for the next decade (1995–2005) made through Westlaw Campus showed Luhmann with 378 hits, Habermas with 1769.

Jean-François Lyotard, and others). In the end, *Öffentlichkeit* may be more than a structural coupling: it may represent an alternative model of the way modern societies manage their subsystems, and how individuals participate in such systems. Another advantage of treating Habermas in this chapter is that his study reveals much about the structural transformations in eighteenth-century Germany that will be a basis for understanding my first examples, Jacob Grimm, Immanuel Kant and Goethe.

Öffentlichkeit is not a coined term, nor was Habermas the first to write an extensive essay on it. Indeed, the word appears in article 42 of the *Grundgesetz* (Basic Law) of the Federal Republic of Germany, which guarantees the openness of parliament and of court trials. It is listed in Grimms' *Wörterbuch* as a coinage of the eighteenth century, a nominalization of the adjective *öffentlich* ('public'). The relatively recent coinage of the noun, which seems deliberately formed on the French term, *publicité*, bears out Habermas's point that the bourgeois public sphere only fully came into existence in the eighteenth century. Furthermore, the term's antonym, *Innerlichkeit* (literally 'interiority', but better translated as 'subjectivity') dates from the same period. Habermas's originality lies not in coining a new, obscurantist theoretical term, but in unveiling the history and maximally exploiting the multivalence of an existing, almost quotidian German word, *Öffentlichkeit*.

Following the path blazed by Hannah Arendt in works such as *The Human Condition* (1958), Habermas's study revived the Kantian idea of a public sphere, where genuine, reasoned political debate takes place – though never on the terms of equality or unhindered access theorized by the bourgeoisie. Perhaps the most straightforward definition of this sphere given in the *SdÖ* is as

> the sphere of private people gathered together as a public. Against the public powers these private people claim for themselves the public sphere regulated from above, in order to engage such powers in a debate over the general rules governing relations in the basically privatized but publicly relevant sphere of commodity exchange and social labor. The medium of this political confrontation was peculiar and without historical precedent: people's public use of their reason [*das öffentliche Räsonnement*]. (Habermas, *SdÖ*, 86)

This passage makes clear that Habermas constructs his notion on Kant's definition of *öffentliches Räsonnement* given in the essay 'What is Enlightenment?' (1783; 'Beantwortung der Frage: Was ist Aufklärung?'). There, Kant limits public reason to the use a

'Gelehrter' makes of his knowledge in public. The concept of *Öffentlichkeit* is thus not a mass-democratic 'volonté de tous'. It requires the existence of a cultural elite whose work represents the public use of reason. In subsequent writings, however, Habermas emphasizes that the language of the public sphere is 'ordinary language' (in contrast to any artificially constructed 'transfer grammar' developed in order for subsystems to communicate, according to the tenets of ST), founded in communicative action and grounded in the respective lifeworlds of participants. As he points out in his major work on law, *Between Facts and Norms* (1992; *Faktizität und Geltung*), such a public sphere presupposes an 'ordinary language' that does not belong to any social subsystem in particular (Habermas, *Between Facts and Norms*, 54–5). Indeed, *Öffentlichkeit* is one of the most frequently indexed terms in this book, second only to 'law' (*Recht*) itself. Furthermore, central to the later book's thesis is 'the claim that under certain circumstances civil society can acquire influence in the public sphere, have an effect on the parliamentary complex (and the courts) through its own public opinions, and compel the political system to switch over to the official circulation of power' (Habermas, 373).

One could almost think of *Öffentlichkeit* as a synonym for structural coupling, for it is a dream of a forum where issues can be discussed in 'ordinary language', free of the citational chains of system. Habermas adopts for a moment the schema of ST in order to overcome it: 'The one text of "the" public sphere, a text continually extrapolated and extending radially in all directions, is divided by internal boundaries into arbitrarily small texts for which everything else is context; yet one can always build hermeneutical bridges from one text to the next' (Habermas, 374).

In this theory, the entrance of literature, art and philosophy into processes of marketing and reification is what allows them to function within the public sphere:

> Inasmuch as philosophical and literary works, artworks in general, are produced for the market and distributed through the market, they come to resemble information in general: as commodities they are in principle accessible to all. They no longer remain elements in the representation of the public sphere of church and court. [...] The private persons who have access to the work as a commodity profane it, in that they autonomously, in the way of rational conversation, search out its meaning, discuss and therefore make known what as long as it was ineffable had been able to develop authoritative power. (Habermas, *SdÖ*, 97–8)

Without acknowledging Walter Benjamin's notion of reproducibility as destructive of the artwork's *aura*, Habermas here invokes it in order to describe a historical transformation which, though it seems to reduce the aesthetic qualities which we identify with art, brings the work into our own lifeworld for the first time and allows it to function as public discourse. From a literary-historical point of view, however, something rather different happens as well in the early modern period, namely the invention of new forms such as the essay and literary criticism, along with the increasing production of novels and other realistic, dialogic and open-ended genres. For Habermas, as for Luhmann, the discourse of artworks is specialized like that of law or technology. The difference is the high degree of emotional content and subjectivity, which are nevertheless communicative. Niklas Luhmann has pointed out this function of communication, with a jab at Habermas: 'in the case of serious problems of understanding and apparent misunderstandings, social systems very often tend to avoid the burden of argumentation and reasoned discourse to reach consensus – very much to the affliction of Habermas. Instead, they tend to push the matter into rejection and to embark on the easy vessel of conflict' (Luhmann, 'Autopoiesis', 14).

Habermas's ideal type too closely resembles the public sphere's own self-image, as if Habermas were an apologist for, rather than a critic of, bourgeois ideology – a lapsus that makes Habermas's critique of Luhmann appear ironic. *SdÖ*, for example, tells us more about how bourgeois intellectuals thought the public sphere operated, rather than how it did in actuality. In other words, 'Habermas largely replaces the historical analysis of the forms of public sphere by the history of ideas on the public sphere' (Koivisto and Valiverronen, 'The Resurgence of Critical Theories', 22). One might quibble with the word 'replaces' here, as there do not seem to be any large-scale historical studies that Habermas could have used. On the contrary, the controversy surrounding his model of the public sphere has provoked scholars such as Joan Landes, Patricia Roberts, Michael Schudson and others to examine more closely how the public sphere actually operated in, for example, early modern France and in Puritan New England. Investigations such as Schudson's provide evidence that leads to another objection to the Habermasian model: *SdÖ* fails to emphasize properly, as Alexander Kluge, Rainer Nägele, J. F. Lyotard and a host of feminist scholars have pointed out, the extent to which the public sphere, like any other social category, defines itself by principles of exclusion – in ST terms, by banishing potential communications that fail to meet standards of rationality to its environment. The rationality and 'ordinary language' that Habermas sees as the only conceivable medium of public debate limits *Öffentlichkeit* in terms of genre, class and gender. Issues not capable of rational resolution – such as religious conviction – are simply banished to the private sphere.

German radicals of the 1960s and 1970s spoke of the need for the creation of an 'oppositional public sphere', a concept which spawned a number of varieties. Author and filmmaker Alexander Kluge has developed an entire approach to creative writing and film-making based on the need for creating a non-reductive public sphere. In Kluge's view, neither the classical public sphere of the eighteenth century, nor the privately owned, 'pseudo-public' sphere of post-war Germany, is capable of producing true democracy (Kluge, 'Film and the Public Sphere', 213). Kluge sees his oppositional public sphere as a necessary expansion of the existing ones. With Oskar Negt, he has elaborated the notion of a proletarian public sphere which uses not reason, but physical action related to seizure of the means of production. Sit-down strikes, for example, which cannot be fit into Habermas's model of reasoned debate, may constitute a worker's only means of entrance into the public sphere. Negt and Kluge's *Öffentlichkeit und Erfahrung* argues that 'a plant where there is a strike or a factory that is being occupied is to be understood [...] as the essential core of a conception of public sphere that is rooted in the production process' (Negt and Kluge, xliv). Habermas, in contrast, argues that the public sphere (we will see in a minute that he insists on its singularity *e pluribus unum*), while it is the source of most political change, connects production and other pragmatic issues with democratic processes through the medium of language.

As an example of identity politics, the feminist critique of Habermas raises the question of whether a concept of public sphere can be made compatible with the forms of cultural analysis and ethnic studies based on such politics. The subsequent proliferation of critical discourses and sub-specializations point to the impossibility of such a meta-language. Rainer Nägele points out that even Kant had framed the possibility of the public use of reason as but one discursive practice among many:

> Kant's ear hears the voice of reason among other registers of discourse such as telling stories (*Erzählen*) and joking (*Scherzen*), and it almost seems as if reasoning finds its place among these other registers as a latecomer. In any case, it finds its place, but it does not take over. It is part of a conversational chorus. In commenting on this passage of Kant, Habermas casually silences the other voices and hears only the reasoning which seems to have occupied all the places. Although we can no longer hear the voices speaking to Kant, we can still read the

texts of the Enlightenment. We can also read its obsession with jokes, wit, comedy, tears, ghosts and ghostbusters, *Schwärmer* [dreamers] and *Geisterseher* [mediums], criminals, clowns, and *Hanswürste* [jesters]. (Nägele, 'Public Voice and Private Voice', 72).

Nägele's public sphere depends upon carnivalized rather than rational discourse.

In his later work, Habermas responds to such critiques by positing *Öffentlichkeit* as: (1) an *e pluribus unum* phenomenon, with all subspheres porous to each other; and (2) grounded in 'ordinary' rather than in metalanguage. He makes the following assertions in *Between Facts and Norms*:

> The public sphere is differentiated into levels according to the density of communication, organizational complexity, and range – from the *episodic* publics found in taverns, coffee houses, or on the streets; through the *occasional* or 'arranged' publics of particular presentations and events, such as theater performances, rock concerts, party assemblies, or church congresses; up to the *abstract* public sphere of isolated readers, listeners, and viewers scattered across large geographical areas, or even around the globe, and brought together only through the mass media. Despite these manifold differentiations, however, all the partial publics constituted by ordinary language remain porous to one another. (Habermas, 374; emphasis in original)

As we can see in the above quote, Habermas's concept of *Öffentlichkeit* is a totalizing one. In addition, one might say that Habermas's goal was precisely to reify the public sphere – as an antidote to the almost complete collapse of subjectivity into mere publicity.

Luhmann, somewhat surprisingly, proposes an empirical test for the existence of a public sphere, at least as this relates to the law: has a court ever applied the *Recht/Unrecht* (in Habermas's terms, valid/invalid) distinction to rational – or, as in Nägele's point above, irrational – consensus stemming from the public sphere? No, this is not the way that courts make decisions, despite the idyllic picture Bertolt Brecht provided of such decision-making in his *Caucasian Chalk Circle* (1944; *Der Kaukasische Kreidekreis*), where the peasants gather to reach a consensus on the best use of the common lands. 'Such a criterion [of consensus] for the distinction between validity/ invalidity cannot be tested in a court. [Only in a play!] Thus, this criterion can only work as a legal fiction. [...] Validity is founded on some kind of idealization of something that is absent' (Luhmann, *Law as a Social System*, 125). This is not to say that courts are impervious to expressed public perceptions stemming from the lifeworlds of law's empire – these may become what Luhmann calls 'irritants' that perturb the legal system. But we must account for the fact that such expressions are cited in legal decision-making even less than are works of literature.

In the end, Habermas and Luhmann agree on much in their basic assessment of the *Ausdifferenzierung*, autopoiesis, and recursivity of social subsystems in complex societies. Whereas in relatively simple societies morality and law can remain coupled or directly related through mutual reference to a metasocial realm, such as a shared religion, the heterogeneity and technical specialization of modernity breaks such extra-systemic references. Habermas analogizes that moral concepts cannot be projected onto the law like the outline of a geometric figure. Formal legal systems abstract, universalize and reduce subjective moral sentiment to mere formal compliance without examination of mental states. However, legal formalism is part and parcel of a necessary formalization of moral action in the modern world. With or without an autonomous legal system, the timeless moral imperative to help those in need can only rarely be exercised in a straightforward fashion that corresponds to individual sentiment. In a mediatized society (to return to a point made earlier), those most in need might be half a world away, and the only pathway to help may be through international organizations. There is a loss not only of a sense of immediacy, but also of a sense of crisis, where the individual would feel inadequate to the task of living up to the moral imperative to help at such a long distance. The formalism of law and of other subsystems then intervenes to act as a scaffolding that holds individuals and their desires erect. Law no longer acts directly on moral sentiment, but (hopefully) through the democratic public sphere, elections and referenda. Individuals do not lose their moral sentiments, but allow them to be translated into the formal channels of enacted legislation: 'Under conditions of high complexity, moral contents can spread throughout a society along the channels of legal regulation' (Habermas, 'Law and Morality', 212).

With this idea of channeling, or – to use James Boyd White's terms – of translation, Habermas allows for a mediated permeability between law and lay conceptions of justice that ST seems to deny. Furthermore, the inability of individuals to connect the legal system to moral rules is (and must be) compensated by their ability to affect the law as a whole through the democratic election of legislators:

> In contrast to naturally emergent rules, whose validity can be

judged solely from the moral point of view, legal norms have an artificial character. They comprise an intentionally produced layer of action norms that are reflexive in the sense of being applicable to themselves. Hence the principle of democracy must not only establish a procedure of legitimate law-making, it must also steer the production of the legal medium itself. (Habermas, 'Law and Morality', 206–7)

Habermas points out that Luhmann's theory ignores the genealogy of present legal systems, which originally allowed divine and natural law to exist alongside positive law. With increasing democratization and secularization, these ideas have migrated to the legislative sphere that now gives law its basic justification: 'A legal system does not acquire autonomy on its own. It is autonomous only to the extent that the legal procedures institutionalized for legislation and for the administration of justice guarantee impartial judgment and provide the channels through which practical reason gains entrance into law and politics. There can be no autonomous law without the realization of democracy' (Habermas, 'Law and Morality', 208).

William Rasch adds a further distinction between the two thinkers:

The whole movement of Habermas's thought tends to some final resting place, prescriptively in the form of consensus as the legitimate basis for social order, and methodologically in the form of a normative underlying simple structure that is said to dictate the proper shape of surface complexity. But for Luhmann, complexity does not register the limits of human knowledge as if those limits could be overcome or compensated for by the reconstruction of some universal rule-making process. Complexity always remains complex and serves as a self-replenishing reservoir of possibilities. (Rasch, *Niklas Luhmann's Modernity*, 49)

While Habermas is the self-identified leftist, then, Luhmann's system seems paradoxically to be more radical and more open to the possibilities of freedom.

From this brief comparison, it should be apparent why lawyers, at least those who publish in law reviews and other journals, would prefer Habermas to Luhmann. No less than literary critics, they want to maintain the structural coupling of what they do with the larger concerns of civil society. No less than literary critics, they do not gladly see the abandonment of moral grounds in favour of a purely functional analysis of their discursive practice. In the end, however, the choice between the two may be a matter of the famous half-empty or half-full glass. A frequent critique of Luhmann's theory has been that, in explaining exactly why overarching social consensus can never form the basis of political and social power, it undermines the dreams of intervention espoused in the more radical positions. Yet, 'the same argument, in rather mollified expression, is also implicit in the works of Habermas […] In these works, however, this view appears through a prism of limited activism, resigned moral humanism, and chastened or disappointed anti-capitalism. Refracted through this prism, arguments close to Luhmann's own view propose themselves as plausible and laudable to the moral conscience of contemporary social and political theory' (King and Thornhill, *Niklas Luhmann's Theory of Politics*, 220).

We will see in what follows, however, that the search for or reconstruction of a public sphere or, at the very least, for an unambiguous functional coupling or transfer grammar between autonomous subsystems is the dream of many authors of modern German literature. I have proleptically placed the present chapter first in my argument, but it could also usefully have been placed last, both to conform with the chronology of the writings that it treats, and also because the theoretical conflict elaborated in the debate between these two sociologists has precedents in the many writers and scholars who attempt to bring law and literature (back) together. As noted above, Habermas's key concept of public sphere finds its ideal type in the literary and publicistic cultures of the Enlightenment. His critique of functionalism's inability to provide connection between systems and the lifeworlds of those affected by them was articulated *in nuce* long ago by Jacob Grimm, as we shall see in the next chapter. Indeed the Grimmian and Romantic notion of the 'spirit of the people' (*Volksgeist*) as the source of legal wisdom invokes perhaps the most fundamental paradox in Habermas's theory of law: it asks of systems that they connect to the lifeworld of the *demos*; but it asks in turn of the *demos* that it move beyond the most fundamental aspects of its lifeworld, leaving behind religious scripture and prohibition, adherence to a particular people or ethnicity, and all other non-rational forms of belonging that tend to equate justice with 'just us', in order to engage in the rational discussion of issues. The discourse theory of law is based upon a post-traditional morality that 'points beyond all particular forms of life'. Democracy no longer signifies the rule of a particular people constituted as a body politic. Rather, it becomes a form of communicative action that has been 'generalised, abstracted and freed from all limits' (Habermas, *The Inclusion of the Other*, 41).

There are, in fact, a few signs that such a world public sphere is being constructed in, for example, internationally shared sites dedicated to memories of genocide, injustice and national trauma. Such sites take the form of museums, memorials, parks and the like; they find their narrative counterparts in works of world literature such as memoirs, reportage, *testimonios*, novels, and documentary and feature films such as the internationally successful *The Lives of Others* (2005; *Das Leben der Anderen*) about the security apparatus of the former East Germany. One might take the competition staged for the 9/11 Memorial, which welcomed design proposals from around the globe, as a salient example of the internationalization of the public sphere, at least insofar as it concerns the memory of atrocity.[9] Luhmann might respond that one cannot yet identify a coherent system for such discourse nor define its operations; nevertheless, it may act as an 'irritant' on the operations of municipal legal systems, and the future is contingent.

Thinking about a global public sphere and international law takes us to the farthest point this study can reach, and perhaps a bit beyond, as the examples above indicate. The next chapter is situated in the nineteenth century, where we find one of the most obsessive scholarly constructions of legal community based on shared language ever attempted, by Jacob Grimm.

---

9 On the tensions between local memory and international interest in museums, see Annette van den Bosch, 'Museums: Constructing a Public Culture in the Global Age'.

2.1
In Search of the Invisible Precedent: Grimm Writes to Savigny

> The law is one big anthropological document.
>
> Oliver Wendell Holmes

It is tempting to read these words of Chief Justice Holmes as dependent upon the work of Carl Friedrich von Savigny (1779–1861), Jacob Grimm (1785–1863) and other German scholars of the nineteenth century, whose methodology could (anachronistically, since anthropology had yet to be founded as a discipline) be phrased as 'no law without anthropology'. This turn to 'the people' as a transcendental subject of law was brought about by a combination of factors, including the proto-anthropological writings of Johann Gottfried Herder (1744–1803), the French Revolution, and the philosophy of Kant and Fichte.[1] The vocabulary is taken up by Hegel, for whom *Volksgeist* is a step on the path towards *Weltgeist*.[2] Nineteenth-century legal scholars saw the purpose of their work as consisting of demonstrating, through comparison with historical examples, how current laws and legal systems conform (or not) to the standards and ideals of the people they regulate. This surprisingly value-neutral approach

---

1 This aspect has been thoroughly examined by Dieter Nörr in his aptly titled *Savigny's Philosophical Apprenticeship* (*Savignys philosophische Lehrjahre*). Among other questions, Nörr tries to determine whether Savigny was influenced by Kant's writings on law, or instead was reinterpreting the later writings of Fichte (Nörr, 328–35). Nörr intended his title as an allusion to Goethe's novel, *Wilhelm Meister's Apprenticeship* (1796; *Wilhelm Meisters Lehrjahre*). He adduces a number of contemporary authors of the period, including Heinrich Jacobi, Schiller and Friedrich Schlegel.
2 A useful summary of the use of '*Volk*' and '*Volksgeist*' in German law can be found in Markus Dirk Dubber, 'The German Jury and the Metaphysical *Volk*'.

to legal norms contrasts with Enlightenment ideas of natural law and the search for rational bases for legal systems that are readily translatable from one culture to another. The term *Volksgeist* (spirit of the people) refers to a virtual construction of basic beliefs, ideas and customs that permeate an oral culture and leave their imprint in written documents. In the case of law in particular, however, the move from an oral to a written culture presupposes an *Ausdifferenzierung* that produces a professional legal class with its own *Fachsprache* (professional jargon) alien to 'ordinary language'. In short, whatever evidence can be produced to demonstrate the existence of underlying shared concepts and values inevitably witnesses simultaneously to this proto-public sphere's sublation into more modern, autonomous forms and formalisms. In the previous chapter we contrasted this latter, ST model of society with the Habermasian notion of the public sphere. While Habermas has never claimed Grimm and Savigny as precursors to his own thinking, this chapter should make evident a common concern among the three for restoring a shared communicative medium that reconnects the specialized communications of various subsystems to the lifeworld of the people affected by them, and that thereby conjoins a society both scholars recognize as functionally segmented. However, while Habermas stresses rational discourse as the medium for (re)constructing a public sphere and a people's lifeworld, Grimm stresses poetry.

The epigraph to this book's introductory chapter – and thus in a sense to the book's thematic – was taken from Grimm's long confessional letter of 9 March 1807, addressed to his mentor, the legal scholar and future Prussian minister, Friedrich Carl von Savigny. Grimm writes that 'A sort of stain marks someone who leaves one field of study for the other, as if it were a religious conversion' (Grimm, *Briefe*, 28–31; 'Eine Art von Makel liegt auf dem, der von einer Wissenschaft ab, zu einer andern übertritt, wie bei einer Religionsveränderung'). The letter is argued with remarkable care and insight, and its chief argument is to point out the inevitable autopoiesis of legal scholarship.

Grimm's confessional letter to his mentor speaks to the contradictory success of the time Grimm had spent as Savigny's student at the University of Marburg and also as his teacher's research assistant in Paris, locating documents on Roman law. The very perfection of Roman law, Grimm argues, means that the study of law cannot be a science in the sense of an investigative procedure:

> Jurisprudence, however, is not at all something inexhaustible like philosophy or poetry; rather, it is both natural and probable for the former that history may demonstrate something factual

that brings jurisprudence to its highest point, that can then be arranged so as to serve as an epitome for any nation.

[Die Gesetzgebung ist aber keineswegs wie die Philosophie, Poesie etwas unerschöpfliches, sondern es ist in der Natur der Sache gelegen und wahrscheinlich, dass die Geschichte irgend ein Factum aufzuweisen habe, welches die Jurisprudenz auf einen höchsten Gipfel bringt, so dass sie für jedes Volk als unübertreffliches Muster dienen und eingerichtet werden kann.]

Grimm, *Briefe*, 28–29

The practical nature of legal studies would dictate Roman law as the only thing worthy of study; but the research into Roman law has already been accomplished to such a degree that nothing scientific is left to be done. The quandary Grimm finds himself in resembles, perhaps, that faced by Friedrich Nietzsche in the Bismarck era, when philology seemed on the one hand to represent a path forward, but on the other hand, in following it one was expending energy interpreting a culture that had passed away irretrievably. One of the major differences, of course, is that Nietzsche published his *Birth of Tragedy* (1872; *Die Geburt der Tragödie*) in the context of a newly unified Germany that did not yet exist as a political unit in Grimm's time. Unlike Nietzsche, whose book was the first step on the path to renouncing his position as a teacher of classical philology, after writing this letter Grimm was employed directly by the French – in fact by Napoleon's brother Jérôme, who was King of Westphalia at the time.

As a result of the French invasion of German territories on the left bank of the Rhine, the Napoleonic Code, introduced in France in 1804. became law in those territories. Many of its provisions were thought to be 'unGerman' ('undeutsch'), including 'the removal of land-rent, division of estates, forced shared inheritance, civil marriage, and divorce' (Hedwig Vonessen, 'Friedrich Karl von Savigny und Jakob Grimm', 139). Grimm's confessional letter thus hides as much as it reveals. Grimm faces important historical and political circumstances if he continues to study law: he risks becoming obsolete when either the *Code Napoléon* is introduced into Germany through force or persuasion, as it has been on the west side of the Rhine and in the Palatinate, Rhenan Prussia and Hesse-Darmstadt, or else the earlier (1794) Prussian General Code (*Preussisches Allgemeines Landrecht*) is gradually adopted as that kingdom exerts increasing influence over the other German states. Grimm confesses this aspect of his transition only much later, in an essay of 1850 on the occasion of the celebration of the fiftieth anniversary of Savigny's doctorate. There, Grimm describes the persuasive power of the Napoleonic invasion: 'At that time, because we were oppressed by a superior power and were forced to change even our name in favour of another, all Roman and Germanic law was cancelled in a single act and the *Code Napoléon* introduced as statutory, how could that not have ruined my study of law?' (Grimm, 'Das Wort des Besitzes', 114; 'damals, weil uns die übermacht erdrückte und selbst unsern namen mit einem andern zu vertauschen zwang, der uns gar nichts angieng, wurde alles römische und deutsche recht mit einem streich aufgehoben und der code Napoleon als gesetz eingeführt, wie hätte mir das die rechtsstudien überhaupt nicht verleiden sollen?').

It might be questioned whether the state of nomological equilibrium Grimm describes in his farewell letter to Savigny could ever be reached. Grimm seemed to bracket an aspect of communication, that is, of a manipulation and transfer of *Sinn* (meaning) in such a way that it causes something to change. The meaningful (*sinnvolle*) legal proverbs and symbols cited by Grimm (we will see some examples below) supposedly regulate affairs and resolve disputes while leaving the actors and the society unchanged. They are effective but without effect.

The whole world has realized how Grimm's 'conversion' out of law and into literature and philology proved to be the 'right' choice: with his brother Wilhelm he went on to produce both the *Hausmärchen* (1812; Grimm's Fairy Tales) and the first comprehensive historical dictionary of the German language (1854), to name only the most important and lasting of their contributions. As Hermann Klenner has pointed out in 'Als Recht und Poesie aus einem Bette aufzustehen schienen', Germanistik as a discipline arises from the disjunction effected through the letter of 1807. It has also been recognized, however, that the impression Grimm's letter gives, namely that he was making a complete break from Savigny and from the study of law, is misleading. Though their career paths parted, the two would remain in contact, frequently in harmony but at times in opposition. The story has been told before from many angles.[3] The

---

3 By Klenner as noted above, by John Toews in his *Becoming Historical*, by Ruth Schmidt-Wiegand in *Jacob Grimm und das genetische Prinzip in Rechtswissenschft und Philologie*, by Jutta Strippel in 'Zum Verhältnis von deutscher Rechtsgeschichte und deutscher Philologie', by Gunhild Ginschel in *Der junge Jacob Grimm*, and by Hedwig Vonessen in 'Friedrich Karl von Savigny und Jakob Grimm', among others. The relationship of the scholarly work of Grimm and Savigny to their pragmatic political work is told in Hans-Bernd Harder and Ekkehard Kaufman, *Die Brüder Grimm in ihrer amtlichen und politischen Tätigkeit*.

idea of a complete break is contradicted above all by Jacob Grimm's contributions to Savigny's legal studies journal, and his publication in 1828 of the *Deutsche Rechtsalterthumer*, a collection of citations from legal texts of the German Middle Ages. Grimm sought in this collection something different from the epitome that he found in Roman law, namely to resurrect a full gamut of legal texts rather than selected passages that were particularly appropriate for current usage. My own retelling of this story emphasizes the contours and contradictions of the *Volk* as a kind of proto-public sphere. The medium of cultural unity of a people is arguably its language, and Grimm emphasizes that this language provides a platform for the structural coupling between systems. The correspondence between Grimm and Savigny, indeed their whole relationship, sounds as a distant, differentiated echo of this original unity. My goal in this chapter is to conduct a close reading of Grimm's language at those points where he seeks to conjoin law with literature. This conjunction between law and poetry requires a rhetorical force that drives Grimm's own language towards the poetic. My presentation will be in three parts: an analysis of Grimm's writings that invoke the utopia of a public sphere; a reading of some of Grimm's letters to Savigny that allude to the conjunctions and disjunctions in their goals and aims; and a trip through Grimm's peculiar hommage to Savigny, 'The Word of Possession' ('Das Wort des Besitzes'). I will begin, however, by tracing the counterpoint of the two careers of the men and their relationship with each other.

Conjunctions and Disjunctions

The correspondence between Jacob Grimm and Friedrich Carl von Savigny epitomizes a coupling between subsystems that takes place intensively and productively, despite the very different *habitus* of the two men. Their mutual influence was highly complex. Savigny developed the notion of the necessity of history as precedent for current jurisprudence. This concern for history characterized his lectures at the University of Marburg, through which Grimm first got to know him. Whereas other lecturers merely gave their own commentary on the existing legal textbooks, Savigny used what today we would call a case method, presenting historical examples of actual legal arguments and briefs. The actual practice of law in Germany took precedence, for the first time in centuries, over the absorption of dry and abstract rules.

Savigny was born in Frankfurt am Main in 1779 and studied jurisprudence at the University of Marburg, at that time a rather unimportant university where law was taught in a centuries-old fashion: Roman law held the centre of attention, and students were led through its intricacies for most of their course of study. The semester Savigny spent at Göttingen under the tutorship of Johann Stephan Pütter was perhaps more important than all his semesters in Marburg. Pütter, along with Gustav Hugo and some other professors, taught the history of constitutions in order to explain the present situation of constitutional law.

Savigny became famous in 1803 with a book on property law, *The Law of Possession* (*Das Recht des Besitzes*), which followed and expanded Pütter's method: by going back to the origins of Roman property law, Savigny was able to clear away the centuries of commentary and make Roman law more applicable to the present. As Gerhard Dilcher summarizes,

> this possibility of making Roman law more applicable through historical investigation of classical sources is based on the fact that the legal structure of the emerging civil society more closely resembled that of the society of the polis-citizen than it did the declining estates-society [*Ständegesellschaft*] of the Ancien Régime. Thus, historical research into law goes hand in hand with modernization – concepts that seem to us today to oppose each other. (Dilcher, 'Jacob Grimm als Jurist', 28)

It was as though – playing on the metaphor of 'source' – the irrigation of a field through a tributary of a tributary had been replaced by a direct taking from the main river.

Savigny married Kunigunda Brentano in the following year. In 1815 he helped found the *Journal of Historical Legal Studies* (*Zeitschrift für geschichtliche Rechtswissenschaft*), which marked the beginning of the so-called Historical School in Germany and to which Jacob Grimm made two contributions. Savigny held positions at the University of Berlin and became a darling of the Prussian government from this time until his death in 1861.

During the Winter semester 1802–3, Grimm and Savigny together prepared a text called 'Juristische Methodenlehre'. One of its claims that remains constant in Savigny's legal thinking is, in essence, the principle of the autopoiesis of legal subsystems, which he expresses in the following fashion:

> Every legislation is [...] the result of the earlier history of legislation. Justinian never intended to create his own codebook, but rather to compose a mere compilation of the abundant materials that are already in existence. The historical whole has itself become law.

[Jede Gesetzgebung ist [...] das Resultat der früheren Geschichte der Gesetzgebung. Justinian hatte nie die Absicht, ein eigenes Gesetzbuch zu machen, sondern eine blosse Kompilation aus den sehr reichlich vorhandenen Materialien zu bilden. Das historische Ganze ist selbst wieder Gesetz geworden.]

'Juristische Methodenlehre'; cited in Schmidt-Wiegand, 3

Savigny and Grimm use a recursive formulation here to characterize the operations of law: legislation is created out of legislation, and law's operation is to convert the 'historical whole', meaning presumably the nomological whole of a people over the course of time, into positive law. This model has much to do with the positions Savigny took up later in the debates concerning whether any of the German states were in need of constitutions or codebooks. Savigny played down the usefulness of the creation of new laws in favour of the recursive operation noted above – the making explicit of the historical whole through a deeper and more thorough study of the history of law in order to bring its historical essence to expression. In other words, codification, if undertaken, should involve the scripting and reformulation of what can be determined to already exist by examination of 'existing materials'. This position has generally been described as a reaction against the excesses of the French Revolution, against the French Emperor Napoleon, and against the imposition of 'his' Code – we might read the invocation of the Roman Emperor Justinian and the Pandects compiled under his reign as an implicit contrasting figure. From this first collaboration onwards, 'codification', and its surrounding examples and terminology, becomes a shibboleth for the two men. After the fear of imposition of the Napoleonic Code had passed, the new bogeyman of codification became the Prussian General Laws (*Preussisches Allgemeines Landrecht*, hereinafter ALR). This attempt at codification, which it will be noted preceded the French effort by a decade, suffered a poor and confused reception, as Reinhart Koselleck has thoroughly documented in *Prussia between Reform and Revolution* (*Preussen zwischen Reform und Revolution*). Even those not fundamentally opposed to codification were put off by the conflict between the putative 'generality' of the code and its attempt to maintain a society based on differences between social orders, with their concomitant privileges, obligations and exceptions. Savigny first came to lecture on the ALR as late as 1819; it only became an examination topic in 1826. In 1814, however, the possibility of a general German constitution loomed on the horizon, and Grimm confessed his fear that the ALR would be its basis:

I would also like to discuss with you the new constitution for Germany, and am certain of only one thing at this point: the Prussian General Code should not spread to other parts of Germany, and the local laws of other regions, even if they are worse than the Prussian General Code, must resist. That way, instead of the mediocre lulling us to sleep, the strong feeling of the bad may give rise to something better. My chief complaint about the Prussians is that their manner of administration has a totalizing (modern, French) aspect.

[Ich möchte auch gern mit Ihnen über die neue Deutschland zu gebende Rechtsverfassung sprechen und bin vorläufig nur darüber einig: das preuss. Gesetzbuch darf nicht weiter um sich greifen, und die übrigen Landrechte, selbst wenn sie schlechter sind, müssen sich dagegen sträuben, damit nicht das Mittelmässige einschläfere, sondern aus dem stärkeren Gefühl des Schlechten das bessere entspringe. Es ist überhaupt mein Hauptanstoss an Preussen, dass mir die Art und Weise ihrer Verwaltung etwas durchgreifendes (modernes, französisches) hat.]

Grimm, *Briefe*, 169–70

Grimm notes the need for comparative study of English, Swedish and Norwegian laws. Grimm's perverse logic here – what's bad is good, because it stimulates reform – stems in part from his local Hessian patriotism.

Another poignant example is Grimm's citation of Martin Luther's table-talks (*Tischreden*) in a long letter to Savigny dated 18 January 1816. Luther states that attempts to codify and order the laws of Saxony are as though one wished to treat the Latin verb *sum* (to be) 'by conjugating it regularly according to the paradigm as "sum", "sus", "sut"' (Grimm, *Briefe*, 227; 'regulariter nach der gemeinen Regel conjugirn, sum, sus, sut'). The irregularity of *sum* is well known – the conjugation in reality is 'sum', 'eris', 'est'. Language and law, Luther and Grimm imply here, do not always work according to a rule. In another vein of the same argument, in his lectures on German literary history held at Göttingen between 1834 and 1836, Grimm upheld the historical against the philosophical approaches to law of Kant, Hegel and others:

The essence of legal scholarship is therefore by its nature a historical one, which must go back as far as possible to the earliest conditions and follow these up to our day. Recently, the view has been put forth – by G. F. W. Hegel and Abraham

Gans – that law must be treated philosophically. Every field of knowledge must be philosophical in the ordinary sense of the word; but that does not mean that the whole field must be understood philosophically. That would mean [in the case of legal studies] an invention of law through suppression of all its material aspects. The results would be incomprehensible to everyone.

[Das Wesen des Rechtsstudiums ist daher seiner Natur nach ein historisches, es muss möglichst weit auf den frühsten Standpunkt zurückgehen und diesen bis auf unsre Tage verfolgen. In der jüngsten Zeit ist die Ansicht behandelt, das Recht müsse philosophisch behandelt werden – So Hegel und Gans. Philosophisch im gewöhnlichen Sinne muss jede Wissenschaft sein; aber das heisst noch nicht, die ganze Wissenschaft vom philosophischen Standpunkte aufzufassen: diese wäre dann, mit Hintansetzung alles Stoffes das recht erfinden. Daraus entstünde etwas Allen Unverständliches.]

Grimm, *Vorlesung*, 391

The life of Jacob Grimm is generally thought of in conjunction with that of his younger brother, Wilhelm. Jacob was born in 1785, Wilhelm a year later. From 1802 to 1805 Jacob studied law at the University of Marburg, his brother joining him in 1803. In 1805 he accompanied Savigny to Paris to help with the reading of manuscript materials in the Bibliothèque Nationale that would become the corpus for Savigny's treatment of Roman law in the Middle Ages. The further correspondence between the two men frequently addressed their common interest in archival research and traded information about how to obtain rare books and manuscripts. While Jacob terminated his formal legal study in 1807, his brother Wilhelm brought his study to a conclusion by taking the exam. Paradoxically, however, it is much easier to associate Jacob's later work with jurisprudence, while Wilhelm's writings are occasional political pieces related to the upheavals of the Vormärz period. Neither brother was a practising lawyer, but Jacob's work makes him a founder of legal archaeology and ethnography (*Rechtsarchäologie and Rechtsethnologie*). Grimm's need to stay close to home made an academic career impossible, so he took a secretarial job with the *Kriegskollegium* in 1806, only to give it up shortly after the French invasion. He eventually became the private librarian of King Jérôme, as noted above, and he continued in this profession at various posts over the next thirty years, most notably at Göttingen. At the same time, he was given important political missions, including travelling to Paris once again to recover artworks and manuscripts looted by the French, and being part of the delegation of Hessen at the Congress of Vienna 1814–15, which he severely criticized in letters to Wilhelm and to Savigny.

In 1837, both Grimm brothers, along with five other faculty members at Göttingen, signed a letter to the King of Hannover, Ernst August, protesting that he had abrogated the constitution established by his father. The King's reaction was to dismiss all of the signers from their positions at the university. Jacob Grimm had to leave the realm of Hannover; the defence the two wrote of their action could only be published in Switzerland, and only under Jacob's name since Wilhelm was still living in Göttingen. Savigny, himself fully integrated into the political apparatus of Berlin, appears not to have approved of the action taken by the two brothers; nevertheless, he was instrumental in seeing that they were eventually hired by Savigny's former pupil, the Prussian emperor Friedrich Wilhelm IV. They came to Berlin in 1841, where they worked together on their dictionary of the German language.

Any approach to Savigny's thought in its historical context immediately runs up against the legal scholar's many ties to literature. He married into the Brentano family, of which the author Clemens Brentano is the most famous member. He was loved by and rejected Caroline von Günderrode, whose subsequent suicide was immortalized in Bettina von Arnim's novel *Die Günderrode* (1840). Savigny read Friedrich Hölderlin's novel *Hyperion* (1797) with enough interest to copy out a long paragraph, whose summary statement, 'Nature has become Idea', could serve as an epigraph for Savigny's (and Grimm's) concept of a legal hermeneutic that attempts to extract, refine, and put down in writing historically developed national legal concepts (Hans Kiefner, 'Ideal wird', 141).

Savigny's approach to law, as John Toews points out, had been about trying to restore the integration of law with its other social subsystems. Unity was posited to reside in the shared cultural values of a people, or *Volk*: 'Savigny claimed that in this original historical consciousness, the world of legal relations and institutions through which the individual gave form to his mutual relations with other subjects was experienced not as an aggregate of separate individual parts, as rules and norms that were functionally bound to different activities, but as an integrated totality within an integrated culture' (Toews, 'Becoming Historical', 287). Furthermore, law had originated as action embedded in social reality before it had become its own system. For this reason, Savigny argued against the introduction of code systems of law in works such as *The Vocation of Our Age for Legislation and Jurisprudence* (*Vom Beruf unsrer Zeit für Gesetzgebung und Rechtswissenschaft*). Rather than instituting codes,

Savigny argued for a thorough historical grounding in legal history: 'there is [...] no mode of avoiding this overruling influence of the existing matter; it will be injurious to us so long as we ignorantly submit to it; but beneficial, if we oppose to it a vivid creative energy – obtain the mastery over it by a thorough grounding in history, and thus appropriate to ourselves the whole intellectual wealth of preceding generations' (Savigny, 'Vocation', 132–3). Law was an edifice built on precedents.

Poetry and Right

Grimm's Christmas Eve letter of 1813 to Savigny can be read as a palinode to his 1807 resignation from legal study. He tells his former teacher of how he has been reading a collection of old German laws:

> It can be doubted whether any jurisprudence has been more poetic, and for that very reason it was sensibly practical in the highest degree. German jurisprudence is to Roman law as an epic is to speculative philosophy, but it could be of use for the historical recognition of a few sayings (not related to natural law), formulated in a pure and simple innocence.
>
> [Schwerlich ist irgend eine Jurisprudenz so poetisch gewesen, und eben damit war sie dennoch sinnlich practisch im höchsten Grad, sie verhält sich zum römischen Recht wie das Epos zur Speculation, ist aber vielleicht zur historischen erkennung einiger reinen und einfach unschuldig aufgefassten (nicht naturrechtlichen) Sätze wohl zu brauchen.]
>
> <div align="right">Grimm, <i>Briefe</i>, 149</div>

Grimm says a great deal in this sentence, aided by shared vocabulary and context that allow him to leave out as much as he puts in. That poetic Germanic law managed to be 'sensuously practical' (*sinnlich practisch*), for example, plays with the two meanings of '*Sinn*': sense and meaning. He will use the word again to describe the goal of his collection *German Legal Antiquities* (*Deutsche Rechtsalterthümer*) as being the preservation of the '*sensual element* of legal history' (Grimm, *Deutsche Rechtsalterthümer*, vii; *das sinnliche element der deutschen Rechtsgeschichte* [emphasis Grimm's]). The poetic formulations – by which, as we shall see, Grimm means language that expresses thought through tropes and imagery – reach the realm of thought and engrain themselves in the memory through their sensible aspects of rhyme and alliteration, metaphor, metonym, imagery and other poetic devices. This thought leads Grimm to his comparison of Germanic law to epic, as opposed to 'speculation', by which he means speculative philosophy. Grimm does not mean, of course, that German law follows the structure or displays the character of epic. Rather, he posits an analogy between the immediate, mimetic appeal of epic and the mediated apprehension of abstract reasoning, as in Roman law. This difference will become clear when we review a few of Grimm's examples below.

A year later (29 October 1814), Grimm writes a review of Savigny's *The Vocation of Our Age for Legislation and Jurisprudence* in the form of a letter to his former teacher (who has asked for Grimm's opinion). Grimm also supports Savigny's ideas for establishing the *Journal of Historical Legal Studies* (*Zeitschrift für geschichtliche Rechtswissenschaft*) that eventually becomes the central organ of the historical school, and to which he contributes an article, 'On Poetry in Law' ('Von der Poesie im Recht'). In his letter, Grimm returns relentlessly to the analogy and connection between law and poetry. He praises Savigny's comparison of law with custom and language, as these three are all popular (*volksmässig*), as opposed to elite or technical. This fact militates against natural law ideas, which become the equivalent of attempting to manufacture the organic, or to invent a universal language: 'Just as senseless as it would be, to set about inventing a language or a poetic tradition, so too no one with his limited reason can invent a legal system that would flourish with gusto, as does that which has grown up out of the ground' (Grimm, 'Von der Poesie im Recht', 172; 'So unsinnig es wäre, eine Sprache oder Poesie *erfinden* zu wollen, ebensowenig kann der Mensch mit seiner einseitigen Vernunft ein Recht finden, das sich ausbreite frisch und mild, wie das im Boden gewachsene' [emphasis in original]). The familiar valences of the German word '*Recht*' are in evidence in this passage. Grimm is not speaking of inventing a single law, any more than '*Poesie*' means a single poem. '*Recht*' here is right, meaning a whole system of justice including laws.

History, legend (*Volkssage*), even an individual biography that contains a practical case history, are all superior to the use of abstract reason to determine law:

> Even a poem or novel only succeeds when its author describes what he has experienced, and feels again what he really felt in his heart. However, since these experiences and thoughts are absorbed by people at different times and places, only great authors like Goethe have the gift of collecting the single living thing into one life, and even in such cases something goes missing.
>
> [Auch ein Gedicht, ein Roman gelingt bloss, wenn der Dichter

beschreibt, was er erlebt hat, und fühlt, wie er wahrhaftig im Herzen gefühlt hat. Da aber nun diese Erfahrungen und Gedanken zu verschiedener Zeit und an verschiedenen Orten in den Menschen eingehen, so ist es nur grossen Menschen wie dem Goethe gegeben, das einzelne Lebendige auch in ein ganzes Leben zu versammeln, und gerät dennoch nie so völlig.]

Grimm, *Briefe*, 172

A few pages further into Savigny's text, Grimm analogizes the transformation that law undergoes from being consciousness and custom to being politics and technique, when the professional troubadours (*Minnesänger*) adapt the older folk poetry. Such, Grimm says, is the replacement of nature with art. This latter type of law, then, is the true 'natural law', as opposed to the one produced by abstract reason of the *philosophes* and the declaration of the Rights of Man. Grimm declares it to be synonymous with both 'divine' (*göttlich*) and 'historical' law (Grimm, *Briefe*, 173). Grimm digresses in order to distinguish between the older poetry and literature that had 'epic force' (*epische Kraft*), and that of his contemporaries – he specifically names Jean Paul and Achim von Arnim – which does not display this characteristic.

In another long and complex passage, Grimm also compares pandecticism to the edition of an authoritative dictionary and grammar of a language: 'We [Germans] have not advanced so far and [our dictionaries] are more like private collections, against which anyone may appear and lodge a critique; the French were the first to introduce the General Code of their Academy' (Grimm, *Briefe*, 174; 'Mit den Wörterbüchern sind wir noch nicht so weit und sie gelten als Privatsammlungen, wogegen jedermann auftreten und reclamiren darf, die Franzosen haben zuerst das allgemeine Landrecht ihrer Academie eingeführt'). Here irony complicates Grimm's message; the basic comparison is between the *Dictionnaire de l'Académie Française* with its official status (since 1694) as providing the correct usage and vocabulary of the French language, and German dictionaries that are all 'private collections'. Even the Grimms' 'own' *Wörterbuch der deutschen Sprache* could not remedy that situation until decades after the death of both brothers. By the same token, Grimm's irony in this passage indicates that he is hesitant about attempting to be on a par with the French. Grimm does not call the effort of the *Académie* a dictionary, for example. Instead, he substitutes the term 'General Code' (*Allgemeines Landrecht*) in direct reference to the Prussian General Code of 1794, and thus in indirect reference to that other product of French academicism, the *Code Napoléon*. Grimm posits Epko von Repko (compiler of the *Sachsenspiegel*, the earliest collection of German legal texts), who noted that he was inventing nothing but was only transmitting the laws his ancestors had laid down, as a model for the collection of tales and sagas that should be carried out.[4]

Beyond characterizing the differences in the historical materials as things-in-themselves, Grimm also analogizes the difficulties faced in their formulation for contemporary usage: defining the border between law (*fixiertes Recht*) and custom (*Sitte*) is as difficult as deciding which phrases to include in a dictionary as a part of a word's definition. The impossibility of prohibition, or of turning the clock back, strikes Grimm as an analogous problem in law and literature as cultural expressions: 'Roman law cannot be abandoned – nor the older symbolic language reintroduced – any more than hexameter verse can be forbidden, or alliteration reintroduced,despite the unGerman feeling it has. (Grimm, *Briefe*, 174; 'Das röm[ische] Recht kann so wenig verlassen werden, als die Hexameter verboten (wiewohl ein undeutscher Ton darin ist,) oder die Alliterationen neu eingeführt (so wenig also die alten Symbole)' (Grimm, 174). In a similar vein, Grimm criticizes A. F. J. Thibaut's 1814 *On the Necessity of General Laws for Germany* (*Die Notwendigkeit eines allgemeinen bürgerlichen Rechts für Deutschland*) as confusing theory with praxis. According To Thibaut, Roman law should not be studied without knowing exactly what practical use it might have in a German context; by the same reasoning, responds Grimm, one would forbid the study of Homer and allow only the *Nibelungenlied* (Grimm, 170). Grimm's historicism is not insular; he is aware of the role of tradaptation in the revitalization of German literature in the second half of the eighteenth century, and in particular of Johann Heinrich Voss's influential versions of Homer's *Odyssey* (1781), which gave a major impetus to the use of hexameter in German verse, even though the language's natural rhythms do not easily allow for such a metre. (The application of quantitative metres of Greek and Latin to a stress-based prosody like German is problematic.) Alliteration (*Stabreim*) is the traditional German way of constructing verse units, along with rhyme.

At the end of section five of the *Vocation*, Savigny makes this point against codification: 'That which is thus constructed by men's hands before our eyes, will always hold a very different place in popular

---

4   Composed between 1220 and 1235 CE, the *Sachsenspiegel* is the oldest German '*Rechtsbuch*' and was compiled by Eike von Repgow (whose name becomes Epko von Repko in Grimm's dialect). As Grimm notes, Eiko or Epko, like the Emperor Justinian, wished only to compile standing legal practices, not to create new law.

estimation from that which has not so plain and palpable an origin' (Savigny, 'Vocation', 60). As an anecdote that supports this point, Grimm recalls his 1805 trip to Paris with his teacher. There they could observe the new festivals designed after the French Revolution to replace the old ones associated with the church:

> I remembered exactly what you had told me in Paris in 1805, as we were walking by the Notre Dame cathedral and were told about the newly introduced festivals and honours, that such stuff struck the people as empty and rootless. The people, too, only respects the *invisible* in poetry and has no liking for anything new.
>
> [Ich erinnerte mich dabei genau an das, was Sie mir zu Paris 1805 sagten, als wir einmal vor Notre Dame vorbeigingen und von den neueingeführten Festen und Würden die Rede kam, wie leer und wurzellos dem Volk dergleichen Machwerk auffalle. Das Volk achtet in der Poesie auch nur allein dieses *Unsichtbare* und mag das Neue nicht.]
>
> <div align="right">Grimm, <i>Briefe</i>, 175</div>

Grimm's ideal of the invisible precedent that is the only guide accepted by the people is related to the saying, 'a fish does not know water'. Festival, law and poetry are constitutive of culture, which is the element in which a people lives and hence invisible to it. This principle yields its inverse: for something – law, language, poetry – to belong to the people, it must derive from an invisible precedent. Grimm saw his task, then, to be that of making the invisible visible, on the principle of Savigny's model of good legislation, which blackletters something the people have always known and done.

Grimm contributed an article to the second volume of the *Zeitschrift für geschichtliche Rechtswissenschaft*. In it, he argues more strongly for the conjunction of law and poetry than perhaps anyone else had ever done in European history to that point. His article is divided into fourteen sections, of which the following twelve show conjunctions: (1) introduction (*Eingang*); (2) common origin (*Ursprung*) of poetry and law; (3) proof through language; (4) value of German language vs. Latin law; (5) proof from poetic form; (6) proof from particular poetic legal phrases; (8) proof from poetic definitions; (9) proof from symbols of law; (10) proof from piety; (11) proof from atrocity; (12) proof from honesty; (13) proof from satisfaction. As long as one goes back far enough (and Grimm does not make it clear how far), law and poetry are one: 'one encounters something given, added, which could be called extra-historical, although it always grows out of the particular history. This "something" tolerates neither simple legislation nor vain invention. The origin of both poetry and law rests on two essentials, the miraculous and the trustworthy' (Grimm, 'Von der Poesie', 154; 'stösst man auf etwas gegebenes, zugebrachtes, das man ein aussergeschichtliches nennen könnte, wiewol es eben jedemal an die besondere geschichte anwächst; in keinem ist blosse satzung noch eitle erfindung zu haus. Ihr beider ursprung beruhet auf zweierlei wesentlichem, auf dem wunderbaren und dem glaubreichen'). Once again, Grimm seems to wish to reproduce the mystery of the invisible in his own writing, as the reader is left to imagine the relationship between what one wonders at and what one believes in, and whether they are synonyms or opposites. Grimm then permits himself a pun on legal language here – '*Grund*' meaning, as in English, the grounds upon which an action is to be taken. Originally, of course, it was synonymous with the earth, the ground upon which everything stands. Reason and reasonableness are telluric in nature, Grimm tells us. 'Present-day scholarship tends to differentiate everything to a hair; the ancients, however, separated nothing, but rather savoured everything out of a single, fully sufficient reason' (Grimm, 'Von der Poesie', 154; 'Die heutige wissenschaft pflegt alles haarklein zu spalten, sie aber trennten nichts, sondern genossen alles aus einem vollkommen zureichenden grund').

In the next section, Grimm goes into more detail of his model of the basis of law and poetry in language: 'Everything that was originally and intimately related reveals itself, on further investigation, to be justified out of the structure and essence of language itself, in which the most vivid, lively contact with the matters to be expressed always occurs. Thus the relationship between law and poetry extends into the depths of all languages' (Grimm, 'Von der Poesie', 155; 'Alles was anfänglich und innerlich verwandt ist, wird sich bei genauer untersuchung als ein solches stets aus dem bau und wesen der sprache selbst rechtfertigen lassen, in der immerhin die regste, elbensvollste berührung mit den dingen, die sie ausdrücken soll, anschlägt. Und so reicht die aufgestellte verwandtschaft zwischen recht und poesie schon in die tiefsten gründe aller sprachen hinab'). Grimm goes on to indicate the shared vocabulary between law and poetry in the earliest documents: judges are called 'finders' because they 'find judgment', and poets have the same title: troubadors. Law is everywhere a binding, and the bindings for poetry are called '*witten*' (modern German '*Weisen*'), which is in turn cognate with the word for (legal) proof, '*Beweis*'.

Grimm next argues for tautology as a technique common to law and poetry. The formal aspect of tautology in poetry is, for example, repetition of sound as in rhyme and alliteration. He gives an entire list of such repetitive phrases: 'helfend and haltend, dema and dela, widuon and weson, hebba and halda, wind and wetir, hus eiftha hof, horn anda hlud' (Grimm, 161).[5] He then goes on to the issue of poetic imagery, one still-current example of which is the term for outlaw, *'vogelfrei'* (bird-free), which Grimm interprets as given over to the birds of the sky, i.e. no longer housed under a roof. (A more usual interpretation is that the outlaw is free for anyone to kill like most birds, as opposed to deer and other large game.) He then goes on to give whole sentences that, in his opinion, show such imagery: 'the last one [in or out] shuts the door; straight paths don't use bridges; if you tread on my hen, you become my rooster' (Grimm, 166; 'der letzte schliesst die thüre zu; gerade geht nicht über Brücke; trittst du mein huhn, wirst du mein hahn'). These proverbs remind us not just of the need for memorization in preliterate times, according to Grimm, but also of 'the constant striving for metaphors, in order to better grasp and express the thing itself' (loc. cit.; 'sondern vielmehr stetes streben nach gleichnissen, um die sache selbst desto fester zu fassen und auszusagen'). The 'thing itself', the *'Ding an sich'* of law, is what Grimm, in almost Kantian fashion, asserts the existence of only through its phenomena. Grimm digs still deeper in the next section, noting the tendency of ancient legal formulae to express notions of time and space metaphorically: 'as long as the Main River flows into the Rhine' (ibid. 171; 'so lang der Main fliesst in den Rhein') for eternity, and 'while the King sleeps' (ibid. 172; 'während des Schlafs des Königs') for a short period. Grimm next considers the general symbolic nature of legal formulae and practices, the recurrence of words such as earth, water and fire, of sword for man and distaff for woman, and so on. All of this he then contrasts with the 'disenchanted world' of law in his own time:

> Let us compare the old custom at the transfer of land, where the two parties went to the place and fulfilled the form of the honoured custom, with today's notarized instruments. Back then, people seem to have owned things with greater joy. Things did not seem to them dead and without feeling, but as things that must be welcomed and bid farewell.
>
> [Man vergleiche den alten gebrauch bei übergabe des eigenthums an grund und boden, wo beide theile hin zur stelle giengen und die weise des ehrwürdigen brauchs vollbrachten,

---

5 I have not translated these completely, since the point is the alliteration; among the meanings are 'helping and holding, have and hold, wind and weather, house and yard'.

mit einem jetzigen notariatsinstrument; dazumal scheinen die menschen ordentlich die sachen lieber gehabt zu haben, sie galten ihnen nicht für todt und fühllos, sondern als solche, die ihren abschied und empfang habe mussten.] (ibid., 179)

This animism, however, exacts a double price of belief and violence. The next two sections of piety and atrocity are meant as a pair: both are lacking in modern law, which is motivated neither by the divine nor by aggressivity, but is simply a dead mummy.

Grimm ends his essay with a discussion of the 'satisfaction' (*vergnügtheit*) of the law. Grimm compares the modern use of coins that are valueless in and of themselves and ready only for commerce with the direct bartering of goods (ibid., 189). He goes on to note the equality of women in old Germanic law. He closes the essay with this sentence: 'The ancient folk poetry expresses itself everywhere in such pleasant, considered and satisfied definitions, and its life is inaccessible to every analysis, at once dry and motivated' (ibid., 191; 'In solchen gemütlichen, bedächtigen und vergnügten bestimmungen lässt sich auch allerwärts die alte volkspoesie aus und ihrem leben widersteht jede bald dürre, bald motivierende ausführung'). Clearly, Grimm's equation of poetry with law leads to a second conclusion concerning the decadence of the present day. We can agree with Gerhard Dilcher that 'Grimm sees clearly how a naive legal culture [*naïve Rechtswelt*] opposes the analytical thought and the *Ausdifferenzierung* of modern scholarship' (Dilcher, 'Jacob Grimm als Jurist', 31). As we have seen above, Grimm was aware that the supposed loss of naivety is irrecoverable, and that his own scholarship in the end is subject to the rules of rationalization and autopoiesis that have – literally – killed things that used to be alive. How much more so, then, the scholarship of his mentor Savigny.

Citation Gone Wrong

Grimm's memorialization of Savigny in 1850 is one of the more eccentric encomia one can read, amounting almost to a 'roast'. Grimm confesses his desire to write something 'pastoral': 'My goal is in fact to examine the pastoral life of the distant past, and to throw some light on several slopes and cliffs of law and poetry that still lie in shadow' (Grimm, 'Das Wort des Besitzes', 121–2; 'Mein Vorsatz ist nehmlich einmal das hirtenleben der vorzeit zu untersuchen, und auf manche seiten und abhängen der sitte und poesie, über welchen noch schatten lagern, licht fallen zu lassen'). Grimm's 'distant past' has a double referent: the past of German culture, as we have seen it reconstructed in his writings above; and the biographical past of his own relation to Savigny. Grimm remembers encountering in

Savigny's office in Marburg the collection of medieval love lyrics made by Johann Jakob Bodmer (1698–1783). Grimm describes the pleasant impression of being in Savigny's office, where he found these books that inspired him to unearth German antiquity: a warm, sunny room, with views of the Lahn river. He then adds a curious remark: 'the book stood out in its uselessness on the shelf, I'm sure you never read it, but at that time my growing interest still did not dare to borrow it from you' (Grimm, 'Das Wort des Besitzes', 116; 'bei Ihnen prangte [das Buch] unnütz auf dem bret, Sie haben es sicher nie gelesen, damals aber getraute meine keimende neigung noch nicht es von Ihnen zu entleihen').

Grimm goes on to contrast that room with the palatial one he visited to celebrate the King's birthday on 15 October 1847 in Berlin. Grimm's sister-in-law Dortchen sews his medals onto his jacket. He arrives among the 'carriages a-rolling' (*rollende Wagen*), notices the exotic plants as he climbs the stairs, and is impressed by the many guests who are elegantly dressed, and who, like the flood of years, have come between himself and his former mentor: 'In this crowd you were barely able to reach me your gloved fingertips' (ibid., 117; 'mir konnten Sie vor dem gedräng kaum eine fingerspitze im handschuh reichen'). Grimm sits down to eat, noting the oversupply of food and the scarcity of talk. Savigny gets up to toast the King's birthday (Grimm makes no mention of the King's appearance, as though the latter had been invisible at his own birthday party). Grimm is seized by the desire to toast the re-edition of Savigny's 1803 book, but is cautioned against such a spontaneous move by several of those present. 'Not to mention that old memories are always dearer to us than recent ones, no one will hold it against me that I feel ten times more attached to you in your Marburg overcoat than in your minister's outfit, that I prefer the fresh mountain air to the stale air of a salon, frank speech to playing things close to the vest' (ibid., 118; 'Zu geschweigen nun dass uns die alten erinnerungen immer theurer sind als die neuen, wird mir niemand verargen, dass ich an Ihnen im Marburger oberrock zehnmal stärker hänge als im ministerkleid, die frische luft des berges vorziehe der schwülen des sales, die offene ansprache der zurück gehaltenen'). Grimm's last comparison gets him closest to his own area of expertise, language: he notes once again, this time in his own friendship, the distinction between living and dead speech. Grimm notes the irony that Savigny, who had written several times against the idea of new legislation, now actively takes part in drafting new laws and ordinances, even though his mentor's personality differs so from that of worldly politicians.

Grimm's unusual eulogy/elegy of his great friend Savigny resembles his writings on law: both depict a present that is bewildering and uncomfortable because it is unable, in Benjamin's terms, to effect the citability of the past. Unlike Savigny, Grimm only collected materials for the study of legal history, but never attempted to derive implications from them for empirical law. The eulogy, like the writings on law and poetry, construct binary distinctions and an absolute boundary between past and present that hide what could have been viewed as more of a continuum. Almost from the original publication date of Grimm's publications on law and poetry, critics have noted the absolute distinction Grimm draws between the present day, when legal language has become notarial and instrumentalized, and the distant past, when it disclosed a lifeworld, a vista on natural law (in Grimm's sense) like the view from Savigny's window in Marburg.

2.2
Kant, Codification, and Goethe's *Elective Affinities*

Yet the present does not allow its monstrous law/justice/right to be stolen from it.

[Und doch lässt sich die Gegenwart ihr ungeheures Recht nicht rauben.]
    Goethe, *The Elective Affinities*, 198 (*Die Wahlverwandtschaften*, 131)[1]

One meaning for 'present' (*Gegenwart*) in the epigraph, taken from the novel by J. W. von Goethe that is the focus of this chapter, is the historical present, the first decade of the nineteenth century when parts of Germany are under French occupation, when the Holy Roman Empire has been dissolved, and when the old regime – and its established systems of law – seems to be evaporating. We saw in the last chapter how the weight of this present moment caused Jacob Grimm to abandon his law career in favour of literature and linguistics in 1807, at the same moment as Goethe (1747–1832) was conceiving his novel *The Elective Affinities* (*Die Wahlverwandtschaften*, hereinafter *WV*). Goethe had also experienced the uncertainties of law under the pressures of foreign domination. The French invasion of Weimar and the billeting of officers in Goethe's house in 1806 played a key role in suggesting the themes of the novel. Goethe had earned his Ph.D. in law at the University of Strasburg in 1771 for a disputation on fifty-six theses written in Latin. After a brief stint as a practising attorney in his hometown of Frankfurt am Main, he

---

1 English translations are from the 1990 Continuum edition by Elizabeth Mayer and Louise Bogan. I have silently emended this translation where necessary in order to give a more literal sense of the original German.

served as an intern at the Reichskammergericht in Wetzlar in 1772. (Readers may remember this institution, important for its role in introducing Roman law into German practice, from the introductory chapter.) Goethe then rapidly made a name for himself in the literary world; his international bestseller, *The Sorrows of Young Werther* (1774; *Die Leiden des Jungen Werthers*) drew the attention of the Duke of Weimar, who invited Goethe to become one of his ministers in 1779.

The title of this chapter places Goethe's novel alongside two perturbances of the legal system of the period: codification, both through the *Code Napoléon* and the Prussian General Code; and the Philosophy of Law (*Rechtslehre*) of the philosopher Immanuel Kant, published in 1797. These three writing events – code, treatise and novel – belong to different subsystems and did not directly influence each other. Instead, I am analyzing *WV* as a 'second-order observation' of marriage in the period in which it appeared. In ST lingo, to observe is to draw a distinction, which in the case of marriage is *ehelich/unehelich*, a binary that in German denotes both the legality of a marriage and also the legitimacy of offspring (we shall see below why this is important). This basic distinction has nothing to do, of course, with the feelings and aspirations of the marriage partners – all that matters is the legal documentation and witnessing. Goethe's novel draws the distinction between these emotional relationships of partners towards each other and towards the institution of marriage. To put it another way, *WV* correlates the *ehelich/unehelich* with the *recht/unrecht* binary, as in the epigraph above.

Goethe's prolific and extremely varied literary production cannot be adduced in detail here. As befitting his background and his ministerial duties, Goethe kept abreast of legal matters his entire life; the catalogue of his library lists 125 titles on legal subjects.[2] An anonymous document in the Goethe and Schiller Archive in Weimar, defending the tradition of written legal argumentation against the introduction of oral argumentation, has been credited to Goethe's authorship (Peter Schwartz, 'An Unpublished Essay by Goethe?'). Along with Franz Kafka, he is one of the few German authors whose *Amtliche Schriften* (Administrative Writings) have attracted scholarly interest. Perhaps the most famous and controversial of the former involves a case of infanticide where Goethe voted against clemency and the mother was executed in 1783. Goethe's reasoning in that case (which was relatively short and in support of the other council members' votes) is remarkable for being at variance with his sympathetic portrayal of Gretchen's crime in the tragedy *Faust*. At the same time, it is consistent with every other statement he made or didn't

---

2   An overview of Goethe's law background can be found in Pausch.

make concerning the necessity of the death penalty. One can sense in Goethe's language upholding the death penalty a preoccupation with the legitimacy of relationships in civil society.[3] By the same token, nothing that Goethe ever published in his lifetime spoke directly on legal or political matters. Famously, Goethe's view of the world was integrative: *Faust*, the later novels, and the autobiographical writings contain whole worlds. *WV* is a case in point: there is much discussion of custom and morality, and almost none of politics or law, and yet indirectly the novel communicates much about those topics.

The integration of activity found in Goethe's career was only possible in a socially stratified, functionally non-differentiated society such as Weimar. In a horizontally segmented society, a lawyer may be a novelist (or vice versa), but her novelistic discourse does not function within the legal subsystem except through citation carried out according to the latter's rules. As a judge, Richard Posner does not cite his own literary criticism.[4] Goethe's long experience as a minister, his legal training, but above all his interest in the profound political alterations wrought in Europe by the French Revolution and the rise of Napoleon worked together to shape the 1809 *WV*. In his study *After Jena*, Peter Schwartz points out that almost no scholarship on the novel has viewed its treatment of marriage from the point of view of legal history. In particular, the uncertain status of laws of marriage and inheritance as the *Heiliges Römisches Reich* ended and the Napoleonic Code, or some form of codification, loomed on the horizon almost certainly played a role in Goethe's conception of the novel – given that his own relationship with Christiane Vulpius and the subsequent status of their son August hovered in the twilit 'state of exception' possible under the old regime, where marriage conventions were seldom specified in great detail and the prince's word could overrule custom. His irregular marriage and the fate of his estate were bound to run up against difficulties under the rule of black-letter law. We can agree with Schwartz's thesis that 'Goethe's text ... links Eduard's and Charlotte's marital instability with a weakening of their hold on their landed property, both thematically and symbolically' (Schwartz, *After Jena*, 24). The novel moves back and forth between its double foci of land and marriage.

---

3   For an overview of the influence of official activities on Goethe's writing, see Jutta Linder's *'Falsche Tendenzen'*.
4   Primarily *Law and Literature*, now in its third edition – another reflection approach, one of whose main theses is the lack of structural coupling between literature and law.

Citing Crime

As Uwe Diederichsen has made clear, legal themes abound in *WV*. These themes are arranged like spokes around the hub of a legal concept that unites them all: marriage, and its accompanying crime of adultery. The epigraph to this chapter takes advantage of the polysemy of the German word *'Recht'*: law, justice, right. Which does Goethe (more properly, the narrator of Goethe's *WV*) mean? 'What are these monstrous rights of the present?' asks Tony Tanner in his treatment of Goethe in *Adultery in the Novel* (192). Tanner's answer is that they are 'the undeniable promptings of physical desire [...] which do not recognize the kind of respect for the past and obligation to the future that, pre-eminently, a wife and husband do, but that man himself [...] inevitably *is*' (Tanner, 192; emphasis in original). The novel explores this disjunction between law and desire, between *is* and *ought*. The novel's title, *Wahlverwandschaften*, or *Elective Affinities*, refers to a chemical process known today as bonding. More specifically, chemical compounds made of two or more elements may dissolve and their parts each 'elect' to join with a new element to form new compounds. The context for the epigraph is that the married couple, Eduard and Charlotte, have invited, for completely different reasons, two outsiders, the Captain and Ottilie, into their home. In true system-theory (or perhaps chaos-theory) fashion, Goethe shows how this seemingly negligible alteration to the closed system of the married couple's estate receives amplification to bring the entire system crashing down. Within a few months, the 'chemistry' has worked to dissolve the marriage into two adulterous attractions – Eduard/Ottilie and Charlotte/Captain – neither of which, however, is physically consummated. Instead, Eduard and Charlotte each thinks of the respective object of adulterous desire as they make passionate love to each other. A child is born of this union who carries the features not of the parents, but of the two imaginary lovers, and who is fated to a death by drowning that seems like a punishment for what the narrator describes as a 'crime' (*Verbrechen*): 'But when Eduard woke the next morning, at his wife's side, the day before him seemed ominous; and the sun seemed to illumine a crime. He stole away; and Charlotte found herself alone when she woke' (*Elective*, 198; 'als Eduard des andern Morgens an dem Busen seiner Frau erwachte, schien ihm der Tag ahnungsvoll hereinzublicken, die Sonne schien ihm ein Verbrechen zu beleuchten' [*WV*, 132]). Tanner notes that 'the legal conjugal coming together now seems to be exactly the opposite, a crime. [...] The implications of this particular sensation are very far-reaching, for it means that law can engender criminality, or, to put it more extremely and worryingly, it implies the possibility that the legal may incomprehensibly turn into its supposed opposite and become the very thing it was formulated to prohibit and exclude' (Tanner, 194–5). Clearly, Goethe is making an effort to draw the reader's attention to this paradoxical conjunction of *Recht* and *Verbrechen*. In fact, the word '*Recht*' is used three times within a few sentences in describing the scene of married seduction. One usage has been given in the epigraph above. It is preceded by two others:

> Eduard did not think of his rights. At last, he simply blew out the candle. And immediately, in the dim light of the night lamp, their passions and their imaginations asserted their rights over reality. It was Ottilie who was closed in Eduard's embrace; while the Captain's image – now clearly, now vaguely – hovered before Charlotte. The absent and the present, strangely interwoven, blended in their blissful ecstacy. (*Elective*, 198)

> [Eduard dachte nicht daran, daß er Rechte habe, und löschte zuletzt mutwillig die Kerze aus. In der Lampendämmerung sogleich behauptete die innre Neigung, behauptete die Einbildungskraft ihre Rechte über das Wirkliche: Eduard hielt nur Ottilien in seinen Armen, Charlotten schwebte der Hauptmann näher oder ferner vor der Seele, und so verwebten, wundersam genug, sich Abwesendes und Gegenwärtiges reizend und wonnevoll durcheinander.] (*WV*, 131)

Furthermore, Goethe inserts for contrast a novella entitled 'The Marvelous Neighbour Children' ('Die wunderlichen Nachbarskinder') told to Charlotte and the others by a visitor. I will not summarize the plot here, but it concerns two neighbour children whom fate brings together, despite their attempts at resisting each other. Many elements of the main story of *WV* – love, marriage, elective affinities, water, death, decision – appear in this novella in compressed, inverted and distorted form, like a dreaming of the day's events. Will Bishop ('The Marriage Translation') argues that the marriage in *WV* that the world should take a lesson from is not that of Eduard and Charlotte, but the one that occurs in the interpolated story. This marriage comes about when the woman, rejected by the man, jumps in the river and the man swims after her to save her from drowning. They are carried downstream, and to replace their soaked clothing are given wedding clothes to wear. These events cause them to realize that they are destined for each other and they ask their parents' blessing for their matrimony. The elemental forces that drive the characters in the novella leave no room for the social distinction of *Recht/Unrecht* that marks the relationship of Eduard and Charlotte.

This citation of the *Recht/Unrecht* distinction reminds the reader that in real life, as opposed to the dream world of the novella, marriage is an institution situated at the crux of a variety of social subsystems, of which law is one. Just as contract couples the legal to the economic subsystem, marriage links a number of social subsystems, including the literary in the form of the novel. This structural coupling is one of the main things revealed in the second-order observation that the nineteenth-century novel makes of marriage. To observe is to make a distinction, and in the case of marriage the distinction drawn is between legally sanctioned cohabitation and unsanctioned cohabitation. A novel, on the other hand, rather than reinforcing the legal distinction, may draw a further distinction within the former category, between passionate and loveless sanctioned cohabitations, for example. Kant's definition of marriage, which we will visit in more detail below, proceeds on the basis of a series of such binary distinctions, first between 'natural' and 'unnatural' sexual intercourse, and then between intercourse done according to nature, and that done according to law, with the latter constituting marriage.

Marriage distinguishes the legitimate and banishes the illegitimate – the 'natural,' to use a common term that Kant picks up on – to its environment. An observation cannot observe itself: marriage can determine the status of a particular human relationship, but cannot determine its own positionality vis à vis other social subsystems. The novel, in turn, banishes the happy marriage, i.e. the marriage that is identical to other marriages and hence communicates nothing, to its environment. In doing so, the novel restores *Sinn* to illegitimacy, as Peter Brooks has shown, for example, in *Reading for the Plot*. *WV* inaugurates the nineteenth-century theme of adultery that dominated novelistic plots for the next hundred years, supplanting the eighteenth century's theme of the seduction or resistance of the unmarried heroine whose last great purveyor was Jane Austen. Coming at the twilight of the *ancien régime* and before the emergence of realism and naturalism, as the title of this study indicates, the novel's treatment of adultery shows a vast difference from what one finds in Eça de Queiroz, Theodor Fontane, Benito Pérez Galdós or Leo Tolstoy later in the century.

Marriage as Passion

Goethe understood the emergence of bourgeois culture more fully than any of his predecessors or successors, but he was nonetheless unable to conceive of it otherwise than from within the framework of an idealized feudal state.

Benjamin, 'Goethe', 182

Benjamin wrote this summary of Goethe for a Soviet encyclopedia, and thus its terms are more straightforwardly Marxist than one finds, for example, in his essay 'Goethes *Die Wahlverwandtschaften*' that we will examine in due course. Benjamin's summary of *WV* just a few lines before this epigraph also differs vastly from the complexities of his essay on the novel, to be examined in chapter 3.3. Benjamin claims hyperbolically that *WV* was 'directed at a public consisting of the Silesian-Polish aristocracy, lords, émigrés, and Prussian generals who congregated in the Bohemian spas around the empress of Austria. Not that this prevents the poet from giving a critical view of their mode of life' (Benjamin, 'Goethe', 182). Goethe's active spa life may have furnished some details for the novel, but his public was much broader, as shown by the record of reactions to the novel. Furthermore, Goethe's thinking, as stated at the beginning of this chapter, was probably stimulated by his own sudden marriage to Christiane Vulpius on 19 October 1806, following sixteen years of living together and one son, August, whose legitimacy was now guaranteed by this act. Peter Schwartz has argued convincingly that the main reason for Goethe's decision to finally wed his longtime companion lay in his uncertainty over whether the Napoleonic Code would be instituted in Weimar following Napoleon's successful invasion – a legal seismic shift that would invalidate Goethe's will that had hitherto benefited his illegitimate son. 'A legal and political climate more hostile to the feudal state of exception within which Goethe had lived until then could hardly be imagined' (Schwartz, *After Jena*, 124). So too Gabrielle Bersier: 'How does Goethe himself cross the epochal threshhold? He alters, that is he modernizes his legal civil status according to the new relations of sovereignty to civil law. He regularizes his marital status. He takes care to regularize his property, both physical and intellectual' (Bersier, 'Der Fall', 73; 'Wie tritt nun Goethe selber über die Epochenschwelle hinüber? Er verändert, d.h. er modernisiert seine zivilrechtliche Lage nach den 'neuen Verhältnissen des Staatsrechts zum Zivilrecht'. Er verbürgerlicht seinen Ehestand. Er besorgt sich um die Verbürgerlichung seines Hausbesitzes und bemüht sich um die Verbürgerlichung seines geistigen Eigentums'). A variety of the verb *'verbürgerlichen'* occurs three times in this passage; I have used 'regularize' to translate it, but that does not render the verb's whole meaning. It means primarily to give someone *'Bürgerrechte'*, which today are civil rights, but which originally were those rights accruing to residents of a town who paid taxes and met other requirements. Accompanying this legal definition is a social one, of taking on the ways of a townsperson: a member of the nobility might become *'verbürgerlicht'* in a social rather than (or in addition to) a legal sense. Bersier wishes to state both that Goethe brought his marriage within the norms of civil society and that he regularized it legally. We note as well the analogy between marriage and property relations, particularly intellectual property. Everything is to be brought into the system of civil society.

Concern about consequences of the imposition of French law (which in fact did not occur) caused Goethe to study the *Code Napoléon* and suggested marriage to him as a topic for treatment in *WV*.[5] Benjamin's view that the novel 'provides a sketchy but very incisive picture of the decline of the family in the ruling class of the period' (Benjamin, 'Goethe', 182) is certainly accurate, precisely in accordance with Luhmann's view of the decoupling of marriage from the political and economic subsystems.[6] Universally, marriage founds society through the regulation of the upbringing of the next generation. If there were not family stability of some kind, children would all grow up as street urchins. Less universal, of course, is the format for bringing these stable unions about or for guaranteeing their endurance. Beyond this basic use-value, specification of the structural coupling of marriage depends upon such factors as the social status of the families involved and the historical development of the culture. Luhmann takes marriage as his topic in the study *Love as Passion* (1982; *Liebe als Passion*), arguing that the evolutionary shift in early modern Europe from a stratified to a functionally differentiated society brought with it a wholesale shift in marriage policy:

> By the eighteenth century families from the upper social strata had already lost their significance as 'supporters of the state'. Socio-cultural reasons for controls on marriage had thus ceased to exist, and what was there to prevent society from making the switch from arranged marriages to marriages of the heart?

---

5 Schwartz details that Goethe and the editor of the *Jenaische Allgemeine Literaturzeitung* made unsuccessful efforts as early as the year of the Code's enactment in 1804 to secure a review of it for the journal (*After Jena*, 47).
6 While no dates are given for any of the novel's events, from the time of its first publication readers assigned various of their living contemporaries to the persons of the Captain, Charlotte, Eduard and Ottilie, and the military campaigns Eduard takes part in, while unspecified, can only allude to the Napoleonic Wars of the first decade of the nineteenth century. Nicholas Boyle's essay, 'Die Wahlverwandtschaften', is useful for its historical placements of the events and characters of the novel.

> [...] [T]he differentiation of other functional systems made it possible to do without family ties (created by marriage) as the pillar of political, religious or economic functions. These systems were now sufficiently autonomous to be able to assert themselves and ensure their own reproduction. [...] [P]eople could, indeed were compelled to, conceive of families as something that had to be founded anew with every new generation. (Luhmann, *Love as Passion*, 146–7)

Another way of putting this is that marriage in Western societies slowly acquired the power of autopoiesis, becoming part of what Helmut Müller-Sievers calls the epigenetic turn around 1800. Müller-Sievers contrasts Goethe's novel with Beaumarchais's earlier play, *The Marriage of Figaro* (1778), whose plot turns on the servant Figaro's efforts to foil Count Almaviva's attempt to claim his right of being the first to sleep with any of his liegewomen. Such feudal privileges, which denied the autonomy and mutual rights of the married couple, are for Müller-Sievers a sign of the 'exteriority' of pre-modern marriage:

> if there was [now] to be an epiphany of subjective activity [*Selbstthätigkeit*] in the offspring (and a natural function for the mother to nurture it), then it had to be preceded by mutual consent, and that consent had to be anchored in an inalienable ground (love) that could be spoken of only in such prearticulative notions as fate, predestination, destiny, and the like. For the epigenetic philosophers and aspiring legislators, the unbearable groundlessness of marriage and its restriction to a public, political, juridical 'thing' found its expression in the feudal practice of arranged marriages. [...] Seen from this perspective, the *ius primae noctis*, rather than representing the libertine breach of the law, is its perverse enlargement, because it aims at nothing but one gigantic arranged marriage. (Müller-Sievers, *Self-Generation*, 128)

The changes in French marriage law during the Revolution demonstrate this difference clearly. Up until 1789, families had asserted their control over matrimony through setting age limits that to our perspective seem absurdly high: a male needed to be at least thirty years of age in order to contract marriage against the will of his parents; a female needed to be at least twenty-five. (The rather striking difference in ages again points at the goal of the marriage laws, since only males who married represented a potential siphoning-off of the family resources through inheritance.)

Even then, marriages could only be performed against the will of the parents after these had been notified by two 'respectful summonses'. During the Revolution, the age of marital self-determination was set at the age of majority – twenty-one. Some general excesses that occurred in response to the liberalization of marriage and the introduction of divorce in the revolutionary period caused the framers of the *Code Napoléon* to move the ages back up again: until 1907, in France a son could only marry against his parents' wishes after attaining the age of twenty-five.

The replacement of arranged marriages with ones of passion brought with it the twin problems of how to explain the presence of unhappy marriages once freedom of choice had been introduced, and what to do about such failures. Goethe appears to have deliberately placed the older type of arranged marriage as background to Eduard and Charlotte's present happiness, for the reader of *WV* is immediately made aware that both partners in the present marriage had been married previously, against their wills, as Charlotte reports in the first pages of the novel:

> 'How I enjoy thinking of our earliest relationship! We fell deeply in love with each other when we were young. We were separated – you from me because your father, in his insatiable passion for wealth, married you to a rich woman considerably older than yourself. I was separated from you because, being without particular prospects, I was forced to marry a wealthy man whom I respected but did not love.' (Goethe, *Elective Affinities*, 134)

> 'Mag ich doch so gern unserer frühsten Verhältnisse gedenken! Wir liebten einander als junge Leute recht herzlich; wir wurden getrennt; du von mir, weil dein Vater, aus nie zu sättigender Begierde des Besitzes, dich mit einer ziemlich älteren, reichen Frau verband; ich von dir, weil ich, ohne sonderliche Aussichten, einem wohlhabenden, nicht geliebten, aber geehrten Manne meine Hand reichen mußte.' (*WV*, 9)

The gap between the two marriages is epochal, reflecting the lessening of family pressures on those taking the vows. Charlotte's depiction of the double wedding that took two lovers away from each other serves both as a resumé of the arranged marriage and as an allusion to many of the greatest novels of the eighteenth century, from Samuel Richardson's *Clarissa* (1748) through Jean-Jacques Rousseau's *Julie* (1762) to Sophie von La Roche's *Fräulein von Sternheim* (1771), and in some sense to Goethe's own 'breakthrough' novel, *The Sorrows of Young Werther* (1774; *Die Leiden des Jungen Werther*). The inconvenience of the two lovers' mutual affections being defeated by family interests lies in the past, as does the novel's preoccupation with that theme. The conflict now shifts to the issue of affection, the instability of which clashes with the permanence implied in the institution of marriage.

As Astrida Tantillo has documented, the earliest criticism of Goethe's novel emphasized two themes: the moral aspect of the work, and its literary quality (Tantillo, *Goethe's* Elective Affinities, 4–5). When considering early criticism of *WV*, we confront the issue that our critical vocabulary of the present tends to distort the historical material. Due to the *Ausdifferenzierung* that has taken place in the 200-plus years since the first publication, twenty-first century critics may readily separate legal from moral issues in the novel. In the still vertically stratified Germany of Goethe's time, the two were bound together, and critical vocabulary was well equipped to condemn the adultery in the novel as undermining the moral foundations of society. In 1828, for example, Wolfgang Menzel attacked *WV* as a symptom of French immorality that had seeped its way into Germany in the train of the French Revolution (Tantillo, 21). Once again, the critical vocabulary of the time did not include the term 'ideology' that may have been at the bottom of Menzel's feelings about the 'Frenchness' of *WV*. Later critics who have approached the novel from its ideological positioning have come to conclusions about Goethe's position vis à vis the aristocratic protagonists of the text that are vastly different and mutually exclusive, as Werner Schlick points out (Schlick, *Goethe's* Die Wahlverwandtschaften, 517). Schlick agrees in essence with Benjamin's pithy summary: Goethe takes up an anti-aristocratic but not a revolutionary position. He does not side with the peasants (none of whom appears as a character in the novel), but writes a 'Middle-Class Critique of Aesthetic Aristocratism'.

Spurred on by Goethe's own comments on his work, critics have upheld a recuperative reading of *WV*, in which the characters' imaginary adultery is punished by mythic vengeance. In this critical tradition, Goethe's novel is said simply to show the evil consequences of adultery. For example, Oskar Walzel finds that the novel 'was written in order to restore honor to the [in the early nineteenth century] profaned marriage institution' (Walzel, *Goethes Die Wahlverwandtschaften*, 36). However, readers of *WV* who see the novel as a warning against adultery ignore the fact that the version of marriage upheld in the novel corresponds to no legal or civil definition of the institution, since the adultery takes place only within the minds of the characters, which mental realm, as Kant points out, is not subject to legal restriction and, as Luhmann points out, does not achieve the status of communication. Fate in this novel is the conflict between legal institution and human desire. If one responds to Walzel's assertion of Goethe's moral intentions with the naive question of why Goethe or anyone else should care what happens to the institution of marriage, then the response almost inevitably invokes the structural coupling of political, social and legal dimensions. Marriage, then, must be preserved as a legal tie, even when its affective bonds have disappeared.

The tragedy of the novel stems not so much from any moral or legal transgression, but more from the characters' decisionless wandering in limbo between the state of marriage and the state of adultery. Rather than a tragedy of action, *WV* presents a tragedy of the failure to draw a distinction, made all the more poignant by the likeability of all four of the non-actors: the Captain is talented and forthright; Charlotte is stoic and forgiving; Eduard is passionate; and Otttilie is modest and pliant. System is the only villain of *WV*. Andreas Gailus has given us an interesting account of a similar pattern in an earlier work of Goethe's that dealt more directly with the French Revolution, his novella collection *Conversations of German Emigrés* (1794; *Unterhaltungen deutscher Ausgewanderten*). As its title implies, the stories in the collection are told by Germans who have fled from the left bank to the right bank of the Rhine in the face of French invasion – a 'modern' updating of the flight from the plague that leads to storytelling in Boccaccio's *Decamerone*. The novellas serve the refugees as 'media, that is, intermediaries charged with reconnecting consciousness and communication at a moment when these two systems are at war. [...] Transforming the obstacle to communication into an incitement to speak, the novellas thus begin to answer the paradox of exteriority, the problem of how to respond within communication to that which exceeds it' (Gailus, *Passions of the Sign*, 98). A similar theme dominates *WV*, which, however, seems to show the opposite, namely the disjunction between consciousness and communication. The only 'medium' or mediator in this text is the aptly named Mittler (literally, 'middle-man'), who ends up failing at every turn.

Various discourses are woven into the narrative in order to 'sideshadow' the action, i.e. to show the path not taken by the characters. I have already discussed 'The Marvelous Neighbour Children' as one such sideshadowing. The utterer of another, very different discourse is the Count, who is engaged in an adulterous relationship and hopes for divorce from his wife. In a visit to Eduard and Charlotte, he proposes that the law of marriage be constructed so as to encourage the latter's dissolubility. So radical – so 'French', we might say – is the Count's proposal that he attributes it to someone else: 'One of my friends, whose good spirits most often showed themselves in the form of proposals for new laws, used to maintain that every marriage should be contracted for only five years. He would say, "The number five is a beautiful, holy, odd number, and the time period sufficient to get acquainted with each other, to bring up a few children, to separate and, most beautiful of all, to make up again"' (*Elective Affinities*, 242–3; 'Einer von meinen Freunden, dessen gute Laune sich meist in Vorschlägen zu neuen Gesetzen hervorthat, behauptete: eine jede Ehe solle nur auf fünf Jahre geschlossen werden. "Es sei," sagte er, "dies eine schöne, ungrade heilige Zahl und ein solcher Zeitraum eben hinreichend, um sich kennenzulernen, einige Kinder heranzubringen, sich zu entzweien und, was das schönste sei, sich wieder zu versöhnen"' [*WV*, 112]). As Johannes Salzwedel has shown in 'Gellert und die *Wahlverwandschaften*,' Goethe derived the Count's 'friend's' position from the actual theories of a famous general, Moritz Graf von Sachsen (1696–1750), who detailed his theory of marriage in a book, *Mes Rêveries* (published posthumously in 1756), a treatise that the author otherwise devotes to questions of military strategy and the most effective means of killing the enemy. Von Sachsen then states explicitly that he owes the reader a theory of propagation to counterbalance the theories of destruction with which the greater parts of the book are taken up. The idea of the five-year marriage is aimed at increasing the population, as only marriages productive of children would be renewed after five years. Sachsen's is thus a legal theory in which the state's intervention stems from its interest in propagation. This same biopolitical interest, for example, became embodied in the first paragraph of the section on marriage in the Prussian *Allgemeines Landrecht* (literally, the general law of the land), discussed in the previous chapter: 'The main purpose of marriage is the generation and education of children' (*Allgemeines*, 3:1; 'Der Hauptzweck der Ehe ist die Erzeugung und Erziehung der Kinder'). Altogether, the *Landrecht* devoted 1134 paragraphs to marriage, starting with a justification of the institution as being for the propagation and maintenance of children. It may be with this definition in mind that the Prussian subject Immanuel Kant – who was often enough philosophically at odds with the authorities – wrote specifically against the view of marriage as necessary to propagation by eliminating children, but not sex, from the legal picture altogether.

Kant and the Philosophy of Marriage

The *Rechtslehre* was a late work of Kant, published in 1797. Goethe also was a latecomer to Kantian philosophy, finding on his return from Italy in 1788 that the University of Jena had become the first institutional stronghold of Kantianism. He was finally brought over to the Kantian critical method through Schiller's encouragement, and through reading Karl Leonhard Reinhold's *Briefe über die Kantische Philosophie* (1792). Goethe became an avid reader of Kant's works, awarding the latter, according to his conversations with Johann Peter Eckermann, first place among German philosophers. Goethe's remarks on Kant include the observation that his philosophy had so shaped contemporary German thought that everyone stood under his influence, whether he had actually read the philosopher's works or not: 'He has also influenced you, without your having read him. Now you no longer need him, because what he could give to you is already in your possession' (Eckermann, *Gespräche*, 224). Goethe specifically mentions, besides the three major Critiques, other writings of Kant such as the *Streit der Fakultäten* (1798) and *Anthropologie in pragmatischer Hinsicht* (1798).[7]

The 'critical turn' of philosophy that Kant brought about had a profound effect on the philosophy of law. According to Ernst Bloch,

> Kant does away with the concept of natural law itself: His philosophy of rights deals with original law purely as rational law. That which, since the Stoics and even since the Sophists, seemed to lend to the ideal of law its stability and content – nature as a category of social opposition – ceases to be synonymous with the judicial logos. Nature as the measure, even as the measure of that which would be superior to nature, remains for Kant and his successors only in aesthetics and not in the philosophy of right. This Kantianism influenced the way in which all succeeding philosophers of right […] approached the subject. (Bloch, *Naturrecht*, 70)

Of course, there is no such thing as a Kantian Code to replace the *Allgemeines Landrecht*, but Kant's philosophy did inspire a number of law professors, such as Gustav Hugo (1764–1844) at the University of Göttingen. Furthermore, the early years of the twentieth century saw a wave of neo-Kantianism that influenced the legal philosophy of Hans Kelsen and others.[8]

---

7 The pairing of Kant and Goethe as writers in different media who each, in his own way, helped define the autonomy of the subject, has become a commonplace of literary history, e.g. Georg Simmel's 1906 *Kant und Goethe*, Karl Vorländer's 1907 *Kant, Schiller, Goethe*, and Gabriele Rabel's 1927 *Goethe und Kant*.

8 Cf. also Hans Kiefner, 'Der Einfluss Kants auf Zivilrecht'.

The emphasis Goethe places on Eduard's '*Rechte*' over Charlotte's sexual organs seems to invoke Kant's defintion of marriage, as given in the *Treatise on Law* (1797; *Rechtslehre*). In that work, Kant infamously defined marriage as the lifelong possession by each partner of the sexual organs of the other: 'Now a natural sexual relationship is either of a merely animal nature, or according to law. The latter is marriage (*matrimonium*), i.e. the obligation of two persons of different sexes to the life-long mutual possession of each other's sexual characteristics' (§ 24, 87–88; 'Die natürliche Geschlechtsgemeinschaft ist nun entweder die nach der bloßen thierischen Natur, oder nach dem Gesetz. Die letztere ist die Ehe (*matrimonium*), d.i. die Verbindung zweier Personen verschiedenen Geschlechts zum lebenswierigen wechselseitigen Besitz ihrer Geschlechtseigenschaften'). This definition, which studiously avoids linking marriage with offspring, has no precedent in existing law. It is an example of the point Bloch makes about Kant's rationalism that here uses marriage to reconcile the contrasting moments of subjective freedom and objective possession.

As Benjamin points out in his essay on *WV*, most commentators have viewed Kant's definition as a 'curiosity of his senile late period' (Benjamin, 'Goethes *Die Wahlverwandtschaften*', 299), or else reckoned it one of those instances in his moral philosophy where logical thinking had won out over common sense. However, the definition follows rigorously from a typically Kantian antinomy. Marriage is for Kant the third cornerstone of jurisprudence, dialectically combining the substantial (property as fact) with the causal (contracts as pacts). Marriage appears in the Kantian legal scheme as a contract making each partner the mutual property of the other. Dialectically, this bondage approaching slavery becomes, due to its mutuality, a foundation of law itself: 'The acquiring of a wife or husband therefore does not occur *de facto* (through consummation) without prior contract, but also not *de pacto* (through a mere marriage contract without subsequent consummation), but rather only *de lege*: i.e. as the legal consequence of the obligation to a sexual relation only by means of the mutual possession of each other' (§ 27, 90; 'Die Erwerbung einer Gattin oder eines Gatten geschieht also nicht *facto* [durch die Beiwohnung] ohne vorhergehenden Vertrag, auch nicht *pacto* [durch den bloßen ehelichen Vertrag ohne nachfolgende Beiwohnung], sondern nur *lege*: d.i. als rechtliche Folge aus der Vebindlichkeit in eine Geschlechtsverbindung nicht anders, als vermittelst des wechselseitigen Besitzes der Personen'). In its assertion of the mutual rights of both marriage partners, Kant's schema differs drastically from traditional Anglo-Germanic law, in which the woman was legally absorbed into the husband and had no rights over his person. On the other hand, it also departs from Roman law of the empire, which considered marriage a mutual non-possession in which neither partner had any rights over the person or property of the other. Reciprocity solves the problem that marriage presents for Kant's legal scheme, where on the one hand the right to possession provides the basis for all right, but on the other hand law should be a visible and pervasive fulfillment of the categorical imperative, which says that people must always be treated as ends rather than as means. Marriage is thus for Kant the only legitimate contract over a person's body. In fact, contradicting nearly everyone's experience, in Kant marriage becomes people's most direct and long-lasting experience of the legal *per se*.

For Kant, propagation cannot be the purpose of marriage, since it would make both partners merely the means to another finality that lies outside their individual wills. Kant rejects this goal as belonging to nature rather than to freedom: 'The end of begetting children may be an end of nature, to which end it first implanted the inclination of the sexes toward each other; but that the human being who marries must have this end in mind is not to be required for the legality of his union; otherwise, when the begetting of children ended, marriage would also dissolve itself' (§ 24, 88; 'Der Zweck, Kinder zu erzeugen und zu erziehen, mag immer ein Zweck der Natur sein, zu welchem sie die Neigung der Geschlechter gegen einander einpflanzte; aber daß der Mensch, der sich verehelicht, diesen Zweck sich vorsetzen müsse, wird zur Rechtmäßigkeit dieser seiner Verbindung nicht erfordert; denn sonst würde, wenn das Kinderzeugen aufhört, die Ehe sich zugleich von selbst auflösen'). The sublimation of the subject-object antinomy continues even when the elements themselves have disappeared. As one interpreter of Kant puts it: 'it is admissable to dissolve the pact (the promise of living together), from which follows that the fact of cohabitation disappears, but one can never contravene the law, which is independent of the will of the subjects' (Vitofranceschi, 'L'istituto del matrimonio', 254).

Kant's definition seems aimed directly at the prevailing concepts of marriage noted above, which emphasized the procreation and care of children, as well as mutual assistance (*Beistand*) of the partners. Theologically, St. Paul's *'remedium concupsicentiae'* was sometimes cited. Kant stands on the threshold of Romantic concepts of marriage, such as those put forward by Johann Gottlieb Fichte in his *Grundrisse des Naturrechts* published in 1797, the same year as Kant's treatise. Like Kant, Fichte grounds his definition of marriage in sex: 'Marriage is the complete union of two persons of different sexes through carnal desire [*Geschlechtstrieb*], which is its actual [*eigener*] purpose' (§ 8; 'Die Ehe ist die durch den Geschlechtstrieb gegründete vollkommene Vereinigung zweier Personen beiderlei Geschlechts, die ihr eigener Zweck ist'). Love, which had traditionally been a duty proceeding from the contract of marriage, in Fichte's view now had become the basis for it. The French Revolution, under whose shadow Fichte did his thinking, gave power of divorce for the first time to the parties of the marriage, rather than to any institution, recognizing an affective bond that preceded and justified the legal contract. This legal innovation, which has strong echoes with what happens in *WV*, was introduced into France during the revolutionary years, creating a reputation for the decadence of marriage in that country.

In philosophy, G. F. W. Hegel and C. F. von Savigny tamed the Romantic notion of marriage by noting that its relation to love is to remove precisely the transient and subjective aspects from that emotion (Dieter Schwab, 'Jena und die Entdeckung der romantischen Ehe', 185). Thus, Hegel in his 1821 *Philosophy of Right* (*Grundlinien der Philosophie des Rechts*) objects equally to: (1) arranged marriages due to the lack of self-consciousness of the partners in taking this step; (2) prenuptial contracts due to the implication that the individual consciousnesses of the partners will continue to be separated in marriage; and (3) marriage out of romantic love, because its irrationality does not conform to the exercise of free will.[9] The shadow of Romantic ideas of marriage lived a subterranean life during the rest of the nineteenth century, emerging, for example, in socialist and feminist writings, and in the dominant theme of adultery in the bourgeois novel as noted above. Marriage had enjoyed a brief moment, immortalized in *WV*, where subjective moral concepts had impressed themselves upon the law without a process of translation into institutional patterns and procedures.

Unlike the Count, the main characters of the novel do not think in the abstract about the institution of marriage. Instead, they make use of a 'medium' to do their thinking for them. The character Mittler promulgates a view of marriage's indissolubility. As noted above, Mittler's name points to his role as mediator, and in fact of interpreter, as someone who comes between enunciation and understanding. Nils Reschke sees the character, an ex-cleric, as representative of the role of the lower clergy in spreading revolutionary ideas in France (Reschke, 'Zeit der Umwendung', 146–61). Mittler's status as a reformer may be reflected in the following statement about him: 'some people tried to persuade him to move to the capital where he could carry on in more influential circles the ministrations he had begun at a lower level' (*Elective Affinities*, 142; 'man war im

---

9   I am following here the analysis of William Conklin in *Hegel's Laws*, 198–9. The relevant sections of the *Grundlinien* are 161 through 169.

Begriff, ihn nach der Residenz zu ziehen, um das von oben herein zu vollenden, was er von unten herauf begonnen hatte' [*WV*, 23]). The published translation has 'city' where I have placed 'capital', but this further specification is still inaccurate: '*Residenz*' is where the ruler of the principality resides, hence 'capital' but in a specifically feudal sense. The sentence thus implies that Mittler would be elevated to the status of a minister and asked to formally codify his previously informal mediations. What began as an alternative to law will now be codified. In fact, this is exactly what Frederick the Great had in mind as a primary goal of the *Landrecht*: once the laws of the land are unified and published in clear and understandable German, the people could take the law into their own hands, as it were. The sterile guild of lawyers would be replaced by merchants, industrialists, and even artists whose productivity would be more useful to the state. The subsystems of law and commerce would become one.[10] If Goethe – a member of the guild of lawyers – intended Mittler as a parody of the reformist dreams of codification and its do-it-yourself legalistas, he did not bother to insert into the otherwise symmetrically organized *WV* a counterpart to Mittler, i.e. a professional lawyer who knows his business and who counsels the right thing.

In any case, however, Mittler is a '*Mittelding*' (amphibious being), a former clergyman who has familiarized himself with law, but without really becoming a lawyer. Mittler has an oddly modern resonance in that his role involves alternative resolutions to disputes, i.e. mediation. The description of his character begins thus:

> As long as he had been in his ministry, not one married couple had been divorced; and the district courts had never been bothered with quarrels and lawsuits from his part of the country. Early in life he realized the necessity of a thorough acquaintance with the law; and he devoted himself zealously to that science, soon thinking himself a match for the shrewdest lawyer. (Goethe, *Elective Affinities*, 142)

> Solange er im Dienste war, hatte sich kein Ehepaar scheiden lassen, und die Landeskollegien wurden mit keinen Händeln und Prozessen von dorther behelligt. Wie nötig ihm die Rechtskunde sei, ward er zeitig gewahr. Er warf sein ganzes Studium darauf und fühlte sich bald den geschicktesten Advokaten gewachsen. (*WV*, 23)

---

10 Thus Frederick in his Order of 1780 that began the decade-and-a-half of work on the ALR. Cited in Reinhart Koselleck, *Preussen zwischen Reform und Revolution*, 37.

The reader is left to wonder whether Mittler's thinking matches the facts. Overall, his description seems contradictory: law is used to decide the binary *Recht/Unrecht*, whereas Mittler's ability to keep disputes out of formal procedural hearings points (as does his name) at mediation, not exactly a common teaching of the '*Rechtskunde*' of the time. It is not clear whether we are meant to use our own binaries in dismissing Mittler as does the legal professional Uwe Diederichsen:

> In spite of his intense interest in the law [*am Recht*], Mittler remains true to his name, and thus also in his legal activities [*Rechtstätigkeit*] he remains an amphibious being between a legally oriented lay person and a trained lawyer. In other words: he has not understood the essence of the law [*Wesen des Rechts*]. For that reason, true and false statements come mixed together in his remarks; for that reason, he causes damage where he wants to help, and becomes in every sense of the word a living contradiction. (Diederichsen, '*Die Wahlverwandtschaften*', 539–40)

According to system theory, contradiction is the basis of system, beginning with the observation that cannot include itself, hence requiring another observation, and so forth. In addition to the interesting character study of a good *Bürger* who hurts where he wishes to help, Goethe may also have been getting at something more structural with the character of Mittler. For example, Goethe may be implying through his character the futility of making ethical observations on legal matters. Mittler upholds the moral ('*sittlich*') side of marriage. When he arrives at the *château* and hears that the Count and his lover the Baroness (both are married to other people) will be staying there, he immediately departs, flinging out the following as he grabs his hat and cane:

> 'Whoever attacks marriage [...] whoever undermines by word or by action this foundation of all moral society, is my enemy wherever I find him; and if I cannot master him, at least I shall have nothing to do with him. Marriage is the Alpha and the Omega of all civilization. It makes the savage gentle; and the gentility of the most civilized finds its highest expression in marriage. It must be indissoluble because it brings with it such an abundance of happiness, that in contrast each individual unhappiness is hardly worth mentioning. [...] There is no plausible reason for divorce. The human condition is so brimming over with pleasure and pain, that no married couple

can calculate their debt to each other. It is an infinite debt, and can only be paid in eternity.' (Goethe, *Elective Affinities*, 186)

'Wer mir den Eh'stand angreift [...] wer mir durch Wort, ja durch Tat diesen Grund aller sittlichen Gesellschaft untergräbt, der hat es mit mir zu tun; oder wenn ich sein nicht Herr werden kann, habe ich nichts mit ihm zu tun. Die Ehe ist der Anfang und Gipfel aller Kultur. Sie macht den Rohen mild, und der Gebildeste hat keine bessere Gelegenheit, seine Milde zu beweisen. Unauflöslich muß sie sein, denn sie bringt so vieles Glück, daß alles einzelne Unglück dagegen gar nicht zu rechnen ist. [...] Sich zu trennen gibts gar keinen hinlänglichen Grund. Der menschliche Zustand ist so hoch in Leiden und Freuden gesetzt, daß gar nicht berechnet werden kann, was ein Paar Gatten einander schuldig werden. Es ist eine unendliche Schuld, die nur durch die Ewigkeit abgetragen werden kann.' (*WV*, 107)

There are a number of remarkable aspects to this speech. Mittler's use of '*Schuld*' – 'debt,' but also 'guilt' in German – in the last sentence of his speech belongs ambiguously to both the legal and religious registers: as debt, marriage is the eternal contract invoked by Kant; however, it is guilt, as in Eduard's feeling that he has committed a crime with his wife, that provides a more appropriate characterization of the marriage in *WV*. Overall, and as indicated in the hellfire notions of eternity and guilt, Mittler's speech does not fit very well with his reputation as a mediator. He is justifying with this speech his refusal to remain in the presence of adulterers, which may be a sensible or moral attitude, but is hardly one of compromise. Mittler's deontological declarations about marriage – that divorce is never an option, that marriage is the beginning and culmination (rendered 'Alpha and Omega' in the translation) of civilization, his vocabulary of domination ('*Herr werden*') and conflict – are all completely at odds with the role he apparently plays in the region. With respect to marriage law, Mittler is not in the middle, but rather conforms to the *Recht/Unrecht* binary. The events of the novel, it should be noted, seem to bear out his aversion to the presence of the adulterers. A few pages after Mittler leaves, the Count presents the libertine views of marriage discussed above, which Charlotte is concerned to deflect lest Ottilie get the wrong view of marriage from them. The adulterous couple does seem to act as an infectious agent in the domestic sphere of Eduard and Charlotte. However, Benjamin is correct when he states, contradicting a century or more of moralizing interpretations of *WV*, that 'unlike Mittler, Goethe did not wish to justify marriage, but rather to show those forces that arise from marriage in a state of decay' (Benjamin, 'Goethe's *Elective Affinities*', 301; 'Wollte [Goethe] doch nicht, wie Mittler, die Ehe begründen, vielmehr jene Kräfte zeigen, welche im Verfall aus ihr hervorgehen' [Benjamin, 'Goethes *Die Wahlverwandtschaften*, 130]).

Overall, Mittler's view of marriage sounds suspiciously like Christian Fürchtegott Gellert's in the *Moralische Vorlesungen* (*Moral Lectures*), first published in 1770, which Goethe is known to have absorbed. Gellert sees marriage as a means to two ends: '*Geschlechtserhaltung*' (propagation) and '*Privatruhe*' (domestic peace): 'The main intention of the creator in planting the trait of mutual love can be defined as the preservation of the human species and of domestic peace' (Gellert, 263; 'Man setze die Hauptabsicht des Zugs der gegenseitigen Liebe, den uns die Hand des Schöpfers eingepflanzet hat, in die Erhaltung des menschlichen Geschlechts und der Privatruhe'). '*Privatruhe*' is a dialectical concept. Its composite form points to a peace and quiet enjoyed in private; yet the term comes to mean for Gellert precisely the opposite, the kind of law and order necessary for the maintenance of the bourgeois public sphere, and which a large number of uncared-for, 'wild' children would threaten. Thus, privacy becomes a public concern, as does marriage itself in this theory. Though the Baron's and Mittler's views seem opposed, they have in common the consideration of marriage as a basis of society in need of regulation so as to preserve other social norms. Both of these contradict the Kantian schema, in which the social is constructed through the contractual reification of personhood.

Those early nineteenth-century readers of Mittler's words who were not already outraged about the so-called immorality of Goethe's novel must have noted their ironic inefficacy in a way that many later readers did not. The French Revolution had destroyed Gellert's assurances about the integrity of *Privatruhe*. As noted above, one by-product of the anti-clericalism of the revolutionary period had been the freeing of marriage from the domain of canon law and its redefinition as a civil contract between individuals. Contemporary thinking tended to link this secularization of the marriage union with a general crisis in the marriage bond and a loosening of sexual mores. Kant's position on marriage could be seen as a scheme for preserving marriage's indissolubility, introduced by the Catholic Church, through the secular means of legal philosophy. If we may judge the views of marriage from other literary productions of the period, as Johannes Salzwedel points out, the concepts of stability and indissolubility have given way to the polar extremes of superficiality and obsession: 'In the period of *WV*, after the French Revolution, the Directory and the dissolution of the Old Reich, more than just the idea of diplomatic balance of power had become yesterday's policy. In addition, the union of reason with conjugal love must have seemed like a dusty, reactionary solution: either Lucinde's liberated attitude or Fidelio's heroism are the new models' (Salzwedel, 'Gellert', 302).

These examples provide insights into the politics of the erotic in the Napoleonic period. The proper contrasting example, of marriage as a union of reason and conjugal love, which Benjamin cites (Benjamin, 'Goethes *Die Wahlverwandtschaften*', 300), is that of Mozart and Schikaneder's *Die Zauberflöte* (1791). The trials of fire and water undergone by Pamina and Tamino in that opera provide an allegory of the indissolubility of marriage. As Benjamin points out, Tamino and Pamina undergo their trials not in order to find each other, but in order to stay together forever (ibid., 129). The setting of *Die Zauberflöte*, Mozart's 'masonic' opera, is nominally Egypt; its marriage ceremony is universally humanistic rather than municipally legalistic or religious in a sectarian sense. Fidelio's loyalty to her husband Florestan in Beethoven's 1805 opera *Fidelio* (libretto by Joseph Sonnleithner) – whose subtitle is 'Married Love' (*Die eheliche Liebe*) – results from her political loyalty to his cause, which is clearly in sympathy with at least the broad principles of the French Revolution. Marriage is here a means to an end; the ebbing of political engagement would empty the bond of its 'content'. Neither contract nor indissoluble bond, the hero's marriage is instead a form of political engagement. At the opposite pole stands Friedrich Schlegel's *Lucinde* (1799), who seeks her principle of freedom in an amorous bond with Julius which stands outside the legal and customary norms of bourgeois society.

In the end, *WV* upholds neither the sanctity and eternity of marriage, nor its use-value, nor its conventional aspect. Goethe introduced opposing views and conflicting discourses, which prepare a dénouement that accepts none of them, thus foregrounding the ideology of marriage. Goethe had seen 'that Sachsen's cogent proposal and Gellert's opposing position could provide the horizon for a conversation whose significance far overshadows its actual subject-matter' (Salzwedel, 'Gellert', 307–8).

3.1
A Recursive Process: Kafka's Law – and Ours

Achilles: I see. You mean GOD sits up at the top of the ladder of Djinns?
Genie: No, no, no! There is nothing 'at the top', for there is no top. That is why GOD is a recursive acronym.
Douglas Hofstadter, Gödel, Escher, Bach

And that the ladder of law has no top and no bottom.
Bob Dylan, 'The Lonesome Death of Hattie Carroll'

In number 13 of the 1995 volume of the *Neue Juristische Wochenschrift*, Rechtsreferendar Robert Höcherl published a hommage to 'Dr. jur. Franz Kafka'. The article details Kafka's study of law at university and his subsequent bureaucratic-legal career. Höcherl also examines Kafka's *Amtliche Schriften*, which, like Goethe's, have been published, and a substantial portion of which (unlike Goethe's!) have even been translated into English – and reviewed by American law professors.[1] As the editors of these documents note, even the 'Kafka industry' stumbles a bit when it comes to considering these writings, which provide no easy access or ready-made insight into Kafka's 'creative' work.

Similarly, of the many approaches to interpreting the long narrative *The Trial* (*Der Process*), the least favoured relates it directly to law, despite Kafka's Ph.D. in the field.[2] Criticism has certainly recognized Kafka's insights into the essence of bureaucracy, part and parcel of

---

1 E.g. Richard Posner, 'Kafka: The Writer as Lawyer', and Jefferson M. Gray, Review of *Franz Kafka: The Office Writings*.
2 Also spelled *'Der Prozess'*; recently, critics and editors have returned to

the observation his writings perform on the condition of European humanity in the early twentieth century. To be sure, Kafka's own statements (or lack thereof), as well as certain features of his writing, have encouraged this disconnect. Nevertheless, there is much to be gained in reading *The Trial* (hereinafter *DP*) as a statement about law.³ That statement is, in ST terms, that the law is recursive in its operations and without an ultimate or supreme instance capable of providing an 'outside' to its autopoietic processes. The ladder of law, to speak with the character of the judge in Bob Dylan's song, has no top and no bottom.⁴ To argue that this insight converges with that of system theory is almost trivial, since Kafka and Luhmann are observing the same phenomena of modernity, and just using different language to describe it. More important is that through the connection Kafka depicts between legal and literary lifeworlds, the law did not just provide content around which to fashion a story; rather, it determined the form of narrative as a recursive process.

Kafka, born in 1883 to a German-Jewish family, studied law at the Karl Ferdinand University of Prague and received his doctorate in 1906. A faculty member and one of Kafka's examiners for his law degree was Alfred Weber, the younger brother of the sociologist Max Weber and author of an article on 'The Bureaucrat' (*'Der Beamte'*) in the *Neue Rundschau* in 1912, which Kafka undoubtedly read. Kafka's tutor in criminal law, Hans Gross, was author of the standard textbook on criminal law, the 1893 *Handbook for Investigative Magistrates, Police Officers, and Gendarmes* (*Handbuch für Untersuchungsrichter, Polizeibeamte, Gendarmen*). Gross became

---

Kafka's original spelling of the word. As we shall see, the idea of a trial only partly captures the meaning of the German.

3 Ideally, this analysis would be correlated with studies of other Kafka texts that directly invoke the structure and process of law, most notably 'In the Penal Colony' ('In der Strafkolonie'), written around the time of *DP* and published in 1919, and *The Castle* (*Das Schloss*), a novel which, like *DP*, remained unfinished at Kafka's death. So closely does the narrative form of *DP* match the recursive formations of modern law, however, that I have decided to present it as my sole extended example.

4 The lyrics of 'The Lonesome Death of Hattie Carroll' can be found at www.bobdylan.com. The song, based on a true incident that occurred in Baltimore in 1963, condemns the light sentence handed out to the scion of a planter family for assaulting a hotel worker because she brought him his drink too slowly. The line I am quoting seems to be free indirect discourse from the reasoning of the judge in the case, and is ironized by the outcome. The song shows that there is a ladder of law, with white on top, black on the bottom, rich on top, poor on the bottom. However, the line as sung corresponds both to the ST model of horizontally organized systems and to the structure of the law in *DP*.

a *cause célèbre* when he ordered his own son, Otto, to be arrested and interned in 1913. Kafka became personally acquainted with Otto Gross in 1917, and in 1920 considered collaborating with him on a literary journal. The possible influence on Kafka's work most likely stemmed from the public portion of the Gross affair, which resembles the persecution of sons by fathers in stories such as 'The Judgment' (1912; '*Das Urteil*') and 'The Metamorphosis' (1915; '*Die Verwandlung*').

Kafka enjoyed a remarkably steady and, by bureaucratic standards, successful career. After a brief stint with another firm, he worked as a bureaucrat in the Workers' Accident Insurance Institute of the Kingdom of Bohemia (*Arbeiter-Unfall-Versicherungsanstalt für das Königreich Böhmen*) from 1908 until tuberculosis, which would eventually take his life, forced him to quit in 1922. Kafka soon rose above the level of *Manipulationist* (roughly, an employee entrusted only with copying, crunching numbers, and so forth) to that of *Concipist* (an employee entrusted with developing 'conceits' or ideas). Ernst Pawel, in his biography of Kafka, describes the Institute – in language reminiscent of another great Austrian writer, Robert Musil – as 'an integral part of the pullulating Austro-Hungarian bureaucracy that like a giant net of near-epic intricacy covered the entire Hapsburg domain and, for all its rips, bulges, and frazzled strands, somehow managed to keep the disparate fragments from breaking loose' (Pawel, *Nightmare*, 183). In this view, bureaucracy, which had grown and was still growing rapidly following the government's decision to socialize numerous aspects of Austrian life on the German model, came to represent the order and unification which for other nations are embodied in their militaries or in a single national language.

Or in science. Bureaucracies are machines, systems whose smooth running depends upon the most modern methods, which Kafka was constantly studying. Ideas of system were incorporated in Kafka's supervisor, Dr Robert Marschner, a progressive technocrat who gave courses – some of which Kafka took – at the Prague Institute of Technology, and who is referred to by the editor of Kafka's bureaucratic writings as an 'insurance scientist' (*Kafkas Amtliche Schriften* 18; 'Versicherungswissenschaftler'). At one point in Kafka's career, his work concerned finding methods for dividing all firms in Bohemia which used heavy machinery into fourteen classes according to the risk of accident, in order to determine on a rational basis how much their insurance premiums should be. Kafka officially requested technical training in order to be able to do his job properly. He first came into contact with Gustav Janouch's father because he was interested in Janouch elder's improved design for a '*Kartothek*', a cabinet for holding data cards (Janouch, *Gespräche mit Kafka*, 16). We can find traces of the *Karthotek* in the description of a writing desk in *Amerika* (*Der Verschollene*),[5] one of the many technological marvels that the novel's protagonist finds in America:

> For instance the top part of [the desk] had a hundred different compartments of all sizes, so that even the President of the Union would have found room for each of his files in it; but even better than that, it had an adjuster at the side, so that by turning a handle one could rearrange and adjust the compartments in whatever way one wanted or needed. (Kafka, *Amerika*, 29)
>
> [Er hatte z. B. in seinem Aufsatz hundert Fächer verschiedenster Grösse und selbst der Präsident der Union hätte für jeden seiner Akten einen passenden Platz gefunden, aber ausserdem war an der Seite ein Regulator und man konnte durch Drehen an der Kurbel die verschiedensten Umstellungen und Neueinrichtungen der Fächer nach Belieben und Bedarf erreichen.] (*Der Verschollene*, 57)

Imagine that one placed, instead of documents in the various compartments, the chapters of a narrative one was writing, which could then be constantly reordered according to the technology of the *Aufsatz* – a word that can mean not only the hutch of a desk, but also an essay. The ordering of the narrative would become aleatory and a function of (literally) bureau-cratic technology.

Kafka's writing first came to the attention not of the literary public, but of his superiors, who praised the fine style of his reports. Kafka responded, no doubt ironically, by sending a sample of one of these technical essays to the editor of a literary journal as a potential contribution (Kafka, *Amtliche Schriften*, 28). Inevitably, bureaucratic technology found its way into Kafka's literary works, subtly in the short story 'The Great Wall of China' ('Beim Bau der chinesischen Mauer'), where Kafka notes that 'for the supervision even of every four day laborers an expert versed in the art of building was required' (Kafka, *Complete Stories*, 236; 'Zur Leitung von vier Taglöhnern war ein verständiger im Baufach gibildeter Mann notig' [*Sämtliche Erzählungen*, 289–90]) The number four was not chosen at

---

5   On publishing the novel after Kafka's death, Max Brod gave it the title *Amerika*. Editors now refer to it as *Der Verschollene*, i.e. The Man Who Disappeared – or more accurately, The Male Person Who Disappeared.

random. Kafka is alluding to the well-known axiom of bureaucratology, that one person can efficiently supervise at most four others.[6]

The editors of Kafka's *Amtliche Schriften* note that some chapters of his novel, *Der Prozess*, are among the truest and most truthful of his official writings (Klaus Hermsdorf and Wagner, Introduction, 60). The perspective I wish to add in this chapter, following the clue of the magical bureau, is that the very form of this 'novel' (a questionable but often-used generic category for this piece of writing) shapes itself to its content in order to speak a powerful message about the recursive process that is life in administered society in which legitimacy derives from process and procedure, rather than from authority or decision.

Citing Austrian Law

In the famous opening scene of *DP*, the protagonist Josef K. awakens one morning to find two men in his room. They are his *'Wächter,'* i.e. literally his Watchers, but usually translated as 'warders.' K. is under arrest, and he spends the rest of the novel working on his case, trying to discover what he is accused of. The 'final' chapter of the novel depicts K.'s execution. The variety of interpretations of, and opinions and perspectives on, *DP* seems to be infinite. Wolfgang Kraus has summarized just a few of the possibilities: '*DP* [...] has been interpreted as a prophetic warning of the Nazi terror (Adorno, 'Notes on Kafka'), as a homesick longing for salvation from earthly guilt (Buber, *Schuld und Schuldgefühle* and Schoeps, 'Theologische Motive'), or as the 'mad delusion of a neurotic driven ever deeper into isolation' (Wolfgang Kraus, 'Schuld und Sinnfrage', 201). Just as the miniature 'Murder of Gonzago' seems to reproduce the plot of *Hamlet*, so too the inserted parable 'Vor dem Gesetz' ('Before the Law'), told to K. by a priest, seems to represent the entire meaning of *DP* in a compressed form. Walter Benjamin has expressed this relationship with the metaphor: 'one could guess that the novel is nothing other than the parable unfolded' (Benjamin, 'Über Franz Kafka', 166; 'Man könnte vermuten, der Roman sei nichts als die entfaltete Parabel'). The parable is treated as the great precedent that explains the rest of the novel, a Grimmian *Rechtsspruch* that, if only it could be understood correctly, would provide the missing foundation for an otherwise aimless bureaucracy.

Before they bring him into contact with the priest who divulges this parable, K.'s attempts to find out more about his case, including the charges against him, take him not only to the more obvious

---

6   I am indebted to John Beebee, Professor Emeritus of Mathematics and the University of Alaska, Anchorage, for this insight.

sources of information and influence, such as the court itself and a lawyer named Huld, but also to more out-of-the-way individuals, such as a painter. In what is conventionally given as the last chapter of the text, K. is taken to a stone quarry and killed with a knife. Frank Stringfellow, for example, sees Josef K. as a Socrates figure who goes willingly to his death, presumably in the cause of truth. Furthermore, the cruelty of this ending, added to Kafka's Jewish background and the fate of his family members, would seem to support interpretations of the novel as prophetic of the Holocaust and of other parajudicial acts of incarceration and murder carried out under a 'state of exception'. K.'s arrest does not seem to proceed in accordance with any conventional type of law, but according to the hidden mechanisms of repression and torture associated with the Gestapo, the KGB, as well as the police and armed forces of South Africa under apartheid and of several South American countries through the 1970s and 1980s, to give a few examples. The scenario of the story 'In the Penal Colony', with its horrendous torture machine, lends credence to this view, and Scott McClintock's use of Kafka to analyze the non-person status of Guantánamo Bay detainees is one of the more recent attempts to make Kafka a prophet of human rights abuses.

However, Kafka never finished *DP*, and it is not clear that he meant the execution scene to be the final one. It could, for example, have been revealed as a dream of Josef K., or if Kafka had finished the novel he could have decided to replace it with another ending. Furthermore, in its finality and clarity the ending contradicts the basic message of the text about the endless ambiguities and infinite delays of 'the law'. Stefan Andriopoulos has managed to provide an interpretation that merges the bureaucratic endlessness of the law with the finality of K.'s knifing, though at the cost of metaphorizing the latter:

> At the end of a prolonged juridical and physiological process, Joseph K. becomes part of a 'vast judicial organism' that 'sucks in' the bodies of natural persons. But the juridical 'particularity of ascribing a certain life to lifeless matter' not only allows for the legal conceptualization of an invisible aggregate person [the corporation or *Behörde*]. It also leads to a 'certain' lifelessness of the animate. (Andriopoulos, *Possessed*, 155)

K.'s death is not a result of the *Recht/Unrecht* decision on his case, but rather of his ultimate aggregation into the structure of the law and the court, a process made visible in the parable 'Before the Law'. The quotation marks in the above passage come from Max Weber's writings on bureaucracy, a philosophical and sociological critique that appeared while Kafka was writing his mature works. Kafka did not know either Weber or his writings, but may have read Alfred Weber's piece 'Der Beamte' mentioned above, which incorporates many of his brother's ideas (Litowitz, 'Max Weber and Franz Kafka', 51). Such readings harmonize to some extent with our view of Kafka as a hero of Modernism, who himself worked as an anonymous bureaucrat only to indulge his artistic fantasies in a night-time world of 'creative' writing that could find no outlet in the real world governed by instrumental reason. In this view, *DP* would be Kafka's protest against his own diminishment as a cog in the bureaucratic machine.[7]

Nevertheless, Theodore Ziolkowski is right to question whether *DP* should be read as such a protest: 'Is it conceivable that a legally trained writer like Kafka [...] could deny in his own work the lawyer's mentality or what Germans call the "juristic style of thought" (*juristischer Denkstil*)?' (Ziolkowski, *The Mirror of Justice*, 226). Ziolkowski proceeds to demonstrate that *DP* is a tapestry of citations from German and Austrian law. Take the novel's first sentence, for example: 'Someone must have slandered Joseph K., for one morning, without having done anything truly wrong, he was arrested' (Kafka, *The Trial*, 5; 'Jemand mußte Josef K. verleumdet haben, denn ohne daß er etwas Böses getan hätte, wurde er eines Morgens verhaftet' [*DP*, 7]). Words such as 'slander' (*Verleumdung*) and 'wrong' (*Böses*) are not colloquial (nor much less the use of '*Rechtsstaat*' a few pages later), but can be shown to occur prominently in the Austrian Criminal Code of 1852 that was still in effect when Kafka was a law student, and which he undoubtedly read with care under the tutelage of Hans Gross. Ziolkowski concludes from this and other citations that *DP* satirizes not bureaucracy, but Austrian law:

> It is plausible to conclude [...] that the first sentence of the novel points, just like the first sentence of the Austrian Criminal Code, at the notion of evil intent and, thereby, at the motivation of the accused criminal rather than at any act he may have committed. Given this premise, the remainder of the novel

---

7 It is thus typical that Eberhard Schmidhäuser, a lawyer, comes to the conclusion ('Kafkas »Der Prozeß«') that the arrest in *DP* represents K.'s mental collapse, and that the trial is a symbolic representation of the progression of a mental illness – a psychological reading of the text that contradicts the overt political ones mentioned above.

falls into place as an extension, albeit to absurd extremes, of the Austrian theory of criminal law. (Ziolkowski, 238)

The term 'Extension' interests as a synonym of 'structural coupling', and also looks forward to the relationship between the Frankfurt Auschwitz trial and Peter Weiss's drama, *The Investigation*. However, to be an extension of the criminal law the novel would need to have illocutionary force, to be a verdictive speech-act with the power of indictment or sentencing.[8] Ziolkowski admits that it is difficult to find an exact motivation for this 'E xtension'. For example, it is not clear whether Josef K. is an innocent victim, or a representative of the well-known human tendency towards denial and rationalization. Robin West also argues for a literal Kafka, who critiques above all the workplace marked by sexual harassment (the law student who carries off the woman in chapter three of *DP*) and dehumanization (the whipper scene of chapter five). Like McClintock, who deploys Kafka in order to protest the dehumanizing processes of Camp X-Ray, West's reading uses Kafka's texts to attack the viewpoint of Richard Posner that market forces provide the best solutions to a vast array of legal issues.[9] Posner, on the other hand, reads other Kafka parables such as 'The Problem of Our Laws' and 'The New Advocate' as contemplations of the difference between positivist and natural law views of the existence of the law. Kafka is critiquing not law *per se*, and certainly not the philosophy of comparative law that would have lent excitement to his dull years of study, but rather the new 'bureaucratic man' that has been formed in the crux of legal and administrative systems that gained power in Europe, and especially in Austria, in the latter half of the nineteenth century. In particular, *DP* explores the recursive nature of these systems.

Recursivity and Power

Luhmann explains that a process 'is called "recursive" when it uses the results of its own operations as the basis for further operations – that is, what is undertaken is determined in part by what

---

[8] The terms 'speech act', 'illocutionary' and 'verdictive' all derive from the language philosophy of J. L. Austin, and especially from *How to Do Things With Words*.
[9] Not surprisingly, Richard Posner has defended himself (*Law and Literature*, 182–205) by attacking West's reading. He does so using two contradictory arguments. Kafka's works are not realistic; to read them as such is to mistake 'Kafka for a lecturer at the Harvard Business School' (Posner, *Law and Literature*, 184). At the same time, however, Posner is happy to enter into the legal details of various scenes and to reinterpret West's readings.

has occurred in earlier operations. In the language of system theory [...] one often says that such a process uses its own outputs as inputs' (Luhmann, *Theories of Distinction*, 139). The 'ladder of law', the pyramid of appeal, the use of precedent and citation, all are examples of this use of outputs and inputs. So, too, is Hans Kelsen's normative theory of law, in the sense that it posits that norms are created only from norms, never from facts.

We may consider two opposing types of procedures in computing: recursive and iterative. Whereas iterative procedures start with a base and apply the same algorithm repeatedly until a goal is reached (as one does when one counts from 0 to 100 by adding 1 to each previous result), recursive procedures begin with some form of the goal, work backward until a base is found, and then work forward again to achieve a complete result. Thus, the 'backward' motion is a movement from the complex to the simple, from the unknown to the known, until definite results, a single, unambiguous precedent that can serve as a base, can be obtained. Important here is the notion that any problem and hence any solution contains within itself a number of subproblems or subsolutions, and that these must be unfolded and 'stacked' upon each other in order to solve the problem. A metaphor for the difference would be: in iterative algorithms, the solution is 'out there', whereas in recursive algorithms, it is 'in there'. As an example, Fibonacci numbers are defined recursively; that is, each number is defined as the sum of the two preceding Fibonacci numbers, except for the first and second numbers of the series, which are defined as 1. The series thus goes: 1,1,2,3,5,8,13,21... But suppose we were asked to determine the 100th number in this series? We would only be able to say that the 100th number was the sum of the 99th and the 98th numbers. This tells us little. But then the 99th number is the sum of the 98th and the 97th numbers, and the 98th number is the sum of the 97th and 96th numbers, and so on, backwards until we reach the first and second numbers, which are defined to be 1. We would then know the 3rd number to be 2, the 4th to be 2 plus 1, and so on back up the ladder until we get to the 100th number. To summarize, recursion involves defining something in terms of itself. That is the procedure. However, there must also be a base, a smallest unit which is defined outright; otherwise the recursive process goes on infinitely.

The Aristotelian sense of plot, that it is of a (linear) chain of events, corresponds to the iterative programme. One thing follows from another and adds to an aggregate. Recursive narratives, on the other hand, are chains in which each link is another chain and where we move backwards from the largest to the smallest link. *DP* presents narrative as a recursive process. The composition of the text bears a strong relationship to its narrative form and is responsible for the uncertainty as to the 'real' sequence of chapters in *DP* (cf. Uyttersprot, Binder ['*Der Prozess*'], and Lotze). Many chapters were left uncompleted, as though the author knew no way out of the recursive hermeneutic process he had created. Kafka wrote the first and last chapters of *DP* almost simultaneously, starting on 11 August 1914. Middle chapters were also worked on simultaneously, and kept in separate envelopes – which, had Kafka possessed the mechanical desk described in *The Man Who Disappeared*, would each have found its unique pigeonhole and been subject to constant reordering. Thus, we could say that the narrative was written neither from front to back nor from back to front, but rather with a kind of jumping motion from subroutine to subroutine. Also contributing to the confusion was Kafka's storage technique: he had the habit of separating the chapters physically from one another in envelopes, almost as Claude Lévi-Strauss ('The Structural Study of Myth') would later put the separate incidents of the Oedipus myth on index cards so that they could be compared with each other out of narrative sequence in order to reveal their hidden meaning. In Kafka we may detect the influence of the bureaucratic procedure of 'pigeonholing' on the creative process. This recursive writing procedure may account in part for the inability of Kafka to complete the text, just as K. cannot reach the law. He abandoned *DP* in January 1915, and never returned to finish it.

Recursivity shows itself from the first pages, for *DP* begins with its end: the main character Josef K. is arrested. We can see this as a reversal of the normal narrative sequence of detective fiction. The initial arrest of K. constitutes simultaneously an incipit, *and* a result towards which the whole of the novel will work, namely to formulate a *Recht/Unrecht* distinction. That the beginning of the novel is coterminous with its end is emphasized by the striking parallels between opening and closing chapters: in each case two men (the '*Wächter*' or warders who serve the court) come to K.'s home without warning and disturb his routine, once to arrest him, and next to execute him. What comes between these two incidents can be seen in two ways: iteratively, as K.'s attempt to resolve the problem of his arrest; or recursively, as a demonstration of the guilty behaviour on which the arrest is based. Iteratively, his arrest confronts K. with a problem he must resolve. Recursively, it confronts him with a truth he must fathom.

Suppose that the law's structure were something like a Fibonacci sequence. In some sense, it is. One of the legal norms that Hans Kelsen, among others, theorizes as crucial to the law's essence, for example, may not seem very normative to a practitioner or subject of the law if it is the 99th norm in a series that stretches back to 1. This chain is represented in the text, for example, by the continual series of blocked viewpoints (such as in the products of the artist Tintorelli), by the labyrinthine stacks of legal papers in the law offices, and overall by the inability of K. to obtain a clear view of his case.[10] But Luhmann's point is that 'autopoiesis [...] positively *requires* the absence of any supreme or last instance at the hub of the process of society's self-continuation. Luhmann's problem is about the performance of agencies, it is the problem of the improbable mastery of the complexity modern society is confronted with' (Schütz,114; emphasis Schütz's). *DP*, no less than *The Castle* (*Das Schloss*), is a narrative that takes the novel as precedent and struggles continually to become one – a struggle shown, among other things, by Kafka having abandoned both texts unfinished. This struggle is an attempt to enter the door of the law and be allowed a second-order observation free of entanglement in the recursive processes being observed. Disentanglement never occurs, and the text becomes caught up in the recursive processes it is intended to describe. In this sense, it is more an 'intension' than an 'E xtension'.

My discussion of Fibonacci numbers is drawn from the book *Gödel, Escher, Bach: An Eternal Golden Braid*. In this book, Douglas R. Hofstadter compares examples of recursion found in genetics, mathematics and music. His definition of the term is correspondingly somewhat loose: 'Recursion is based on the "same" thing happening on several different levels at once. But the events on different levels aren't exactly the same – rather, we find some invariant feature in them, despite many ways in which they differ' (Hofstadter, 148–9). In his own sample narrative, Hofstadter gives a recursive definition of God that allows ready application to the concept to literature:

$$GOD = \frac{GOD}{Djinn}$$

Or 'God equals God over Djinn'. Here we begin with God, the Unknown, and define Her as lower versions of Herself, incorporating more and more – indeed an infinity of – Djinns, since one may substitute the right side of the equation into its numerator to obtain 'God over Djinn over Djinn', and so on. The above formula is interpreted in a dialogue between the traditionally dense Achilles

---

10 Interestingly, when we move beyond the highly restricted systems of mathematics, Luhmann claims that the novel form was first responsible for the second-order observation that arises from recursion. See *Theories of Distinction*, 140–41.

(aided at one point by the Tortoise) and the Genie over the meaning of the word GOD:

> *Genie:* Oh, aren't you acquainted with recursive acronyms? I thought everybody knew about them. You see, 'GOD' stands for 'GOD over Djinn' – which can be expanded as 'GOD Over Djinn. Over Djinn' – and that can in turn, be expanded to 'GOD Over Djinn, Over Djinn. Over Djinn' – which can, in its turn be further expanded ... You can go as far as you like.
> *Achilles:* I see. You mean GOD sits up at the top of the ladder of Djinns?
> *Genie:* No, no, no! There is nothing 'at the top', for there is no top. That is why GOD is a recursive acronym. GOD is not some ultimate Djinn. GOD is the tower of Djinns above any given Djinn.
> *Tortoise:* It seems to me that each and every Djinn would have a different concept of what GOD is, then, since to any Djinn, GOD is the set of Djinns above him or her, and no two Djinns share that set.
> *Genie:* You're absolutely right – and since I am the lowest Djinn of all, my notion of GOD is the most exalted one. I pity the higher Djinns, who consider themselves somehow closer to GOD. What blasphemy!
>
> (Hofstadter, 113–14)

Hofstadter's use of Djinns points to his actual source of inspiration, *The Thousand and One Nights*, a book which is recursive in the extreme. The very title of this collection of Arabian, Indian and Persian tales hints at its recursive structure. According to the premise of its frame tale, it should contain only one night, that single night between Sheherazade's marriage and her execution, which she is then able, through narration, to expand miraculously into a thousand. In many of her tales, action is suspended while another tale is told by one of the characters in the story, and so on, up through as many as four levels of quotation. The myriad other tales in this book unfold from Scheherazade's story, just as the whole Fibonacci series unfolds from the simplicity of its formulation and an infinity of Djinns unfolds from GOD. If we allow for the fact that a *'Türhüter'* is also a type of watcher or warder, we can reduce the structure depicted in the parable to the formula:

$$\text{LAW} = \frac{\text{LAW}}{\text{Watcher}}$$

For those familiar with *DP*, that is, the endless sequence of Djinns recalls the sequence of gatekeepers in the Kafka parable 'Before the Law'. I posit LAW as equal to 'Law Above Watcher', which can be unfolded in an analogous fashion to GOD. Kafka's *DP* both depicts and imitates this structure. For those concerned that the use of human actors softens the mechanics of recursion, we can provide the alternative formula LAW equals 'Law Above Writ'. I use 'writ' here in a sense somewhat expanded from the strict legal one of (originally) a command, precept, or formal order issued in written form by a competent authority. The point of both formulae is that LAW is to be found nowhere, but its instruments – be these graphemes or organic threats of violence – everywhere.

The illusory resting-point – truth, absolute proof, or transcendent top of the ladder of Warders and Writs that is sought by Josef K. – receives another name from Jacques Lacan and the Lacanian cultural theorist Slavoj Žižek: the Big Other. Recognition of the impossibility of locating this Other calls into question the identity of the seeker in a state of exception:

> This impossibility of experiencing the 'big Other' in the real signals the virtual character of our symbolic identity. This virtuality is far from limited to theology – it also forms the basis of bureaucratic metaphysics. [… This virtuality] also accounts for the elementary trick of bureaucracy (which is not an exception but the very rule of its 'normal' functioning): bureaucracy corners the subject into a situation in which, in order to survive, he has to break the (explicit) Law – this violation is then tolerated, but also manipulated as a permanent threat. Whenever one deals with a true bureaucratic machine, one is sooner or later caught in a vicious circle (for the attestation A one needs the paper B; one cannot get B without C; and, finally, of course, the circle is closed, C cannot be obtained without A …). (Žižek, 'Why Does the Law Need an Obscene Supplement?', 79)

The temptation to read *DP* as an allegory where Law = God, and K's guilt is original sin or human weakness, stems from the fact that both religion and bureaucracy deal in belief rather than in knowledge. Belief involves the Big Other in a way that knowledge does not – hence the intense relation between the man and the doorkeeper in the parable 'Before the Law': 'in an uncanny way, belief seems always to function in the guise of such a 'belief at a distance': in order for belief to function, there *had to be* some ultimate guarantor of it, yet this guarantor is always deferred, displaced, never here *in persona*'

(Žižek 81; emphasis in original). Like the man from the country, one is never permitted to enter the door and bask in the presence of the Big Other, GOD, or LAW. This structure helps us understand the persistence of transcendental interpretations of *DP*, whether the transcendent goal be God or Justice. Kafka attempted to give insight in his writing to the recursive, self-referential, Gödelian structure of modern society, in which religion must be called to provide a basis. In Luhmann's words, 'Society can exist only as a self-referential system, it can operate and reproduce communications only within a Gödelian world. This general condition makes "religion" (whatever this means) unavoidable. Social life, therefore, has a religious quality' (Luhmann, 'Society', 147).[11] And both religion and LAW, to return to Žižek's point, are examples of the Big Other.

In the Law Machine
Dietrich Wachler has intepreted Kafka's works as critiques of a secondary stage of the industrial revolution, which sees 'the identification between man and machine as a feedback control system, as a cybernetic mechanism, between apparatus and socio-economic system by means of automation, with the consequences of a radical change in consciousness' (Wachler, 'Mensch und Apparat bei Kafka', 150), and for post-structuralist thinkers such as Gilles Deleuze and Felix Guattari, *DP* is a 'scientific investigation, a report of the experiments on the functioning of a machine in which the law runs the strong risk of playing no more than the role of exterior armature' (Deleuze and Guattari, *Towards a Minor Literature*, 43–4). The law does not direct the machine: it simply is the machine, a point made in the story 'In the Penal Colony' when the Commandant becomes a victim of the torture apparatus he formerly directed. Kafka was of course not influenced by cybernetics or by the invention of the computer, but rather by all the forces and changes – including those in literature, philosophy and psychology – that made such an invention possible and desirable. The notorious computerization of bureaucracy is only possible because bureaucracies have already been 'rationalized', to recall Max Weber's famous term; that is, have already become inhuman (by definition) machines.

The first sentence of the novel, cited above, expresses the equation that will serve as a motivating force for the investigation and which seems to deliver truth while actually withholding it. Theo Elem, in

---

11 'Gödelian' refers to structures that invoke the so-called 'Incompleteness Theorems' of the logician Kurt Gödel, one of which states that consistent systems of axia cannot be complete. The Hofstadter book cited in this chapter applies these ideas well beyond their original domain of mathematical logic.

writing a summary of Kafka criticism in which he sees only contradictions and the endless play of difference, considers this sentence to typify *DP*'s critique of the accepted logical procedure of moving from the general to the specific. If so, then *DP* is a second-order observation of the interpretive process itself (Elem, 'Der Prozess', 435–40). The sentence, with its upholding of formal logic, of cause and effect, of the regime of civil rights and procedural guarantees (*Rechtsstaat*) and of our sympathy with the main character as a persecuted individual, alludes to the legal and metaphysical presuppositions with which most readers will approach Kafka's text. Law is, as Luhmann says, the guarantor of normative expectations in modern societies. Yet Kafka's arrangement of his text and his recursive formulation of the problem turn generalizations like those contained in the first sentence against themselves. Every part of the first sentence of the novel is denied or at least placed in logical suspension by the rest of the text: no one has libelled K. No one needed to denounce him to the court since, as we learn, the court is automatically drawn to the guilty. Furthermore, we see K. doing plenty of 'wrong' things in the course of the novel.[12]

Part of this paradox lies in the double nature of the *Rechtsstaat* itself, since, as Michael Stolleis details, in Habermasian fashion, civil rights and bureaucratic control are mutually conditioning:

> The packaging of administrative actions in formal legal procedures is a modern phenomenon. Its goal is to increase the equitableness and effectiveness of the administration and to have this latter steered by legislative parliaments and monitored by the courts whose function it is to apply law. Historically, therefore, form-bound administrative law and formal *Rechtsstaat* depend upon each other. [...] Without formalism the tools of the *Rechtsstaat* would be ineffective. Protection under the law means no more and no less than monitoring the observance of certain forms of legal inquiry and application. Only for this reason did that often criticized [...] concentration on the juridical framework of administrative action arise at the end of the nineteenth century alongside the political trend towards universal suffrage. At this moment, administrative

---

12 Adrian Jaffe makes this point forcefully in a segment of his study with the subtitle 'The Inversion of Crime and Punishment' (87–9). Jaffe reads K.'s guilt sociologically: it is not original sin, but the kind of stigma that arises from a degraded social environment. Many critics have pointed to Kafka's Jewishness as the source of this feeling of degradation, while my own interpretation emphasizes the structural features of modernity.

law and administrative science were born. (Stolleis, *Geschichte des Öffentlichen Rechts*, I: 335)

Stolleis does not name Franz Kafka as one of the critics of the empty formalism of administrative procedure, but he is certainly the most remembered of these, to the extent that 'Kafkaesque' can now be used in American jurisprudence as an enthymeme. The problem with Stolleis/Habermas is evident enough: formalism and proceduralism in and of themselves can just as easily become obstacles to legal remedy as pathways thereto. The following sentence from the beginning of *DP* is one of the most realistic-legalistic in the text: 'K. lived in a state governed by law, there was universal peace, all statutes were in force, who dared assault him in his own lodgings?' (Kafka, *The Trial*, 5; 'K. lebte doch in einem Rechtsstaat, überall herrschte Friede, alle Gesetze bestanden aufrecht, wer wagte, ihn in seiner Wohnung zu überfallen?' [*DP*, 11]). As noted above, the appearance of the legal-technical term *Rechtsstaat* in this sentence gives some justification to interpretations of *DP* as predictive of fascism – the *Rechtsstaat* appears to have failed to live up to its responsibilities here. (For some, it had never even begun in either Germany or Austria, because the publication of, and adherence to, law and procedure were not accompanied by their usual pendant of legislation by a popularly elected parliament.) After all, most of K.'s thoughts and assumptions are proven wrong in the course of the narrative. (Kafka began *DP* at the exact moment World War I began, making the reference to peace ironic.) But if one reads the sentence together with Stolleis's analysis, the more likely interpretation becomes one where the *Rechtsstaat* becomes its own worst enemy, as it were, a critique that is condensed into the parable 'Before the Law', where the infinite chain of doorkeepers can represent the endlessness of procedure, and the contradictory command to wait forever at the door meant only for you can invoke the inevitable logical short-circuits of procedure that Žižek has outlined.

The Chain Gang

Josef K. is not the man who seeks admittance to the law, but is located somewhere in the chain of doorkeepers. As Deleuze and Guattari put it, 'the secret of *The Trial* is that K. himself is a lawyer, also a judge' (Deleuze and Guattari, *Towards a Minor Literature*, 57). Though the exact reason for K.'s arrest is never given in the novel, we see continually how his powerlessness before the court actually puts him in a position of power over others and how his persecution causes him to become prosecutor. This is brought home most directly to the reader in the chapter of the novel entitled 'The Whipper' ('*Der*

Prugler'). K. walks into a storage room at the bank where he works and finds a scene of torture: his two warders are being beaten because K. has complained to the court about their behaviour. This chapter, located in the centre of the novel, represents 'the first moment [...] when the circle of collusion, deviation, and retribution linking the characters comes fully to a close and when, consequently, the delineations separating accused, accuser, and the arm of the law fall away' (Henry Sussman, 'The Court as Text', 41). This recursive circle can be thought of in two ways: (1) K. is a legal subject as well as an object of investigation; or (2) the court takes this opportunity to reveal the monopoly on violence that is the seat of its power. In the second reading, the whipping is simply '*Abschreckung*' (deterrence) of the crudest sort; in the first, it is a function of K.'s own position on the ladder of law, from which he can activate certain levers of the judicial machine. The circle of guilt and punishment is a vicious one: because K. is guilty, the warders abuse him by confiscating his underwear. Because K. complains about his treatment, the warders are beaten. K.'s punishment for punishing, in turn, is that he must personally witness their beating. K.'s watchers are appointed to make an observation of Josef K. They are, in turn, observed by a higher instance, which no doubt is under observation by a still higher instance, and so forth. The ladder's infinity is further emphasized by K.'s opening the door to the same room the next day and finding the identical scene being repeated.

If the law's violence works overtly in this scene (as it does also in K.'s execution), elsewhere in the novel it manifests itself as symbolic and structural. Pierre Bourdieu reminds us that *DP*'s structure of infinite deferral outlined above is social rather than metaphysical, both an accumulation of cultural capital and an exercise of symbolic violence:

> [T]he art of 'taking one's time', or 'letting time take its time', as Cervantes puts it, of making people wait, of delaying without destroying hope, of adjourning without totally disappointing, which would have the effect of killing the waiting itself, is an integral part of the exercise of power. [...] Kafka's *The Trial* can be read as the model of a social universe dominated by such an absolute and upredictable power, capable of inducing extreme anxiety by condemning its victim to very strong investment combined with very great insecurity. (Bourdieu, *Pascalian Meditations*, 228–9)

What distinguishes Bourdieu from Luhmann is the question of power, since according to ST the ladder of system has no top and no bottom. However, Bourdieu further points out that the seemingly extraordinary social world depicted in *DP* may resemble the daily lives of members of stigmatized social groups (e.g. the Jews of Kafka's Prague), whose experience of this arbitrary power begins with their own assignment to one of these said groups by the arbitrary, essential operations of society's Big Watcher.

We may note in the following conversation how K.'s treatment of the tradesman Block resembles that of a lawyer or court interrogator, although within the novel K. is never really interrogated at all. K. meets Block, who has been on trial for many years, in the home of their lawyer. He suspects Block of a liaison with the lawyer's maid and nurse, Leni, whom K. considers for some reason to be his:

> He was a scrawny little man with a full beard, holding a candle in his hand. 'Do you work here?' K. asked. 'No,' the man replied, 'I'm not part of the household, the lawyer just represents me; I'm here on a legal matter.' 'Without a jacket?' K. asked, and indicated with a wave of his hand the man's inappropriate state of dress. 'Oh, do forgive me,' said the man. [...] 'Is Leni your lover?' K. asked curtly. [...] 'Oh goodness,' said the other, and raised one hand before his face in shocked repudiation, 'no, no, what are you thinking of?' 'You look trustworthy,' said K., smiling, 'but yet – let's go.' He gestured with his hat for him to lead the way. 'What's your name?' asked K. as they went along. (Kafka, *The Trial*, 167–8)

> [Es war ein kleiner, dürrer Mann mit Vollbart. Er hielt eine Kerze in der Hand. 'Sie sind hier angestellt?' fragte K. 'Nein,' antwortete der Mann, 'ich bin hier fremd. Der Advokat ist nur mein Vertreter. Ich bin hier wegen einer Rechtsangelegenheit.' 'Ohne Rock?' fragte K, und zeigte mit einer Handbewegung auf die mangelhafte Bekleidung des Mannes. 'Ach, verzeihen Sie,' sagte der Mann. [...] 'Leni ist Ihre Geliebte?' fragte K. kurz. [...] 'O Gott,' sagte der und hob die eine Hand in erschrockener Abwehr vor das Gesicht, 'nein, nein, was denken Sie denn?' 'Sie sehen glaubwürdig aus,' sagte K. lächelnd, 'trotzdem kommen Sie.' Er winkte ihm mit dem Hut und ließ ihn vor sich gehen. 'Wie heissen Sie denn?' fragte K. auf dem Weg.] (*DP*, 123)

K.'s order to 'come along' (*'kommen Sie'*) despite Block's appearance of guiltlessness, along with his use of the adjective *'glaubwürdig'*, translated as 'trustworthy' but closer to 'reliable', as in a reliable witness, sounds remarkably policial, particularly insofar as it is linked to K.'s initial denial of Block's honesty. Aggressive interrogation and rudeness are shown by K. in several scenes throughout the novel and are only two of his unsavoury characteristics. Ritchie Robertson has pointed out some others: 'Calculating, egoistic, aggressive, authoritarian, self-deceived, and repressed, [K.] is somebody who, willingly or not, has discarded large tracts of his personality in order to fit into the organization which employs him' (Robertson, *Kafka*, 100). The organization Robertson refers to is the bank where K. enjoys a relatively high position and not to the court, though the ambiguity here is significant.

Though Robertson sees K.'s guilt as inherent to the fact that he voluntarily belongs to the system, he does not point out that the majority of K.'s antisocial acts are caused by his trial, and he ends up with a fairly conventional critical notion of K. as morally guilty, as though Kafka's goal in the novel had been to penetrate the traditional black box of character motivation, rather than the structures of power that motivate them. At times, the narrative holds out this hope that extra-systemic considerations could irritate the system. The lawyer Huld explains to K. how the officials of the court often must seek advice from the hierarchically inferior lawyers because the former lack the 'proper understanding of human relationships' (Kafka, *The Trial*, 117; 'Sinn für menschliche Beziehungen' [*DP*, 88]). K.'s punishment comes neither at the beginning nor at the end of the novel, but throughout: his punishment is that he must punish. In other words, the structure of punishment, like the structure of the court and the law, is recursive, reproducing its whole hierarchy at each of its levels.

Given that the beginning of the novel represents its goal, namely the arrest of K., then we have a situation similar to that of our recursive definition of a Fibonacci number. The first sentence of the novel posits K.'s guilt in an unclear and unfathomable way. In reading the text we will move backward through more and more elemental situations until we encounter the clearest definition of K.'s guilt in the parable 'Before the Law'. Just as in recursive programmes the solution of higher levels is delayed until the lowest level (the base) can be resolved, so K.'s search for the meaning of his arrest is thrown from one unresolved episode to the next, and the sequence of his quests is from specific to general, from higher level to lower level. For example, K. comes before the court almost immediately after being arrested, in Chapter 2 in Max Brod's arrangement of the text, entitled 'First Interrogation' ('*Erste Untersuchung*'). Chapter 3, where K. visits the law offices, takes place in the same building a week later. In Chapter 2, K. actually sees the courtroom and talks with his judges. In Chapter 3 he speaks only with the law-office workers, and the remaining chapters show an increasing distance from the court, ostensibly because K. has offended the magistrates with a violent speech in his own defence during the first interrogation. K.'s movement through the last half of the novel is thus centrifugal in relation to the court; he moves farther and farther away from, rather than closer and closer to, the top echelons of justice. Yet, at the same time, he discovers at each turn that everyone and everything – including the narrative *DP* – is connected to the court in some way, and the discussion that takes place at that level reproduces K.'s problem in miniature.

Chapter 4 shows K. again at the rooming-house where he had been arrested, speaking not with his neighbour, Fräulein Burstner, who as a lawyer's secretary could not possibly help him with his case, but rather with her friend, Fräulein Montag.[13] The process of meditation and – to use Henry Sussman's term – 'interpretive supplanting' has begun. Sussman, however, fails to provide any direction or structuration for this continual evasion of meaning, which thus appears to be random and pervasive, and hence ultimately uninteresting. The process of supplanting is not random, but has a recursive structure. In later chapters K., no longer able to represent himself, will hire the lawyer Huld, who is feckless enough that K. subsequently fires him. Later K. also seeks help from the court painter Titorelli, a man who would seemingly have but the slightest relation to the real centres of power. In fact, he has a great deal of influence, and furthermore, as K. is leaving Titorelli, he discovers that the latter's studio is physically connected to the offices of the court.

The most elemental, 'normative' definition of K.'s relationship to the law, the parable 'Vor dem Gesetz' ('Before the Law'), is appropriately a subroutine inserted into his dialogue with the priest in the penultimate chapter, and a solution of the parable would be necessary in order to understand what the priest has to say. By extension, understanding the priest could help K. to understand the artist, and on back up the ladder, until he would finally know why he was arrested. This is perhaps what Walter Benjamin meant when he said, 'one could guess that the novel is nothing other than the parable unfolded'. But in fact the parable remains folded, rather than opening up to yield information. Whereas the Fibonacci programme ends when F(O) is reached and defined outright as the number one, no such base is obtained from the parable. The story or, rather, its interpretations repeat themselves infinitely.

---

13 As has often been noted, K.'s relation to the two women seems to derive from Kafka's use of Grete Bloch as a messenger and intermediary with his fiancée, Felice Bauer. Accusations of both women against Kafka, delivered at a meeting in Berlin, were the triggering incident for his beginning *DP*.

Let us review the parable: a man comes to the law and asks for admittance. The doorkeeper says that he cannot admit him now and the man remains, hoping to be admitted later. The man tries to enter on his own, causing the doorkeeper to remark: 'If you're so drawn to it, go ahead and try to enter, even though I have forbidden it. But bear this in mind: I am powerful. And I'm only the lowest doorkeeper. From hall to hall, however, stand doorkeepers each more powerful than the one before. The mere sight of the third man is more than even I can bear' (Kafka, *The Trial*, 215; 'Wenn es dich so lockt, versuche es doch, trotz meinem Verbot hineinzugehen. Merke aber: Ich bin mächtig. Und ich bin nur der unterste Türhüter. Von Saal zu Saal stehen aber Türhüter, einer mächtiger als der andere. Schon den Anblick des dritten kann nicht einmal ich mehr vertragen' [*DP*, 156]). The man chooses to wait. He grows old and is dying when he perceives a light coming from the open door. The final sentences of the story define its paradox: 'The doorkeeper sees that the man is nearing his end, and in order to reach his failing hearing, he roars at him: "No one else could gain admittance here, because this entrance was meant solely for you. I am going to go and shut it now"' (Kafka, *The Trial*, 217; 'Der Türhüter erkennt, daß der Mann schon am Ende ist, und um sein vergehendes Gehör noch zu erreichen, brüllt er ihn an: "Hier konnte niemand sonst Einlaß erhalten, denn dieser Eingang war nur für dich bestimmt. Ich gehe jetzt und schließe ihn"' [*DP*, 157]). The attempts at interpreting this parable are almost as numerous as interpretations of *DP* itself – indeed, most of its commentators recognize the centrality of the parable as Benjamin has defined it. Three prominent readings might be termed the 'existentialist', 'religious', and 'interpretation' views. In the first category one should mention Ingeborg Henel and Ritchie Robertson, both of whom see the parable as a demonstration of K.'s inability to accept his guilt. Robertson also enters the religious category by describing the law as the Torah, the doorkeeper as an Eastern Jew. In 'Der Prozess Against The Court', Heinz Politzer points out that the designation *'Mann vom Lande'* is probably a translation of the Hebrew *'Am-ha'aretz'*, a word which designated Jews living outside Jerusalem and hence not privy to the secrets of their own religion. Ulf Abraham interprets the man as an 'uncalled prophet' (*'ungerufener Mose'*). The 'interpretation' school views the story as exemplifying the problems of interpretation as the assignment of final meaning. Henry Sussman sees the parable as a demonstration that the law 'has space only for its readings, not for its readers or most devoted servants', i.e. that the slippages of the signifying chain work to obliterate the individual subject (Sussman, 'The

Court as Text', 50). To put it another way, the law is nothing other than its gatekeepers. We are all Watchers.

There is, however, a fourth school of interpretation, which claims that 'Before the Law' is about law. One should mention here Jacques Derrida's idiosyncratic reading, 'Devant la loi'. More interesting for our purposes, however, is Giorgio Agamben's reading of the parable in *Homo Sacer*. According to Agamben (49–62), this short text was the 'Revelation of Nothing' of the law. The story shows our living in the 'state of exception' in which life and law are indistinguishable. The concept of the 'state of exception' that Agamben draws from both Benjamin and Carl Schmitt refers to a situation in which it is impossible to determine whether an action is legal or illegal, whether the violence of a regime is, in Benjamin's terminology (in his 'Critique of Violence') 'law-preserving' or 'law-establishing'.[14] Such ambiguity arises when power is exerted on *zoé*, or bare life, in the practice of biopolitics and technologies of the self, practices Agamben traces to the ambivalence of *habeus corpus*. Because its effectiveness rests on the identification of the individual with the bare life of the physical body, 'Corpus is a two-faced being, the bearer both of subjection to sovereign power and of individual liberties' (Agamben, *Homo Sacer*, 125). The parable becomes in this reading a lesson in biopolitics, where the law literally deploys the man's body at the point most convenient to it, while leaving to him the sovereign choice as to whether to wait or to leave. Agamben deploys Kafka again in his work *State of Exception*, interpreting the latter's writings as the realization of the absolute saturation of life with law (through biopolitics, biometrics, the welfare state, and so on) to the point of there being no outside the law – and hence no inside either: 'Kafka's most proper gesture consists not [...] in having maintained a law that no longer has any meaning, but in having shown that it ceases to be law and blurs at all points with life' (Agamben, *State of Exception*, 63). This is equivalent to the *aporia* of the state of exception, which is both a state beyond the law and also the very foundation of it.[15] This fundamental paradox trumps discussions of *DP* that focus on its citations of specific legal situations. There is no 'outside' the law, and for that reason there is no precedent, no defined base number for

---

14 Chapter 3.2 will explore in detail the mutual citations between Benjamin and Schmitt that gave rise to the concept of the *Ausnahmezustand* or 'state of exception'.
15 Agamben's theories are extremely prescient with regard to post-9/11 abrogations of fundamental rights. 'The state of exception has today reached its maximum planetary dispersal,' he notes in *State of Exception* (111), perhaps hyperbolically.

the recursive series, no grounding for the law. The law regenerates and reproduces itself through self-citation and recursive processes of autopoiesis.

The key to a recursive interpretation of this story lies in a remark made by the doorkeeper about his own relation to the law: 'The sight of the third man is already more than even I can stand.' If we take this literally, we see that the doorkeeper himself cannot have penetrated past the third door. He merely cites what others have told him. In fact, though he can stand the sight of the doorkeeper immediately above him, that does not mean he may go past him. The doorkeeper is thus as much an outsider to the law as the man himself. Indeed, the priest hints at this in his interpretation, when he says that the doorkeeper may know little more about the law than the man himself. In other words, the recursive structure of the law would mean that each doorkeeper keeping others from the outside would also be a man seeking admittance to the law, just as in recursion each subsolution turns into a subproblem, each right-hand term of an equation becomes, in the next stage of problem-solving, a left-hand term. We are told nothing about either the man's past or the doorkeeper's future. Is it not possible that the man has functioned as a doorkeeper for someone below him and that the doorkeeper, after shutting the man's door, will go to the next one and beg for admittance just as the man has done? The man and the doorkeeper are thus not adversaries, but are dialectically related, just as the notion of crime and punishment are in this novel, just as Josef K. becomes both victim and perpetrator. The failure to enter the law lies neither in the man nor in the doorkeeper, but in the law's recursivity, which keeps everyone always already within it. The law is not a structure that may be perceived and defined from the outside, but rather an infinitely repeating recursive process, '*Der Prozess*', which encompasses everything and everyone. Taking the term 'Watcher' (*Wächter*) to designate any court functionary (i.e. all the characters of the novel), we may define LAW as 'Law Above Watcher.' The law is an infinity of watchers who guard – nothing. The man's misunderstanding of the law is like Achilles' misunderstanding of GOD, as a being sitting at the top of a ladder of Djinns. Rather, GOD is that ladder of Djinns which has no top. The system of LAW is the infinity of its writs or of its watchers, who simultaneously act as its victimizers and its victims.

K., like Achilles, fundamentally misunderstands the true nature of the law's power structure (i.e. of its interpretive structure). His attempt to penetrate the law is a fighting with mirrors, just as the attempt to see God would be in Hofstadter's parable. This notion explains certain mysteries of the novel: why the law offices are in a warehouse rather than in a separate building; why the officials are so shabbily dressed and so open to human vices; why everyone seems to know someone from the court and something about K.'s trial; why, as the painter Titorelli puts it, 'Everything belongs to the court' (Kafka, *The Trial*, 150; 'E s gehört alles zum Gericht' [*DP*, 110–11]). It also allows us to understand why no one is able to help K. Everyone has at some point the same relation to the law as the man has to the doorkeeper. It also helps us realize that K.'s death is not his punishment: nowhere is it stated in the final chapter that K.'s execution is intended to punish him or is the result of a sentence. Furthermore, while the painter Titorelli speaks of three different kinds of acquittals, he never mentions that the law achieves convictions. K.'s death is not a punishment but a failure, as is pointed to by his final words, 'like a dog' (Kafka, *The Trial*, 231; 'wie ein Hund' [*DP*, 165]), i.e. like a dumb animal, without having comprehended. K's failure was inevitable considering that his trial was an infinite loop, a recursive procedure without a base, an application of law to a non-precedent. The law knows no finalities, only infinities, as Huld says: 'this vast judicial organism remains, so to speak, in a state of eternal equilibrium' (Kafka, *The Trial*, 119–20; 'Dieser große Gerichtsorganismus bleibt gewissermaßen ewig in der Schwebe' [*DP*, 89]).[16] 'The Law [...] has to kill [K.] because it can neither convict nor acquit him,' remarks Politzer (Politzer, '*Der Prozess* Against The Court', 216), outlining in moral terms the infinite loop we have described. As the ladder of Djinns and the ladder of Watchers are infinite, so, too, in a sense is the text of *Der Prozess*.

---

16 Huld's description of the law as an 'Organismus' participates in the same metaphorical equation between life-system and social system that underlies much of Luhmann's use of biological theories by Maturana, Uexküll and others.

3.2
Citing the Weimar Constitution

In 1926, in commemoration of the 11 August *Gedenktag* (anniversary) of the Weimar Constitution (*Verfassung des Deutschen Reichs*), the Expressionist writer Fritz von Unruh (1885–1970) published a poem that apostrophized Germany, first as a masculine 'Genius', and then as the feminine national icon, Germania:

> Im apokalyptischen Sturm
> haben wir dir,
> heiliger Genius des Vaterlandes,
> gefügt
> das neue, dürftige Dach
> …
> Dann stehest du [Germania]
> bettelarm,
> wie es Priestern ziemt,
> am Altar
> der Republik
> aller Geschlechter –
> und deutet wissend,
> was die Mutter des Haines
> in ihren Sprüchen –
> lange bewahrt,
> niemals verstanden –
> endlich enthüllt.
> (Unruh, 'Der Gedenktag der Weimarer Verfassung', 303–4)

[In the apocalyptic storm, / we covered you, / sacred genius of the fatherland, / with the new, bare roof…

And so you [Germania] stand there, / dirt poor, / as priests should be, / at the altar of the Republic / of all tribes – / and interpret knowingly / that which the mother of the grove / finally reveals / in her sayings, / which have long been preserved / but never understood.]

In between this opening and closing, the poem speaks of those who would destroy the dwelling-place of German genius, namely the warmongers and international capitalists who are figured as 'giants', alluding to the barbaric fratricide of Fafner and Fasold in the Siegfried myth. The poet may be reminding readers of the compromises that had enabled passage of the 1919 Constitution, namely between the rights of workers and those of capitalists and industrialists. Unruh never uses the word 'constitution' in the poem, other, of course, than in its title. The document appears first as a roof, which is metonymic for house or dwelling, and on that basis for protection. In the last stanza, the constitution is presumably the altar where Germania stands and functions as an oracle, interpreting sayings that have never been understood. The metaphor of the altar corresponds to that of the roof, a positive, tangible object with a symbolic function. The idea of *Volksgeist*, literally the spirit of a nation, which had been a constant in German thought since the period of Romanticism, is invoked here in the format of obscure oracles that stand in need of interpretation. Unruh's political outpouring is a prime example of what Rolf Poscher has called 'constitutional celebrations in anti-constitutional times'. The writings of the times, so Poscher tells us, referred repeatedly to the unavailability of the signing ceremony to symbolization: 'the ceremony lacks the attractiveness of a great event such as the storming of the Bastille or the great image, such as the founding of the Reich in the Hall of Mirrors at Versailles' (Poscher, 'Verfassungsfeiern in verfassungsfeindlicher Zeit', 20). Most interesting for the purposes of this chapter, however, is the question of why Unruh chose to use mythic and religious vocabulary to describe the secular and rationalist event of the Weimar Constitution. While it may seem almost banal or unthinking for a poet to metaphorize constitutional legal order as an altar, Unruh's figure takes on other colourings when compared with Carl Schmitt's notion of 'political theology' or with Walter Benjamin's idea of divine violence that were circulating at exactly this time. This chapter examines how the writing of these last two thinkers cites the Weimar Constitution, or the ideas of constitutionalism, parliamentarism and legal foundationalism in general.

We call the fragile democracy under which Germany was governed between 1919 and 1933 the 'Weimar Republic', even though the seat of federal government was in Berlin. This is because the constitutional convention subsequent to the Kaiser's abdication was held in Weimar, and its product became the document that Germans loved to hate – despite the fact that the rule of Germany by a constitution had been the enduring dream of a significant portion of the intelligensia and middle classes since the mid-nineteenth century. There were still plenty of monarchists, the Communists wanted a rule by workers' councils, and nearly everyone became disillusioned with his or her political party once it entered a parliamentary coalition and began wheeling and dealing. Unfortunately, Weimar 1919 would also become linked in the minds of many Germans with the highly unfavourable Versailles Treaty of 1919, since the two documents were signed only months apart from each other.

Due to its controversial nature, but also paradoxically to the fact that it had abolished pre-publication censorship for the first time in Germany history, the 1919 constitution became a factor in the structural coupling between law, literature and culture. This chapter addresses this structural coupling as it appears in three pieces by Walter Benjamin (1892–1940) that appeared while Weimar was still a democracy ruled under its constitution: 'Critique of Violence/Force/Power' ('Zur Kritik der Gewalt', 1921); 'Goethe's *Elective Affinities*' ('Goethes *Wahlverwandtschaften*', 1924); and *The Origin of the German Mourning-Play* (Der Ursprung des deutschen Trauerspiels, 1928). These three masterpieces from the Weimar period share a vocabulary that in turn cites and couples the discourse of the political, legal and philosophical subsystems of the time. Benjamin's 'Critique of Violence' essay, as Jacques Derrida has claimed ('Force of Law', 277) is haunted by spectres: for example, the essay's anti-parliamentary spirit seems to predict Germany's turn to totalitarian rule in 1933, while Benjamin seemingly attached his signature to the treatise in the repetitions of varieties of '*walte(r)n*' (to rule, dominate). It is haunted as well, as I argue in this chapter, by citations of Weimar political discourse, the text of its constitution, and related political commentary that time has allowed to fade. What these essays have in common is usefully summarized by Richard Wolin:

> Under mythical justice, which Benjamin contrasts with divine justice, life is governed by a universal network of misfortune and guilt. This is the realm of fate which for Benjamin characterizes not only the pagan religious systems of prehistory, but remains predominant in the modern world under the order of law, where, under the guise of justice, misfortune and guilt are merely rendered abstract and take on the personalized form of 'right.' (Wolin, *Walter Benjamin*, 51)

In his 'Critique of Violence', penned shortly after the adoption of the constitution, law is the most obvious and inescapable sign of fate, whereas in the essay on Goethe's novel it is marriage. In the former, Benjamin addressed the fundamental question of how law 'gets off the ground', an answer to which can only be found outside of law, and for which myth provides one of the few available vocabularies. In his piece on Goethe's adultery novel which we have examined in Chapter 2.2, Benjamin uses Kant's definition of marriage in order to overturn the judgment of generations of critics who had argued for the novel's moralistic upholding of marriage as central to social life. Finally, of the 1928 book, Benjamin states specifically in his second *Lebenslauf* (roughly, his biography) that

> This essay [...*Origin of German Mourning-Play*] is connected on the one hand with the methodological ideas of Alois Riegl, [...] and on the other hand with the contemporary essays of Carl Schmitt, who in his analysis of the political landscape attempts an integration of phenomena, which only appear isolatable according to their different subsystems.[1]
>
> [Dieser Versuch [...*Ursprung*] knüpft einerseits an die methodischen Ideen Alois Riegls, [...] andererseits an die methodischen Versuche von Carl Schmitt an, der in seiner Analyse der politischen Gebilde einen analogen Versuch der Integration von Erscheinungen vornimmt, die nur scheinbar gebietsmässig zu isolieren sind.] (Benjamin, 'Lebenslauf III', 219)

Alois Riegl was an art historian whose idea of *Kunstwollen*, or 'will-to-art', influenced Benjamin. The title of Schmitt's *Political Theology* (*Politische Theologie*, 1922), on the other hand, gives a good idea of that work's integration of phenomena. Benjamin would use Schmitt's idea of the 'state of exception' (*Ausnahmezustand*) both in the *Ursprung* and in one of his last essays before his death, 'On the Concept of History' ('Über den Begriff der Geschichte,' 1940), in which he wrote: 'The tradition of the oppressed teaches us that the "state of exception" in which we live is not the exception but the rule' (Benjamin, 392). In a letter to Schmitt dated 9 December

---

1   I have allowed myself a liberty in translating the nominal part of the adjective 'gebietsmässig'. '*Gebiet*' is normally translated as 'field', but in my opinion a field can also be a subsystem, and here Benjamin evokes the distinction between art history (Riegl's field), political theory (Schmitt), and his own redemptive criticism that extracts the philosophical content from literature.

1930, announcing that he will be receiving a copy of the *Trauerspiel* book, Benjamin speaks of how his research in the philosophy of art [*Kunstphilosophischen Forschungsweisen*] has benefited from Schmitt's writings on the philosophy of the state [*Staatsphilosophischen*] (Benjamin, *Gesammelte Briefe*, 4:558). Legally speaking, the idea of the state of exception was embodied in Article 48 of the constitution that allowed the *Reichspresident* to suspend basic rights temporarily in cases of threats to public safety and order.

Walter Benjamin is regarded today as Germany's greatest literary critic, whose essays and works enjoy translation into many languages and worldwide influence. The afterlife of Benjamin's writings, as well as their 'life away' (*Fortleben*) in translation, has obscured to a certain degree their engagement with political and legal issues of Weimar – perhaps more accurately, with the political and legal issue that Weimar was. Benjamin's adult years and his first great writings coincided with the Weimar Republic, with the eventual cession of power by the German electorate to the National Socialists, and the subsequent totalitarian regime – which saw no need to formally abrogate the Weimar Constitution, since it already contained a provision for its suspension. Born in Berlin, Benjamin spent the years of World War I in Switzerland. He completed his doctorate there and returned with his wife Dora to the city in March of 1920. Berlin – and the newly minted 'Weimar Republic' – was recuperating from the open civil war that had followed the abdication of the emperor and the subsequent vacuum of power. It was a civil war that would continue underground for the next thirteen years, and in which Benjamin ranged himself on the left. Weimar was Germany's first, all-too-brief experiment with living under a true constitution and a parliamentary system of government with genuine political parties. The new democracy has often been described as loved by no one and hated by many, and thus doomed to failure from the start, but it is difficult to say how long it might have lasted had it not been for the accumulation of essentially economic burdens, culminating in the Great Depression of 1929 and the millions of desperate unemployed, eager for any way out of their misery.

While there is no direct evidence that Benjamin read the newly minted constitution either in whole or in part, the apprehension of its meaning for Germany was constantly referenced both in popular culture and in the writings of the educated elites, as the epigraph to this chapter was intended to show: 'Weimar is the only extended period prior to the end of World War Two where theorizing and disputation about the law of the state took place in a democratic political context. [The] struggle over methods and aims in the Weimar Republic was conducted in the consciousness, and under the rubric, of crisis' (Arthur Jacobson and Schlink, *Weimar*, 3–4). In his study of the Weimar debates surrounding constitutionalism, Peter C. Caldwell reproduces a political cartoon from the cover of the satirical magazine *Kladderadatsch* that could be opposed to Unruh's eulogy. It shows the drafter of the constitution, Hugo Preuss, as a Jewish tailor fitting the woman named 'Germania' in various scraps of clothing, on which are written words revelatory of their provenance: 'American Constitution'; 'French Constitution'; 'English Parliamentarism'; 'Marxism' (Caldwell, *Popular Sovereignty*, ii). The cartoon reflects two of the most common criticisms that the German public levelled at the new constitution: that it was not organic, but rather composed of citations from other constitutions, rather than taking as its precedent the illusive German *Volksgeist*. Such critiques ignored the many ways that the Weimar Constitution cited its failed or partially successful predecessors: the making of the German constitution was indeed, as Margaret Crosby puts it, a 'slow revolution'. A number of writers of the period expressed a preference for the constitution of 1871 as being more organic and consistent – this document had been designed and put into effect by the monarch rather than the people, and did not contain a section on citizens' rights. Others, however, whether on the left or on the right, objected not to this particular constitution, but to constitutionalism *tout court* as a pretence at rationality that masked real power relations. 'Civil constitutionalism found no haven [*Heimatrecht*] in the ranks of the avant-garde. [...] The entire domain of contract [*Vertragssphäre*] of the Republic appeared grounded in violence [*Gewalt*]. Therefore, scepticism generally took aim at the illusion that solutions for elemental conflicts could be found in the sphere of rational speech' (Helmut Lethen, 'Der Habitus der Sachlichkeit', 420).

Though without formal training in law or political theory, Benjamin studied philosophy under Hermann Cohen, whose systematic neo-Kantianism provided a basis for theoretical pronouncements on a variety of subjects. Cohen saw law as analogous to mathematics, i.e. as a fundamental basis for knowledge in the humanities, because law came closest to expressing a pure ethics at the basis of human relationships. In 1918, Benjamin and Gershom Scholem jointly read the third edition of Cohen's *Kant's Theory of Experience* (*Kants Theorie der Erfahrung*), and the WV essay is full of Cohen's 1919 *Religion of Reason from the Sources of Judaism* (*Religion der Venunft aus den Quellen des Judentums*).[2] No wonder, then, that Benjamin's early text, 'On

---

2   For a thorough assessment of Cohen's influence on Benjamin, see Deuber-Mankowsky, *Der frühe Walter Benjamin und Hermann Cohen*.

the Program of the Coming Philosophy' ('Über das Programm der kommenden Philosophie'), posits Kant as the fundamental precedent that future philosophy must confront, by discovering the weakness of the role Kant gives to experience (Erfahrung).[3] In this context, Benjamin's idea of 'redemptive criticism' (*rettende Kritik*) began from the assumption that literary works embody philosophical content that is unavailable to philosophy due to the parabolic or symbolic nature of meaning in art. In deciphering the work, literary criticism can help philosophy attain this truth. Benjamin takes Goethe's *WV* as an embodiment of experience that serves as a counter-example to Kant's doctrine of marriage, a central element of the latter's legal theory.

Electoral Affinities

The procedures of redemptive criticism are admirably demonstrated in Benjamin's reading of the theme of marriage in Goethe's novel. Writing in the years 1921 and 1922 (the essay was published in the *Neue Deutsche Beiträge* in 1924–5), just after completing the 'Critique of Violence', Benjamin accomplished four things simultaneously: first, he gave a practical demonstration of the idea of immanent criticism which he had elaborated in his dissertation on German Romanticism; secondly, he polemicized against vitalist readings of Goethe's work, embodied in the biography by Friedrich Gundolf;[4] thirdly, he set out the categories of a phenomenology of mythic forms; and fourthly, he attempted to counter a notion, widely accepted in the critical reception of Goethe's novel, that the *WV*'s main theme of adultery and its consequences upholds the moral conception of marriage as the pillar of civil society (John McCole, *Walter Benjamin*, 117–19). I will focus my examination primarily on the last two of these objectives, which are, it turns out, mutually dependent. This last concern with the indissolubility of marriage inheres in Immanuel Kant's notion of marriage, as discussed in Chapter 2.2. There we saw that Kant first defines marriage as the inalienable right of one partner to make use of the sexual organs of the other. Benjamin aligns the perverseness of Kant's definition of marriage with the gap between experience and truth that has

---

3   German has two verbs for experiencing something: *erleben* and *erfahren*. Benjamin takes the root meanings of the verbs, 'to live' vs. 'to travel', as being essential to the two different types of experience: a mere living through vs. being made aware of something new through an event. It is the latter type of experience that Benjamin is concerned with.
4   For an account of the *WV* essay as being aimed at Gundolf and the Stefan George school, see Richard Lane, *Reading Walter Benjamin*, 75–100.

hitherto characterized the critical reception of *WV*: 'Of course, the philosopher [Kant] made his gravest mistake when he supposed that from his definition of the nature of marriage he could deduce its moral possibility, indeed its moral necessity, and in this way confirm its juridical reality' (Benjamin, Goethe's *Elective Affinities*, 299; 'Freilich war es der ungeheuerste Irrtum des Philosophen, daß er meinte, aus dieser Definition, die er von der Natur der Ehe gab, ihre sittliche Möglichkeit, ja Notwendigkeit durch Ableitung darlegen und dergestalt ihre rechtliche Wirklichkeit bestätigen zu können' [Goethes *Die Wahlverwandtschaften*, 127–8]). Kant's definition, again, was that marriage was a contract between a man and a woman for the mutual enjoyment of each other's sexual organs, and thus a resolution of the antinomy between the freedom of the individual and the rights of property through the use of parts of individuals as means rather than as ends. The Weimar Constitution adhered to the Kantian idea of reciprocity in its insistence on the equality of marriage, while also preserving the more traditional idea rejected by Kant, that marriage is a means to the end of propagation. Propagation, preservation and individual rights all play a role in Article 119 that brought marriage under the protection of the constitution: 'As the foundation of family life and of the preservation and increase of the nation, marriage receives the special protection of the constitution. Marriage has as its basis the equal rights of both sexes' ('Die Ehe steht als Grundlage des Familienlebens und der Erhaltung und Vermehrung der Nation unter dem besondered Schutz der Verfassung. Sie beruht auf der Gleichberechtigung der beiden Geschlechter'). The first sentence goes back at least as far as the physiocratic state policies of the eighteenth centuries, and emphasizes the importance of marriage for the state. The second sentence, on the other hand, not only makes of marriage a fundamental right and choice of the individual, but also implies that the numerous inequalities of gender and class that had shaped marriage practice were now to be put aside.

As Peter Fenves points out, Benjamin saw Kant's definition of marriage as a particularly problematic embodiment of the paradox of the categorical imperative in general:

> the hyperbolic doubts to which Benjamin subjects the [Kantian] categorical imperative point toward a sexualization of the body as a whole and a corresponding moral paralysis: under current conditions no part can be employed as a means at all. Since marriage, for Kant, is the juridical form within which 'sexual properties' can finally be used, Benjamin's doubts about the categorical imperative are of a piece with the critique

of marriage that traverses his analysis of Goethe's *Elective Affinities*. (Fenves, *The Messianic Reduction*, 211)

Part of Benjamin's critique is accomplished by replacing Kant's idea of marriage as a contract with the image of marriage as a seal (in the sense of a wax seal on a letter, i.e. insignium) on human relationships governed by fate: 'From the objective nature of marriage, one could obviously deduce only its depravity – and in Kant's case this is what it willy-nilly amounts to. That, however, is precisely the crucial point, its content [*Gehalt*] never can be deduced from the real matter [*Sache*], but instead must be grasped as the seal which presents this matter' (Benjamin, 'Goethe's *Elective Affinities*', 299; Ableitbar aus der sachlichen Natur der Ehe wäre ersichtlich nur ihre Verworfenheit – und darauf läuft es bei Kant unversehens hinaus. Allein das ist ja das Entscheidende, daß niemals ableitbar ihr Gehalt sich zur Sache verhält, sondern daß er als das Siegel erfaßt werden muß, das sie darstellt. [Benjamin, 'Goethes *Die Wahlverwandtschaften*', 127–8]). Benjamin's point is clear enough: the use of sexual organs in a marriage has far more to do with animal nature than with '*Sittlichkeit*', custom-made morality, which is the basis of law. Positive law rarely defines what marriage is; instead, as in the Weimar Constitution, law defines the relation of marriage to the state, or the state's responsibility to preserve and protect marriage and the family. Kant's idea of marriage may seem depraved due to its single-minded insistence on the right to the use of the partner's sexual organs as the exclusive basis of the marriage contract. Kant himself explicitly argued in his lectures on ethics to counteract this impression: 'When a person dedicates him or herself to another, she commits not only her sex, but her whole person; one cannot be separated from the other' (Kant, *Ethikvorlesung* 20, 210; 'Wenn sich nun eine Person der anderen widmet, so widmet sie nicht allein ihr Geschlecht, sondern ihre ganze Person, dieses lässt sich nicht separieren'). Kant writes of marriage as the unifying of fate through the *copula carnalis* 'as an act joining the fate of one body part with the other (*copula carnalis*) and simultaneously the basis of a legal union as between persons who undergo obligations towards each other (*copula legalis*). This tie is marriage' ('als ein Akt der Anknüpfung des Schicksals des einen Teils mit dem anderen (*copula carnalis*) zugleich den Grund einer gesetzlichen Verbindung wie unter Personen die sich untereinander verpflichten (*copula legalis*). Dieses Band ist nun die Ehe' [Kant, 'Metaphysische Anfangsgründe der Rechtslehre', 462]).

In using 'seal' as a metaphor to represent the relationship between legal form and real content of marriage, Benjamin cites his own early 'Critique of Violence'. The last sentence of the earlier essay reads: 'Divine violence, which is the sign and seal but never the means of sacred imposition of a sentence, may be called "sovereign violence"' (Benjamin, 'Critique', 252; 'Die göttliche Gewalt, welche Insignium und Siegel, niemals Mittel heiliger Vollstreckung ist, mag die waltende heissen' ['Zur Kritik', 203]). In David Pan's reading, the seal here represents a 'trace of a proper name in the insignia that guarantee that the move from mythic to divine violence is a move from mere material life to a sacred life. [...] But this link between insignia and sovereignty is precisely the structure of the normal functioning of sovereignty, according to Schmitt's idea that the key issue is "who decides"' (Pan, 'Against Biopolitics', 49–50). The decision on the state of exception institutes 'the proper name of sovereignty in competition with other possible names, and in so doing so establishes a specific subject whose symbolic connections define a particular tradition, for instance the specific rituals of a peace ceremony' (Pan, 50). Or of a marriage ceremony. To be a seal on human relationships means that marriage provides a visible sign whose purpose is both merely to secure what already is (one seals an envelope so that one will know if it has been broken open), but is also an added communication (as in the seals added to documents to verify their authenticity), and thus a supplement to its original meaning.

Kant, according to Benjamin, got everything right about marriage that philosophy, and perhaps indeed law, would allow, but missed the *Gehalt* or content, which can only be revealed by literature. Kant's system depends on marriage's indissolubility. The sublimation of the subject-object antinomy continues even when the elements themselves have disappeared. Kant's view of marriage could be thought of as a secularization of Christian thought on marriage (officially adopted only after the Council of Trent) that makes of it a sacrament and a lifelong bond. However, Kant's terminology is strictly that of contract and possession, which, as Peter Leisching concludes after a thorough survey, has no precedent in the writings on natural law that Kant was familiar with.[5] The sublimation of individual desire in the eternity of *lex* restores the human relationships destroyed by the instinctual pleasures of sexual relationship.[6]

---

5   The title of Leisching's article, 'Rechtshistorische Parallelen zu Immanuel Kants Ehelehre', proves to be ironic, since it finds Kant's conception to be unique and without precedent.
6   I follow here the analysis of Hans-George Deggau, *Die Aporien der Rechtslehre Kants*, 175.

Kant's marriage concept thus attempts to free the partners from certain aspects of what Benjamin calls fate.

The tragedy of *WV* and its central theme are provided not by the seal of marriage as such, Benjamin argues, but rather by the main characters' inability to come to the decision to annul a marriage that stands in the way of their deepest intuitions. As we have seen, Benjamin first dismisses the critical oversimplification that had identified Goethe's purpose with Mittler's views, and had thus reduced *WV* to a treatise in defence of marriage. Here is a more complete version of the quotation examined in Chapter 2.2: 'For [Goethe] an imprint of the juridical norm in this work was indispensable. After all, he did not want, like Mittler, to establish a foundation for marriage but wished, rather, to show the forces that arise from its decay. Yet these are surely the mythic powers of the law, and in them marriage is only the execution of a decline that it does not decree' (Benjamin, 'Goethe's *Elective Affinities*', 301; 'Für ihn war eine Ausprägung der Rechtsnorm unerlässlich. Wollte er doch nicht, wie Mittler, die Ehe begründen, vielmehr jene Kräfte zeigen, welche im Verfall aus ihr hervorgehen. Dieses aber sind freilich die mythischen Gewalten des Rechts und die Ehe ist in ihnen nur Vollstreckung eines Unterganges, den sie nicht verhängt' [Benjamin, 'Goethes *Die Wahlverwandtschaften*', 130]). The verb *'verhängt'* with which Benjamin ends his sentence resonates in a triple register that reinforces his identification of law with myth. Most immediately, *'verhängen'* means to pronounce a sentence, as a judge or jury would do in a criminal case. Secondly, however, the verb also refers to a declaration of the suspension of normal law and to the imposition of a state of siege (*Ausnahmezustand*), which the work of Carl Schmitt and Giorgio Agamben have rechristened in English as a 'state of exception'. Finally, the verb's nominal form, *'Verhängnis'*, refers to an evil or imposing fate to which people may be subjected. This fate, which Benjamin sees as the subject matter (*'Sachgehalt'*) of Goethe's novel, arises from the 'mythical powers' of law: 'Myth is the subject matter [of *WV*] in the sense that marriage as a juridical institution is governed by mythical law, and its decay releases the powers which have always already resided within such law – more or less parallel as the "state of exception" does for the law of sovereignty' (Burkhardt Lindner 'Goethes *Wahlverwandtschaften*', 37). The identification of myth with law refers us to 'Zur Kritik der Gewalt', published in volume 47 of the *Archiv für Sozialwissenschaft und Soizalpolitik* in 1921. This essay synthesizes Benjamin's neo-Kantian philosophical training with the syndicalism of Georges Sorel's *Reflections on Violence* (1908; *Réflexions sur la violence*), and the political ambience of the early Weimar years alluded to above.[7] Carl Schmitt read this journal regularly, and Giorgio Agamben has suggested that his notion of the 'state of exception' may owe something to Benjamin's discussion in the 'Critique'. Perhaps more crucially, as Jan-Werner Müller points out, both Benjamin and Schmitt were inspired by Sorel's discussion of myth as a discursive phenomenon that grounds authority because it is more directly connected to the lifeworld of a people, and hence more capable of moving people to action than are the autonomous, self-reflexive subsystems of modern societies (Müller, 'Myth, Law, and Order', 462–3). Indeed, it is difficult to accommodate myth within ST. It appears to belong more to the 'Law-as-Poetry' archaic society described by Grimm. Here we can imagine Luhmann agreeing with Roland Barthes in *Mythologies* that myth should be defined precisely as a second-order language that can take nearly anything as the basic sememes for its construction, leaving the rest to its environment. Of course, it is not always better to act than not to act, or to recognize authority rather than defying it. Hence the parlous ambiguity both of Benjamin's critique and of Schmitt's state of exception.

Constitutional Critique

> The state of exception is the space in which [Schmitt] tries to capture Benjamin's idea of a pure violence and to inscribe *anomie* within the very body of the *nomos*.
>
> Giorgio Agamben, *State of Exception* (54)

Nomos is the Greek word for law or custom. It derives from a verb meaning 'to deal out, dispense'. *Nomos* is, Carl Schmitt argues in Nomos *of the Earth*, the governing disposition of a society, more powerful and persuasive than black-letter law. *Anomie* literally means, then, 'without law', though in the thought of the sociologists Emile Durkheim and Robert Merton it refers to a situation of relative social breakdown where moral regulation fails to keep pace with specialization and the division of labour.[8] We have seen above the description of the literal anomie of Weimar as its constitution did not take root. We have examined Benjamin's analysis of anomie on the analogy of

---

7   On the relation to Sorel, whose anarchist ideas later appealed to fascists, see Chryssoula Kambas, 'Walter Benjamin liest Georges Sorel'.
8   Robert Merton's theory of *anomie*, developed in *Social Theory and Social Structure*, explains how deviance from societal norms is produced by those norms. This concept of *anomie* as an inevitable product of *nomos* very much parallels the paradoxes put forth by Benjamin, Schmitt, Agamben, and indeed Luhmann.

the marriage of Eduard and Charlotte: the freedom accorded by law is crushed by law's fateful imbrication in the forces of history.

The invocation of philosophical critique in the title Benjamin gave to his essay indicates that he aims at nothing less than an examination of the 'first principles' of violence, and at drawing the distinction between its pure and impure forms. The idea of 'critique' conveyed in the title immediately brings Kant to mind, and it is indeed Kantian and neo-Kantian conceptions of law that are the targets of the essay, as summarized by Beatrice Hanssen: 'while Benjamin's critique appeared to be informed by Kant's fundamental distinction between morality and legality in that [Benjamin] too sought to define the morality of an action by disengaging it from the judicial system, he purported to surpass the correlation between justified means and just ends that still informed Kant's moral philosophy' (Hanssen, *Critique of Violence*, 20–21). To accomplish this, Benjamin posited an antinomy between positive and natural law, each of which is incomplete, lacking a part held by the other: 'Positive law is blind to the absoluteness of ends [...] natural law is equally so to the contingency of means' (Benjamin, 'Critique', 237; 'das positive Recht ist blind für die Unbedingtheit der Zwecke [...] das Naturrecht für die Bedingtheit der Mittel' ['Zur Kritik', 181]). Examples of pure means (language and revolutionary general strikes) are divorced from pure ends (divine justice). Benjamin renamed these poles of the antinomy: 'law-preserving force/violence' (*'rechterhaltende Gewalt'*), the societal forces of injunction and punishment that preserve law; and 'lawmaking force/violence' (*'rechtsetzende Gewalt'*), the forces of conflict that bring about new laws and that are represented in penalties which are out of proportion to the crime they punish, e.g. the death penalty for theft. The use of police force represents one such disproportion, an extension of law-preserving force into the sphere of law establishment, and Benjamin notes that this contamination is more uncanny in a democracy such as Weimar than in a monarchy, where the police represent the monarch's personal will. Such disproportion can only be understood as law's extension of its power over society. In taking this position, Benjamin departs from the perspective of a number of his anti-constitutional contemporaries, who took up again the cause of the *Volksgeist* and its unwritten laws. As Anselm Haverkamp explains, Benjamin 'saw no reason to deny the progress of positive law. [...] Instead, he takes a position [...] on the question of how the "mystical origins" of authority are to be replaced and of how the "state of exception" [...] is to be taken up and mastered' (Haverkamp, 'Ein unabwerfbarer Schatten', 172).[9]

---

9 Haverkamp mentions Fritz Kern's 'Recht und Verfassung im Mittelalter',

Benjamin's thesis rests on the polyvalence of the German word *'Gewalt'*, which can mean equally 'power', 'force', or 'violence'. Furthermore, the noun derives from the verb *'walten'*, which means to oversee or administer something. By the same token, quite a few of the venerable legal proverbs beloved of Jacob Grimm contrast *Gewalt* with *Recht*: 'Might goes before right' ('Gewalt geht vor Recht'); 'When violence comes, justice is dead' ('Wenn Gewalt kommt, ist Recht tot'); and 'A handful of power is better than a sackful of justice' ('Eine Hand voll Gewalt ist besser als ein Sack voll Recht') are a few of these (Günter Grundmann, *Rechtssprichwörter*, 19). Benjamin's point can be better understood if the translator selects two different meanings of *'Gewalt'* to render the antinomy: law-preserving power vs. law-creating violence. An example of the latter, and a good illustration of Benjamin's association of law with fate, is the revenge taken on Niobe by Artemis (who killed her seven daughters) and by Apollo (who killed her seven sons). The divine violence does not punish the infraction of any existing law; it acts without precedent. The new law created by violence, if it is one, is hard to formulate in language. Niobe's 'crime' (the fullest account is found in book six of Ovid's *Metamorphoses*) was that she boasted about the number of her children (fourteen, in Ovid) in comparison to the twins of the goddess Lego. Leto's revenge is to have her two children, namely Apollo and Artemis, kill all fourteen of Leto's offspring.

> the violence that befalls Niobe comes from fate. This fate can only be uncertain and ambiguous (*zweideutig*), since it is not preceded or regulated by any anterior, superior or transcendent law. [...] There is thus a 'demonic' ambiguity of this mythical positing of law, which is in its fundamental principle a power (*Macht*), a force, a positing of authority. [...] At this originary and mythical moment, there is still no distributive justice, no punishment or penalty, only 'expiation' (*Sühne*) rather than 'retribution'. (Derrida, 'Force of Law', 287)

Benjamin claims that the modern 'ignorance of the law is no excuse' derives from this idea of law as mythical violence, whose

---

published in the *Historische Zeitschrift* in 1919, as one valorization of the 'good, old law' that delegitimated every new one. However, Kern's essay maintains the opposite point. He begins by noting that in pre-modern Germany, and in those parts of it that still hold to custom as law, law was old, and what was old was good, but that in fact the 'absolutely binding positive law' (72) of modernity is superior in most respects to any alternatives the Middle Ages had come up with.

infraction calls forth expiation rather than punishment. To return for a moment to the later essay on Goethe's novel, we can now understand more fully Benjamin's claim that the dissolution of the marriage is a matter of fate rather than conscience. The characters of *WV* inhabit this locus where fate exerts its monstrous rights and demands the expiation of Eduard and Ottilie.

In their seminal work of legal anthropology, *The Cheyenne Way*, Karl Llewellyn and E. A. Hoebel make a point that resembles Benjamin's, based on their actual observations of the development of law in an oral culture:

> In order that inventions (or lines of growth) [in law] may take on perspective, one recalls that the earliest emergence of law-stuff may have a character which can on a different level become proverbial as contra-legal. So 'club-law', conquest and ruthlessness, outfacing and submission; so, in general, the establishment of what social psychologists call the pecking-order of the flock. One recalls also that the brute violence or fraud which at any moment yields present outrage can generate not only future legal imperative but even future "right". The course runs from power into recognition, repetition, expectation, and tradition, until authority finds itself backed by going morality. (Llewellyn and Hoebel, 299)

For Benjamin, the inescapability of *Gewalt* – which, again, means both illegitimate force and legitimate enforcement – at the root of all legal systems problematizes the notion of contract. Not surprisingly, contract becomes the root and centre of law as a sign of its *Ausdifferenzierung* from other social subsystems. Niobe's punishment is typical of the role of law in a vertically organized society, wherein 'the magnitude of the danger proves the law by demonstrating the identity of law and being oneself, of law and life; it does not prove guilt in the infringement of law nor does it provide facts as preconditions for the use of legal norms, but law itself. It is not the means, but the manifestation' (Luhmann, *Theories of Distinction*, 85–6).[10] Benjamin does not hesitate in this critique to confront directly the Kantian notion of justice as the embodiment of the categorical imperative to use people always as ends rather than as means, 'for positive law, if conscious of its roots, will certainly claim to acknowledge and promote the interest of mankind in the person of each individual. It sees this interest in the representation

---

10 Luhmann references Benjamin's 'Critique of Violence' essay at this point (footnote 134, citation on page 317).

and preservation of an order imposed by fate' (Benjamin, 'Critique', 241; 'denn das positive Recht wird, wo es seiner Wurzeln sich bewußt ist, durchaus beanspruchen, das Interesse der Menschheit in der Person jedes einzelnen anzuerkennen und zu fördern. Es erblickt dieses Interesse in der Darstellung und Erhaltung einer schicksalhaften Ordnung' ['Zur Kritik', 187]). Benjamin rains on the parade celebrating the individual rights guaranteed by the Weimar Constitution, such as those pertaining to marriage, by making these contingent on an 'order imposed by fate'.

The example of fate Benjamin provides in 'Critique of Violence' – to be replaced by marriage in the essay on *WV* – is the death penalty, anticipated in the myth of Niobe, which in Benjamin's view recreates the contradictory essence of law each time it is applied: 'in the exercise of violence [*Gewalt*] over life and death, more than in any other legal act, the law reaffirms itself. But in this very violence something rotten in the law is revealed, above all to a finer sensibility, because the latter knows itself to be infinitely remote from conditions in which fate might imperiously have shown itself in such a sentence' ('Critique', 242; 'in der Ausübung der Gewalt über Leben und Tod bekräftigt mehr als in irgendeinem andern Reschtsvollzug des Recht sich selbst. Eben in ihr aber kündigt zugleich etwas Morsches im Recht am vernehmlichsten dem feineren Gefühl sich an, weil dieses sich von Verhältnissen, in welchen das Schicksal in eigner Majestät in einem solchen Vollzug sich gezeigt hätte, unendlich fern weiß' ['Zur Kritik', 188]). Benjamin's use of 'fate' (*Schicksal*) here and throughout the essay may conjoin his own earlier exploration of the term in 'Fate and Character' (*Schicksal und Charakter*) with Kant's usage of the term in connection with marriage. In the essay that was composed at approximately the same time as the critique, Benjamin explores the conjunctions and disjunctions between the two terms, finding in the end that they are indistinguishable:

> Not only is it impossible to determine in a single case what finally is to be considered a function of character and what a function of fate in a human life […]; the external world that the active man encounters can also in principle be reduced, to any desired degree, to his inner world, and his inner world similarly to his outer world, indeed regarded in principle as one and the same thing. Considered in this way character and fate, far from being theoretically distinct, coincide. (Benjamin, 'Fate and Character', 202)
>
> [Es ist nicht nur in keinem Falle anzugeben, was letzten Endes als Funktion des Charakters, was als Function des Schicksals

in einem Menschenleben zu gelten hat [...] sonder das Aussen, das der handelnde Mensch vorfindet, kann in beliebig hohem Masse auf sein Innen, sein Innen in beliebig hohem Masse auf sein Aussen prinzipiell zurückgeführt, ja als dieses prizipiell angesehen werden. Charakter und Schicksal warden in dieser Betrachtung, weit entfernt theoretisch geschieden zu werden, zusammenfallen.] ('Schicksal und Charakter', 173)

He goes on to note that 'The laws of fate – misfortune and guilt – are elevated by law to measures of the person' (Benjamin, 203; 'Die Gesetze des Schicksals, Unglück und Schuld, erhebt das Recht zu Massen der Person' [174]).

We can identify the common concepts linking the earlier essay on violence to the immanent criticism practiced on Goethe's *WV*. There as here, something rotten in the law – the law of marriage as eternal contract – shows itself. Like Niobe's children, Otto, the child of the adultery committed through the imaginations of Charlotte and Eduard, is fated to die for the crimes of others. Ottilie, the instrument for imposing Otto's sentence, then dies in expiation of Otto's death, and Eduard in expiation of Ottilie's. Since this is a novel, however, the sentencing does indeed appear as 'fate imperiously showing itself', as though Goethe had wished to show that third type of violence at work, which Benjamin calls divine:

Divine violence may manifest itself in a true war exactly as it does in the crowd's divine judgment on a criminal. But all mythic, lawmaking violence, which we may call 'executive', is abject. Abject, too, is the law-preserving, 'administrated' violence that serves it. Divine violence, which is the sign and seal but never the means of sacred imposition of a sentence, may be called 'sovereign' violence. (Benjamin, 'Critique', 252)[11]

[Sie vermag im wahren Kriege genau so zu erscheinen wie im Gottesgericht der Menge am Verbrecher. Verwerflich aber ist alle mythische Gewalt, die rechtsetzende, welche die schaltende genannt werden darf. Verwerflich auch die rechtserhaltende, die

---

11 I have emended the published translation in several places. I have substituted 'abject' for Jephcott's 'pernicious' to translate the German '*verwerflich*'. 'Pernicious' is both too mild a term, and also indicates something that the law does, rather than how its subjects consider the law – or indeed, how they do not consider it, since it is a foreclosed topic, the secret execution as opposed to the public one. In addition, 'abject' is etymologically parallel to '*verwerflich*', both deriving from a root verb meaning 'to throw (down)'. I also believe that '*verwaltete*' is 'administered' rather than 'administrative'.

verwaltete Gewalt, die ihr dient. Die göttliche Gewalt, welche Insignium und Siegel, niemals Mittel heiliger Vollstreckung ist, mag die waltende heißen.] ('Zur Kritik', 203)

A 'true' war would be, of course, the opposite of the 1914–18 conflict, whose end result was the abdication of the Kaiser, parliamentary rule, and administered violence. Germany was only able to carry on the war for so long through the military draft, which is the epitome of administered violence.[12] Benjamin's idea of divine violence, then, is to substitute the law which for Benjamin is always, as Günter Figal notes, 'the domain of mediated violence' (Figal, 'Recht und Moral', 371) with an unmediated one, a spontaneous outburst of mystical origins like that of the lynch mob he describes. Benjamin's notion of divine law thus may remind us of Jacob Grimm's – an unknowable, primal agreement among people that this is how things are (not) done. In marriage, this originary violence/violation is the power over the partner's sexual characteristics, so long as it is mutual.

In capital punishment, human desire vanishes into the legal aporia it has created, as does morality. Just so, Benjamin argues, with the marriage of Eduard and Charlotte, which is no longer a form of life, but simply an adherence to fate: 'The subject of *WV* is not marriage. Nowhere in this work are its ethical powers to be found. From the outset, they are in the process of disappearing, like the beach under water at floodtide. Marriage here is not an ethical problem, yet neither is it a social problem. It is not a form of bourgeois conduct. In its dissolution, everything human turns into appearance, and the mythic alone remains as essence' (Benjamin, 'Goethe's *Elective Affinities*' 302; 'Der Gegenstand der *Wahlverwandschaften* ist nicht die Ehe. Nirgends wären ihre sittlichen Gewalten darin zu suchen. Von Anfang an sind sie im Verschwinden, wie der Strand unter Wassern zur Flutzeit. Kein sittliches Problem ist hier die Ehe und auch kein soziales. Sie ist keine bürgerliche Lebensform. In ihrer Auflösung wird alles Humane zur Erscheinung und das Mythische verbleibt allein als Wesen' [Benjamin, 'Goethes *Die Wahlverwandtschaften*', 131]). This position on marriage forms the bedrock of Benjamin's seventy-page essay. It is to be understood as shifting the role of marriage in the

---

12 Benjamin's point about universal conscription is both in tune with general immediate postwar attitudes in Germany, and intensely personal. One of Benjamin's best friends, Wolfgang Heinle, committed suicide in 1914 along with his lover Rita Seligsohn rather than suffer separation due to his conscription.

text from object to limit. Stripped of its moral and social aspects, the legal bonds of marriage, especially in their Kantian dimension of sexual property rights, remain as the beach sand on which the waves of passion pound.

States of Exception

> The sovereign is the representative of history. He holds the course of history in his hand like a sceptre. This view is by no means peculiar to the dramatists. It is based on certain constitutional notions. (Walter Benjamin, *The Origin of German Tragic Drama*, 65)

> [Der Souverän repräsentiert die Geschichte. Er hält das historische Geschehen in der Hand wie ein Szepter. Diese Auffassung ist alles andere als ein Privileg der Theatraliker. Staatsrechtliche Gedanken liegen ihr zugrunde.] (Benjamin, *Ursprung*, 245)

The 1928 book on *The Origin of the German Mourning-Play* (*Der Ursprung des deutschen Trauerspiels*, hereinafter *Origin*) deals with the character of German dramas of the Baroque period as these relate to then-current political ideas, including, as we see in the epigraph, political representation and constitutionalism. *Origin* refers back to the 'Critique of Violence' by associating Greek tragedy with Greek law, principally through the structure of the *agon*. Trials were contests without compromise, as has come down to us above all in the case of Socrates as depicted in Plato's *Apology*. Benjamin's view was influenced by Florens Christian Rang; the language of their correspondence is cited almost unchanged in a passage of the *Origin*.[13] In an act of 'redemptive criticism', Benjamin intended his portrayal of the nobility of the Baroque period to represent the middle classes of his time, because he viewed the constellation of absolutistic power depicted in Baroque 'tyrant-drama' as continuing into the beginnings of constitutional rule, most especially in its idea of political power as a form of representation. Willem van Reijen has characterized the allegory of the *Bürgertum* in the *Origin* essay with the following formulation:

> Benjamin intuited that the pattern of absolutist rule in the Baroque period had extended itself over the beginnings of the

---

13 Cf. Antonia Birnbaum, *Bonheur Justice Walter Benjamin*. Rang's contribution came above all in a letter to Benjamin dated 28 January 1924 (Benjamin, *Gesammelte Briefe*, 2: 425–7);

citizens' constitution into the inter-war period. Benjamin could not share the presupposition that parliament was the place for constructing rational opinion and the *volonté générale*. The newly developed and ever-present film and radio technology makes the public display value of the politicians into a criterion for their success. The media complex chooses not only the star, but also the dictator. (Van Reijen, 'Die Allegorisierung des Bürgertums', 665)

As his work for radio, his interest in photography, and his seminal essay of the artwork in the age of its reproducibility show, Benjamin was intensely concerned with the effects of media technology on political representation. The increasing importance of radio and film for the self-presentation of politicians to their publics diminishes both the importance and the possibility of rational discourse within a parliament. Parliaments and theatres decline simultaneously.

Benjamin thus differentiates Baroque *Trauerspiel* from Greek *Tragödie* – a difference betrayed by the title of the published English translation that denies the specificity of the German genre. For Benjamin, the silent relationship of the tragic hero to his or her fate, as opposed to the volubility of the martyr, depends upon the very different notions of the world order associated with tragic and Christian thought, respectively. Instead of engaging in an *agon* that ends, the martyr or tyrant of Baroque drama soliloquizes endlessly instead of deciding: 'The prince, who is responsible for making the decision to proclaim the state of exception, reveals, at the first opportunity, that he is incapable of making a decision' (Benjamin, *Origin*, 71; 'Der Fürst, bei dem die Entscheidung über den Ausnahmezustand ruht, erwiest in der erst-besten Situation, dass ein Enschluss ihm fast unmöglich ist' [*Ursprung*, 250]).

The mourning-play mourns not for a hero, but for a fallen, 'creaturely' world, a ruined landscape whose redemption is only hinted at through the process of allegory:

> In the terms of the martyr-drama it is not moral transgression but the very estate of man as creature which provides the reason for the catastrophe. This typical catastrophe, which is so different from the extraordinary catastrophe of the tragic hero, is what the dramatists had in mind when – with a word which is employed more consciously in dramaturgy than in criticism – they described a work as a *Trauerspiel*. (Benjamin, *Origin*, 89)

> [Im Sinn der Märtyrerdramatik ist nicht sittliche Vergehung,

sondern der Stand des kreatürlichen Menschen selber der Grund des Unterganges. Diesen typischen Untergang, der so verschieden von dem außerordentlichen des tragischen Helden ist, haben die Dichter im Auge gehabt, wenn sie – mit einem Wort, das die Dramatik planvoller als die Kritik gehandhabt hat – ein Werk als »Trauerspiel« bezeichnet haben.] (*Ursprung*, 268).

What unites martyr and tyrant, according to Benjamin, are their equal rejection of the common creaturely world and their attempt to bring about, through their suffering and histrionics, the 'state of exception'. *WV*'s Eduard, who abandons his marriage for the battlefield in a search for death, links in his person the sufferings of the martyr with the state of exception. Here, as in his essay on Goethe, Benjamin notes the difference between moral transgression and the mere acting out of the impositions – the 'sentencing' – of fate. The *WV* can be seen as a kind of *Trauerspiel*, since other than the silent Ottilie the characters comment at length about their condition and attempt to circumvent the workings of fate. The common reading of that 'fate', as explored in Chapter 2.2, is the French Revolution, Napoleon, and the end of the *ancien régime*.

Benjamin's notion of the tyrant derives from the 'decisionist' political philosophy found in the works on *Dictatorship* (1920; *Die Diktatur*) and *Political Theology* (1922; *Politische Theologie*) by Carl Schmitt. In the formulation of Lutz Koepnick, 'Schmitt's construction of sovereignty, his account of the seculatization of theology in modern political thought, as well as his anchoring of political legitimacy in the formal criterion of existential decisiveness during periods of exception are all essential to Benjamin's understanding of the modern state and his analysis of power in baroque drama' (Koepnick, *Walter Benjamin*, 42).[14] Born in 1888, Schmitt studied law at Strasburg (where Goethe had received his doctorate) and later became a student of Max

---

14 Benjamin draws, however – as Sigrid Weigl notes – a crucial difference between Baroque and contemporary concepts of sovereignty: 'In the Baroque one did *not* claim that the sovereign is he who decides the state of exception, but the other way around: whoever is sovereign has the power to decide the state of exception!' ("Über Franz Kafka" 174) (*Walter Benjamin*, 84, emphasis in original). Perhaps even better is Samuel Weber's formulation: 'The primary function of the prince [in *Ursprung*] is to exclude the exception, which is not the same as to "decide" upon it. Indeed, in the Baroque world of the Restoration that Benjamin describes, the "state of exception" does not need to be decided upon: it is there permanently, as the possibility not of permanent revolution, but of permanent catastrophe' ('Taking Exception to Decision', 130).

Weber, who cured him of his neo-Kantianism. Schmitt wrote his thesis in 1910 and his *Habilitationsschrift* (a second dissertation necessary to obtain a university position) in 1914. The war delayed his finding of a position until 1920, at the University of Greifswald. Schmitt's earliest publications were literary in nature, whether the satirical fiction of the *Buribunken* or his interpretation of the poet Theodor Däubler, wherein Schmitt expressed in the clearest fashion his resistance (and that of many of his generation) to modernity: '*Ecce saeculum*. In this century Däubler's *Nordlicht* came into being. This work is as deep as our times are superficial, as full of divine spirit as our own time is empty of it. [...] It achieves the spiritual balancing of a world abandoned by spirit' (Schmitt, *Theodor Däublers »Nordlicht«*, 64–65; 'Ecce saeculum. In ihm entstand Däublers 'Nordlicht'. Es ist so tief, wie die Zeit flach, so groß, wie die Zeit klein, so voll des göttlichen Geistes wie die Zeit leer davon. [...] Es trägt in sich das ganze Gewicht des geistigen Ausgleichs einer Welt, die der Geist verließ'). Like Goethe and Kafka, Schmitt finally decided in favour of a doctorate in law, and held positions as Professor of *Staatsrecht* at universities in Greifswald, Bonn, Berlin and Cologne. He was named *Preußischer Staatsrat* in 1933, and became actively engaged in Nazi legal manoeuvrings. He defended the summary executions of the Röhm-Putsch, as well as the dismissal of Jewish civil servants. Nevertheless, his influence on the Nazi regime ended in 1936, and he was stripped of all titles other than his professorship and *Staatsrat*. After the war, Schmitt was brought to Nuremberg and interrogated for more than a year, but was eventually cleared of any war-crimes charges. His rehabilitation was long, occurred in indirect and labyrinthine ways, and was due in part to his continuing popularity in the remaining fascist countries such as Portugal and Spain. However, an important step in his 'rediscovery' was the questioning of parliamentary democracy in Germany in the late 1960s, which relegitimated to a certain extent Schmitt's concept of the 'state of exception'.[15]

Schmitt affected the social world outside of the subsystem of legal theory due to his literary style and his ability to explain contemporary issues by revealing their underlying structural and mythic patterns, as will be explained in Chapter 3.3. David Pan links Schmitt's aesthetics with his political thinking thus:

> Schmitt rejects the establishment of the autonomy of art in the bourgeois private sphere, not because of its elitism but

---

15 For balanced accounts of Schmitt's more disreputable side, see Quaritsch, *Positionen und Begriffe Carl Schmitts*, and Jürgen Seifert, 'Theoretiker der Gegenrevolution: Carl Schmitt'.

because both the autonomy of art and the bourgeois private sphere provide the haven for ideas to develop independent of institutional control. He attempts to reestablish this control through his description of art 'raised to the level of myth'. (Pan, 'Political Aesthetics', 156)

Paul Noack notes the parallelisms between the thought of Schmitt and Benjamin: 'Both are adversaries of thinking in a series of compromises [...], and in that sense, opponents of the parliamentary system, of political liberalism and of the political system produced out of these. Both conceive that the spirit of an age only expresses itself in a state of exception' (Noack, *Carl Schmitt*, 113) In addition, as Rüdiger Safranski points out, Schmitt's focus on the 'moment of decision' bears a resemblance not only to Benjamin's law-creating violence, but also to Ernst Jünger's 'sudden fright' and Paul Tillich's *kairos*, concepts which in turn derive from Søren Kierkegaard's 'moment'. In all of these, the 'flat and-so-forth of bourgeois stability is confronted by the blinding pleasure of intensive infinity – in the moment' (Safranski, *Martin Heidegger*, 173).

Eschewing the cautious reasoning characteristic of most legal scholars, Schmitt begins his investigation of sovereignty with a controversial formulation that has become infamous in German legal theory and beyond, and that Benjamin clearly is citing in his study of *Trauerspiel*: 'The sovereign is he who decrees the state of exception' (Schmitt, *Politische Theologie*, 1; 'Souverän ist, wer über den Ausnahmezustand entscheidet').[16] A striking twenty-first century example that demonstrated the validity of Schmitt's idea was the declaration of a 'war on terror' following the 9/11 attacks. This declaration, which brought with it various infringements of 'normal' legal guarantees of US citizens, was both founded on and supportive of the sovereignty of the central US government that had been attack. While legislation was eventually passed to support this idea, there was never an investigation of or debate about the state of emergency itself, i.e. that the reaction was to be 'war' and not some other procedure. In a situation where war cannot be declared since the enemy is not a nation-state, the ability to decide that a state of war exists demonstrates sovereignty. The idea of exceptionalism confronts us more readily with the central paradox of an idea that would generalize conditions that are exceptional. With this sentence,

---

16 The dynamic equivalent of *Ausnahmezustand* is 'state of emergency' in English, 'state of siege' in French and Italian. However, I will use the literal translation, since the notion of exception includes the other terms that are specific types of exception.

Schmitt reverses the normal procedure of scholarly investigation, beginning as it were with his conclusion. However, from the reader's perspective the sentence fulfils an important function: 'a sentence like this creates suspense. It is striking. It is shocking. One reads the following sentences in order to get over the surprise' (Peter Schneider, *Ausnahmezustand und Norm*, 20). It is also a declaration of the remarkable about-face in Schmitt's conception of dictatorship, which he had seen as commissarial in the earlier book, *Dictatorship*. In Roman law, dictatorships suspended the law, but only within a framework of limited time, a patent example of law as norm. With the opening sentence of *Political Theology*, on the other hand, Schmitt places the law under the control of a sovereign who can decide when it applies or not. The sentence forces its reader to confront the fundamental question of whether states of emergency are inside or outside the legal order, an important issue given that some Weimar governments ruled under continual state of emergency decrees (cf. John McCormick, 'The Dilemmas of Dictatorship'). Schmitt's original definition of sovereignty derived from a question all too often asked in the Weimar period: 'Who is in charge [...] when the legal order does not answer the question of jursidiction?' (Schmitt, *Politische Theologie*, 17–18; 'wer ist zuständig [...] wenn die Rechtsordnung auf die Frage nach der Zuständigkeit keine Antwort gibt?'). *Ausnahmezustand* is thus, in Agamben's terms, 'the legal form of what cannot have legal form' (*State of Exception*, 1), a state of either mythical or divine violence.

Like Benjamin's 'Critique of Violence', which may have provided Schmitt with his central paradox of the fact that law can never legislate itself, Schmitt's decisionist philosophy rejects the normative approach of Hans Kelsen, the most prominent defender of a positivist conception of law in which – since laws embody norms – exceptions could never be legal. As George Schwab summarizes, while 'Schmitt hinges his definition of sovereignty on the sovereign's power to make the decision about whether a state of exception exists, Hans Kelsen is found at the opposite pole, not only avoiding the problem of the exception, but always trying to subject sovereignty to norms' (Schwab, *The Challenge*, 49–50). Kelsen was Schmitt's great antagonist in the Weimar period, and more directly influential on the legal subsystem: Kelsen drafted the new Austrian Constitution that was passed in 1920. His neo-Kantian *Pure Theory of Law* (*Reine Rechtslehre*) was only published in 1934 when he had already been forced into exile, but its thesis had been anticipated in numerous publications and lectures. The adjective '*rein*', which parallels the title of Hermann Cohen's book on ethics, was meant to indicate both an approach in which one attempts to discover the transcendental grounds that allow laws to come into being and have an effect, and concomitantly the freeing of legal theory from 'impure' political biases. According to this theory, laws are created not through political compromise, but by being connected to a pre-existent 'ought', which Kelsen called a 'norm'. An example of this search for purity would be Kelsen's use of matrimony (*die Ehe*) as an example in the *Pure Theory of Law*:

> The legal relation of matrimony, for example, is not a complex of sexual and economic relations between two individuals of different sex merely shaped into a specific form by law. Without law there simply is no such thing as 'matrimony'. Matrimony as a legal relation is a legal institution, that is to say, a complex of legal obligations and rights in the specifically technical sense – this means, a complex of legal norms. (Kelsen, 168)

This brief discussion is indicative of Kelsen's approach to law, and stands in direct opposition to Benjamin's discussion of marriage viewed through the lens of Goethe's novel. Law for Kelsen is the realization of norms in the form of 'oughts' and 'ought nots'. Only rarely are norms embodied directly in legal language; rather, they can be logically inferred from existing law, or from the sanctions provided for by law. For example, the sanctions against murder and manslaughter are derived from the unwritten (in secular law) norm, 'Thou shalt not kill'. Rights and obligations, which refer to actions and behaviours rather than to persons, are to be defined mutually – the right to marry, for example, depends on the obligation of the state to recognize and document marriage and to provide concomitant benefits.

There is a compelling logic to Schmitt's attack on Kelsen, which is that 'the existence of the state is undoubted proof of its superiority over the validity of the legal norm. [...] The norm is destroyed in the exception' (Schmitt, *Political Theology*, 12). States can destroy or nullify norms, but not vice versa. As paraphrased by William Rasch, Schmitt's idea is that normative law can only be carried out within sovereign jurisdictions: 'states neither arise nor are legitimized by way of a logical deduction from universal norms; rather norms presuppose the legitimacy of states. [...] It is the situation, the condition, the 'state,' which structures [law's] enabling space' (Rasch, *Sovereignty*, 24). As in Newtonian mechanics, laws can be analyzed as proceeding from norms only as long as the analysis takes place within the framework of a normal situation. The problem is that norms cannot bring a normal situation about. Like Freud for the psychic system, Schmitt believes that the royal road to understanding the legal system lies in its aberrations and ruptures, in moments of what Benjamin calls 'law-establishing violence'.

Benjamin Hett contextualizes Schmitt's attack on Kelsen as one of 'various versions of antipositivist conceptions of law, at the expense of an embattled positivism. [...] The essential point of antipositivist theory was that politics and morals *had* to inform law, and thus antipositivists of right and left stood strongly against the neo-Kantians' celebration of reason and order and their drawing of careful, categorical lines' (Hett, 'Hans Litten', 190–91). If Kantian philosophy was the backbone of legal positivism, antipositivism could count on big guns such as Arthur Schopenhauer, Friedrich Nietzsche and G. F. W. Hegel. The Nazi period saw the ultimate triumph of the antipositivists, as every law was to be interpreted and every provision carried out under the amorphous concept of benefiting the German *Volk*. The revolution in (il)legal thinking was accompanied by reversals of personal fortune. Kelsen, who in the interest of building his department had played an active role in Schmitt's appointment at the University of Cologne, was suddenly dismissed by the Nazi government while on vacation in 1933. Schmitt was the only faculty member not to sign a letter asking the government to reconsider.[17]

Normative law leaves Goethe's text along with mediation and compromise – all three being represented by the figure of Mittler – in Benjamin's derisive dismissal of the latter's famous speech in defence of marriage, quoted in Chapter 2.2. Benjamin writes of it as though he were critiquing the actions of the *Reichstag*: 'Such talk [as Mittler's] can indeed be indefinitely pursued – talk which, in Kant's words, is a "disgusting mishmash", "patched together" out of baseless humanitarian maxims and muddy, delusive juridical instincts' (Benjamin, 'Goethe's *Elective Affinities*', 301; 'Unbeschränkt läßt sich [...] solche Rede verfolgen, die, um mit Kant zu sprechen, ein »ekelhafter Mischmasch« ist, »zusammengestoppelt« aus haltlosen humanitären Maximen und trüben, trügerischen Rechtsinstinkten' ['Goethes *Die Wahlverwandtschaften*', 130]). Suddenly Kant, whose definition of marriage was held up to ridicule, is used as the philosophical enforcer who will cut off the pointless filibuster that delays decision.

Benjamin not only implicates the contractual basis of marriage as violent, but even begins to draw on the same vocabulary of decay to describe it, and links it to the general situation in Weimar:

like the outcome, the origin of every contract also points toward

---

17 For an interesting double perspective on the Kelsen-Schmitt duo before and during Weimar, see Peter Caldwell's *Popular Sovereignty and the Crisis of German Constitutional Law*, 40–62 and 85–119.

violence. It need not be directly present in it as lawmaking violence, but is represented in it insofar as the power that guarantees a legal contract is, in turn, of violent origin even if violence is not introduced into the contract itself. When the consciousness of the latent presence of violence in a legal institution disappears, the institution falls into decay. In our time, parliaments provide an example of this. They lack the sense that a lawmaking violence is represented by themselves; no wonder that they cannot achieve decrees worthy of this violence, but cultivate in compromise a supposedly nonviolent manner of dealing with political affairs. (Benjamin, 'Critique', 243–4)

[wie der Ausgang, so verweist auch der Ursprung jeden Vertrages auf Gewalt. Sie braucht als rechtsetzende zwar nicht unmittelbar in ihm gegenwärtig zu sein, aber vertreten ist sie in ihm, sofern die Macht, welche den Rechtsvertrag garantiert, ihrerseits gewaltsamen Ursprungs ist, wenn sie nicht eben in jenem Vertrag selbst durch Gewalt rechtmäßig eingesetzt wird. Schwindet das Bewußtseinvon der latenten Anwesenheit der Gewalt in einem Rechtsinstitut, so verfällt es. Dafür bilden in dieser Zeit die Parlamente ein Beispiel. Sie bieten das bekannte jammervolle Schauspiel, weil sie sich der revolutionären Kräfte, denen sie ihr Dasein verdanken, nicht bewußt geblieben sind. In Deutschland insbesondere ist denn auch die letzte Manifestation solcher Gewalten für die Parlamente folgenlos verlaufen. Ihnen fehlt der Sinn für die rechsetzende Gewalt, die in ihnen repräsentiert ist; kein Wunder, daß sie zu Beschlüssen, welche dieser Gewalt würdig wären, nicht gelangen, sondern im Kompromiß eine vermeintlich gewaltlose Behandlungsweise politischer Angelegenheiten pflegen.] ('Zur Kritik', 190–91).

'Compromise' was an epithet strongly associated with the Weimar Constitution in the mind of the general public. The main drafter of the document, Hugo Preuss, was himself a compromise, in that he was a left-leaning liberal appointed by Friedrich Ebert of the Social Democratic Party. Industry and unions came to another such compromise. Many of the delegates to the constitutional convention in Weimar abstained from a vote on the final document due to the 'character of compromise' (*Kompromisscharakter*) that they felt inhered in the final draft. The time between Germany's capitulation and the creation of the constitutional convention in 1919, after all, had been taken up with generalized violence between political factions interested in the imposition of their idea of law, *tout court* and without compromise, ranging from the maintenance of feudal conditions to the imposition of workers' soviets.

In his affirmation that the foreclosure of the violent, abject origins of institutions of political compromise such as parliaments eats away at the fabric of society, Benjamin is in full agreement with the sovereignty theory of Carl Schmitt. The marriage of Eduard and Charlotte is, then, a microcosm of the Reichstag of Weimar Germany, their marriage contract a summary of the Weimar Constitution that resulted not from a decision, but a compromise. In bringing Kant's definition into dialogue with Goethe's text, and in citing in this work of literary criticism concepts of natural versus positive law developed both in 'Towards a Critique of Force' and also in his treatment of the Baroque tyrant, Benjamin creates a constellation of ideas – philosophical, novelistic, and critical – that 'redeem' Goethe's by making it speak about law's relation to the fragile hopes of Germany's political future. Like Goethe's novel, that future ended tragically and fatefully.

3.3
From Schiller to *Schund*: *Zensur* and the Canonization of Literature

The fact that we [in the Federal Republic of Germany] have a general prohibition on censorship, but no generally accepted social-scientific *concept* of censorship, exposes a facet of the censorship problem that makes difficult the creation of juridical consensus on the matter.

[Damit, dass es zwar ein Zensurverbot, aber keinen allgemein sozialwissenschaftlich akzeptierten Zensurbegriff gibt, ist eine Pointe des Zensurproblems sichtbar geworden, die juristischen Stellungnahmen schwer zu schaffen macht.]

Helmut Ridder (21; emphasis added)

Helmut Ridder's emphasis on a social-scientific definition of censorship as necessary grounding for its legal positions is both reinforced and complicated by examination of the complexities of censorship practised during the Weimar Republic – reinforced because the Weimar Constitution had explicitly abolished censorship, and complicated by at least two factors: the distribution of the censoring function among a number of social subsystems beyond the legal and legislative; and the recognition of the special status of works of the literary canon (*'schöngeistige Literatur'*), which meant that the censoring mechanism cited neither social science nor legal precedent in its approach to this area, but rather literature's own self-definitions and theoretical positionings. Specifically, what was not canonized as literary belonged to a category called *Schund* (roughly, pulp fiction) and was open to censorship. The title of this chapter uses the poet most associated with German national aspirations, Friedrich Schiller (1795–1805) as a metonym for the canonization process, sharing as he does an initial consonant cluster ('*sch*') but little else with *Schund*. Schiller's canonization was visible above all in his citability; his work had given rise to a series of anthologies and collections of his verses and sayings, bearing titles such as: *Schiller's Aphorisms, Sayings and Maxims on Nature, Art, the World, and People* (1806; *Schillers Aphorismen Sentenzen und Maximen, über Natur, Kunst, Welt und Menschen*); or more provocatively, as German nationalism grew during the nineteenth century, *Schiller's Power-Quotes for Germans, Geared for the Present Circumstances* (1814; *Schillers Kraftsprüche für deutsche auf die jetzigen Zeitumstände passend*); but then more delicately, *The Language of Flowers According to Schiller* (1839; *Blumensprache nach Schiller*). Schiller thus represented that supposed core of German national literary tradition that conservative writers such as Rudolf Borchardt saw as being eroded by industrialized and politicized writing, a topic we will revisit in the next chapter.

The present chapter treats these issues in the order adumbrated above, beginning with an examination of the polyvalent term *Zensur*, then examining its structural coupling with copyright law in the period, before moving to an examination of the actual practice of censoring *Schund* during the period under consideration.

Zensur vs. Censorship

The German word '*Zensur*' provides an excellent window on the idea of the system-theory notion of 'distinction'. Beyond a meaning very close to its English equivalent (censorship), *Zensur* can also refer to the giving of a grade, as in an academic setting, i.e. the drawing of distinctions in achievement. Both words derive from the same Latin nouns, *censura*, meaning 'test', 'judgment' and 'rigidly moral behaviour', and *censor*, the office that carried out official censorship in the Roman Republic. While a common notion of censorship sees it as the law's intervention in the literary process, I wish to emphasize here that mutual observations and structural couplings between law, literature and other subsystems are necessary for the construction of the system of censorship in democratic societies. Censoring as a related series of structural couplings differs from the top-down approach of repressive regimes, such as the Catholic Church with its famous Index, post-Metternich Austria and Germany, and Nazi and East Germany, or in Württemberg in the eighteenth century, motivating Schiller to flee after being imprisoned for attending the première of his own play, *The Robbers* (*Die Räuber*). This authoritarian kind of censorship has drawn the lion's share of critical attention, most of it justifiably denunciatory. On the other hand, as Klaus Petersen points out, libel suits have rarely been part of the study of *Zensur*: 'Libel lawsuits are seldom considered in censorship research, because on the one hand their number is beyond our ability to keep track, and as well because they escape the normal fixation on authority as the only source of repression' (Petersen, *Zensur*, 77). The use of a single term, *'Zensur,'* to cover more complex and mediated forms of this practice such as libel and copyright lawsuits is somewhat misleading – though it would be equally misleading to claim that such forms are not really *Zensur*, as we shall see from some Weimar examples – and is indicative of a historical development from supervision by a single authority to the negotiations and self-regulation that became necessary due to the huge increase in volume and media possibilities in the modern era.

Adjectival qualifiers have been called in to provide the necessary differentiation. Klaus Kanzog's entry on *'Zensur'* for the *Reallexikon der deutschen Literaturwissenschaft* numbers just two varieties: formal, i.e. carried out by governments with regulated sanctions; and informal, i.e. carried out by divergent economic, political and social pressures. Under the latter, however, Kanzog discusses and defines 'self-censorship' (*Selbstzensur*), so that we could really speak of at least three types. The approach of Aleida and Jan Assmann provides a distinction for the censor's observations highly relevant to the situation in Weimar Germany: canonical vs. censored. Something is censored if it cannot be admitted into the canon. The history of writing would seem to be one of continuous further distinctions within each of these categories. Furthermore, writing gives birth to practices of censorship, because 'in oral cultures no investment in censorship is necessary, since alternative or false opinions have no chance of survival' (Assmann and Assmann, 'Kanon und Zensur', 19). Oral cultures 'censor' in different ways, many of them unrecognizable to those inhabiting print cultures. Before printing, the decision to produce or to copy manuscripts effectively censored what was not copied – or even preserved in writing. Susanne Kord makes a point similar to the Assmanns's, namely that the process of censorship can be inseparable from that of canonization:

> Unlike the relationship between censor and author, which is frequently portrayed as antagonistic, the link between censorship and the work seems more analogous. Indeed, in many cases, literary history seems to have taken its cue from censorship restrictions in establishing a poetological basis for that literary 'quality' which is used to justify canonization; in other cases, the considerations of the censors coincide precisely with those of the most influential literary reformers and arbiters of taste. (Kord, 'The Curtain Never Rises', 369)

In other words, finding some similarity between a piece of writing and the work of Schiller may be enough to rescue it from the category of *Schund*. We will encounter several instances below that show, in very precise language, how judgments made on the basis of aesthetics and poetics inform legal decisions as to the publishability of a work.

The censoring system becomes far more extensive and regulated with the invention of printing – the more mobile word and script are, the more mobile censorship must become to deal with them. In addition, print is itself the product of increasingly complex societies whose subsystems are differentiating themselves, giving rise to collaborating or competing censoring systems: church, monarch, school administrations, government agencies, the publishing market, and so forth. To give one example, private individuals have increasingly exerted censorship over works whose publication they feel would disadvantage them – the most famous German case is that of the actor Gustav Gründgens (1899–1963), who successfully prohibited the publication of the novel *Mephisto* by Klaus Mann in the Federal Republic of Germany.[1] An interesting counterpart to this protection of personality was the decision taken on 21 October 1922 by the Prussian police to allow the portrayal of public figures on the stage. Yet by and large, the literature on censorship has failed to elaborate a model for the complex couplings between these subsystems.

Within censorship, following the Assmanns, one can distinguish between: arbitary censoring acts done out of fear by a regime; systematic censoring acts done to stabilize tradition and maintain order; and – the type I will explore in this chapter – those done from the perspective of a canon: 'The canon motivates *Zensur*, but also monitors it, and each act of censorship in the shadow of a canon is also the canon's drawing of limits around itself' (Assmann and Assmann, 'Kanon und Zensur', 21). *Zensur* becomes an essential drawing of distinction by the canon, and canons censor as part of their autopoietic function of maintaining their own canonicity. Here Luhmann's thesis that binarism increases with increased complexity and autonomy of subsystems seems to be reversed, for the Assmanns's point is most readily understandable when applied to oral cultures: what does not enter cultural memory for preservation has been, in effect, censored. That we find in many modern print cultures a large body of literature that is neither canonized nor censored is perhaps due to the multiplicity of censoring systems

---

1   On this and more recent cases in the Federal Republic, see Ladeur and Gostomzyk, 'Mephisto Reloaded'.

that leads to incompleteness and, at times, paradox. A number of examples will show the complexity of censoring and canonizing systems in Weimar Germany, a society which lived under the motto of 'there shall be no censorship' (eine Zensur findet nicht statt). I will show how censorship, in the binary meaning given above, in fact converged on texts from a number of different directions.

Legitimating Language

If the concept of censorship does not yet exist in oral cultures because it is impossible to disaggregate it from the general principles of expressive behaviour, it nearly disappears from sight in complex societies because the censoring behaviours are so varied and take place according to the rules of so many different subsystems, so as not to be capable of being gathered under a single concept. Pierre Bourdieu agrees that this absence of definition of censorship is due neither to accident nor to neglect, but rather results from the discursive limitations imposed by the differentiation of subsystems. In modern societies, genre and form act as implicit censoring mechanisms:

> the need for [...] censorship to manifest itself in the form of explicit prohibitions, imposed and sanctioned by an institutionalized authority, diminishes as the mechanisms which ensure the allocation of agents to different positions [...] are increasingly capable of ensuring that the different positions are occupied by agents able and inclined to engage in discourse (or to keep silent). [...] Censorship is never quite as perfect or as invisible as when each agent has nothing to say apart from what he is objectively authorized to say. (Bourdieu, 'Censorship and the Imposition of Form', 138)

The agent 'authorized to (not) say' is a Weberian bureaucrat, a product of the shift from hierarchical to segmented societies. This literally formal censorship is characteristic of societies with separate, autonomously functioning autopoietic subsystems (e.g. legal discourse, aesthetic discourse, literary criticism, philosophy). At the same time, it makes the censoring mechanism of such societies resemble those of undifferentiated ones, where the taboos against certain forms of expression tend to be implicit rather than explicit. The signs and processes by which language achieves legitimation within the subsystem of differentiated societies are extensive, and always carry with them the concomitant process of deligitimation. Ridder notes, for example, the affinity of a *'Promotionsverfahren'*, i.e. the approval of a doctoral dissertation, where the accepted dissertation will be published as a piece of scientific work. There is a close resemblance between this process and nineteenth-century pre-publication censorship. In fact, the conversations between authors and their censors in such situations could resemble those between students and professors. Yet none of the professors involved will be accused of censorship, because no general verdict labelling it as such has been forthcoming.

If we consider society as a system whose main concerns are autopoiesis and homeostasis, then we can assume that society will constantly be seeking out negative feedback mechanisms for information that would disturb its homeostasis. An example of this is the tendency of German censorship in its various forms to prohibit the import of foreign influences. During the Weimar period, a coalition of forces resisted the importation of foreign film and theatre. While the German film industry obviously was worried about competition, judges and censors seemed above all to attempt to erect barriers against Bolshevist ideology, as in the famous prohibition of Soviet filmmaker Sergei Eisenstein's *Battleship Potemkin*; various non-official bourgeois groups feared anything 'un-German'.[2] If, however, we consider censorship as part of a complex relation whereby literature observes developments in law and government and makes autopoietic adjustments, then the picture becomes somewhat different. For example, if we consider the development of copyright in parallel to the development of censorship, then the state could be seen as directing the flow of literature by protecting and encouraging (some) authors, by defending their rights to income from their work, and by hindering (other, less literary) authors from publishing. The same state that hinders certain publications through censorship may also encourage reading and publication by exempting books and newspapers from the VAT or sales tax, or by providing for free mailings. In addition, in abolishing formal censorship the law may allow a third, grey area to come into being wherein individuals may sue over the contents of literary texts.

With specific references to the need for a functionally oriented approach to the idea of censorship, Reinhard Aulich has provided several examples of functional differentiation and similarity that can be subsumed under the heading of 'censorship'. He proposes three broad categories, corresponding to the stages of creation, distribution, and influence of literature: supervision [*Kontrolle*] of the genesis [*Genese*] of literary production; supervision of the distribution of literature; and supervision of the diffusion of literarature

---

2   On this see Klaus Petersen, 'Censorship and the Campaign against Foreign Influences in Film and Theater during the Weimar Republic'.

(Aulich, 'Elemente einer Functionalen Differenzierung', 215–17). Different political and legal regimes will place their emphasis on different areas; by the same token, the same goals can be achieved by developments in one or the other of these areas. For example, in response to the demands of reformers in 1848, explicit upholding of freedom of the press (*Pressefreiheit*) was introduced into German law for the first time, above all with the *Bundespressgesetz* of 1854. One book dealer reacted thus: 'Now, with freedom of the press, we're worse off than we were before under censorship' (cited in Siemann, 'Von der offenen zur mittelbaren Kontrolle', 294; 'Jetzt bei Preßfreiheit sind wir viel schlimmer daran als früher unter der Zensur'). The previous lack of freedom of the press had meant an overwhelming emphasis on the genesis phase of public writing, in the practice called '*Vorzensur*'. The new law balanced its explicit guarantee of freedom of opinion and of the press with a host of explicit measures distributed across the three areas. In return for their freedom to publish, for example, newspapers now had to make a deposit with the proper authorities, from which eventual fines could be subtracted. Such fines could not have existed in the period of '*Vorzensur*', since illegal literature theoretically could never reach the stage of distribution, and the provisions for infraction were aimed more at the personal freedom of the author or publisher. If the presses worried about money, women authors, according to Susanne Kord, were worse off due to the new requirement that all works be published under the author's real name, since anonymity or pseudonymity had been an important camouflage to avoid persecution due to their gender (Kord, 'The Curtain Never Rises', 363). Following the general dictum, we see that greater freedom is paid for, as it were, with greater uncertainty.

This will be taken a step further in the Weimar Republic, with the abolition of book censorship. Between 1919 and 1926, anything of a literary nature could be published (though not necessarily performed or exhibited); by the same token, anything and anyone could be taken to court for any reason that resonated with statutory language – blasphemy, for example, or the overthrow of the state. Censorship became diffused and, in Dieter Breuer's formulation, 'democratized' (Breuer, *Geschichte Der Literarischen Zensur*, 220). Klaus Petersen's major study of censorship in the Weimar period is guided by his general hypothesis (*Zensur in der Weimarer Republik*, 7–8) that censorship was largely carried out in Weimar by non-governmental organizations, such as the churches, and was a product mostly of the vexed inner political turmoil of the state. Mostly, but not exclusively; notions of aesthetic value came into play as well. As Mirjam Storim points out, the earliest aesthetic evaluation of *Schund* around 1900 came in the form of an 'anti-aesthetic': the object of analysis releases sensuality and raw instincts, destroys the reader's sense of reality, subverts authority and lacks any artistic or cultural value whatsoever (Storim, *Aesthetik im Umbruch*, 102). The pennydreadful heroine Wanda von Brannburg (Germany's Master Female Detective), for example, exhibits no political sentiments or loyalties of any kind, and was a favourite neither of the right nor of the left.

The nineteenth-century bookdealer's lament quoted above could just as easily have come out of the Weimar period. Literature was no longer censored; however, it could be – and in fact often was – considered as incitement to treason. A new term was thereby invented: *'Literarischer Hochverrat'*, defined on 5 February 1927 through the *Reichsgericht* (roughly, the German supreme court in this period). A number of writers were condemned under this heading, the basic idea being that their work or public performance had the goal of inspiring the audience or readership to violent acts that could bring down the government. As Alfred Oborniker, a lawyer in Berlin pointed out in a 1925 article, such rulings were difficult to reconcile with precedent: a 1909 law had recognized that the glorification of crime was not equivalent to inciting someone to commit crime. Analogously, the depiction of a failed proletarian uprising, such as the one in Hamburg depicted by Larissa Reissner in her 1925 travel narrative *Hamburg on the Barricades* (*Hamburg auf den Barrikaden*), could hardly be considered incitement, especially since the uprising in Hamburg failed: 'And to think that the audience could construct rules for their own planning from a failed action! They could at most say, negatively: this is how not to do it. But [to be treasonable] the piece must in fact say how one should go about committing the act' (Oborniker, 'Kunst-Verfolgung', 207; 'Und ferner Regeln aus einer mislungenen Aktion! Sie können doch nur negativ sagen: So macht man's nicht. Aber es muß doch gesagt werden, wie man's tun soll'). Reissner had only depicted in her narrative the actual events she had seen, according to Oborniker, without addition of the call to insurrection, or instructions for the same, that would reveal the intention of overthrowing the state. The authorities felt otherwise. The idea of 'literary treason' is a sinister structural coupling, a rare opportunity for finding a legal performative in literature. It is worthy of a separate chapter that unfortunately would not fit into a study of this size.[3]

---

3   Interested readers are referred to article 'Ästhetischer Hochverrat' by Joachim Dyck.

Coupling Copyright with Censorship

Like censorship, copyright practice structurally couples law and literature, and discussions of copyright through the Weimar period on occasion reveal that what is being protected is not expression or creation *per se*, but aesthetic, intellectual, or political value. Considering censorship together with copyright as elements of a single publication system, and allowing books to stand for literary production, we arrive at a notion that we might call 'The Book as a Legal Object' ('Das Buch als Rechtsobjekt'). This is in fact the title of a dissertation by Ernst Rathenau, published in 1919, just as the Weimar Republic was being born. Rathenau begins with copyright and then connects this to the negative aspects of punishable offense. His explanation of copyright derives the notion from the implication of the author in a social network:

> In granting copyright, the general public notifies the author of its gratitude for his furthering of general cultural values. The rightsholder wishes to enjoy his production as a reward for his social deed. Monetary reward allows him the leisure for new creation. The inner feeling of joy from being allowed to impart to people a new value does not cancel out the appreciation of that practical aspect.
>
> [Mit der Verleihung des Urheberrechts bekundet die Allgemeinheit dem Verfasser ihre Dankbarkeit für die Förderung allgemeiner Kulturwerte. Der Urheber will als Lohn seiner sozialen Tat das Geschaffene genießen. Die reelle Belohnung gibt ihm die Musse zu neuem Schaffen. Das innere Glücksgefühl, den Menschen einen neuen Wert schenken zu dürfen, vernichtet nicht die Wertschätzung jedes praktischen Vorteils.]
>
> (Rathenau, *Das Buch*, 21)

Rathenau's language should surprise us, since it does not derive from the more usual justification of copyright as protecting either a type of personal property, the intellectual property created by the author, but from a type of contract between author and the general public (*Allgemeinheit*). Literary works differ in this respect from other forms of property due to their public nature. Thus, Rathenau posits a public will that judges and rewards the worth of intellectual publication. Literature is a 'social act' (*soziale Tat*). Many other forms of publication are considered only economic creations (*rein gewerbliche Erzeugnisse*), and hence are not subject to copyright (Fritz Bockius, *Die strafrechtliche Bedeutung der internationalen Verträge*,

20). *Schund* is undoubtedly one such kind of purely economic publication. Furthermore, the mark of works of art and literature, following the grounds laid out for a 1932 law, is that they are the 'Result of a creative intellectual effort [...] and receive their individual characteristics from the individuality of their creator' (Rathenau, *Reichsjustizministerium*, 32; 'Ergebnis einer schöpferischen Geistestätigkeit [...] und empfangen ihre Eigenart aus der Individualität ihres Schöpfers'). A critic of the wording of this law wanted to add a further characterization of works of literature and art to the first paragraph, so as to specify that what were to be protected would be 'Works of literature, of composition and of the plastic arts, insofar as these represent an individual mental creation' (Hans Otto de Boor, *Vom Wesen des Urheberrechts*, 82; 'Werke der Literatur, der Tonkunst und der bildenden Künste, soweit sie eine eigentümliche geistige Schöpfung darstellen').[4] The grounds for copyright are thus equivalent to the grounds for state observation of the literary process, and indeed of that part of the literary process – intellectual creativity – that is normally a 'black box', discernable only through its manifestations and symptomology. One sees a similar notion in, for example, Heinrich Mitteis's suggestion that the notion of copyright be applied to 'national works of art' (*nationale Kunstwerke*) of whatever age in order to protect them against adaptation – he gives the negative examples of the *Nibelungenlied* being adapted as an operetta or Schiller's *Robbers* as a musical (Mitteis, 'Recht und Dichtung', 696). The designation as 'national' would create a supercanon of untouchable works. This suggestion for creating immobility, which was not adopted, is quite familiar in certain cultural areas, such as architectural or historical sites that are declared unmodifiable, in contradistinction to most phenomena in the flux of culture. The opinion of Hans-Georg Knothe reveals feelings similar to Mitteis's, and along the same lines of reasoning as Rathenau, that there is a core of meaning in canonical works that the public has a right to expect. In Knothe's opinion, theatres should have to advertise the extent to which they were 'meaning-changing' (*sinnändernd*) rather than 'meaning-interpreting' (*sinndeutend*) or be liable for customer dissatisfaction with the product (Knothe,

---

4   Similarly, discussion of an 1863 copyright law had noted that personal letters were of two kinds: those with literary merit that enjoyed protection, and those without that were equivalent to unprotected oral communication. 'In a specific case the quality of the letter is always *quaestio facti* and the determination of this something for the judge to decide' (*Protokolle* 18; '[I]m einzelnen Falle sei die Qualität der Briefe immer quaestio facti und die Entscheidung darüber dem Richter zu überlassen').

'Umfunktionierte' Klassiker-Aufführungen ohne Hinweis', 1075). Thus, the differential treatment accorded works of literature and art inevitably coupled the systems of law and literature by making of the trial judge a literary critic, who must determined the effects of different production styles on meaning. For example, were Mitteis's suggestion to be adopted, the legal binary of 'national' vs. 'non-national' would need to be created and maintained for works of literature.

Thus, Rathenau is not alone in neglecting alternative histories of the origins of copyright that emphasize the notion of individual property and contract. In his history of copyright, Rathenau notes that early conceptions (including those of *'Privilegien'*) only concerned themselves with printers and book dealers. These were given or denied the privilege of publishing works. Authors were never mentioned. Literary expression was not differentiated from public speech, which by its nature belonged to the public and could be reproduced; the book, in turn, was sold as a physical object the same as any other, subject to the control of the purchaser who could do whatever he wished with it, including making multiple copies. The first mention of the author in actual legislation came during the period of the Deutscher Bund. In a law passed in 1832, the writer (*Schriftsteller*) was mentioned together with the publisher (*Herausgeber*) and printer (*Verleger*). As Heinrich Bosse points out, implicitly the movement towards copyright and the concept of intellectual property implied a new status of the book as the expression of an authorial personality: 'The book, previously an element of speech regardless of the fact that others traded in it, now becomes a good, in fact the primary good, that is filled with personality [persönlichkeitsgeladene Ware]' (Bosse, *Autorschaft ist Werkherrschaft*, 124).

After 1870, the German Reich intensified the investment of authorial personality in writing by protecting unpublished works. Finally, the 'Law Concerning Copyright for Works of Literature and Music' ('Gesetz betreffend das Urheberrecht an Werken der Literatur und der Tonkunst') of 1901 gave the most important models for the protection of authors, but also for their responsibility. It named possible infractions that creative works could engage in, such as libel, blasphemy, incitement to riot or to civil war, and also *lèse majesté*. The close identification of authors with works that justified copyright also justified prosecution. It was under just such a law, which ostensibly protected copyright, that many of the Weimar censoring prosecutions took place. To give one of the most famous examples, in 1922 Carl Einstein's play, *The Bad Message* (*Die schlimme Botschaft*), was confiscated and prosecuted by the Prussian attorney-general Ortmann for *'Gotteslästerung'* (blasphemy). Found guilty, Einstein was sentenced to a six-week prison term and his publisher to three weeks (substituted by fines of 10,000 and 5,000 marks, respectively).[5]

Zensur in the Weimar Republic

With *Zensur* formally abolished but criminal and civil prosecutions of authors abounding, never were conditions more uncertain than during the Weimar Republic, and in the following I will construct a model of the structural coupling between legal and publishing systems out of the mass of details. Let us begin with Paragraph 118 of the Weimar Constitution, a reading of which already begins to reveal paradoxes and double-binds:

> Every German has the right, within the limits of existing public law, to express his opinion through speech, writing, print, graphic, or in any other manner. No condition of private or public employment can hinder him in this, and no one may punish him for making use of this right.
>
> There shall be no censorship; however, regulations departing from this can be instituted for moving pictures. Legal measures to combat *Schund* and pornography and to protect youth at public performances and concerts are permitted.
>
> [Jeder Deutsche hat das Recht innerhalb der Schranken der allgemeinen Gesetze seine Meinung durch Wort, Schrift, Druck, Bild oder in sonstiger Weise frei zu äußern. An diesem Rechte darf ihn kein Arbeits- oder Anstellungsverhältnis hindern und niemand darf ihn benachteiligen, wenn er von diesem Rechte Gebrauch macht.
>
> Eine Zensur findet nicht statt, doch können für Lichtspiele durch Gesetz abweichende Bestimmungen getroffen werden. Auch sind zur Bekämpfung der Schund- und Schmutzliteratur sowie zum Schutze der Jugend bei öffentlichen Schaustellungen und Darbietungen gesetzliche Maßnahmen zulässig.]
>
> (Verfassung des Deutschen Reiches, par. 118)

The famous negative formulation of *Zensur* in Article 118 – that it was not to occur – was preceded by a paragraph that also seemed to grant unrestricted freedom of speech: 'Every German has the right, within the limits of existing public law, to express his opinion by

---

5   For a thorough account of this case with substantial quotations from the testimony, see the entry on Einstein in Houben 1:137–74. Einstein's is the only Weimar prosecution contained in the 1924 edition of Houben's encyclopedia of censors and censorship cases.

means of speech, writing, print, graphic, or in any other manner'. Yet we see right below that the cinema was not included as one of those manners. *Schund*, the limits and definition of which are so elusive that I have left the word in German, presents a similar exception that will receive further discussion below. The freedom from censorship is exercised only within the framework of prevailing laws, including the one against *Schund* that was passed at the end of 1926.

Behind the ambiguities and contradictions of the paragraph lies the question of whether the intention of the lawmakers was to do away with *Zensur* in the sense of state influence on literary production, or to put an end only to the practice of prepublication licensing. As Bernd Rieder poses the question (117–29), it is not clear whether the *Zensur* that is being undone is 'material' (*materiell*) or 'formal' (*formell*). 'Formal' censorship means that there is a central authority for carrying out the censoring activity, and publication is dependent upon what is being printed conforming to its standards. '*Materiell*' means that censorship is practised whenever the state sees publication as threatening to it. When one looks at Weimar as heir to the revolutionary period of 1918–19, which simply abolished censorship, then it would seem that the national government is renouncing any attempts at the suppression of freedom. However, if one looks at the sentence as a continuation of the development of *Zensur* to that point in German history, and in particular if one sees the exceptions made for film and *Schund*, then the abolition of licensing or precensorship (except for film) would seem to be the intention. With irrefutable logic, Rieder concludes that only formal censorship could have been meant with the sentence. The actual practice of the Weimar authorities, some examples of which have been given above, bear him out on this.[6] Of these, I will concentrate in what follows on a single issue, that of *Schundliteratur*, because it shows most clearly the dialectic between censorship and canonization.

The ambiguity of the term *Schund* inhabits a 1911 publication by Theodor Sternberg. Sternberg argues that the incorporation of legal themes into adolescent literature would have a positive effect on the public appreciation of law ('*Rechtsgefühl*') and would also improve the quality of that literature: 'Soon we will have an elite corpus of crime fiction' (Sternberg *Die Selektionsidee*, 9; 'Wir werden bald auch eine schöne Kriminalliteratur haben').[7] '*Schön*' (literally, beautiful) here does not express admiration at the state of the detective novel

---

6 An extensive contemporary listing of censorship cases and the reasoning of the board can be found in Hans Rüdesheim, 'Aus den Dunkelkammern'.
7 '*Kriminalliteratur*', literally 'criminal literature', is a somewhat broader concept than detective fiction.

genre; rather, it abbreviates part of the fixed phrase 'schöngeistige Literatur', which translates the French *belles lettres* (which in turn translates the Latin *bonae litterae*). What is meant, then, is Literature with a big 'L,' culture which is not '*Schund*.' Sternberg provides a definition of *Schund*:

> The more literature denies variety, the more a story makes everything dependent on one aspect of life, be it the social, the technological, or the criminal, the more the whole enters the realm or at least the proximity of *Schund*. [...] Jules Verne rescued his science-fiction novels from the sphere of *Schund* by making fun of the character of his protagonists who do not venture beyond the purely technological aspects of their personalities.
>
> [Je mehr [die Literatur] die Mannigfaltigkeit verleugnet, je mehr in einer Erzählung nur alles auf einen Faktor des Lebens, sei es das Soziale, sei es besonders die Technik oder das Kriminale, abgestellt wird, tritt das Ganze in den Bannkreis oder doch in die Nähe der Schundliteratur. [...] Jules Verne hat seine Technikromane dadurch aus der Sphäre der Schundliteratur gerettet, daß er sich über die nichtsalstechnische Charaktereigenschaften seiner Helden selbst belustigt.]
>
> (Sternberg, *Die Selektionsidee*, 9)

Sternberg specifies the falsity of the world picture delivered by *Schund* as its reduction of complexity and its concentration on a single aspect of life. Furthermore, the ease of reading *Schund* stems in large part, as Mirjam Storim points out (as one of the few scholars to read these texts from cover to cover), from a strict and unerring 'identification of appearance with the inner values' of characters (Storim, 'Einer, der besser ist', 259). Irony and authorial distance save works (just barely) from *Schund* status. In this definition, the terminology of *Schund* would also apply to ideologically constructed works, or to works that attempt to document a single event – for example, a particular legal case or the revolution as in Reissner. Such works were frequent during the Weimar period, especially on the stage, and were called '*Zeitstücke*' (literally, 'time-plays', where time refers to the contemporary).

Just how dangerous the notion of contemporaneity could be is shown in the judgment against Kurt Kläber. The miner-poet had his published verse confiscated on 10 August 1925. His publisher Schälicke was prosecuted and sentenced to one year's probation and fined 100 Marks. In deciding that these writings did not fall under the protection accorded literary works, the court noted above all that they were '*Zeitstücke*', with the following legal reasoning: 'It is an entirely separate matter, however, if during politically unstable times a certain group launches literature at the people that portrays present-day matters or ones from the recent past with the recognizable intention of overthrow' ('Eine Sache für sich sei es aber, wenn in politisch erregten Zeitläufen eine bestimmte Gemeinschaft Literatur ins Volk werfe, die mit deutlich erkennbarer umstürzlerischer Absicht Gegenwartsdinge oder Geschehnisse aus naher Vergangenheit gestalte').[8] There are three parts to this declaration: the first is the political situation at the time of publication; the second is the intention to overthrow the government; the third is the focusing of the piece on current or recently past events. Literature can be safe from prosecution, the ruling seems to say, as long as it looks far enough into the past for its plots and avoids the present.

Putting these two aspects together in Figure One gives us some notion of the relative censorability of a literary work according to these two criteria – its complexity, and its relative contemporaneity of theme. When the theme is contemporaneous, monolithic and unambiguous, the work may 'cross the line' (represented by an arc) of actionability in the upper left-hand corner of the chart.

Political literature or '*Zeitstücke*' tended towards contemporaneity, *Schund* towards the single theme or reduction of world-view.

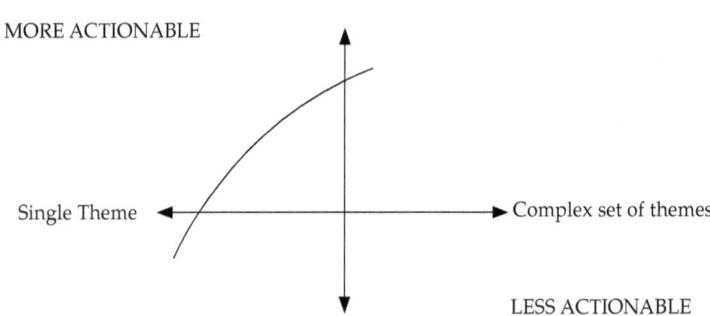

Figure One: Censoring criteria in the Weimar Republic

---

8   *Vossische Zeitung* (evening edition) 28.02.1927; *Vorwärts* (morning edition) 1.03.1927.

What is Schund?

The literal meaning of *'Schund'* is 'offal', that which is left over from the *'schinden'* or skinning of an animal. Metaphorically, it came to mean something completely worthless. In considering the appeal of a listed novel on 4 January 1928, the *Oberprüfstelle* Berlin, the body responsible for making the binary decision regarding *Schund* novel-by-novel, went back to this basic definition found in *Grimms Wörterbuch*: *Schund* is simply writing that is utterly worthless. The two *'sch-'* words were frequently (though not necessarily) used together as a fixed phrase, *Schund- und Schmutzliteratur*, whose exact boundaries are ever-changing according to social and artistic norms. Thus, for Ernst Schultze, who waged a tenacious campaign against it a few years before World War I, *Schund* came in two forms: the morally dangerous and the morally neutral (Schultze, *Die Schundliteratur*, 9–10). These two types had in common that their literary quality was 'bad' or 'worthless'. (Schultze does not discuss the logically necessary category of morally dangerous works of high literary quality.) Schultze designates (with quotations and illustrations) two broad categories of *Schund*: 'backstairs (e.g. dime) novels' (Schultze, *Die Schundliteratur*, 12–20; *Hintertreppenromane*, so called because they were hawked on the backstairs entrances to tenement dwellings); and Nick Carter novels (Schultze, 20–29), that is, detective novels with sensational aspects, one female counterpart being the Wanda von Brannburg series. The term 'backstairs novel' alerts us to the association of *Schund* with urban and industrial society: only the tenement apartments inhabited by the working class were routinely endowed with such an entrance. Furthermore, Schultze's examples of crimes that resulted when life imitated *Schund*-art are all urban. In a separate article on the topic, he notes the role of urban issues in increasing the dominance of bad literature. These range from the absence of working parents from the home, which puts children in the position of entertaining themselves, to the increased noise levels of cities that destroys reading concentration (Schultze, 'Schundliteratur früher und jetzt'). His examples of the negative social effects of reading are also urban: twenty-six Berlin schoolboys were inspired in 1908 by their reading of Nick Carter to form an Indian tribe, the 'Creeping Fox', which committed various petty robberies around the city and then divided the loot at Tempelhof, soon to be the site of the Berlin airport (Schultze, *Die Schundliteratur*, 42). In a separate article, 'Selbstmord und Schundliteratur', Schultze also made *Schund* responsible for some cases of suicide.

A list of categories of *Schund* prepared as an appendix to the 1926 law that tried to define and isolate the epidemic includes the following non-erotic and not excessively violent types of literature: detective stories (*Nick Carter*); adventure stories (*The New Robinson Crusoe*); stories of youth (Jungen und Mädchenerlebnisse) (*Jungenstreiche; Lene und Lotte*); cowboy-and-Indian stories (*The Last of the Mohicans*); writings that glorify war (*Das eiserne Kreuz*); and folk-patriotic Kitsch. Elsa Matz of the Deutsche Volkspartei, in one of the discussions surrounding the formulation of the law, declared that under its terms 70 per cent of the book production in Germany belonged to the category of *Schund* – meaning that censorship should repress almost three-quarters of the books printed.

Some of the actual cases of censorship confirm this view. A sort of criminal novel à la Thomas Reynolds or Eugène Sue, *Das Zigeunerkind oder die Geheimnisse eines Fürstenhauses*, was indexed by the Berlin *Prüfstelle* on 4 December 1928, with the judgment that it did not possess enough unity of action. *Prüfstellen* were, roughly, censoring boards established in the larger German cities to carry out the provisions of the law passed in late 1926.[9] The narration provided a complete 'inconsequentiality of human actions' ('Folgenlosigkeit menschlicher Handlungen'), which in and of itself could break the inhibitions of youth who might read the novel (Petersen, *Zensur*, 169). The formulation about inconsequentiality straddles the borderline between an aesthetic and a moral judgment, as shown in the triple meaning of 'inconsequential' (the German is not an exact translation match, but the point is still valid). 'Inconsequential' points to triviality, showing the base subject matter of the text under consideration. Another possible translation, 'without consequence', refers to the fact that the criminals go unpunished, leading to a view of the world as amoral. Finally, in a purely formal sense, the word points to the 'lack of sequence' of the plot actions. One event follows another without the inner logic and necessity associated with 'high' literature since Aristotle's *Poetics* was rediscovered in the Renaissance – rules that Schiller, for example, had used to help structure tragedies such as *Don Carlos* and *Maria Stuart*.

In a finding of 4 January 1928 against *Die schöne Krankenschwester* (*The Lovely Nurse*) and 25 April 1928 against *Maria, ein Kind der Liebe* (*Maria, a Love-Child*), the *Oberprüfstelle* noted that, in order to be harmful, a writing had to appeal to lower instincts or 'convey a completely distorted picture of the world that causes naïveté' (Karl Schumann, *Das Gesetz*, 36; 'ein vollständig verzerrtes Bild zu vermitteln, Weltfremdheit zu bewirken'). The term '*Weltfremdheit*', which occurs with great frequency in discussions of *Schund* as one

---

9 *Prüfstelle* does not have an easy translation. It comes from a verb meaning 'to test', i.e. to examine something closely. A literal translation would be 'place of examination'.

of its deleterious effects on youth, deserves some comment. In its earliest usage, *'weltfremd'* – which literally means 'strange(r) to the world' – indicated someone completely oblivious to the ways of the world due to isolated upbringing, as in the case of the Arthurian hero Parzifal, who is raised in the middle of the forest by his mother in order to shield him from the dangers of knighthood. Grimm's *Wörterbuch* gives the more modern usage as follows: 'strange to life and reality; unacquainted with the actualities, dangers, requirements or possibilities of the real world' ('lebens-, wirklichkeitsfremd; unvertraut mit den tatsächlichen gegebenheiten, den gefahren, anforderungen oder möglichkeiten der realen welt'). There appears to be no one-to-one translation into English for this concept. 'Alienation' and 'estrangement' already come loaded with connotations derived from Marxism and Formalism, respectively. I have used *'naïveté'* to convey the sense of literature's ability to construct an alternate world readers can escape to, avoiding the 'dangers, requirements or possibilities' of this one. Added to the plots of *Schund* being inconsequential and unrealistic, so too the idea of the unleashing of instinct is an aesthetic one derived from *Bildung*. *Schund* was seen as attacking 'the view of humanity, the educational ideal, and the concept of freedom of the new German Humanism and of Weimar Classicism. Since Kant and Schiller it had been the common knowledge of every educated person that freedom depended on the self-legislation of behaviour (including of one's sensuality)' (Georg Jäger, 'Der Kampf gegen Schmutz und Schund', 175).

Responding to criticism of the *Schund* concept, including a reminder that *'Weltfremdheit'* characterized many of the works of world literature, the *Oberprüfstelle*, responded in its second ruling of 25 April that though 'depiction of a world that is completely alien to reality endangers youth, the *Oberprüfstelle* does not propose completely eliminating escapism, fantasy, and daydreaming from our literature' (Schumann, 36; 'die Ausmalung eines mit der Wirklichkeit unvereinbaren Weltbildes für die Jugend gefährlich sei. [...] Der OPS liegt es fern, Weltfremdheit, Phantasie und Wachträume aus unserer Literatur ganz wegzuwünschen'). But if a writing contained such characteristics, it needed to provide *'Gegenwerte'* (alternative values) in order to avoid falling into the category of *Schund*. 'Should such writing manage – in spite or perhaps because it abandons the realm of actual experience – to shed new light on certain aspects of human nature, to articulate or allude to otherwise ineffable truths not bound to any time or place, or to otherwise compensate for its surrender of the basis of experience, then it is no longer worthless, and hence not *Schund*' (Schumann, *Das Gesetz*, 36). It was even deemed necessary by some that yet another distinction be made: this time between

Schund and *Kitsch*. The latter was also aesthetically worthless, but did not appellate the lower instincts of or induce '*Weltfremdheit*' in its readers, especially given that *Kitsch* was enjoyed by a much broader range of consumers, from lower to middle class and of all ages.

The *Oberprüfstelle* was perhaps responding to the critique of its first ruling by Dr Lindenau of Berlin, published in the *Deutsche Juristen-Zeitung*. Lindenau devoted much of his article on the decision quoted above to the difficulties presented by the notion of '*Weltfremdheit*', a term which, as he points out, was not present in either the legislation or the deliberations of the parliament. He notes the difficulty of distinguishing the concept from those of fantasy and daydream which are the 'inexhaustible sources of all literature and poetry' (Herbert Lindenau, 'Zur ersten grundsätzlich wichtigen Entscheidung der Oberprüfstelle über den Begriff der Schundschrift', 514; 'unerschöpfliche Quellen aller Dichtkunst und Poeterei'). He also critiques the *Oberprüfstelle* for overreaching and usurping the 'educational mission of parental authority, and the influence of the home and school' (Lindenau, 514; 'die Erziehungsaufgaben der elterlichen Gewalt, der häuslichen Einwirkung und der Schule'). Perhaps deliberately taking a path that would avoid the difficulties of '*Weltfremdheit*', the head of the *Film-Oberprüfstelle*,[10] Ernst Seeger, defined *Schund* as writing that 'arouses crudity, intemperance, addiction to pleasure and other low instincts by means of exaggerated verbal representation of inferior value, and [that] creates a false view of the world and encourages unhealthy drives through a fabricated emotional world of fantasy' (cited in Petersen, *Literatur und Justiz*, 94; 'Roheit, Zügellosigkeit, Genußsucht und andere niedrige Instinkte anreizt, durch minderwertige, übertriebene sprachliche Darstellung, und durch eine verlogene Gefühlswelt der Phantasie, ein falsches Weltbild in der jugendlichen Seele schafft und ungesunde Triebe anregt'). As with '*Weltfremdheit*', translation of Seeger's German terms into English presents a challenge, because the moral vocabulary is unique to a period in which secular subsystems are combining the terminology of moral institutions such as the church with the jargon of psychology. The result is an interesting reduplication of concepts: instincts (*Instinkte*) reappear as drives (*Triebe*); a false picture of the world (*falsches Weltbild*) is paralleled by a mendacious emotional world. The anchoring centre of the definition, however, is provided

---

10 The *Prüfstelle* for film went back much further than the one for literature, to 1920. It has also drawn far more attention from historians, including the publication by the Deutsches Filminstitut of the censorship decisions from 1920 to 1938.

not by reduplication, but by contrast: the linguistic representation's exaggerated (*übertrieben*) quality is precisely what vitiates its value. One wonders, for example, whether the exaggeration lies in a 'high' rhetorical style, excess verbiage, or the eschewing of qualifiers in favour of absolutes in descriptions of characters.

Distinction

The actual definition of *Schund* by those who designed the law against it contains an element not examined so far, namely its being destined for the masses. *Schund* is writing 'without artistic merit and intended for mass distribution, writings which according to their form and content move the reader towards crudity or immorality, or which may harm young persons' moral, intellectual, or healthy development or overstimulate their fantasy' ('Bericht des 12. Ausschusses (Bildungswesen)', cited in Petersen, *Literatur und Justiz*, 63; 'Für Massenverbreitung bestimmte Schriften ohne künstlerischen Wert, die nach Form und Inhalt verrohend oder entsittlichend wirken, oder von denen eine schädliche Einwirkung auf die sittliche, geistige oder gesundheitliche Entwicklung oder eine Überreizung der Phantasie der Jugendlichen zu besorgen ist'). This torrent of official words nearly masks the real culprit of mass culture (*Massenverbreitung*). Books could not be assigned to the *Schund* category 'due to their political, social, religious, ethical, or philosophical argument' (Petersen, 161; 'wegen ihrer politischen, sozialen, religiösen, ethischen oder weltanschaulichen Tendenz'). That left only two criteria: commerical/material, and aesthetic. If books could be identified as coming out of an 'industrial machine' (*industrieller Mache*) then they could be considered as *Schund*.[11] Compared with the relation between the volume of *Schund* produced and its main crime of lack of aesthetic form, the campaign against this type of literature seems to be a classic distinction of aesthetic tastes which, as Pierre Bourdieu points out, play a role in the maintenance of class distinctions. Such distinctions play themselves out in food no less than in art:

> The opposition between the immediate and the deferred, the easy and the difficult, substance (or function) and form, which is exposed in a particularly striking fashion in bourgeois ways

---

11 A few years later, a member of the German Communist Party or KPD defined *Schund-* und *Schmutzliteratur* as simply 'Literature that furthers the capitalist society' ('Literatur, die die kapitalistische Gesellschaft verbreitet'). This partisan formulation reminds us of the structural coupling between politics and literature addressed in the previous chapter.

of eating, is the basis of all aestheticization of practice and of every aesthetic. Through all the forms and formalisms imposed on the immediate appetite, what is demanded – and inculcated – is not only a disposition to discipline food consumption by a conventional structuring which is also a gentle, indirect, invisible censorship. [...] It is also a whole relationship to animal nature, to primary needs and the populace who indulge them without restraint; it is a way of denying the meaning and primary function of consumption, which are essentially common. (Bourdieu, *Distinction*, 196)

As in Luhmann, common instincts such as hunger or curiosity are banished to the environment by the drawing of a distinction whose purpose, in this case, is to maintain the boundaries between classes. However, Bourdieu would undoubtedly argue that the problem with *Schund* was not linked to its newness or innovative qualities, nor to any empirical studies that would have shown an actual negative effect on readers, but to its association with the lower classes. It is not merely that the large production runs and cheap editions point to mass consumption, but that the very idea of a broad readership and an easy reading experience are automatically linked to bad taste and degenerate morals. ST, however, maintains the autonomy of subsystems: not everything has the monolithic, single cause as in Bourdieu or Marx.

Distinction in literature had existed since the creation of a literary marketplace; indeed, David Hume had noted it already in the eighteenth century, arguing in his usual contrarian fashion that the difference between elite and popular culture was based on nothing other than conditioning and experience, rather than on a radical distinction in values: 'The most vulgar ballads are not entirely destitute of harmony or nature; and none but a person, familiarized to superior beauties, would pronounce their numbers harsh, or narration uninteresting' (Hume, 'Of the Standard of Taste', 493). Just as Hume recognized the popularity of broadsheet ballads in his day, Germans 'familiarized to superior beauties' and believing such beauties to be foundational to the continuation of their culture noted the overwhelming tide of cheap, popular novels flooding the market and extinguishing the light of true literature.

The 1926 law did not prohibit production or publication of *Schund*, only its sale if it came onto the list of proscribed works. But even if the law itself outlined categories of *Schund* as noted above, the rapidly mutating market for cheap books guaranteed that there would be new titles and categories within months of the law's taking effect. Who could be called on to monitor all these new titles? Decades before, Ernst Schultze had foreseen the need for a panel composed of 'poets, writers, lay people and booksellers' (Schultze, *Die Schundliteratur*, 86–7; 'Dichter, Schriftsteller, Männer des gemeinen Lebens und Buchhändler'), but felt his suggestion was impractical because to serve on such a committee, to be drawn into the conjunction between law and (sub)literature, would seem like punishment to a genuine author. Yet authors and professors already could be, and were, compelled at the very least to provide testimony when called for; in the Carl Einstein case mentioned above, the court sent out a brief questionnaire to a variety of professors of law, philosophy and art, asking their opinion on the blasphemy paragraph of the law, and also whether Einstein's work violated it. Responses were received from public intellectuals such as Thomas Mann and Heinrich Wölfflin.

Beyond these spontaneous assemblages of experts, however the government of Weimar set up more permanent examining boards. The Main Examining Board (*Oberprüfstelle*) in Leipzig was soon supplemented by two regional *Prüfstellen*, in Berlin and Munich. The boards were by law composed equally of representatives of education, government, publishing, youth services and the literary profession. To fill the last category, the boards took on a who's-who of German writers to make these judgments. The *Prüfstelle* in Berlin was made up (at various times) of Heinrich Eduard Jacob, Werner Mahrholz, Bruno Schönlank, Lion Feuchtwanger, Arnold Zweig and Hans José Rehfisch. Lion Feuchtwanger (1884–1958), one of two of these authors still printed and read today, had at first composed plays, but turned to writing historical novels during the Weimar years, publishing *Die hässliche Herzogin* in 1923 and *Jud Süss* in 1925 (the latter appeared in English as *Power* in 1926). While the latter novel was transformed by director Veit Harlan into one of the most sensational anti-Semitic films under the Nazis, Feuchtwanger was more interested in the linkage between power and money in German politics. *Erfolg* (1930) – which supposedly contained thin disguises of the Weimar literati, among them Feuchtwanger's friend Bert Brecht – *Die Geschwister Oppermann* (1933) and *Exil* (1940) followed. He also wrote a trilogy reconstructing the life of the Jewish historian Josef Ben Matthias (Josephus). Heinrich Jacob was an editor of the left-leaning *Berliner Tageblatt*, about which we will learn more in the next chapter, and the author of several novels and short-story collections. His novel *Blut und Zelluloid* (1929), which predicts the Nazi propagandistic use of film, was burned in the *auto da fé* of 1933. He had joined the local *Goethe-Bund*, a group that promoted literature and the rights of authors to free expression. Werner Mahrholz (1889–1930) was an influential Germanist with a reflexive view on the crisis of the self as expressed in his books on contemporary literature, on literary criticism, and on Dostoevsky. He wrote for most of the important newspapers of the time, and from 1925 on was the editor of the *Vossische Zeitung*, while also publishing his own, *Die Hochschule* (Higher Education). Politically, he was active above all in school reform in Bavaria. He was a member of the *Deutsche Demokratische Partei*, which was the party most fervently committed to the success of the Weimar Republic. Bruno Schönlank (1891–1965) was born in Berlin to a father who was a socialist member of parliament. At the outbreak of World War I he organized a demonstration in Berlin, for which the police placed him in preventive custody. Schönlank's first literary success had been in the genre of '*Arbeiterlyrik*' poems about the working class. *Der Gefangene* of 1917 made him famous, and was followed by *Blutjunge Welt* (1919), *Gesänge der Zeit* (1920) and *Sonniges Land* (1920). Schönlank also wrote 'speaking chorus' plays, of which the best known was *Der gespaltene Mensch* (1927). In 1932 he was denied permission to speak on the radio, and emigrated when the Nazis took power. Arnold Zweig (1887–1968), another author who remained on the literary radar after Weimar, especially in East Germany, was a Communist who had been a soldier in World War I. He was known mostly for his prose narratives, especially the 1927 novella *The Struggle Over Sergeant Grisha* (*Der Streit um den Sergeanten Grischa*). Rehfisch, at one time the most popular dramatist of Weimar Germany, cultivated a genre known as the *Gebrauchsstück* or journalistic play. His most celebrated piece was *The Dreyfus Affair* (*Die Affäre Dreyfus*), which told the story of the French general whose false conviction for treason became a *cause célèbre* all over Europe because it was shown to have been motivated by anti-Semitism.

The point in providing these brief authorial profiles of the team of literary experts is to show their generally critical, left-of-centre orientation, which meant that their interventions, not to mention their literary activities, ceased to exist shortly after the Nazi seizure of power in 1933. These author-censors were not in general concerned with preserving their fathers' Germany or upholding the canon of Classicism; rather, they took up their review work with a double purpose: to guarantee authors their freedom of expression, but also to defend the public against the excesses that could definitely be found and to canonize literature as distinguished from *Schund* or pornography. Their work at the conjunction of law and literature lasted only a few short years, replaced by the top-down censoring activities of an authoritarian regime. However, the idea of the *Prüfstelle* as an institution for the protection of youth from 'endangering' cultural products became a model for revival in the post-war Federal Republic, which still today maintains a Federal Examining Board for Media Pernicious to Youth (*Bundesprüfstelle für jugendgefährdende Medien*, www.bundesprüfstelle.de), composed mostly of representatives of the same categories as the Weimar version (representatives of churches have been added), and that continues to index. Obviously, the addition of television and the Internet have made its task even more complex.

It is an ironic preservation of an institution that many intellectuals saw as the absolute antithesis of the personal freedoms envisioned in the Weimar constitution.[12] Luke Springman has compared the language of the Weimar debates on censorship with those occurring in the Federal Republic. Springman argues that one deep reason for the strong resemblance of post-1945 structures of censorship and canonization with those of Weimar lies in a shared cultural pessimism (Springman, 'Poisoned Hearts', 418–19). In Weimar this pessimism was represented by intellectuals such as Oswald Spengler, José Ortega y Gassett (translated from Spanish) – and Rudolf Borchardt, who based his poetic career on the need to re-establish the supposedly broken tradition of German literature, as we shall examine in the next chapter.

---

12 The author Heinrich Mann was perhaps the most prominent author to protest repeatedly against the 1926 law, as chronicled in Jürgen Haupt, 'Schmutz und Schund'.

3.4
German Literature Fights for its Rights: A Thick Description of an Incident of Weimar Literary Culture

> In Borchardt's work, reconciliation consists in giving artistic form to the irreconcilable.
>
> [Versöhnung in Borchardts Werk besteht in der Gestaltung des Unversöhnlichen.]
>
> Theodor Adorno, 'Charmed Language', 199 ('Beschworene Sprache', 72)

> In an era in which the ultimate absorption and contemplation makes you invisible, [Borchardt] is someone who, for the sake of being visible, distorts and reflects that absorption and contemplation even in the face of the abyss. He is not himself the lie, but the lie takes hold of him each time he defines his relation to the public.
>
> [In einem Zeitalter in dem die letzte Vertiefung und Besinnung unsichtbar macht, jene Vertiefung und Besinnung auch vorm Grunde um der Sichtbarkeit willen, abbiegt, reflektiert. Lüge ist er nicht selbst, sondern Lüge ergreift ihn jedesmal wo er seine Relation zum Publikum bestimmt.]
>
> Walter Benjamin to Ernst Schoen, May 1918 (*Correspondence*, 128 [*Gesammelte Briefe*, 1:460])

Two related aspects of Rudolf Borchardt's (1877–1945) principle of non-reconciliation are explored in this chapter: his ideological defence of the so-called 'rights' of German literature that in turn unleashed a court case that could only be decided on the binary basis of *Recht/ Unrecht*; and his rhetorical assumption of attorney's position on behalf of literature. Both aspects conjoin the subsystems of law and literature. On 26 January 1932, Borchardt was sentenced by a Munich court to pay a fine of 600 Reichsmarks as a consequence of his having libelled the Munich correspondent for the *Berliner Tagesblatt*, Werner Richter (1888–1969), in a pamphlet called *German Literature Fighting for its Rights* (*Deutsche Literatur im Kampfe um ihr Recht*, hereinafter *DLKR*). Borchardt had published this text the previous year with the Müller-Langen Verlag. Beyond the fine, which was paid by the press he had 'defended' against putative leftist attacks and conspiracies with the aegis of his writing, Borchardt was also ordered to pay court costs, to eliminate the incriminating passages, and to publish the judgment in three different newspapers. Borchardt's attack had not been the public rehearsal of private animosities. Neither Borchardt nor his work had been attacked by Richter, whose target in reporting for the *Berliner Tagesblatt* had been the Müller press itself, its merger with the Albrecht Langen enterprise, and the acquisition of both by the *Deutschnationaler Handlungsgehilfen-Verband* (German National Association of Booksellers' Employees, hereinafter, DHV). Essentially, the DHV was a union of assistants in bookstores. It was thus an oppositional organization to the Association of German Publishers, which represented those in charge of the 'means of production' of the book trade. The DHV's activities greatly exceeded those we associate with a union. Most important for the Borchardt case is the publishing programme of 'national' literature that the DHV developed through founding the Hanseatische Verlagsanstalt in 1893, which began a programme of publishing nationalist literature in 1916, and which in the following decade acquired two small literary presses in Munich, the Georg Müller and the Albert Langen, of which we will hear more below.

The background to the writing of *DLKR* involved a complex chain of reactions to the suicide of a senior employee of the Georg Müller press, Karl Krause. Krause took his life in his office in June 1931, just hours after being dismissed by the company director, Gustav Pezold. Viewpoints diverged as to the cause. The left-leaning *Berliner Tageblatt* (hereinafter *BT*) published a report on 14 June 1931 containing strong implications that the firing had been due to Krause's political views, which were said to be too far left for the new owners of the press. The leadership of the press, on the other hand, maintained that Krause had been fired for sexually harassing a female employee. Borchardt barely mentions the original motivating incident in his pamphlet.

This chapter details Borchardt's defence of German literature, and then fills in the context that brought about the writing of *DLKR* and the subsequent lawsuit. Although it was a minor legal manoeuvre involving a minor writer, the Borchardt libel trial was also a highly symptomatic crucible conjoining a number of different subsystems of the late Weimar era: literature, publishing, news reporting and politics. It arose out of a deep divide between writers, touched on in the previous chapter, who felt that the task of literature was to identify and hopefully to correct tendencies in the present, and those who felt that the purpose of literature must be to (re)construct a national tradition. I read this legal case as exemplary of the literary *habitus* of Weimar, and in particular of the literary effect of capitalism on literature. As Herbert Göpfert has said of a Borchardt publication of 1929 that took a similar stance to that in *DLKR*, his trial also brought 'the political, economic, and social conflicts of those times into a single focus. The literary and book-historical theme expanded into a general view of the epoch' (Göpfert, 'Die Aufgaben der Zeit', 131).

Examining the conjunction of these subsystems in the Borchardt trial amounts to a 'thick description' of this event. The locution, which derives from the anthropological work of Clifford Geertz, indicates an ethnographic writing that provides as much context for a behaviour as possible, hopefully to the extent that such behaviour becomes comprehensible to readers situated outside the culture in which it occurs. As Geertz explains, 'What the ethnographer is in fact faced with [...] is a multiplicity of complex conceptual structures, many of them superimposed or knotted into one another, which are at once strange, irregular, and inexplicit, and which he must contrive somehow first to grasp and then to render' (Geertz, 'Thick Description: Toward an Interpretive Theory of Culture', 10).[1] In the modern world, these 'conceptual structures' frequently take the form of what Luhmann calls subsystems, and the more formalized and explicit 'structural coupling' between them replaces superimposition and knotting, though this may be more a case of one's choice of the metaphors used to visualize phenomena (recall my own attempt at diagramming in Figure One of Chapter 1.1). Borchardt, his pamphlet, and the publicity surrounding the case, all of which appear to us today as bizarre, but which were readily comprehensible and even defensible to readers at the time, are ripe for thick description. To translate Geertz for a moment into the terminology of Pierre Bourdieu, I wish to use this incident to elaborate the 'rules of literature' in Germany in 1932.

---

1 Geertz begins his article by acknowledging the philosopher Gilbert Ryle as the inventor of the term 'thick description', but Geertz's application of it has been more widely influential, and the latter's applications of the idea are more germane to the task at hand.

The Case

It may never be known whether the firing of veteran employee Karl Krause was anything more than an understandable reaction to indecent behaviour on his part. The only legal actions to ensue from Krause's suicide were the slander and libel cases described in this chapter. A female employee in the division of the Georg Müller Verlag in Munich that was responsible for novel publishing complained of Krause's harassment, which reached the point of groping, and asked that she be transferred. Pezold heard of this and spoke with the employee on 13 June 1931. After a conversation with Krause in which he steadily denied everything, Pezold dismissed him without notice. (Pezold later denied that the firing was immediate, but it seems to have been; undisputed is the fact that Krause was asked to remove himself from the office without delay.) On the same day, Krause shot himself in his office at virtually the same time Pezold was informing other employees about the firing. Krause had worked for sixteen years in the novel and stage-play departments, and was especially close to Paul Ernst (1866–1933), one of the authors whom Borchardt praises highly in *DLKR*. There are some grounds to suspect that the sexual abuse charge was only an excuse for a firing that had long been planned. The novelist Guido Kolbenheyer (1878–1962) in particular did not trust Krause, and felt that he was capable of giving away secrets. Kolbenheyer had written in a letter to Pezold: 'Furthermore, what could keep Krause, since he is of that type that likes to tell all, from whispering the plans and contracts of the press into the ear of Mrs Thomas Mann, née Pringsheim. I am convinced that Thomas Mann knows more about the Georg Müller Verlag than its board of directors does' ('Welche Sicherheit ferner *kann* es geben, dass [Krause] nicht die Pläne oder Verträge des Verlags – und solche Naturen erkunden alles – Frau Thomas Mann geb. Pringsheim einflüstert. Ich bin der festen überzeugung, dass Thomas Mann vom G. M. V. mehr weiss als der Ausichtsrat' [Wilhelm Stapel an Gustav Pezold, 25.10.1930; cited in Andreas Meyer, 77, emphasis in original]). Why Thomas Mann would have a particular interest in the doings of the Georg Müller Verlag, or what use he might make of such knowledge, is not clear, though he did contribute on occasion to the *BT*. Mann was considered a traitor by many on the right for reversing the anti-democratic views expressed in *Betrachtungen eines Unpolitischen* (1918) and for supporting the Weimar Republic. It is no accident that Thomas Mann would be on everyone's mind at the moment, since he had won the Nobel Prize in the year prior to Kolbenheyer's letter, and he and his wife Katja

Pringsheim were lavish entertainers and avid partygoers. Everyone knew everyone in Schwabing, the artistic suburb of Munich.[2]

The *BT*'s first report of the suicide the day after it occurred, in an article that called Krause one of the most beloved figures of Alt-Schwabing, said that he had been fired under a 'flimsy excuse' (*'nichtigem Vorwand'*) ('Ein Selbstmord', *BT* Sonntags-Ausgabe, 14 June 1931). Furthermore, it noted that Krause stood too far left for a press now sharply turned to the right through its absorption by the DHV. In fact, Krause had expressed sympathy for Italian fascism in its ability to give some unity to a national feeling, though he was not a supporter of the NSDAP (the Nazi party). The *BT* also made the totally unfounded claim (*'wie man hört'*) that the DHV was now directly financed by Alfred Hugenberg, an ultra-conservative capitalist whose media conglomerate promulgated right-wing authors and newspapers. Andreas Meyer sums up this first article in the *Tageblatt*: 'Although not everything was quite factual in this first report, it was substantively correct' (Meyer, 'Die Verlagsfusion Langen-Müller', 78). Werner Richter's next article, 'Die Literarische Diktatur der deutschnationalen Handlungsgehilfen' (*BT*, morning edition, 19 June 1931) began with a recap of Krause's death, and dutifully reported the assertions of the Georg Müller Verlag that he had been given notice rather than fired immediately, that the case had nothing to do with politics, that no Hugenberg money was involved, and that the publisher operated in a non-political fashion. Richter then began a long accounting of how the DHV had acquired the two presses, including a listing of the board of directors of the DHV in order to show the scarcity of literary talent among them. Richter made his argument that we have become familiar with from its use in the campaign against *Schund*: that while capitalism should have a free hand in a democratic Germany to spend and purchase as it pleases, the acquisition of literary outlets bears special consideration: 'It is a matter of public concern when two presses of the stature of the Georg Müller and the Albert Langen, which have considerably influenced the development of German literature for decades, are brought to the level of outlets for reactionary interest groups.' Richter concluded with a contradictory juxtaposition meant to show the absurdity of the DHV's

---

2 Mann also knew Borchardt. In 1926 Mann had published a short piece in the *Literarische Welt* on Borchardt that recounts a time when the latter was a guest at the Mann home for tea, and ended up declaiming a Schiller poem 'admirably'. The piece may have been tongue-in-cheek, but on its surface expressed only admiration for Borchardt's learning and oratorical skills. See Thomas Mann, 'Über Rudolf Borchardt'.

literary ambitions: 'In place of two autochthonous and independent publishing houses, directed in a profoundly cultural manner, there now stands the all-powerful and soulless corporation: a publishing warehouse that brings out Strindberg and Wedekind, Hamsun and Lagerlöf in Munich, but in Hamburg, on the other hand, besides nationalistic literature, only something on the order of [Otto Karl] Gessler's *Powerbrokers of the Empire*.'[3]

According to Iris Hamel, it is no accident that the curious organization of the booksellers came into being at a time of transition from a pre-industrial society governed by ideas of *Stand* into a modern, industrial society (Hamel, *Völkischer Verband und nationale Gewerkschaft*, 9). In the course of forty years the DHV developed into the most important employees' societies. It arose out of the societal changes due to the rise of large industry and technical development that robbed the middle classes of their traditional basis. Neither the conservative nor the liberal parties could answer the problems of the middle classes. As a result, both the SPD on the one side and anti-Semitic propaganda on the other were the main forces acting on the members of the DHV.

On 2 February 1916, the DHV founded a '*Deutschnationale Hausbücherei*', which worked on a subscription system (a yearly fee of sixty marks entitled subscribers to six books). The entity would develop its own publications, and also work to save and absorb other presses. One of its shining moments came sixteen years later, as it took on the fusion of the Müller and Langen presses. The main factor was to define its constituents politically. The original 1916 list included 'Germania' by the Roman writer Tacitus, which as the earliest written account of the Germans held a place in nationalist thinking, and Charles de Coster's rendition of the archetypal German trickster figure, *Till Eulenspiegel*. In later years, the antisemitic historian of German literature and novelist Adolf Bartels, Wilhelm von Polenz's 'Der Büttnerbauer', Wilhelm Raabe with several novels including *Der Hungerpastor*, earlier authors Heinrich von Kleist, Eduard Mörike, Gustav Freytag, Jeremias Gotthelf, Gottfried Keller and Viktor von Scheffel came onto the subscription list.

In 1926 an *Auswahlkomittee* of the DH was brought together, which consisted of high-ranking members of the DNVP (the German National People's Party) and Zentrum (the Catholic party), and the writers Hans Grimm, Ernst Jünger, E. G. Kolbenheyer, Wilhelm Schäfer, Wilhelm Stapel, Hermann Ullmann and August

---

3 Otto Karl Gessler (1875–1955) was an important politician during the Weimar years, Minister of the Armed Forces for a time, who withdrew from the scene during the Nazi years.

Winnig. Interestingly, several of these were Müller Verlag authors. In 1924, Wilhem Stapel published a work called *The Fictions of the Weimar Constitution: Towards a Differentiation of Formal and Functional Democracy* (*Die Fictionen der Weimarer Verfassung. Versuch einer Unterscheidung der formalen und der funktionalen Demokratie*). The title resumes Stapel's argument: due to the formal legal thought processes of the writers of the Weimar constitution, Weimar is a fictive, not a real democracy. An advertising prospectus (*Werbeprospekt*) of 1931 shows how the general nationalistic anti-Semitism and xenophobia of the DHV flowed into its publishing agenda: 'Not every book written in German is a German book! We desire that every poet and writer who bases his work on the ground of the German people be supported' (cited in Hamel, 139; 'Nicht jedes in deutscher Sprache geschriebene Buch is ein deutsches Buch! – Wir wollen Förderung des auf dem Boden des deutschen Volkstums stehenden Dichters und Schriftstellers. [...] Wir bringen keine artfremden Autoren. Deutschen können nur von Deutschen geholfen werden'). The writer Rudolf Borchardt did not contribute to this agenda of the DHV until shortly after the death of Krause discussed above.

German Literature Fights for its Rights

Rudolf Borchardt was born in Königsberg in 1877, but spent his formative years in Berlin and lived in Italy for most of his adult life. He died on the Brenner Pass in 1945. Victim of a Jewish heritage whose importance he had always denied – or victim of his urge to assimilate, as we will read more of below – a frail and elderly Borchardt had been ordered deported from his home in Italy by the Nazis, but perished en route. Borchardt is remembered today as one of the main voices of the 'creative Restauration', which emphasized the need for German literature to maintain its relationship to tradition, and of its more politically oriented counterpart, the 'Conservative Revolution'. Though his primary talent was as a lyric poet, he wrote in all genres, and was a talented orator. His best-known works are probably his essays on gardening and the Italian villa, and his translation of Dante's *Commedia* for which he invented a corresponding form of medieval German. The latter project, which produced an unreadable German text, gives some idea of the uncompromising nature of Borchardt's poetics. His friends during his lifetime included Hugo von Hofmannsthal and Rudolf Alexander Schröder, and he at times acted as a spokesperson and polemicist for the more conciliatory Hofmannsthal in the latter's literary controversies with Stefan George and his followers.[4]

---

4   For example, in the extraordinarily intense conflict in 1926/27 over the

The parallels between Borchardt and Walter Benjamin are striking, and include, besides their Jewish backgrounds and persecution unto death by the Nazis, attempts at autobiographies of their respective Berlin childhoods, as well as the precarious financial existence they led due in part to strained family relations.[5] Both worked out a form of 'inner exile' through profound engagement with another time and culture, be this the Paris of the nineteenth century in the case of Benjamin, or the Italy of Dante's time for Borchardt. Benjamin, of course, became deeply interested in both Jewish mysticism and Marxism, two topics that Borchardt abhorred. Yet both were moved by the quest for a stable system to replace the departed monarchical one. In a *'Lebenslauf'* written in 1938, Benjamin mentions Borchardt's essay *Villa* (1908) as among the books that most influenced him (Benjamin, 'Curriculum Vitae (VI)', 381; 'Lebenslauf VI', 225). Borchardt's method for historically reconstructing the landscape architecture of the Italian villa was, we must conclude, influential for Benjamin's own approach to historical inquiry.

Theodor Adorno compares Borchardt with yet another Jewish intellectual, the Viennese Karl Kraus, with their mutual concern being the degenerate condition of language in their time (Adorno, 'Beschworene Sprache', 64 [194]). The restoration of language from its decayed status caused by its use in commerce and exchange results in language mysticism: an absolute commitment to form and a cultivation of the traditional metrics of Classical and medieval Europe. Adorno's dialectical reading of Borchardt, a small portion of which is conveyed in the epigraph to this chapter, highlights the contradictory position of someone who condemned writers such as James Joyce, Marcel Proust and Thomas Mann (and, one would guess, Walter Benjamin) while sharing more with them than he was perhaps aware.

Borchardt viewed the Weimar Republic as the anathema of his hopes and aspirations for Germany, and the newer tendencies of literature to address contemporary issues, some of which we have examined in the last chapter, as completely foreign to the aspirations of aesthetics. He cites a litany of these supposedly negative literary practices near the end of *DLKR*: 'The German

---

successor to the Germanist Franz Muncker at the University of Munich, a three-way race between Ernst Bertram, Josef Nadler and Friedrich Gundolf. See Ernst Osterkamp, '"Verschmelzung der kritischen und der dichterischen Sphäre". Das Engagement deutscher Dichter im Konflikt um die Munckernachfolge 1926/27'.

5   See Kai Kauffmann, 'Rudolf Borchardts und Walter Benjamins Berliner Kindheiten um 1900'.

people's misery and heartbreak is assailed by the old mechanisms of yesterday, journalism, pulp literature, entertainment, the new novel, the new eroticism, paragraph 218, depth psychology, smoke and titillation, Joyce, Proust, the young writers, New Objectivity, genetic inheritance, bold but utterly decent homosexuality, intellectual connections with France, Lenin, Gandhi, the newest Edgar Wallace novel, adventure that takes one's breath away, the world on a conveyor belt' (Borchardt, *DLKR*, 45; 'Um [des Volkes] Elend und sein herzgebrochenes Leidwesen sausen die alten Apparaturen von vorgestern, Presse, Massenliteratur, Unterhaltung, der neue Roman, die neue Erotik, par. 218, Tiefenpsychologie, Rauch und Reiz, Joyce, Proust, die jungen Erzähler, Sachlichkeit, Vererbung, die kühne, jedoch hochdezente Homosexualität, geistige Brücken nach Frankreich, Lenin, Gandhi, der letzte Wallace, atemraubende Abenteuer, die Welt am laufenden Band').[6] Borchardt makes use of asyndeton in this passage to convey the image of a fragmented and incoherent psychic system of the individual reader in the Weimar Republic, seduced by a reading list *in extenso* that apparently means jumping from the difficulties of Joyce to the simplicities of Wallace.

The profound changes in literary production and consumption during the Weimar Republic caused Borchardt to alter his own output, especially given that he was trying to make a living from his writing. He turned to writing prose fiction, publishing the aptly titled *Das hoffnungslose Geschlecht* (*The Hopeless Race*) in 1929, and the novel *Vereinigung durch den Feind hindurch* (*Unity through the Enemy*) in 1937. His main source of income, however, was from the many lectures he gave. The power of his rhetorical style can still be perceived today; by all accounts, his verbal delivery was also spellbinding. (The fact that Borchardt had dictated *DLKR* in two days in the office of the publisher and taken his honorarium with him to Italy, giving the impression of his having been a 'hired gun' for Müller-Langen, found its way into more than one press review.) Two of these lectures given in 1929 are useful for placing *DLKR* in perspective: the so-called '*Bremer Rede*', held in the bookstore of G. A. von Halem, whose title is 'Our Current Responsibilities to Literature' ('Die Aufgaben der Zeit gegenüber der Literatur'); and a speech to celebrate the two-hundredth anniversary of the birth of the greatest writer of the German Enlightenment, Gotthold Ephraim Lessing (1729–81). The Bremen speech was on the very real crisis faced by German publishers and booksellers. German book production

---

6 Paragraph 218 refers the part of the penal code that prohibits abortion. It was a topic of controversy both during the Weimar Republic and through the first decades of the post-war Federal Republic.

(including every kind of book) had reached its highest point in 1925 with 31,595 titles published, about 4000 more than in 1920. In 1930 it descended to 26,961 (Gisela Bruchner, 'Rudolf Borchardt und der Buchhandel', 324). Naturally, the 1930 decline has much to do with the economic crisis that had begun in late 1929. The historical nature of the crisis of the booksellers related to the relatively high prices of books after the reform of the *Reichsmark* that was intended to cure hyperinflation. According to Gisela Bruchner, Borchardt found himself in a paradoxical situation when recommending a plan of action for the German reading public: 'On the one hand, Borchardt had to agree with the German reading public for not buying books any longer, because it naturally has become mistrustful of German literature following the "pseudo-blossoming" of Naturalism. He also recognized, however, that literary taste had changed due to the sociological transformation of readership, and that the public sought entertaining literature rather than edifying or educating literature (Bruchner, 'Rudolf Borchardt', 339).[7]

Borchardt elaborated six reasons for the crisis of the German publishing industry: (1) the weak buying habits of the German public, due in large part to the world economic crisis and high unemployment; (2) the high prices of books; (3) the flood of mass literature, given an impetus by the need for publishers to avoid risks; (4) the indebtedness of booksellers to private capital and technical producers; (5) the loss of a predictable market; and (6) the confusion of a public that has lost any sense of literary continuity (Bruchner, 'Rudolf Borchardt', 293). Borchardt also discussed the role of literary criticism, which in his view had deteriorated in tandem with its object of study. According to Borchardt, the German-speaking countries had produced some great critics, such as Ludwig Speidel (1830–1906), who worked primarily as a theatre critic in Vienna, the Swiss critic and author Josef Viktor Widmann (1842–1911), and Wilhelm Scherer (1841–86), one of the most influential Germanists of the last half of the nineteenth century. 'We had these men not because of, but in spite of newspaper literary supplements' (Borchardt, 'Die Aufgaben der Zeit gegenüber der Literatur', 371; 'Wir haben sie nicht durch das *Feuilleton*, sondern trotz des *Feuilletons* gehabt'). The literary supplement, or *Feuilleton*, of a newspaper frequently carries literary criticism or reviews of books. Borchardt implicity blamed the newspapers, aimed at a broad readership and therefore calling

---

7 The original bogeyman for the 'death' of German literature was Heinrich Heine, accused by Ludwig Börne and later by Karl Kraus with initiating the commercialization of literature. See Anthony Phelan, *Reading Heinrich Heine*, 7–11.

for an accessible criticism aimed at accessible literature, for lowering readers' literary standards. All the apparatus of publishing is present in Germany, but without either the literature or the readership to fill it. Borchardt also proposed three solutions to the publishing crisis: (1) collaboration between presses to reduce costs; (2) a central lending library with branches throughout Germany, which would guarantee a minimum print run for any book; and (3) reduction of Germany's numerous small presses to a few large ones (Bruchner, 'Rudolf Borchardt', 295). The consolidation of the two smaller Munich presses would conform to this strategy. His speech provoked a response by different publishers in a so-called 'Juvenile Literature Booksellers' Circular' (*Jugendbuchhändler-Rundbrief*).[8] Many reports on *DLKR* compare it with this earlier speech.

Borchardt's essay on Lessing pursued in greater detail Borchardt's purported perspective on the decline of German literature. It argued that the idea of a 200th anniversary had something phantasmagorical about it, since the erasure of tradition in German letters meant that the present times had lost any and all vocabulary for understanding the writers of earlier periods such as Lessing. To speak of Lessing's effect on present-day Germany would be to recognize in some sense the Weimar Republic, which Borchardt was not prepared to do. Borchardt used a metaphorical language that made Lessing into a soldier rather than a writer. It would reappear in more virulent form, as Heinz Moenkemeyer ('RBs Lessing-Essay', 146) points out, in *DLKR*, where Lessing joins Goethe and Schiller as horsemen of the apocalypse returning to destroy the capitalist industry that has ruined literature: 'When *Lessing* was its leader, German literature did not tolerate the dictatorship of academic cliques, and when Goethe and Schiller were its leaders, it did not tolerate the dictatorship of coalitions of literary mediocrity. Today, literature declares that we have a responsibility towards it of not tolerating any dictatorship of democracy-tinged, metropolitan big business' (Borchardt, *DLKR*, 10, emphasis added; 'Die deutsche Literatur hat, als Lessing sie führte, keine Akademieklüngel-Diktatur geduldet, als Goethe und Schiller sie führten, keine Diktatur der koalierten Literaturmittelmässigkeiten. Sie erklärt heute, das wir sie verantworten, keine Diktatur des mit der Demokratie verfilzten Grossstadtundernehmertums zu dulden'). This sample passage demonstrates Borchardt's attempts through

---

8   Göpfert claims this has only one precedent in German history: the *Neues Archiv* of the bookseller Johann Jakob Palm of Erlangen at the end of the eighteenth century (Göpfert, 128). Reactions came both in various numbers of the the *Börsenblatt für den deutschen Buchhandel*, and in the *Jungbuchhändlerrundbriefe* 16 (April 1930).

rhetoric to conjoin subsystems. First of all, we see the citation of political and economic language within the context of literature: 'coalition' (*Koalition*) clearly is intended to parody the parliamentary governance that Weimar experimented with for the first time in German history. The word is used almost exclusively to designate the collaboration of two or more political parties to create a parliamentary majority that can then pass legislation. With the phrase 'coalition of literary mediocrity', Borchardt evokes the hostile critics and authors who surrounded Goethe and Schiller in their day, and whom they targeted with the '*Xenien*' in their *Musenalmanach* of 1797. Borchardt prefaces his catachresis with the term 'dictatorship', which presents the opposite situation to that of a coalition: unilateral vs. multilateral decision-making. The following phrase, 'dictatorship of democracy-tinged, metropolitan big business', has a similarly paradoxical ring, though many would recognize the role of large corporations in the replacement of the public sphere with, as Habermas puts it, a 'pseudo-public' one. The invoking of metropolitan capitalism brings the economic system into the picture, recalling some of the points Borchardt had made in his Bremen speech about the publishing industry.

Considering Borchardt's career and the speeches and essays that immediately preceded *DLKR*, then, there is something to Alfred Beerbaum's contention that the poet spoke for no political party and spared neither side of the conflict. Nor was Borchardt the only literatus to argue that German literature was in grave peril: the scholar Ernst Robert Curtius published his *German Spirit in Danger* (*Deutscher Geist in Gefahr*) in the same year of 1932. Borchardt has a double mission in *DLKR*. One of these, which he had rehearsed in his Bremen speech, was to decry 'the dessication and soul-killing of German literature over the last fifty years, and the concentration of economic power in the hands of publishing corporations and trade publishers' (Borchardt, *DLKR*, 8; 'die im Literatentume des verflossenen Halbjahrhunderts vollzogene Abnüchterung und Entseelung des deutschen Schrifttums und die Konzentrierung wirtschaftlicher Macht in den Händen der Aktienverlage und der Handelsgesellschaften'). Paradoxically, however, in line with his earlier suggestions for overcoming the publishing crisis, Borchardt greets the takeover of two small Munich presses, the Georg Müller Verlag and the Albert Langen Verlag, by a monopolistic concern, though more of a union organization than a firm, the DHV. Borchardt insists that his writing does not stem from any affinity of his own political position with that of the clerks' organization: 'Differences of principle separate me utterly from any party-political activity of the DHV, as well as from its representatives in parliament and its populist-conservative fellow-travellers' (Borchardt, 7–8; 'Von der parteipolitischen Betätigung des Deutschnationalen Händlungsgehilfenverbandes, seiner parlamentarischen Vertreter wie derjenigen seiner volkskonservativen Parteifreunde trennen mich grundsätzliche Gesinnungen [...] unüberbrückbar'). The DHV is less sympathetic to Borchardt than folks from the other side of the fence. Making the same point from a reversed perspective, Borchardt notes that the Hanseaten Verlag, with its healthy *Unterhaltungsliteratur* (roughly, mass-market literature), is as meaningless to him as that press's opponents' pernicious *Unterhaltungsliteratur*. He is on the side of those presses that gave their all for the German nation, a group which for him includes Cotta, Göschen, Perthes and Brockhaus, as well as the two small presses acquired by the DHV. Borchardt published frequently with the Bremer Presse, led by Drs Wolde and Wiegand. 'Their programme was to offer the best in German literature, make highly discriminating selections of new works, and show the scope and basic unity of the body of the nation's literary culture in anthologies and translations' (*25 Jahre Georg-Müller Verlag*, 9). Rowohlt published most of Borchardt's plays, while the twelve-volume *Schriften. Handlungen und Abhandlungen* (1928) and his story collection, *Das hoffnungslose Geschlecht*, were published with the Horen Verlag. With these and other statements, Borchardt tries to give the appearance of neutrality, when in fact he was – as the epigraphs to this chapter show – more or less a hired attorney of the fused presses, and through them of their parent owner, the DHV. He had signed a contract with Langen in 1930 to deliver a biography of Goethe for the hundredth anniversary of that author's death. Ten thousand Reichsmark were paid as an advance for this project, which Borchardt never delivered on. Instead, he dictated *DLKR* in two days in the building of the Albert Langen Verlag. Pezold provided many of the details for the pamphlet, such as the minutes of the meeting of the *Buchhändler Börsenverein* that he uses. (Pezold would later retract these in a letter to Borchardt dated 16 September 1931, on which more below).

The DHV acquired in 1928 a Georg Müller Verlag that was on the verge of bankruptcy, and its authors threatened with being remaindered (*25 Jahre Georg-Müller Verlag*, 12). The press had just celebrated its twenty-fifth anniversary with a handsome volume, complete with portraits of some of its authors. The celebratory book had contained a warning that might as well have been composed by Borchardt, except that it uses 'summer literature' as a synonym for '*Unterhaltungsliteratur*': 'The twenty-fifth anniversary of the founding of the press occurs during difficult times for elite literature [*hohe Literatur*]. The ongoing economic crisis, whose causes everyone knows but whose solution requires men whom Germany currently lacks, continues to gnaw at the marrow of the German publishing industry. […] Sales of good, handsomely produced books suffer from the impoverishment of the more intellectual circles, while the demand for cheap 'summer literature' has risen dramatically' (*25 Jahre*, n. p.). Borchardt singles out for special praise the authors Kolbenheyer, Wilhelm Schäfer and Paul Ernst. Today's reader would perhaps more readily recognize names such as Johannes Schlaf, Franz Pocci, Theodor Däubler and Frank Wedekind, who were also published there.

Let us briefly examine the careers of Kolbenheyer and Schäfer (1868–1952), whom Borchardt seemed to regard as the special stars of the Müller Verlag, and who, along with Borchardt, have been subsequently forgotten by later literary history. Kolbenheyer is mentioned in some of the reporting on the case as a co-conspirator against Krause. He was born in Budapest, studied in Vienna, and later lived in Tübingen and Munich. His work was awarded several literary prizes, and he became a member of the Prussian Academy of the Arts in 1926. Weimar awarded him a *Goethe Medaille*. Unlike Borchardt, Kolbenheyer suffered few difficulties in Nazi Germany, to the extent that the Allies evicted him from his house in Munich after the war. His most successful work was the *Paracelsus* trilogy, published between 1917 and 1925, three historical novels that followed the birth and career of the famous alchemist. They are full of dialogue crafted in a literary imitation of Alemannic dialect. The first of these sold 25,000 copies by 1930, the second and third in a similar range.[9] Along with Wilhelm Schäfer, Kolbenheyer resigned from the Berlin Academy of the Arts in protest over an alleged power-grab by the left-leaning author Alfred Döblin. Schäfer seems to have been the best-selling of all the Müller Verlag authors, principally due to his *Thirteen Books of the German Soul* (*Dreizehn Bücher der deutschen Seele*) of 1922, which sold 90,000 copies by 1935 (Donald Richards, *The German Bestseller*, 208).

We will see below that Borchardt contrasts elite literature that comes out of tradition with the industrial product of *Massenliteratur*. Two additional names mentioned by Borchardt in *DLKR* are Hugo von Hofmannsthal and Emil Strauss. According to Borchardt, both are victims of the capitalization of the publishing industry: 'A higher-up from Hofmannsthal's publisher told me years ago that the

---

9 Figures from Donald Richards, 168–9. The third volume of the trilogy was published in 1926, and its decreased overall sales compared to the first two are probably indicative of the publishing crisis Borchardt spoke about in his Bremen speech.

time-to-print of that author's works has been repeatedly prolonged by the fact that the print runs for his work bear no relation to the usual sales volumes. I believe it. The work of Emil Strauss, that precious jewel of solid German imaginative art, has lain captive for decades at the same publisher's [...] while literary prizes search for worthy candidates, and the Thomas Manns, Frank Wedekinds and Carl Sternheims of the literary world are celebrated (Borchardt, *DLKR*, 43–4; 'Ein leitender Beamter des Verlegers Hofmannsthals hat mir vor Jahren gesagt, die verlegerische Gestion diese Werkes werde dadurch immer wieder merklich erschwert, dass es ausserhalb der übrigen Verlagsmasse ganz für sich stehe. Das will ich glauben. Das Werk Emil Straussens, dies köstliche Juwel gediegener deutscher Phantasiekunst [...] hat durch Jahrzehnte im gleichen Verlage wie unter Bleidächern gefangen gelegen. [...] während für Literaturpreise nach Würdigen gesucht wurde, während die Mann, Wedekind, Sternheim bejubelt wurden').

In spite of the alleged excellence of its authors, Borchardt maintains that the Georg Müller Verlag practically deserved what it got, since 'the press approached more than once the undiscriminating and valueless, inflated publishing plethora of the bad pre-war German style, in which the good was mixed with the bad, the genuine with the phoney' (Borchardt, *DLKR*, 14; 'Der Verlag grenzte mit mehr als einem Zuge an die kriterienlose und wahllose, plethorisch aufgeschwemmte Büchermacherei des schlechten deutschen Vorkreigsstiles, in der das Beste, das Üble, Echtes und Unechtes durcheinanderschwammen'). Müller embodied the contrast of Schwabing between the Bohemian and the *stamm* Bavarian; its list 'dissolves the contrasts between a miscarriage like Wedekind and a classic of dialect and regionalism like Ludwig Thoma into a common stew' (Borchardt, *DLKR*, 14 'die Gegensätze zwischen einer schnöden Spottgeburt wie Wedekind und einem Klassiker der Mundart und Landesart wie Ludwig Thoma in einer Gemeinbrühe aufgelöst'). Borchardt is completely consistent in placing himself on the side of telluric regionalism at the expense of a literature open to international influences.

Borchardt claims that both the *Frankfurter Allgemeine Zeitung* (17.06.31) and the *BT* (14.06.31) spun Krause's death as a political theme, whereby the presses' purchase by the DHV meant that it was being pulled to the right by Hugenberg. Nevertheless, Borchardt is writing to defend 'the great and courageous German press in Munich, on whose self-defence against the opportunists of German literary decay I hereby appoint the public as judge, holding in my hands the terrible documents' (Borchardt, *DLKR*, 6–7; 'das grosse und tapfere deutsche Verlagsunternehmen in München, über dessen plötzlich entstandene harte Notwehr gegen die Nutzniesser des deutschen literarischen Verfalles ich hier, mit den erschreckenden Dokumenten in Händen, das Publikum zum Richter bestelle'). This is the first of many perlocutionary statements in the pamphlet, where Borchardt rhetorically bestows upon himself, his opponents, or (as in this case) his readers offices and positions through which they may affect change. The public, as judge, will decide *Recht/Unrecht* in the case of Krause. This is, of course, the struggle that the title of Borchardt's pamphlet alludes to – a literal legal battle between left-wing newspapers, especially the *BT*, and the publishers of German national literature.

The *BT* had been founded in 1872 to fill a gap in the periodical world of the capital of a newly minted Germany, whose current offerings were more provincial. Its founder, Theodor Wolff, was an important figure in the politics of Wilhelmine Germany. Its main drama reviewer, Alfred Kerr, became one of the most important arbiters of literary taste of the period. The *BT* was liberal, open to the world, and strove to be entertaining. In the period in question, the *BT* was unambiguously against National Socialism from the beginning. While it called the shots correctly, Gotthart Schwarz believes that its political analyses were too focused on 'moral condemnation of superficial phenomena' (Schwartz, 'Berliner', 326).

Borchardt made the mistake of naming names in *DLKR*. The following sentence impugning the motives of *BT* reporter Werner Richter crossed into the realm of libel: 'Whatever the deceased's motives might have been, Mr Werner Richter, Munich reporter for the *BT*, insists on having us consider "this case as one of the most dismal in the sad history of post-WWI Munich". This sad chapter, and the name of Mr Werner Richter set below it, are a journalistic swindle' (Borchardt, *DLKR*, 21–2; 'Es möge mit dem Toten gegangen sein, wie es wolle, Herr Werner Richter, Münchener Berichterstatter des *Berliner Tageblatts* will "an diesem Falle eines der trübsten Kapitel aus der traurigen Geschichte Nachkriegsmünchens" aufzeigen. Dies traurige Kapitel und Herrn Richters daruntergesetzter Verfassername sind ein Zeitungsschwindel'). The swindle alluded to here is not the invention of non-existent people as witnesses, but the substitution of a tendentious accusation by the DHV's nemesis, the Association of German Bookdealers, for Richter's own investigative work. Further, 'This genial fellow must have closed an eye on account of the collective, or perhaps he cashed in an honorarium for the reproduction of his "intellectual property"? [...] Such a move serves to characterize Mr Richter as what he is, a pitiable tool' (Borchardt, *DLKR*, 15; 'Er muss, der gutmütige Mann, um der gemeinsamen Sache willen, ein Auge zugedrückt habe, oder er hat, vielleicht, ein Nachdruckshonorar liquidiert, zum Schutze seines "geistigen Eigentums"? [...] Damit ist Herr Richter als das gekennzeichnet, was er ist, ein armseliges Instrument'). Specifically, Richter is a cog in the machine of the leftist journalistic forces working against the presses that publish national literature. Richter's lawsuit against Borchardt centred on these two rhetorical excesses: 'journalistic swindle' and 'pitiable tool'. While Borchardt accused Richter of doing work-for-hire, a number of reviews said the same thing about *DLKR*, mentioning the honorarium Borchardt had received for writing it (2400 Reichsmark).

Borchardt mentions that he has in his hands the minutes of the general meeting of the Association of German Bookdealers (*Arbeitgeberverband der Deutschen Buchhändler*) of 1 May 1931. These minutes contain an entry under the harmless-sounding 'Miscellaneous' ('*Verschiedenes*') that urges an investigation of the DHV, including a preparation of the list of the presses that are now under their control. Borchardt characterizes the presumed monopolistic tendencies behind such an attitude as 'You are the state' ('*Der Staat seid Ihr*') There is, however, one individual who leads the fight against the DHV:

> And because this man stands at the head of the only German publisher that one is forced to call outright a book factory, I hereby publicly strip him – and him alone – of the protection of anonymity and call him by name the unscrupulous nemesis of every sacrificing German intellectual worker: he is the General Director of the DVA, [Gustav] Kilpper. For me and for German literature, for which I am the spokesperson, he is a cipher.

> Und da dieser Mann an der Spitze des einzigen deutschen Verlages steht, den man klipp und klar eine Bücherfabrik nennen muss [...] so erkenne ich ihm, und ihm allein, den Ehrenschutz der Anonymität hier öffentlich ab und nenne den bedenkenlosen Beschädiger eines aufoperfernden Arbeiters am deutschen Geiste beim Namen: is ist der Generaldirektor der Deutschen Verlagsanstalt, Kilpper. [...] Mir gegenüber und der deutschen Literatur, für die ich das Wort führe, ist er ein Nichts.

> (Borchardt, *DLKR*, 36)

The 'book factory' referred to is the Deutsche Verlags-Anstalt, or DVA. If Borchardt earlier had employed legal terminology with terms like *int. prop.*, here he cites more the performative modality. Twice he performs a legal, or pseudo-legal, act through perlocutionary rhetoric: he reveals Kilpper's name. We are familiar with anonymity as a legal issue when reporters are forced to reveal the names of their sources, for example. Secondly, Borchardt assumes the position of speaking on behalf of German literature, becoming its attorney. How Borchardt's words relate to the words of literature itself is unclear. Borchardt's literary coup in assuming the direction of literature is an example of the personal characteristics that Benjamin perceived at a much earlier stage of his career, as stated in the epigraph: 'the lie takes hold of [Borchardt] each time he defines his relation to the public'.

Reactions to the Pamphlet

As though accepting Borchardt's position as spokesperson, the German press responded to *DLKR*. 'Reviews' of Borchardt's pamphlet, ranging from one paragraph to several columns in length, appeared in at least twenty-eight German newspapers.[10] In reading the various appraisals of Borchardt's pamphlet that appeared in different newspapers, one would think that the reviewers had been reading several radically different variants of *DLKR*. Conservative reviewers (the majority) found Borchardt's arguments convincing, his rhetoric persuasive, and the threat to German literature very real. Periodicals that tended more towards the left noted the hypocrisy of Borchardt presenting himself as the preserver of German values just before running off to his residence in Italy, and found that his rhetoric undercut itself in its excesses.

As is clear from the foregoing, *DLKR* was not a work of literary criticism per se. Yet there were a few who interpreted it at least as a directive for the practice of German criticism. Dr Gunther Haupt, for example, wrote a piece published in the *Fränkischer Kurier* just a few days before Borchardt's trial began.[11] Haupt posits that the immediate goal of *DLKR*, the defence of the three presses, is only secondary to its underlying message concerning the relationship between criticism and literature. Haupt points out an unintended consequence of giving second- and third-rate authors the impression that their 'Germanness' (*'deutsche Gesinnung'*) is more important than their literary talent, and that German literature is in need of

---

10 There was some duplication or 'syndication' of reviews. One written by Niels Hansen, for example, appeared in *Der Deutsche* (Berlin) on 31 July 1931, in the *Tägliche Rundschau* (Berlin) on 2 August, and in the *Zeitung für Ostpommern* on 4 August.
11 Gunther Haupt, 'Die Aufgaben des deutschen Schrifttums in der Gegenwart', *Fränkischer Kurier* (Nuremberg), 18 January 1932. Further reviews discussed will be noted in-text by newspaper name and date.

more patriotic compositions: 'we assume Germanness in every decent person, be he poet or critic, as well as in the reader. But a work of literary art that depends solely on Germanness is not art' ('Eine vaterländische Gesinnung setzen wir bei jedem anständigen Menschen voraus, beim dichter, beim Kritiker, ebenso wie beim Leser, aber ein Kunstwerk, das sich nur auf sie berufen kann, ist keins'). Such poets should refrain from burdening the public with the need to buy their products simply to keep them alive. Good writers should encourage criticism of their work, and critics should carry out their function according to the rules of art rather than to the exigencies of political partisanship.

The literary-critical aspect of the pamphlet can also be seen in the fact that it was reviewed by some well-known contemporary authors. Perhaps the most prominent of these was Hanns Johst (1890–1978), an Expressionist dramatist best remembered today as being the target of Bertolt Brecht's parodic early play, *Baal*, and for the quip, 'Whenever I hear of culture ... I release the safety-catch of my Browning!' from the play *Schlageter*, which phrase became associated with Nazi attitudes towards literature and art. Johst's review of *DLKR* was published under the title 'Fifty Pages of Courageous Prose' in the *Münchener Neueste Nachrichten* on 12 September 1931, making it a rather late contribution to the culture wars surrounding the pamphlet. Johst's contribution is epistolary, a letter to an 'Esteemed Friend of Literature' (*'Verehrter Bücherfreund'*). Johst then cites Borchardt indirectly to characterize the rights of literary works: 'Once they appear as books, the writer sees his works as engaged in a struggle for existence, in an existential struggle for their rights' ('Erst einmal in Buchform, sieht [der Dichter] seine Werke im Kampf um ihre Existenz, im Existenzkampf um ihr Recht'). Johst follows Borchardt in attributing rights to works, an unheard-of legal conception. Johst next devotes several paragraphs to the idea of what makes literature political, arriving at the conclusion that 'when someone writes in a popular, telluric style, if he limits his events to personal experiences of his actual existence as a German, then he counts as an author of the "very low country" and is dismissed mistrustfully as "national"; for the representative author of the Republic must have at least a European, and hopefully a human sensitivity. [...] He must behave himself according to the requirements of the world-press' ('Schreibt nun einer volksgemäss, erdgebunden, entwickelt er seine Vorgänge aus den persönlich begrenzten Erlebnissen seines wirklichen Daseins, als deutscher Mensch, so gilt er a priori als Dichter des "sehr platten Landes" und wird mistrauisch als völkisch abgegolten; denn der republikaisch-repräsentative Dichter muss, wenn nicht menschheitlich zumindest:

europäisch empfinden. [...] Er muss sich überhaupt so aufführen, wie es das Weltbild der Weltpresse voraussetzt'). Johst then tells his imaginary friend that Rudolf Borchardt's *DLKR* will reveal to him the machinations of this world-press, which includes its characterization of the merger of the two presses under the umbrella of the DHV as a 'counter-revolution'.

The *Vossische Zeitung* (Morgen-Ausgabe 25 October 1931) claimed to not have a dog in the fight, since they had always maintained an open mind towards 'any intellectual achievement' ('jede geistige Leistung') and had not been specifically attacked by Borchardt the way the *BT* and the *FAZ* had been. As an ostensibly neutral observer, its impression of Borchardt is of a 'megalomaniacal broadside-writer who uses every rhetorical trick and an incomparable demagogy' ('grössenwahnsinniger Pamphletist mit allen erdenklichen dialektischen Kniffen und einer nicht mehr zu überbietenden Demagogie'). Similarly, the *Niedersachsen* of Bremen (22 October 1931) published a short piece by Franz Wellmann, who remarked how difficult it was to judge such a flaming polemic ('flammende Streitschrift') objectively. He recommends it to those interested in the purity of German literature, but notes some slips in style and the many, mostly unnecessary foreign words. I have only found a few other articles that criticize *DLKR* for its style and inflammatory rhetoric. To today's reader at least, the pathos of passages such as the following works to its own detriment through exaggeration:

> Hands up! Nobody move in this den of iniquity! [...] Authors like [Paul] Alverdes lost? Not as long as I have a sword left in my hands. [...] If we're going to war, then not once, but twice. *A corsaire corsaire et demi*.[12] To speak with Goethe in German: against a bandit, one and a half bandits.
>
> [Hände hoch, und keiner rühre sich in dieser Mordschenke der Niedertracht. [...] Menschen wie Alverdes verloren? Nicht solange ich lebe und eine Klinge schlage. [...] Wenn Krieg sein soll, – nicht einmal, zweimal Krieg. *A corsaire corsaire et demi*. Zu gut deutsch und goethisch: Auf einen Schelmen anderthalbe.]
> (Borchardt, DLKR 27)[13]

---

12 'Against a pirate, one and one-half pirates.'
13 Paul Alverdes (1897–1979), who was severely wounded in World War I, was another of the decidedly minor authors whose work Borchardt was enamoured of. His early work tended to report on war as a transformative human experience.

On the other hand, however, a rather astounding number of writers – Borchardt wannabes? – echoed in their own rhetoric the overwrought metaphors of '*Kampf*' found in the pamphlet. The *Deutsche Rundschau* praised Borchardt's 'masterfully condensed and affecting language' (12 September 1931; 'meisterhaft geballte und eindringliche Sprache'), the *Deutsche Allgemeine Zeitung* his 'virtuoso polemical abilities' (5 August 1931; 'virtuose polemische Fähigkeiten'). The *Kölnische Volkszeitung* (15 January 1932) embraces Borchardt's legal metaphorics, expressing gratitude to this supposed 'master of the German word' ('Meister des deutschen Worts') for his 'judgment' ('Richtspruch') and 'flaming verdict' ('flammenden Verdikt'). The *Münchener-Augsburger Abendzeitung* (18 September 1931) begins with the following: 'Listen up! In the area of literature we have not witnessed a manly deed for a long time now' ('Alle Achtung! Auf literarischem Gebiet haben wir seit langer Zeit keine mannhafte Tat erlebt'). Naturally, the article goes on to say that the publication of *DLKR* represents one such longed-for deed. It goes on to note that the battle for Germanness is carried out with 'blazing sword' ('blitzendem Degen'). The *Generalanzeiger* of Dortumund agrees that Borchardt's work may help German literature and *'Geist'* attain its rights (16 August 1931; 'zum Rechte verhelfen'). The *Schlesische Zeitung* (8 August 1931) speaks of the 'nearly ruined German literature'. The *Berliner Lokal-Anzeiger* speaks of the two sides in the battle over German literature as in a declared 'state of war' (12 August 1931; 'der Kriegszustand ist erklärt'). The *Goslarsche Zeitung* (10 August 1931) calls Borchardt a 'leader-type' ('Führerpersönlichkeit') and adds the names of opprobrium to the list of 'un-German' literature: '[Carl] Sternheim, [Alfred] Wolfenstein, [Carl] Zuckmayer, Friedrich Wolff, Vicky Baum, Emil Ludwig Cohn, [Erich] Remarque, Lion Feuchtwanger, Jakob Haringer'. In sum, a not insignificant number of readers seem to have bought into and even expanded the vocabulary of law and of struggle that Borchardt makes use of.

The Legal Cases

The Borchardt pamphlet provoked not one, but several trials. Gustav Kilpper's reaction to his denigration in the *DLKR* led to a hearing before the German Publishers' Disciplinary Committee (*Ehrenrat des Deutschen Verlegervereins*) on 19 December 1931. Though such paralegal committees do not exert the degree of compulsory power that a state court has, for example of fining and imprisoning, their observations can result in actions being taken that affect the standing of members within the institution. The result of this particular hearing was that an understanding was reached between the parties, as part of which the director of the Langen Verlag, Pezold, abandoned Borchardt in order to come to a mutual agreement with his accuser. Pezold and Kilpper published mutual apologies in early January and Borchardt's pamphlet was removed from circulation. Pezold's admission consisted of three points: (1) he denied the correctness of Borchardt's indictment of Kilpper or of any other publisher for the negative newspaper articles against the Müller and Langen presses; (2) he acknowledged and retracted the specific errors in *DLKR* in this regard, and expressed regret over the attacks on Kilpper in that pamphlet and in a letter of 7 October 1931; and (3) he stated his intention to remove *DLKR* from circulation, on the basis that substantial portions of the pamphlet had been proven to be inaccurate. The last point was carried out around 10 January 1932, and again was widely reported in the German press, mostly without comment. Only the *Neckar-Zeitung* of Heilbronn saw fit to editorialize that the essence of *DLKR* did not lie in its attack on specific persons, nor in the smaller details of the issues it addressed, but in its 'struggle against the leveling and commercializing of [German] literature, a struggle for poetry against writing' (14 January 1932; 'ein Kampf gegen die Verflachung und Merkantilisierung des Schrifttums, ein Kampf für die Dichtung gegen die Literatur').[14]

The case heard by the Frank court in Munich on 20 January 1932 was symmetrical in terms of its claims and counter-claims. The department chiefs (*Schriftleiter*) of two newspapers, the *BT* and the *Münchner Post*, were being sued by Gustav Pezold, CEO of the two merged presses, represented by his attorneys Edgard Julius Jung and Otto Leibrecht, because of their reporting which claimed that Krause's firing had been politically motivated and that Pezold had been negligent in not taking more seriously the possibility that Krause would kill himself over the incident. The *Berliner Tageblatt*, represented by Dr Hirschberg, countersued in the course of the trial, but the court ruled that the statute of limitations had run out for filing a claim.[15]

---

14 It is difficult to translate the opposition in German between *'Dichtung'* and *'Literatur'* – *'Dichtung'* is a somewhat broader concept than poetry and could very well be rendered with English 'literature', while *'Literatur'* is used here in its most deflated English sense of anything written down, as in 'Let me give you some literature that describes our products'. On the other hand, *'Literatur'* clearly assumes its most high-flown cultural valence in the title of Borchardt's pamphlet.

15 There are conflicting accounts in the newspapers, some claiming that the countersuit had been allowed, but possibly confusing it with the separate suit filed against Borchardt back in September. Again, it is important to keep in mind that no official transcript of the trial was taken. I have not followed this matter further, since it is a formal aspect subsidiary to the literary questions raised by the trial.

The charge of *'Beleidigung'* (literally 'insult') under which this trial was conducted corresponds to paragraphs 185, 186 and 187 of the German criminal code (*Reichsstrafgesetzbuch*) in force at the time. *Beleidigung* corresponds to the Roman concept of 'iniuria', but restricts the destroyed or damaged object to one's honour. Another word for *Beleidigung* is *'Ehrangriff'* (literally, an attack on one's honour). A synonym for *'guter Ruf'* is *'Ehre'*, and it is clear that in this instance Richter's reputation as a reporter was attacked through the direct statements in the *DLKR* quoted above. Paragraph 193 made an exception that allowed for attacks out of *'berechtigtes Interesse'*. This legal concept, which literally means 'justified interest', constitutes a defence in the case of slander or libel. A readily comprehensible example would be a defence attorney who makes disparaging remarks about the complainant. The attorney presumably makes these in the interest of defending his client, and is not liable as long as his actions appear to lie within that interest. The German press of this era wanted this defence interpreted in the broadest sense: that everything published in a newspaper or journal was in the public's interest and thus should remain immune from prosecution (Nicolaus Schierloh, *Die Beleidigung in den §§185, 186, 187 RStGB*, 93).

German trials of the era were not stenographically transcribed, so reports of what happens in courtrooms depends upon newspaper and other reporting, the memories of those involved, and the verdict that was typed out and became a public document. As with everything else related to this case, the reports of the trial and its outcome differed vastly according to the political position of the newspaper reporting them. The *BT* could hardly be expected to provide neutral coverage of the trial, even if neutrality had been considered a virtue at the time. Its pages (21 January 1932) purported to reveal much about the 'latest in widespread reactionary fashionability' ('viel verbreitete reaktionäre Modeströmungen'), went over the whole ground of the death of Krause once more, and focused on several letters he had written that indicated his increasing discomfort within a business in which there was constant invocation of 'Germanness' (*'deutsches Volkstum'*). The *Münchener Post* 'blamed the victim' by claiming that the secretary had been with Krause for years without reporting any untoward incidents and that she was known for carrying out gymnastic exercises in the office in front of everyone.

Witnesses included Pezold who had done the firing, the secretary allegedly harassed by Krause (heard behind closed doors), most of the permanent staff of the Müller Verlag, and a Dr Steffens who, as head of the DHV union, had made decisions on how to cut off

Krause's widow as quickly as possible from benefits – strategies which he proudly shared with the court. Mr Fritzsche testified at having found the secretary crying in the corridor and having reported this to Pezold, who decided on firing Krause the next day. This testimony (especially of the secretary) undoubtedly led the Frank court to decide that the harassment issue had been a real one, and that the imputation of political motivation in the *BT* was unfounded.

The judgment in both cases was given on 26 January. Each of the bureau chiefs of *BT* and the *Münchner Post* was fined 500 marks and ordered to pay court costs. Weighing against the two newspapers was the clearly political intent of their reporting on the matter. So far this looked like a victory for the conservative Pezold and for the DHV. However, Rudolf Borchardt was also found guilty of libel against Werner Richter, the Munich correspondent of the *BT*. Borchardt was sentenced to a fine of 600 marks or ten days in gaol, payment of court costs, the destruction of the plates from which *DLKR* had been printed, and publishing of a retraction in three periodicals, so the score in the end stood 1000–600 in favour of the right wing. The court recognized to a slight degree the defense of *'berechtigtes Interesse'*. Borchardt, who was holed up at his villa in Italy and not present at the trial, had his costs borne by Müller-Langen. While widely reported in newspapers, the trial of Borchardt did not call forth the essayistic responses that the initial publication of *DLKR* had. Oddly, many newspapers only announced the result of the Borchardt trial rather than of both, leaving the mistaken impression that the *BT* had carried the day.

The View from Italy

At a moment of great political and economic danger in which your presses and the DHV found itself, you appointed me as your attorney.

[Sie haben mich […] in einem Augenblicke schwerster politischer und geschäftlicher Gefahr für Ihre Betriebe und die Geltung des DHV, um eine öffentliche Anwaltschaft beschworen.]

Borchardt to Pezold (*Briefe*, 132–3)

Forbidden by his lawyers from attending the trial, Borchardt followed the events from Italy. In his correspondence – between letters written in Italian asking for repairs to the villa he was renting in Saltocchio and for extensions on his payment of rent, and letters to his publishers in Germany asking for money, including a long and detailed letter to Pezold asking, essentially, for publication of various works that would justify yet another advance from the press to help maintain his existence – Borchardt weighed in on the legal issues swirling around *DLKR*. Even at this distance, the trial weighed heavily on him. He reported his feelings in a letter to his friend Edgar Jung dated 15 February 1932: that the verdict horrified him, and that the matter was a 'crisis' that he may or may not survive (Borchardt, *Briefe*, 143).

The centrepiece of Borchardt's long-distance interventions in his trial was a writ for his lawyer, Otto Leibrecht, which takes up ten printed pages in Borchardt's published correspondence (Borchardt, *Briefe*, 73–84). The writ is labeled 'draft', and it is unclear whether it, or a version of it, was ever sent to Leibrecht, and if so, whether it was forwarded to the complainant. The arguments Borchardt raises in it, couched in a densely legalistic prose (e.g. with a highly consistent use of 'plaintiff' [*Kläger*] and 'defendant' [*Beklagter*]), seem not to have been presented at the trial, in which – as noted above – the defence relied mostly on the concept of *'berechtigtes Interesse'*. Among the points Borchardt raises are: (1) that his own tone in *DLKR* was inevitable, given the tone of Richter's published articles; (2) that the length of time between publication of *DLKR* and the lawsuit is suspect; (3) that there was a misunderstanding of Borchardt's use of 'swindle' (*Schwindel*), in that he had never meant that Richter himself was not the author of his pieces but that he was using information supplied by publishers interested in smearing Müller-Langen and the DHV; (4) that the accusation that *DLKR* claims that Kilpper fed Richter information is found nowhere in the text; (5) that anything touching Kilpper in the complaint is null due to the fact that Kilpper himself has consistently refused to sue; and (6) that the specific terminology used in *DLKR* that became the target of the lawsuit has objective validity and is therefore not libellous. Borchardt ends with the statement that he would appear in person at the trial – a vow that was not to be fulfilled. Shortly thereafter, in another letter, Borchardt wrote of the trial – in indirect discourse, assuming the language of the enemy Richter – as a confrontation between 'Aryan' and Jew.

Playing the Race Card in Weimar

Johannes R. Becher is a German author. He is neither a Jew, nor a foreigner.

[Johannes R. Becher ist ein deutscher Autor. Er ist weder Jude noch landfremd.]

Franz Hollering (*Der literarische Hochverrat von Johannes R. Becher*, 11)

The claimant's protest that he, Werner Richter, is Aryan while the defendant is a member of the Jewish race has no bearing on the question of whether claimant's civil rights have been violated by the defendant through slander and libel.

[Die klägerische Protestation, (Werner Richter) selbst sei Arier, während Beklagter ein Angehöriger der jüdischen Rasse sei, kann für die Frage, ob Kläger von Beklagtem durch üble Nachrede und Beleidigung in seinen bürgerlichen Rechten benachteiligt worden sei, nicht als erheblich angesehen werden.]

Rudolf Borchardt (*Briefe*, 79–80)

Jews are not mentioned in the Weimar Constitution (which was in large part drafted by a Jew, Hugo Preuss). That silence is significant, since it brings to an apparent end the treatment of Jews throughout German history as separate fiefdoms, whose obligations, rights and privileges were to be embodied separately from those of Germans. For example, Jewish secular law in Germany begins not with legislation, but with charters.[16] As with the elimination of the pockets of exceptionality vis à vis marriage examined earlier, so too the various exceptions for 'race' and the restrictions on the holding of many offices to Christians were eliminated. Yet the quotes above tell us that, on a practical level, the special treatment of Jews continued in the legal system. In defending his client Becher, a Communist who would later become the poet laureate of the German Democratic Republic, on a charge of having committed 'treason through literature' ('*literarischer Hochverrat*') by publishing his 1925 anti-war novel *Levisite*, Franz Hollering played the Weimar race card. The similarities to the card played by Richter's lawyer against Borchardt are obvious enough, and constitute a set of opposites. Most crucially, the race card played in defending Becher emphasizes his Germanness as a defence, implicitly condoning differential treatment and justice as 'just us', whereas Borchardt appeals to the race neutrality that was embodied in the modern legal system.

Borchardt also played the race card against himself, however. Besides the *Börsenverein der Deutschen Buchhändler*, Borchardt also identified as the enemies of German literature 'the Jewish literary publishing corporations' ('*die jüdische Literatur-Verlagsaktiengesellschaften*'), which 'are in the process of building an alliance and exerting pressure on the public sphere and on the book trade' (Borchardt, *DLKR*, 26; 'mit Hilfe "ihrer" Presse sowohl

---

16 For a concise overview of the beginnings of Jewish secular law in Europe, see Mark Cohen, *Under Crescent and Cross*, 43–51.

den GMV wie auch dessen Autoren publizistisch unterdrücken und mundtot machen wollen'). During the trial itself, Richter's lawyer Löwenfeld is reported by the newspaper *Deutsche Republik* to have called the defendant 'Adolf Hitler's pet Jew' (13 February 1932; 'Lieblingsjuden Adolf Hitlers').[17] Again, no protocol was taken of the trial and it is impossible to provide the 'thick description' we would want of the use of such a term, assuming it was used at all. But a later press report against Löwenfeld notes that he had impugned Borchardt's honour during the trial, which may be a reference to this remark.[18] According to Iris Hamel, the DHV on whose behalf Borchardt was indirectly working was an actively anti-Semitic organization: 'Its founders saw Jews not only as representatives of capitalism, but also as the destroyers of national unity. [...] The DHV contributed significantly to the formation of nationalistic thought. It contributed to the conversion of cultural anti-Semitism into political anti-Semitism' ('Schon seine Gründer sahen im Juden nicht nur den Repräsentanten des Kapitalismus, sonder auch den Zerstörer der nationalen Einheit. [...] So hat der DHV massgeblich an der Ausbildung des völkischen Gedankenguts mitgewirkt. Er trug dazu bei, dass der vorwiegend gefühlsmässige Antisemitismus durch eine politische Judenfeindschaft ersetzt wurde' (Hamel, *Völkischer Verband*, 268).

In his own summing up of the trial in the *BT*, the 'Aryan' Werner Richter claimed that 'Borchardt is obviously a victim of his drive to assimilate' (n.p.; 'Borchardt ist offenkundig – und das ist wohl die Lösung aller dieser Rätsel – ein Opfer seines Assimilationstriebes geworden'). Richter does not elaborate much on this idea, expounding instead on the conservative lifestyle that Borchardt flaunted, which in the actual Prussian Junkers had a certain majesty, but which in Borchardt betrays at every turn its true purpose of covering up his inner anxieties. In a questionable piece of literary psychoanalysis, Richter uses the technical term 'overcompensation' for Borchardt's alleged psychic state. He needed to become more German than German in order to compensate for his racial marginality. It is a judgment on Borchardt that has been repeated first of all by Adorno, in the article from which this

---

17 The author of this article was Wolfgang Petzet, who was mainly active in theatre and film criticism, and author of a 1931 book against film censorship, *Verbotene Filme*.
18 *Münchener Telegramm-Zeitung*, 21 January 1932. The article is titled 'Münchener Rechtsanwalt als Kläger', and reports that Löwenfeld sued for defamation of character. The Frank court was again called into action, and obtained the same result: the monthly *Deutsches Volkstum* and Löwenfeld were each sentenced to pay a fine of 600 Marks.

chapter's epigraph was drawn, by Benjamin as discussed above, and by Heinz Politzer, whose article on Borchardt, 'Poet of Assimilation', appeared in English in the journal *Commentary* in 1950. Politzer notes that Borchardt's fate demonstrated 'the extreme irony of an extreme Jewish destiny. In the end his roots proved stronger than all those forces in him that had asserted themselves by seeking to deny his origins' (Politzer, 'Poet', 64).

Conclusion

As soon as Borchardt's pamphlet was withdrawn, it became, even to those who had previously shown interest, a 'literary curiosity' (Neckar Zeitung, 14 January 1932; 'literarisches Kuriosum'), but of course the term 'curiosity' is double-edged: it implies that something no longer 'communicates' in the Luhmanian sense of effecting change; yet as the word indicates (and as the article also indicates), that 'something' becomes a record that is worth our curiosity. Within the context of this study, that curiosity derives from the linkages we can draw between Borchardt before the law and: (1) the cultural pessimism concerning the fate of German literature that was a factor in the censorship debates of Weimar; (2) the invocation of a *Literaturgeist* analogous to Grimm's *Volksgeist*; and (3) the shared dream of an effective conceptual catachresis that would give literary spirit its rights by transcending the gulf between subsystems.

The abundance of mixed metaphors, vivid descriptions and prosopopeia in the DLKR stems, I would argue, from this desire. Take, for example, the following passage:

> If they wish to dispense with the normal rules of combat of equality under the law and use violence instead, one can have the right of club-law – tomorrow, immediately; and I can assure you that the powers of the German spirit, which I represent here, will not let its unilateral refinement allow its unworthy opponent to get the upper hand.
>
> [Wenn man sich der Waffenehre normaler Rechtsgleichheit begeben und die Gewalt sprechen lassen will, kann man Faustrecht haben, morgen, sofort, und die Mächte des deutschen Geistes, die ich hier verantworte, werden, das kann ich versichern, nicht durch falschverstandene einseitige Vornehmheit dem Lumpen die Vorhand lassen.]
>
> (Borchardt, DLKR, 27)

Throughout European history, there have existed rules of combat and the concept of honourable conduct in war (*Waffenehre*). These, of course had nothing to do with equality before the law. Yet Borchardt brings them together, clashingly, in a single metaphorical phrase, adding, for good measure, the idea of club-law (*Faustrecht*, literally 'fist-law'). 'Club-law' is perhaps more widely recognized through the phrase 'might makes right'. It refers to the originating violence that Benjamin speaks of, consistent with Borchardt's invocation of the divine powers of the German spirit. In some sense, Borchardt's rhetorical confusion of law with literature resembles Grimm's, though with the difference that whereas Grimm saw perpetual peace as a product of law and poetry, Borchardt sees only perpetual *Kampf*, whether aesthetic, legal, political, or rhetorical. Borchardt's consistent imagery of *Recht* and use of pseudoperformatives to appoint himself the attorney of German literature in the fight for its rights came true for him in a Munich courtroom, in a manner and with a result that he had not foreseen.

4.1
Carl Schmitt and/as Benito Cereno

> I am the last, self-conscious representative of the *jus publicum Europaeum* [...] and I am experiencing its end in the same manner as Benito Cereno experienced the journey of the pirate ship.
>
> [Ich bin der letzte, bewußte Vertreter des *jus publicum Europaeum* [...] und erfahre sein Ende so, wie Benito Cereno die Fahrt des Piratenschiffs erfuhr.]
>
> Carl Schmitt, *Ex captivitate salus* (75)

'Jus publicum Europaeum' (literally, 'European public law') refers to the peculiarly modern idea of national territorial sovereignty, equality between national states, and the 'humanization' and nationalization of war. In a process Schmitt calls the *'nomos* of the earth' ('Nomos *der Erde'*), the entire globe has been progressively divided by national boundaries, with the end result that there are no remainders (except, as we shall see, the world's oceans).[1] The nation-state came to exercise absolute control over who may enter and leave its space, and its own laws applied to everyone, almost without exception, inhabiting or travelling through that space. We might contrast such a 'jus publicum' with the state of law under European empires, which, as Lauren Benton has shown in *A Search for Sovereignty*, tended to allow for multiple and overlapping jurisdictions and sovereignties. Schmitt considers the principles of 'jus publicum' to have been founded with the Treaty of Westphalia of

---

1   I have earlier given the standard translation of Greek *nomos* as 'law'. Schmitt, however, correctly points to the more archaic Greek meaning of 'division', and it is this meaning, and the relationship between division and law, that forms the theme of Schmitt's book.

1648, and he saw World War II as the definitive end of this concept of sovereignty, to be replaced by a new world order led by the United States of America. As the epigraph demonstrates, Schmitt read Herman Melville's novella, *Benito Cereno* (1855) as predictive of this new world order. This chapter will follow the twists and turns and influences of Schmitt's reading, for example its intersection with the thought of Ernst Jünger, and with their help extract the nomological content of Melville's story and apply it to issues of globalization and its impact on national systems of law.

In chapter 3.2 we observed the circularity of citation between Walter Benjamin and Carl Schmitt – Schmitt may have derived his notion of the state of exception from Benjamin's 'Critique of Violence'; subsequently, Benjamin borrowed this notion and others from Schmitt's *Political Theology*. This chapter examines similar pathways of citation and mutual influence as Schmitt reads Melville's *Benito Cereno* (hereinafter *BC*) in a number of allegorical directions at once, from the most intimate biographical ones, as shown in the epigraph, to reflections on the law of the sea and globalization. Schmitt also interpreted the story in different ways for different audiences and interlocutors, among them the novelist Ernst Jünger. The rescue of a Spanish slave ship by Americans at the story's core furnishes, in Schmitt's reading, a literary precedent for twentieth-century geopolitics.

In his reading of Shakespeare's *Hamlet*, Schmitt notes that his approach goes against the grain of German literary studies that stress philology and formal aspects of literature and ignore interdisciplinary approaches that would reveal the workings of history and ideology in the text:

> The philosophers of art and teachers of aesthetics have a tendency to regard the work of art as an autonomous creation, closed upon itself, free of historical or sociological reality, and thus to understand it only on its own terms. [...] We therefore come up against sharp distinctions and fundamental divisions, against barriers and limitations of opposing methodologies, against fully formulated value-systems that recognize only their own passports and certifications, that allow only their own visas to be recognized, and that grant others neither entry nor transit.
>
> [Die Philosophen der Kunst und die Lehrer der Ästhetik neigen dazu, das Kunstwerk als eine in sich geschlossene, von der geschichtlichen oder soziologischen Wirklichkeit losgelöste, autonome Schöpfung zu betrachten und nur aus sich selbst heraus

zu verstehen. [...] Wir stoßen also auf scharfe Unterscheidungen und grundsätzliche Trennungen, auf Barrieren und Schranken entgegengesetzter Betrachtungsweisen, auf ausgebaute Wertsysteme, die nur ihre eigenen Pässe und Bescheinigungen anerkennen, nur ihre eigenen Visa gelten lassen und einem andern weder Eintritt noch Durchfahrt gestatten.]

(Schmitt, *Hamlet*, 34)

Schmitt describes here, in almost Luhmanian terms, the general situation of specialization and *Ausdifferenzierung* of subsystems in the modern world by which literary criticism began to autonomize itself at a fairly late stage. Schmitt wrote the above words many decades after he had formulated his reading of *Benito Cereno*. In following the development of the Cereno complex, we can see Schmitt breaking down the barriers he identifies here between professional literary criticism, political science and law.

During World War II, Schmitt, together with his friend Ernst Jünger (1895–1998), whose work will be discussed below, read the fiction of nineteenth-century American writers Melville and Edgar Allen Poe as prophets of the situations of world war and of the post-war periods, and in particular – as the epigraph points out – of the end of national claims to sovereignty. Schmitt's student, Armin Mohler, claims that Schmitt cited Herman Melville's novella more than any other work of world literature. Mohler states further that the title character of the novella 'preoccupied Schmitt very intensively' (Schmitt, *Briefwechsel mit einem seiner Schüler*, 153n74; 'hat C. S. aufs intensivste beschäftigt'). Two paradoxes accompany these facts: the first is that Schmitt, a German nationalist who saw the US replacing Britain as Germany's chief foe, would be so taken by an American piece; the second is that, despite his fascination for the story, Schmitt never published a complete essay on the novella, as he did on *Hamlet*, Theodor Däubler's *Nordlicht*, and other works. Schmitt's reading of *Benito Cereno* – or, more accurately, his repeated citations of *BC* as both a political and legal allegory and as a *persona* for himself – does not result in a single treatise, but rather gives rise to a series of reflections and diary entries, and subtly integrates itself into Schmitt's treatment of the law of the sea. This essay will trace the genesis of Schmitt's reading, compare it with other possible readings of *BC*, and explain Schmitt's use of Melville to prophesy the phenomenon of globalization. Finally, I will compare Schmitt's decisionism, for which he finds *BC* an ideal exemplum, with ST.

The Literatus Carl Schmitt

As noted in chapter 2, Schmitt's writing attacked at nearly every point the principles of legal positivism. The latter, similar to ST, upheld the law's autonomy and relative independence from political and economic processes. In positivism, legal norms arise from the cumulative body of citation, precedent and rulemaking. Justice is (merely) a product of history and procedure. The advantage of this theory is legal certainty. Its weakness, as we have seen in Kafka, is the lack of a genie at the top of things, of LAW outside of its own recursive acronym, to get the system started. The most visible of such genies is the dictator, who simply dictates law, and the function carried out by a dictator or other top executive is the decision that results in law-creating violence.

Schmitt's writings denied the law's autonomy on every front. Schmitt early went for the point of indeterminacy in positivism, asking the question of how an autopoietic system gets off the ground – that is, to use the terms Benjamin came to apply to this problem, what is the exceptional act of violence that founds a norm? An entire normative system may be swept away as the result of an election, as happened in Germany in 1933. Schmitt's thought appeals due to its rhetorical and literary force, and because, like natural law, it attempts to seize law, politics and government together at their common root. The disadvantages of his approach, as we might expect, are the shadowy nature of the reconstructed root and the uncertainty typical of antifoundationalism. Hence, my use of the term 'myth', which (as Adorno and Horkheimer showed in *Dialectic of the Englightenment*) is the only form of reason capable of burrowing beneath the positive foundation of common sense – of what 'everyone knows'. 'Myth' here is the alternative to *'Logos'*. Myth is what it is and will not stand for questioning the way *Logos* does.

A Situational Story
All law is 'situational law.'
Carl Schmitt, *Political Theology*, 13

We can date Schmitt's discovery of *BC* with some precision. He seems to have first read the story in early 1941. At the time, Schmitt was living in Plettenburg. On 25 February 1941 he writes to Ernst Jünger of the impression the story has made on him: 'I am taken by the entirely unconscious, subliminal symbolism of the situation as such' ('Ich bin von dem ganz ungewollten, hintergründigen Symbolismus der Situation als solcher überwältigt' [Schmitt, *Ernst Jünger-Carl Schmitt*, 115]). 'Situation', we have seen in 3.2, is a keyword for Schmitt, a lever that activates the state of exception. Thus, his repeated application of the term to *BC* amounts to a self-citation from his early work, especially from the *Political Theology*.

'Situation', in his thinking, explodes ideas of normativity with the fluidity of moment that calls for decision. Sovereign is the person who produces and guarantees a situation. So powerful is situation that, according to the quote, its contours, rather than the intentions of the people living within it, produce its symbolism. Melville based his story on a true incident in which the human cargo of a slave ship revolted and took the captain, Benito Cereno, and crew prisoner, ordering them to steer towards Africa. When an American ship, captained by Amaso Delano, hailed and boarded the wreck, the Africans, led by Babo, staged an elaborate performance, giving the impression that the whites and Cereno were still in charge. Only at the last minute did Cereno leap on board the longboat and reveal the plot, at which point the ship was recaptured, the slaves returned to service, and Babo executed. Melville took these basics, and the names of the characters, from Delano's narrative of the incident.

In his answering letter, Jünger repeatedly expressed a strong preference for the work of Edgar Allen Poe that would run throughout his writing career. The resulting extended literary debate over the relative merits of the two authors parallels the contrast between, in the characterization of Ulrich Ufeld, two conservative revolutionaries, one (Schmitt) a statist and the other (Jünger) an anarchist (Ufeld, 'Carl Schmitt und Ernst Jünger', 567). Schmitt found in the horrors of Melville's story a confirmation of the consequences of the destruction of national sovereignty and of the dethroning of elites by the masses. Jünger, on the other hand, preferred Poe's depiction of the visions gained through aimless wandering and passive suffering at the hands of inhuman forces, as in Poe's unfinished novel, *The Narrative of Arthur Gordon Pym* (1838) or in his 'A Descent Into the Maelström' (1841). However, for Jünger, the inhuman forces were those created by modern industrial society.

Jünger (1895–1998) enjoyed the longest lifespan of any German writer whose life dates are recorded, continuing to publish books into his early nineties. A decorated World War I veteran, he published his memoir of the war, *In Storms of Steel* (*In Stahlgewittern*), in 1922. Disillusioned with Weimar democracy, he engaged in right-wing political journalism and essayism and became friends with a number of Nazi higher-ups, though he never joined the party and returned to soldiering instead. Most of his letters to Schmitt were written from his post on the Western Front or in occupied France, where he saw little combat. His essays, *Total Mobilization* (1931; *Die totale Mobilmachung*) and *The Worker* (1932; *Der Arbeiter*), and in general his project of aestheticizing war, terror and politics, are widely considered as having provided an intellectual programme for Nazism. Jünger first met Schmitt in October 1930 in Berlin, when the former wrote to the professor of law to congratulate him on his *Concept of the Political*, in which Schmitt developed his notorious friend/foe definition of politics. The friendship grew and Schmitt became godfather to Jünger's second son, but they were separated by their differing reactions to the advent of National Socialism. Jünger called it quits, while Schmitt wrote appallingly in favour of Hitler's dictatorial powers and in excuse of the murders carried out under his name, and served for a while as the attorney-general of Prussia.[2]

H. F. Peters summarizes Jünger's fascination with Poe's maelstrom as a prophetic symbol of the modern era. Modern humans experience terror not in the face of natural forces, but rather ones of industrial gigantism and inhuman weapons of mass destruction. Resistance to such forces is impossible; the only alternative is to 'ride the wave' like the protagonist of Poe's story. Jünger's analysis of the maelstrom first appeared in the 1939 book *Gärten und Strassen* (Peters, 'Ernst Jünger's Concern with E. A. Poe', 146).

After reading and depreciating Jean Giono's short story about Melville, 'Greetings to Melville' (*'Saluer à Melville'*), because it 'privatizes' the story's symbolism (Giono's story recounts Melville's brief encounter in England with an Irish woman freedom-fighter), Schmitt repeats for Jünger his observation of *BC*'s portrayal of an existentialist situation:

> [Giono's] story is a nasty reduction of Melville to kitsch – Melville, whose incomparable greatness lies in his ability for objective, elementary, and concrete *situation*. For that reason, *BC* is greater than the Russians and all other storytellers of the nineteenth century, so that in contrast even Poe works anecdotally, while as an epic of the ocean *Moby-Dick* is comparable only to the *Odyssey*. Only Melville is capable of making graspable the ocean as element. A very contemporary thematic. By the way, air did not become a new element of warfare through the airforce and airplanes; the element of aerial warfare is not air, but fire.
>
> [Das ist eine üble Verkitschung Melvilles, dessen unvergleichbare Größe die Kraft zur objektiven, elementaren und konkreten *Situation* ist. Benito Cereno ist dadurch größer als die Russen und sämtliche andern Erzähler des 19. Jahrhunderts, sodaß neben ihm auch Poe anekdotisch wirkt, und Moby-Dick ist als Epos des Meeres nur mit der Odysee zu vergleichen. Das

---

2 Elliot Neaman suggests (*A Dubious Past*, 94–5) that Schmitt's overt anti-Semitism in his university and public lectures also was displeasing to Jünger.

Meer als Element ist nur durch Melville faßbar zu machen. Ein sehr aktuelles Thema. Die Luft ist übrigens nicht etwas durch die Luftwaffe und Flugzeuge als neues Element erschienen; das der Luftwaffe zugeordnete Element ist nicht die Luft sondern das Feuer.]

(Schmitt an Jünger, 4 July 1941, 121)

Jünger responds with a defence of Poe as the more transcendent writer, which draws Schmitt still deeper into his own interpretation: 'I am thinking of *BC* as *Situation*-Symbol' (4 April 1941, 129; 'Ich denke an *Benito Cereno*, als *Situations*-Symbol'). Schmitt never loses this opinion of Poe as the lesser writer, as can be seen from his diary entry of 2 May 1948:

The genius of Villiers de l'Isle Adam; to 'the guest of the last festivities' goes (alongside Benito Cereno, the Head Ranger, who else?) first place as one of our new myth-images; Poe has mythical Situations (in the Maelstrom, in the dungeon of the Inquisition) but no mythical figures (the attempt with Pym is too weak).

[Die Genialität von Villiers de l'Isle Adam; zu unseren neuen Mythenbildern gehört (neben Benito Cereno, dem Oberförster, wer noch?), vor allem anderen 'le convive des dernières fêtes'; Poe hat mythische Situationen (im Maelstrom, im Kerker der Inquisition) aber keine mythischen Figuren (der Ansatz bei Pym ist zu schwach).]

(Schmitt, *Glossarium*, 92)

The Head Ranger (*Oberförster*) is a tyrant figure in Jünger's own novel, *Auf den Marmorklippen* (1939). This narrative, which concerns the extirpation of a peaceful forest people, delivers an apocalyptic allegory of the rise to power of Hitler – the 'Head Ranger' – and a prediction of his end.[3] Sinister nature corresponds to that of the title figure of Villiers de L'Isle-Adam's short story, 'Le convive des dernières fêtes' (1874; 'The Guest of the Last Rites'). In this story, a mysterious Baron Saturn joins a carnival party. It seems from the conversation that he is an executioner in town to work the guillotine at the public execution scheduled for the following morning. It is

---

3 The ability of Jünger to publish this text – ironically, with the Hanseatische Verlagsanstalt that was one of Rudolf Borchardt's favoured presses – in a Germany where censorship was in full force remains something of a mystery. Eventually the Nazis caught on and prohibited further printings.

later revealed, however, that he is merely an amateur who travels from execution to execution, often bribing the professionals to let him do the job.

BC shares with these stories the theme of violence and tyranny carried out as a masquerade. However, while the reader experiences the horror of the European stories through their effect on the narrator, the experience in BC is conveyed through the suffering of the title figure, who, despite his rescue, dies of the horror and guilt of his experience, expiring three months after the end of Babo's trial. Amaso Delano, ever the optimistic Yankee, whose thought at times becomes scarcely distinguishable from that of the third-person narrator, tries to comfort Benito: '"You are saved," cried Captain Delano, more and more astonished and pained; "you are saved: what has cast such a shadow upon you?" "The negro"' (Melville, BC, 103). The nominal exclamation could be generic, referring to the 'African race' in general, and hence indirectly to the slave trade as the framework that set in motion this series of atrocities. The likely first response of a reader, however, would be to think of this as referring to Babo, the leader of the uprising.

As the Head Ranger and the *convive des dernières fêtes* are to the narrators of those stories, so Babo is to Benito, with deadly consequences. In Edgar Allen Poe's 'Descent into the Maelström' and 'The Pit and the Pendulum' (1843), it is the situation *in extremis*, rather than the actions of a single evil character, that transforms the protagonist. For example, the narrator of 'Maelström' explains how his hair 'which had been raven-black the day before, was as white as you see it now' (Poe, 'A Descent into the Maelström', 88). Poe's only novel, *The Narrative of Arthur Gordon Pym*, attempted to create a narrator with more substance and psychological depth than in the stories, though most critics agree with Schmitt that Pym's character is not fully achieved.

Schmitt connects Melville with his own thinking in his next letter, without explicitly naming him: 'On the ocean our classes and classifications cease to exist. I have been investigating the problem of piracy for quite a while. Now I have come one step closer to understanding it' (24 September 1941, 131; 'Von der See aus hören unsere Klassen und Klassifikationen auf. Seit langem beschäftigt mich das Problem der Piraterie. Jetzt bin ich ihm einen Schritt näher gekommen'). The short interval between this letter and the previous one indicates that it is an examination of BC as an example, a precedent of legal thinking on piracy, that has brought Schmitt one step further. Schmitt expressed his thoughts on piracy and its role in the development of a 'world system' more fully in the book *Land and Sea* (*Land und Meer*), as we will see below.

Finally, in one of the many dreams exchanged between the two men, Schmitt finds a way to combine his Cereno with Jünger's Poe, signing his note 'Greetings from your Cereno' (11/12 March 1943, 159; 'Gruß Ihres Cereno'). This is also the point at which the correspondence becomes most intimate, with a minimum of the formalities that had marked previous letters. The note, with a time indication of 2.30 a.m., suggesting that it is the report of a dream, is highly condensed: 'Fabulous (fatal?) situation: the *San Dominick* in the maelstrom. B. C. tells himself: better to die at their hands, than for them. Tacitean emphases of this sort leave academic jargon like "existential" far behind them' (159; 'Fabel-hafte (Fatum-hafte?) Situation: die S. Dominick im Maelstrom. B C sagt sich: besser durch sie sterben, als für sie. Solche taciteische Zuspitzungen lassen Schulworte wie »existentiell« weit hinter sich'). In this sentence, Schmitt makes a paronomastic move that is difficult to reproduce in English: the repeated sound 'fa' links the two concepts of 'fable' and 'fate.' *'Fabelhaft'* means 'fabulous' in German much as in English colloquial usage, but Schmitt undoubtedly is thinking of the Greek term *'fabula'* that Aristotle uses for plot, an action of the proper magnitude, the heart and soul of tragedy, consisting of events linked by probability and necessity. *'Fabel'* is also the generic term for a fable, a genre that is close to the political allegory Schmitt sees Melville as having provided him with. There is no adjective *'fatumhaft'* in German; Schmitt's neologism, which literally means 'fate-like', allows the idea of fate to refer back to fable, plot and situation as its engendering matrix.

The *San Dominick* is the ship on and around which the plot of *BC* takes place. Its name and appearance invoke Europe's incomplete secularization – its 'political theology' – that the narrator constantly invokes, for example by stating that the ship's appearance 'almost led Captain Delano to think that nothing less than a ship-load of monks was before him' (Melville, *BC*, 48). Invoking the 'ship of state' allegory, Schmitt predicts the impending destruction of Germany as a sovereign nation that has been taken over by its darker forces. He invokes a personal dimension as well. Poe's maelstrom story, in which a small boat is pulled down into the depths of the ocean, shows the power of nature and of extreme situations to cause enlightenment in the sufferer. Cereno, as we have seen, achieves a negative enlightenment, but the overwhelming force in his case is social. The man-made maelstrom, we might say, is the slave trade. Babo's forcing of Benito Cereno to play the captain when he is really a hostage opens Cereno's eyes to the cruelty of the system of which he had been a functionary. Jünger responds that the combination of Poe and Melville works, because 'Poe sees the same things individually that Melville sees politically and socially' (8 April 1943, 161; 'Poe sieht ja individualistisch, was Melville politisch, gesellschaftlich').

In the transcription of his dream, Schmitt presents a triangular relationship between three authors. We have seen that Poe and Melville stand in a dialectical relationship. To understand the reference to Tacitus, we may wish to start with Schmitt's diary entry of 28 August 1947: 'Now I am taken with the beginning of Tacitus's *Historiae*. Is it only rhetoric, as Ortega said to me? Is it not the identity of the situation, and thus existential communion, participation in one and the same primal and core situation of our eon?' (Schmitt, *Glossarium*, 5; 'Jetzt hat mich der Anfang der Historien des Tacitus ergriffen. Ist das nur noch Rhetorik, wie Ortega mir sagte? Ist es nicht die Identität der Situation, also existentielle Teilhabe, participatio an ein und derselben Ur- und Kernsituation unseres Aeons?'). 'Ortega' refers to the Spanish philosopher José Ortega y Gassett (1883–1955), whose work we will examine in more detail below. Four years separate the two citations of Tacitus, whose shared content makes them appear as though they were made from one day to the next, with the word 'Situation' as the thread uniting them. Another important clue is Schmitt's mentioning of Edmund Burke's comparison between Tacitus and the *Journal politique national* of Antoine de Rivarol (1753–1801).[4] We should also note an *aperçu* Schmitt gives in a letter: 'I am sending Rivarol's work to you with this letter, a grand thing and proof of my thesis: the great historian is first of all a contemporary of times he writes about, and secondly someone defeated by them, as Thucydides, Polybius, Tacitus, Otto von Freysing, Machiavelli, and Tocqueville were.'[5] While not a historian per se, Schmitt clearly wishes to imply his own situation as an organic intellectual of the defeated. Rivarol was a monarchist who published against the French Revolution. Tacitus, on the other hand, looked with nostalgia on the days of the Roman republic, as he recorded the vices and iniquities of the Augustan emperors. As Schmitt notes, Tacitus begins his *Historia* with a lamentation of the degradation of Roman society under the Caesars: 'Slaves were bribed to turn against their masters, and freedmen to betray their patrons;

---

4   Carl Schmitt, letter to Armin Mohler (26 October 1966) *Briefwechsel mit einem seiner Schüler*, 374.
5   Carl Schmitt, letter to Armin Mohler (9 February 1967) *Briefwechsel mit einem seiner Schüler*, 380; 'Ich schicke ihnen hier den Rivarol, eine grossartige Sache, ein Beleg meiner These: der grosse Historiker ist erstens Zeitgenosse der von ihm "geschriebenen" Zeit, und zweitens Besiegter, wie Thukydides, Polybius, Tacitus, Otto von Freysing, Machiavell und Tocqueville'). Presumably the time Schmitt refers to is the historical period that the historian actually lives in.

and those who had not an enemy were destroyed by friends' (Tacitus, *History*, 420; 'corrupti in dominos servi, in patronos liberti; et quibus deerat inimicus per amicos oppressi' [I.2]). Such is one of the typical 'Tacitean emphases' (*'taciteische Zuspitzungen'*) Schmitt refers to in his letter. It is an apocalyptic vision of the war of all against all, an existential situation indeed for which Tacitus provides many concrete examples in his individualized and dramatized portrayals of the fate of individuals who lived and died through those times. Schmitt seizes on Tacitus as a fellow conservative intellectual who portrayed the sinking ship of state realistically, as Melville did allegorically – the difference being that while the sinking ship for Tacitus was his own nation, for Melville it was Spain and Europe.

Schmitt's persistent identification of himself with Cereno raises the question as to whether his quotation, 'B. C. tells himself: better to die at their hands, than for them' ('B C sagt sich: besser durch sie sterben, als für sie'), refers to the Benito Cereno of the story, or to Schmitt himself. No quotation of this kind can be found in *BC*. Nor does it seem particularly relevant to the context of Cereno's plight, *'sie'* (they) presumably referring to the Africans who hold Cereno captive. Schmitt thereby gives Cereno a choice he does not really have in Melville's story, where the captain is always in danger of dying at the hands of the Africans, but never contemplates dying 'for' them. If Schmitt refers to himself as Benito Cereno, then the context of war and fascism makes the meaning more understandable: better to resist and die at the hands of the German government, than to continue sacrificing oneself for it. A perhaps relevant detail here is that Schmitt's mortal enemies within the Nazi-Regime were the SS 'Schwarze Korps', named after the black of their uniforms, to which the color of Babo and his compatriots would then allude.

Schmitt's adoption of the persona of Benito Cereno begins at this moment, where his own voice seems merely to cite the words of the fictional character. The Cereno masquerade began in a private exchange between Schmitt and Jünger, but soon became a public stance. Shortly after the end of the war, Schmitt asked that a 'disavowal' (*Waschzettel*) be printed with any future editions of his book *Leviathan*, first published in 1938. It warns against reading the book, and the name found at the bottom of the disavowal is not Carl Schmitt, but Benito Cereno, thus implying, for those who know the story, a disavowal of the disavowal.[6] In Melville's story, Benito Cereno becomes a puppet in the hands of the revolted

---

6 Schmitt sent copies of this text both to Jünger (June 1945, 192–3) and to his student, Armin Mohler (4 December 1948) *Briefwechsel mit einem seiner Schüler*, 38–9.

slaves. His power of speech is removed. In Schmitt's view, who are the puppet-masters ventriloquizing him? Once the mask of Benito Cereno is assumed, it becomes impossible to ground or establish the sincerity of any statement, since each can later be claimed as coerced citation rather than heartfelt opinion. In publishing the *Waschzettel*, is Schmitt disclaiming what he wrote in *Leviathan*, because he was under the control of the Nazis at the time? Or is he winking at the reader and giving him mysterious signs, the way the Spanish sailors desperately do to Amasa Delano (which he uniformly interprets as indicative of skulduggery being plotted by the Spanish), in order to indicate that the warning given is not to be taken seriously, because it is made in conformity with the Americans and the post-war regime?

In Ruth Groh's reading, Schmitt's 'signing' of the *Waschzettel* with the name of Cereno means as much as Schmitt saying the following: 'My book [*Leviathan*] does contain shrill anti-Semitic tones; for that reason an exoteric reader, who does not know my Political Theology and Mythology and who does not know that I wrote this book while playing the role of Benito Cereno, will take me for a racist and accomplice [*mitschuldig*] to the Holocaust' (Groh, *Arbeit an der Heillosigkeit der Welt*, 138). Later, Groh formulates the essence of Schmitt's Cereno persona, using the indirect discourse she imagines Schmitt producing:

> The ship called '*Europe*', in whose captaincy Schmitt figured [*figurierte*], has supposedly been taken over by the mutinous SS and other institutions of the Nazi power structure and sunk to the bottom. He, Schmitt, supposedly was forced to pay lip-service to the terroristic tyrants in order not to become a martyr to his belief in the 'Mythos Europa.' His relationship to those in power was thus determined by inner resistance [*inneren Widerstand*] and action under duress. (Groh, *Arbeit an der Heillosigkeit der Welt*, 138)

Groh's reading correctly identifies Schmitt's appropriation of the Cereno myth in order to excuse himself in the post-war period, but the correspondence with Jünger (not mentioned by Groh, and published only after the appearance of her book) shows that Schmitt's role-playing had begun much earlier, before it was clear that Germany would lose the war, and that it had occurred on several levels, beyond the autobiographical. Indeed, Groh's own identification of Cereno as a modern variant of the Epimetheus myth that was dear to Schmitt's heart shows this. More important than Schmitt's own sincerity or insincerity in his use of the myth, however, is that aspects of his interpretation move beyond his personal fate as what today would be called a 'public intellectual', to a generalized allegory of the end of the *jus publicum Europaeum*. If Carl Schmitt used *BC* as a personal myth, to claim that he was forced, Cereno-like, to adopt Nazi ideology, he also fostered another, more public reading of the myth that is worth exploring.

Benito Cereno and the Post-War Order

In Schmitt's reading of Melville's story, passed on to his students and friends from several European countries, the *San Dominick* represents Europe, with its elite class (Cereno) presently dominated by its masses (the African slaves). As Sava Klickovic further specifies, Schmitt 'elevated Benito Cereno to a symbol of the situation of the intelligentsia in a mass-system' (Klickovic, '"Benito Cereno": Ein moderner Mythos', 268; 'hat Benito Cereno zu einem Symbol für die Lage der Intelligenz in einem Massensystem erhoben'). The slave rebellion is the masses' taking over of leadership, whether this be through democratic means, through revolution, or through enthusiasm for fascist leadership. The aimless wandering of the ship represents the rudderless vagaries of the state, whether under a parliamentary system as in Weimar, or under Nazism. Undoubtedly, the novella confirmed for Schmitt the same message he had found in José Ortega y Gassett's *La rebelión de las masas* (1930), a book that he recommended (in a German translation that had sold more than 300,000 copies) to Jünger.[7] Ortega's essay criticizes the democratization of culture and politics resulting from the industrial revolution. The mass production of everything, including culture, eliminates local specificities and dissolves national boundaries and state sovereignty – the end of the *jus publicum Europaeum*. Rather than elites serving as models that the masses might emulate, their values are discarded, and instead masses and mass-produced values begin to dominate. The second part of Ortega's book is governed by the same refrain that haunts Melville's story – the question, '¿Quién manda en el mundo?' (roughly, 'Who's in charge?').

In an essay on *BC* published in a *Festschrift* for Schmitt's seventieth birthday, the prominent Spanish legal scholar, Enrique Tierno Galván (1919–86) makes Benito 'the conscience of the elite that sees and suffers' (Tierno Galván, 'Benito Cereno oder der Mythos Europas', 354; 'das Bewußtsein der Elite die sieht und leidet'). The similarities between the essays by Klickovic and Tierno Galván, the occasion for which they were written, and the fact that Schmitt mentions

---

7   Carl Schmitt, letter to Ernst Jünger (10 August 1931) *Ernst Jünger-Carl Schmitt*, 11. Sales figures from Thomas Mermall, Introduction to *La rebelión de las masas*, 7.

once in his diaries 'wonderful conversations' (*schöne Gespräche*) with Tierno Galván (on a different subject) all suggest that these essays are recollections of and attempts at preserving Schmitt's reading of Melville (Schmitt, *Glossarium*, 316). Tierno Galván was a law professor at the University of Salamanca. An opponent of Franco, after the latter's death he became the socialist mayor of Madrid. In Tierno Galván's reading, Captain Delano, who sees the distressed ship and tries to help, represents an American position that is equally idealistic and self-interested, as it worked itself out through two world wars. Galván also has an interesting analysis of a relatively minor character, the slave Atufal. Atufal is the most powerful of the Africans on board. In directing his masquerade, Babo keeps Atufal in chains, and has him brought before Cereno and Delano:

> Captain Delano's attention was caught by the moving figure of a gigantic black, emerging from the general crowd below, and slowly advancing towards the elevated poop. An iron collar was about his neck, from which depended a chain, thrice wound round his body. [...]
> At the first glimpse of his approach, Don Benito had started, a resentful shadow swept over his face; and, as with the sudden memory of bootless rage, his white lips glued together. [...]
> 'See, he waits your question, master,' said [Babo]. [...]
> 'Atufal, will you ask my pardon now?'
> The black was silent. [...]
> 'Go,' said Don Benito, with inkept and unknown emotion.
> Deliberately as he had come, the black obeyed.
> (Melville, *BC*, 61–2)

Mouthing Babo's script, Don Benito adds that this scene has been replayed every two hours for the last sixty days, whereas we must suppose that in actual fact this is the first and only time it has been played. The chains are feckless; Atufal could easily throw them off at any moment. This peculiar scene did not appear in Delano's original account that Melville used as a source, and hence it furnishes an important clue as to Melville's intentions for the story. Specifically, the scene amplifies the story's leitmotif of 'Follow your leader' (the motto carried on the ship's prow) by suggesting the ambiguity of leadership and mastery. Shortly after the passage cited, Atufal's royal status is discussed, to which Babo appends that he himself was only a 'black man's slave' in Africa (Melville, *BC*, 62). These are both true statements. Delano notes Atufal's 'royal spirit' (Melville, *BC*, 62), and advises Cereno to pardon him out of 'natural respect' (Melville, *BC*, 63) for this spirit. Delano's remarks hint at the discrepancy between natural law and the municipal law that permits such men to be slaves, while the 'natural slave' Babo climbs higher on the social ladder by aiding his fellow African's enslavement. But like most of Delano's observations, this one is ironized by his complete ignorance of the true situation. In fact, the staging of Atufal's enslavement is gratuitous, serving no real purpose in either fooling Delano or in keeping the whites subdued. It seems to stem merely from an ironic whim on Babo's part, from his desire to enact the Hegelian master-slave dialectic with live actors. The real offence, obviously, has been the enslavement of Atufal in his African homeland, for which Cereno is asked to beg his pardon. Babo (we imagine) delights in enacting a scene of Cereno's tyrannical whim and absolute dominance, knowing that these are the characteristics he gives the Spaniard.

Tierno Galván picks up on this dialectic. In his reading, Atufal represents the principle not of natural law, but of terror. The following sentence reads as though it had been written not by Schmitt, but by Jünger: 'In its purity, terror takes up today the place left behind by extinct values. Perhaps this explains that in Melville's myth a gigantic Black, Atufal, becomes the symbol of terror' (Tierno Galván, 'Benito Cereno', 355; 'In seiner Reinheit nimmt der Terror heute den Platz der toten Werte ein. So erklärt es sich vielleicht, daß in dem Mythos Melvilles ein in Ketten geschlagener riesiger Neger, Atufal, das Symbol des Terrors ist'). Unlike either Schmitt or Klickovic, Tierno Galván recognizes that the terror experienced by Cereno has its roots in the terror and violence practiced upon the slaves. Benito Cereno 'experiences his own guilt [...] in the face of a terror that is nothing more than an amplification of the characteristics of the terrorized' (Tierno Galván, 'Benito Cereno', 356; 'empfindet die eigene Schuld [...] angesichts eines Terrors, der nur die Steigerung der eigenen Eigenschaften des Terrorisierten ist'). Remarkably, Tierno Galván published his essay in 1968; he could not then know how predictive it would be of the evolution of geopolitics and warfare in the last quarter of the twentieth century. Galván's use of the word 'terror' can be interpreted as referring to 'Nazi-Terror', 'Stalin-Terror', or perhaps 'Franco-Terror'. He provides no examples. But by the end of the twentieth century terror would mean something else, almost the reverse of the perversions of national sovereignty conducted under totalitarian regimes: the conduct of war by the stateless. Furthermore, a large part of the effect of twenty-first century terror depends on the incomprehension of its victims, who, like Amasa Delano, fail to recognize, acknowledge or understand the hatred felt towards them by the terrorists. This evolution of terror fits Schmitt's ideas of the evolution of warfare and world power, and accompanies the fading of the sovereignty of national states and of the *jus publicum Europaeum*. Perhaps the image of terror on board ship inspired Schmitt's idea of the partisan in a later work, *Theory of the Partisan*. There, he equates corsairs with partisans (Schmitt, *Theory of the Partisan*, 70) and parallels piracy with partisan action as the 'pre-scientific' stage of sea war and land war, respectively.

Marianne Kesting, whose brother was a student of Schmitt's, entertained a long correspondence with Schmitt that included a number of interviews. Kesting, trained in Germanistik and music, challenged the interpretations of *Benito Cereno*, detailed above, which made Melville a critic of European rather than American politics and society. She reports that Schmitt answered her critique on 6 December 1968, acknowledging its accuracy, but asking whether there was not something in the allegorical and symbolic level of the work that would support at least part of his own interpretations. In a later interview, when Kesting reiterated her concerns that allegorical interpretations ignored the story's textual integrity, she reports that Schmitt answered, 'with a mocking smile: "Yes, yes, the philologists..."' (Kesting, 'Begegnungen', 98; 'mokant lächelnd: "Ja, ja, die Philologen..."'). Schmitt also noted that his interpretations had found an enthusiastic reception among his numerous and far-flung adherents and colleagues. One might also add that Sava Klickovic's Schmittian interpretation of the story, held as a lecture for the Melville Society in 1957, resulted in his being named an honorary member.[8]

Kesting became determined to defend the so-called philological level of interpretation, and she eventually published, in 1972 (second edition 1983), a critical edition of Melville's story (in German translation), with a selection of critical approaches (including Klickovic's) and her own reading. Interestingly, Kesting's own interpretation also finds that the story treats the America-Europe problem, but from the point of view of slavery and its effect on American class systems: the European conflict between estates has been transformed into questions of slavery and of race (Kesting, '"Benito Cereno" und seine Interpretationen').[9] Cereno, the creole aristocrat, stands for the Southern states, Delano for the North. Kesting's interpretation thus agrees with Schmitt's that the slave rebellion on the ship represents,

---

8   Carl Schmitt, letter to Armin Mohler (19 March 1957) *Briefwechsel mit einem seiner Schüler*, 235. Klickovic, who like Schmitt's wife came from northern Serbia, under the Tito regime was involved in trade and travelled widely in North and South America.

9   Nicola Nixon seconds the notion that Melville was critiquing class, but rather than have Cereno represent either Old World aristocracy or Southern slavocracy, she reads him as representative of Northern dandyism.

in some sense, class warfare in Europe, though only in the sense that this is reflected in US culture. There are as many problems with Kesting's reading as with Schmitt's, but I will limit myself to the most obvious one, which is that the story itself neither encourages its reader to think about slavery as its central issue, nor to have sympathy with the Africans who from our present standpoint were acting in legitimate self-defence. Like Schmitt, we are encouraged to identify with the only dynamic characters of the story: Benito Cereno and Amaso Delano. The narrator shares the racist attitudes of these two characters, as in his patronizing characterization of 'the negro': 'There is something in the negro which, in a peculiar way, fits him for avocations about one's person. Most negroes are natural valets and hairdressers' (Melville, BC, 83), and in his lascivious view of the sprawled woman slave, 'with youthful limbs carelessly disposed' (Melville, BC, 73). Conversely, while Babo's head is described as a hive of subtlety, it is not a location of subjectivity. Thus, in an attempt at 'demythologizing' the BC of Schmitt et al., Richard Faber reminds us of the way the story works counter to our own ideological position in favour of freedom for the oppressed: 'Against this "New" European "Order" [the Third Reich] there arose resistance movements everywhere between the North Pole and Sicily, from the Atlantic to the Urals. Only these movements could legitimately cite BC, whose real hero is the partisan, Babo' ('"Benito Cereno" oder die Entmythologisierung Euro-Americas', 82). The BC story, with just a few details changed, can be told from the perspective of a heroic Babo, and in fact has been in the 1997 Steven Spielberg film *Amistad*.[10] Taken as a whole, recent American criticism tends to embrace both sides of the divide Kesting saw between various symbolizations of the figure of Benito Cereno. For example, one of the story's most often-cited interpreters, Eric Sundquist, sees nothing wrong in identifying Cereno simultaneously as a 'symbol of American paranoia about Spanish, Catholic, slave-holding despotism' and also as a 'southern planter, [a] dissipated cavalier spiritually wasted by his own terrifying enslavement' (Sundquist, *To Wake the Nations*, 148). In an increasingly globalized world, American and European readings of the novella have come increasingly to coincide.

---

10 The 1839 *Amistad* mutiny was quite similar to that of the *Tryal*, but the ship was found in US waters and the case eventually reached the Supreme Court, which decided in 1841 that the 'slaves' had been taken illegally in Africa contrary to treaty, and ordered them repatriated. Most crucially, the slave trade had not been outlawed in 1799 when the Benito Cereno incident occurred. See Howard Jones, *Mutiny on the Amistad*.

Benito Cereno and Globalization

In the epigraph to this chapter, Schmitt claims to be suffering the end of the *jus publicum Europaeum*, a concept that arose out of the religious conflicts of the sixteenth and seventeenth centuries. Thomas Hobbes and Jean Bodin, legal theorists who wrote under the shadow of those religious wars, are fundamental to Schmitt's concept of state sovereignty. Schmitt experiences the end of this period of municipal law as though it were the voyage of a hostage aboard a pirate ship. With this metaphor, Schmitt alludes to the role of sea power in the dissolution of a historical legal order. To drive his point home, Schmitt designates the *San Dominick* of *BC* as a pirate ship. This designation is technically accurate, since in taking over the ship the legally enslaved Blacks have made themselves pirates, and they are ready to commit an act of piracy in commandeering Delano's ship as well. Schmitt found *BC* conducive to his thinking about the role of pirates in the development of international law. This interest in pirates may account for Schmitt's willingness to equate the *San Dominick* with a freebooter on the Spanish Main.

Melville took his plot virtually intact from the memoirs of the American captain, Amaso Delano, who, like all the characters (but not the ship), appears in *BC* under his own name. The historical Delano was not shy about revealing the motivation for his retaking the *Tryal* (rechristened the *San Dominick* by Melville, as Delano's *Perseverance* is rechristened the *Bachelor's Delight*). His encouragement to his sailors runs thus in his own account: 'By way of encouragement, I told them that Don Bonito [sic] considered the ship and what was in her as lost; that the value was more than one hundred thousand dollars; that if we would take her, it should be all our own; and that if we should afterwards be disposed to give him up one half, it would be considered as a present' (Delano, *A Narrative*, 327). The courtroom aftermath to this incident, played out in Concepción, Chile, was twofold: the rebel slaves were condemned to death or to prison; and Benito Cereno attempted to thwart Delano's salvage claims. Delano appends to his narrative transcripts of the various depositions describing the incident, translated from the Spanish. Cereno's legal manoeuvrings included taking depositions from Botany Bay convicts, whom Delano was transporting on his ship, and who 'swore every thing against me they could to effect my ruin. Amongst other atrocities, they swore I was a pirate' (Delano, *A Narrative*, 329). The legal wranglings merely underscore the fact that any encounter like this on the no-man's-water of the high seas is inherently ambiguous. Who are the pirates? What constitutes legitimate ownership of things – and of people?

Melville deliberately intensifies the confusion about piracy found in Delano's narrative. In the story, Delano continually fights back his own suspicions that the *San Dominick* is a 'freebooter', and is nagged by a suspicion that the hostage Cereno is really the pirate leader, a motif that culminates in his alliterative ejaculation, 'this plotting pirate means murder!' (Melville, *BC*, 98), when Don Benito jumps into the longboat. On the other hand, Melville renames Delano's own ship the *Bachelor's Delight*, after an infamous pirate ship that had been converted from a slaver, and makes Delano's first mate a former 'privateer's-man' (Melville, *BC*, 89). Delano encourages his crew in the dangerous task of taking the mutinous vessel with promise of booty, just as a pirate would. On the other hand, legitimately owned slaves who mutinied on a vessel came under the category of pirates, and when the mask is finally dropped the Blacks are revealed to be 'flourishing hatchets and knives in ferocious piratical revolt' (Melville, *BC*, 99). In his decision on the Amistad case, for example, chief Justice Joseph Story, in ruling that the rebels were Africans taken illegally and thus free men possessing the right to legitimate self-defence, wrote that they 'cannot be deemed pirates or robbers in the sense of the law of nations' (States v. Amistad, 40 U. S. 593–4). The logical implication of this statement is that mutinous slaves *could* be deemed pirates.

To my knowledge, Schmitt never used the term 'globalization' in any of his letters or publications; yet his description of the triumph of sea and air power over land power can be viewed as a theory and critique of that inexorable process. Christopher L. Connery calls Schmitt's *Nomos der Erde* 'perhaps the last serious attempt to think through the materiality and spatiality of the earth as a whole in philosophical terms [...] the elementalism of the German and English romantic project being an expression of a newly globalized consciousness, where finally materiality – space, the elements – as a universal whole could be thought and considered in its ideational dimension' (Connery, 'Ideologies of Land and Sea', 4). In another book with a similar thematic, *Land and Sea*, Schmitt pauses before his introduction of the third epoch of world history, that of ocean power (the first two are of river and of inland sea), and salutes his 'herolds' (*Herolde*), Herman Melville and Jules Michelet (Schmitt, *Land und Meer*, 30). He praises only the novel *Moby-Dick* by name, in terms resembling those in the letter to Jünger as the greatest epic of the ocean, but we will see that *BC* lurks beneath the surface of his argument. For one thing, Schmitt points out that this third epoch of sea power was achieved with the help of adventurers, whale hunters and pirates. He devotes an extraordinary amount of time to this last group, claiming that they were the front-line troops in the war between Protestant and Catholic powers that defined the early modern period (Schmitt, *Land und Meer*, 44). Schmitt then makes piracy the foundation both of English sea power and of capitalism: 'The English all participated in the great hunt for booty. Hundreds upon thousands of English became at that time "corsair capitalists"' (Schmitt, *Land und Meer*, 46). While Schmitt does not define the exact contribution of pirate capitalism to the overall development of an economic system that would eventually dominate the world, its role is elevated by his not comparing it with any other factors. The strangest lacuna of all is any mention of slavery or the huge contribution it made to the nascent capitalist system. In a sense, slavers and antislavery policing form a fourth group that Schmitt should have mentioned in the context of the other three. This sublimation of slavery into piracy is repeated in Schmitt's reading of *BC*. In this sense, *Land und Meer* carries out the same substitution as the Schmitt-Jünger reading of *Benito Cereno*. Just as that reading rebaptized the *San Dominick* as a pirate ship, so too here the real business of capitalism, which included slavery as one of its constituent parts, is reduced to piracy. One may read here Schmitt's resentment of England as Germany's arch-foe and rival, as well as an analysis of history in light of the geopolitics of World War II, where Germany enjoyed land superiority while England controlled the high seas.

In Schmitt's view, whereas a land power's ability to take over the whole world would appear only as a tyranny to be resisted, England's piratical ability to build a world empire based on sea power appears to the other powers 'as good and natural, the very essence of civilization and humanity, peace and international law. [...] Here you may observe, that the great Leviathan has power even over the minds and feelings of humans' (Schmitt, *Land und Meer*, 89; 'als gut und selbstverständlich; das ist für sie dasselbe wie Zivilisation und Menschlichkeit; es ist der Friede und das Völkerrecht selbst. [...] Hier kannst du sehen, daß der große Leviathan Macht auch über die Geister und Gemüter der Menschen hat'). The Leviathan had been a central symbol in Schmitt's political theory for years, principally in his 1938 book, *Der Leviathan in der Staatslehre des Thomas Hobbes*, where Schmitt had identified the Leviathan as a 'Jewish war symbol' (*jüdisches Kampfsymbol*).[11]

In reality, the Leviathan did not hypnotize the world, and other

---

11 In a letter dated 12 April 1973, Schmitt claims, rather incredibly, that this book was an answer to Walter Benjamin's political symbolic, presumably in the *Trauerspiel* book (Schmitt, *Jawohl*, 14). Raphael Gross brings the *Leviathan* essay together with Schmitt's ideas of the progressive movement from land to sea to air power in arguing that *Leviathan* makes the Jews responsible for acceleration, which conflicts with the Catholic notion of the *katechon*.

nations did not stand by and applaud British sea power and concede the free passage of the high seas. In a brief history of the law of the sea, Edward D. Brown notes that the *jus publicum Europaeum* has always held two contradictory notions on the issue of the high seas: *mare liberum* (freedom of the high seas) on the one hand; and *mare clausum* (extension of national sovereignty as far as possible, for example to protect fisheries) on the other. Individual nations, such as Britain, do not throw themselves wholeheartedly behind one principle or the other; rather, they may argue for either principle or both at any one time, depending on specific contexts and goals. Historically, disputes and treaties tended to sway back and forth between these principles, rather than tending towards ever greater freedom. The most dramatic development in the law of the sea came in the postcolonial period (roughly, from 1960 onwards), when the number of sovereign nations with coastlines increased drastically and altered the balance of international treaty-making on the subject, culminating in the 1982 United Nations Convention on the Law of the Sea (see Brown, *The International Law of the Sea*, 5–11).

While Schmitt does not spend much time on the Americans in *Land and Sea*, he clearly considers them a continuation of the English in their reliance on naval and eventually air power to achieve military and economic goals, which then lead to the de-emphasizing of national boundaries (based on and defended by land-based armed forces) in favour of international treaties, human rights and global trade organizations. In Chapter 19 of *Land und Meer*, Schmitt notes the theories of Admiral Alfred T. Mahan (*The Influence of Seapower upon History* of 1890) concerning the need for the US and England to co-operate in maintaining the world order through command of the oceans, but observes that Mahan's concept still holds to the older idea of municipal law (*Landrecht*).

The relative unimportance of America in the post-war book represents a softening of the position Schmitt had held during World War II. In the 1943 essay 'Die letzte globale Linie', Americans appear as the most fearsome perpetrators of globalization:

> The Americans girdle the entire earth with a system of airbases and air transport, and proclaim an 'American century' for our planet. […] After the last of these global demarcation lines, the line of the Western hemisphere, has been transformed into a global interventionism without borders, a new situation has arisen. Against the claims of a universal, planetary world policing and world domination, a different *nomos* of the earth defends itself, resting on the basic principle of the division of the earth into several regions, each defined by its respective

historical, economic and cultural essence. (Schmitt, *Staat, Großraum*, 447)

Schmitt wrote this at approximately the same time as he was reading Melville intensively, and it distills his readings of both Captain Delano's intervention with its double motivation (charity and salvage) and Captain Ahab's monomaniacal quest to rid the world of evil.

In the much longer *Nomos der Erde*, Schmitt provides more details concerning the process by which humanity has moved from local, geographically determined boundaries to mathematically determined ones such as the Tordesillas line, the Greenwich line and other time boundaries, and the division of the world into Western and Eastern hemispheres. Here he gives more credit to other aspects of globalization, such as the trend towards universal human rights. The French, according to Schmitt, also played a role in globalization with their attempt

> to transfer to the world their liberal-individualistic constitution of the ideas of 1789 in a simultaneously individualistic and universalistic legal system and to make *le Citoyen Français* the model of a cosmopolitan world-citizen with validity for all nations. This new world-citizen would resemble the *Citoyen Français* so much because, despite the fact that the universal rights of this new system of international law in reality is merely an extension and apotheosis of the *droit civil* into a law of world sovereignty, the 'world' inhabited by the world-citizen in essence would be identical with the world-market under Anglo-Saxon domination. (Schmitt, *Staat, Großraum*, 208)

I have cited this passage at length because it shows, like few others of Schmitt, how he views a structural coupling between the subsystems of law, military power and economics as they together bring forward a process we today call 'globalization'. Indeed, the ease with which Schmitt combines these systems and nations into a single conspiracy in favour of 'human rights' at the expense of municipal law should make one suspicious of his argument. How and why does structural coupling work in this instance? Who decides when British economic power seizes on French legal universalism to expand its own sphere of dominance? The sovereign? The market? In Schmitt's own terms, a decision had to be made to allow this structural coupling to occur, yet the moment of decision does not appear in his account. In this passage and others, Schmitt anticipates many of the critiques of globalization of the 1990s and the early twenty-first century, especially those related to the ideological masking of economic and military domination beneath the surface of 'universal values' such as democracy and human rights. Schmitt's position reverses a common genealogy, where protests over economic globalization and flows of capital deplore the extension of the same rights to producers (in developing nations) as are enjoyed by consumers (in developed nations).[12]

And what role do Benito Cereno's people, the Spanish, play in this process of the creation of world-citizens and globally valid law? In Schmitt's reading, while Spain furthered the process of globalization through the sponsoring of Columbus and other explorers, it lost its chance of becoming a sea power with the defeat of its armada in 1588. The long period of decline that followed saw Spain lose virtually all its colonies that had once spanned the globe. Tierno Galván reads Benito Cereno's helplessness as symbolic of the paralysis of the Spanish nation in general:

> It is no accident that the captain of the myth is a Spaniard. [...] Centuries have accumulated at the helm [of the *San Dominick*], without any profound movement that could loose it from its moorings. [...] What better than a Spanish galleon to contrast with the optimism of the 'new man', Mr Delano? (Tierno Galván, 'Benito Cereno', 354–5)

H. Bruce Franklin is even more emphatic: 'When Delano considers withdrawing the command from Benito Cereno "on some benevolent plea" because the "dark Spaniard" was not fit to be trusted with the ship' [*BC*, 69], he serves as a representative American of his own time, of Melville's time, and of the time on the eve of [the twentieth] century when the United States would achieve its "manifest destiny" by seizing what was left of the collapsing Spanish empire, thus itself become a global empire' (Franklin, 'Slavery and Empire', 150).

Conclusion

To summarize Schmitt's allegorical reading of *BC*, the ship represents a sovereign European state, Benito Cereno the decisionless protagonist of a Baroque martyr drama, the Africans the Ortegan masses in rebellion, and Amasa Delano the superior American whose motivations for helping the drifting ship are as ambiguous as the story's plot in general. The restoration of order and imposition of justice are only possible at sea and amount to the imposition of

---

12 For a useful review of the different critiques of globalization, see Scott Cutler Shershow, 'Myth and Nihilism in the Discourse of Globalization'.

a US world order. Thomas Vesting is correct when he notes that, while Schmitt's early recognition of the death of 'classical' state sovereignty deserves a place in the history of thought, his insistence on retaining older ideas of force and theology as measuring rods for the state makes him able to recognize transformations of state sovereignty only as either decline or disappearance. 'In a world more and more concerned with issues of knowledge and less and less with issues of power, the work of Carl Schmitt can no longer serve as a guide' (Vesting, 'Die permanente Revolution', 201). Nevertheless, Schmitt's analyses that link knowledge, law, power and aesthetics may serve as a reminder that *Macht* and *Wissen* are in fact related to each other, and that literary *mythos* has a role to play in that complex. Schmitt's theory represents a 'hermeneutics of suspicion' vis à vis the supposed universality of human rights, the so-called 'war on terror', and so forth:

> For Schmitt, to assume that one can derive morally correct political institutions from abstract, universal norms is to put the cart before the horse. The truly important question remains: Who decides? What political power representing which political order defines terms like human rights and public reason, defines, in fact, what it means to be properly human? What political power distinguishes between the decent and the indecent, between those who police the world and those who are outlawed from it? (Rasch, *Sovereignty*, 147)

While ST posits the autonomy of systems as ever-increasing, the development of international law complicates this picture when it trumps municipal law. When ST takes up the issue of structural coupling, it is always within the context of 'a' society. As pointed out in the introduction, one of the most readily understandable examples of an autonomous system is language: a treatise written in German cannot have influence over the scholarly conversation in Great Britain or the United States, unless one of the structural couplings between languages, such as translation, is brought to bear. ST seems to have developed few models for analyzing the retreat of autonomy before the crumbling of sovereignty that Schmitt sees being worked out in the law of the sea and air, and which leads him to proclaim the end of the *jus publicum Europaeum*. Starting with the influence of the *Code Napoléon* on Goethe's treatment of marriage in *WV*, we have seen the possibility of cross-national citations of law, but in Schmittian geopolitics this process is accelerated, as indeed it has been in post-war Germany with the increasing power of the European Union. In that sense, Schmitt's choice of an American text as foundational myth is entirely appropriate. This tension between German and international systems of laws and rights reappears in the next and last study-example of the book, Peter Weiss's play *The Investigation*.

4.2
Citation as Second-Order Observation: Peter Weiss's *The Investigation*

> The theatre, however honourable its motives may be, has no right to be ashamed of and to deny itself.
> Dieter E. Zimmer, 'The Reading in the People's Auditorium of the German Democratic Republic'

> [Das Theater, so ehrenwert seine Skrupel auch sind, hat Unrecht, sich seiner selbst zu schämen und zu leugnen]
> Dieter E. Zimmer, 'Die Lesung in der Volkskammer der DDR'

Dieter Zimmer wrote these words in a review of one of the sixteen simultaneous premiere performances of Peter Weiss's 1965 oratorio (*Oratorium*), *The Investigation* (*Die Ermittlung*).[1] As a dramatist, Weiss confronted a problem complementary to that of the prosecutors and judges who attempted to assess personal guilt within the framework of the criminal government of Nazi Germany. Weiss's artistic problem, and that of the directors and actors charged with presenting his work to the public, concerned the ethics and aesthetics of representing the Holocaust. As we will see below, reviewers of these original productions consistently addressed the issue of whether the theatre would end up theatricalizing the material. Zimmer here speaks directly to the issue, upholding the right of the theatre to present even this material while preserving the autonomous aesthetic of art. Weiss saw himself compelled to 'no aesthetic judgment vis à vis this play, but rather I see in it a material that consists of facts [*Tatsachen*] and that lies beyond aesthetic norms'

---

1   Zimmer's review appeared in *Die Zeit*, 29 October 1965: 21.

(Hans Mayer, 'Kann sich die Bühne eine Auschwitz-Dokumentation leisten?', 8; 'ich sehe zunächst einmal keine ästhetische Beurteilung diesem Stück gegenüber, sondern ich sehe in diesem Stück ein Material, das aus Tatsachen besteht und das ausserhalb ästhetischer Massstäbe liegt'). Zimmer, on the other hand, goes on to say that he would not be embarrassed to make classic aesthetic observations like 'Witness Number Three was well acted; [Defendant] Kaduk not so well'. ('To observe' in Luhmanian terms is to draw a binary distinction that effects a change within a system.) The *'Unrecht'* in Zimmer's statement is actually more colloquial than I have rendered it in English – it is no doubt coincidence that a reference to the *Recht/Unrecht* distinction appears in the review of a play that observes the *Recht/Unrecht* distinction being made – and with what degree of difficulty. Yet this coincidence points us towards the particular structural coupling that occurs in Weiss's remarkable – if to this day underappreciated – play, and that is the topic of this chapter.

Shaping stage plays upon the agonistic procedures of a courtroom trial, real or imagined, is not unusual for playwrights, with examples ranging from Bertolt Brecht's 1940 *The Good Person of Szechwan* (*Der gute Mensch von Sezuan*) and his 1945 *Caucasian Chalk Circle* (*Der kaukasische Kreidekreis*) to Jerome Lawrence and Robert Edwin Lee's 1955 *Inherit the Wind* (based on the Scopes 'monkey trial' of 1925), to name but a few examples from the twentieth century. What makes *The Investigation* unusual is its degree of exact citation: the play amounts to an immense, artistically shaped quotation from the trial testimony, which Weiss gathered both directly, as an observer of the trial, and second-hand from newspaper accounts, especially Bernd Naumann's for the *Frankfurter Allgemeine Zeitung*. Furthermore, from its initial conception *The Investigation* was conceived as a second-order observation of law by literature.[2] Thus, the play's title has at least three references: it refers to the Frankfurt trial; it refers to the mimetic investigation of reality that drama is capable of providing; and it refers to mimetic observation (the drama) of legal observation (the trial). Weiss himself used the legal term 'Konzentrat' (concentrate of testimony; *Notizbücher*, 391) to describe the relationship of his drama to the 'real' trial.

No Precedent

JUDGE: As examining magistrate
               you saw no means

---

2   It would seem that technically a second-order observation can only occur within a subsystem, not between two or more. However, I feel that the term retains its usefulness for indicating the observation of an observation.

of making your findings public

1ST WITNESS Before what court
could I have brought an action
for the killing of masses of people
and the seizure of their goods and property
by the highest administrative offices
I could not institute proceedings
against the government itself
(Weiss, *The Investigation*, 289)

[RICHTER: Sahen Sie als Untersuchungsrichter
keine anderen Möglichkeiten
Ihre Kenntnisse zu veröffentlichen

ZEUGE 1: Vor welchem Gerichtshof
hätte ich Klage erheben können
über die Mengen der Getöteten
und über die
von den höchsten Verwaltungsstellen
übernommenen Werte
Ich konnte doch kein Verfahren
gegen die oberste Staatsführung einleiten]
(Weiss, *Die Ermittlung*, 191)

This passage from Weiss's play revisits a paradox voiced repeatedly in the texts we have been examining: the law cannot make the second-order observation of declaring itself to be legal – or more appropriately, in the case of the mass exterminations carried out by the German government between 1939 and 1945, to be illegal. When the entire system from top to bottom is illegal, the *Recht/Unrecht* distinction becomes impossible to draw. In the latter sense, the epigraph contains a play on the idea of *Werte*, which in German can mean both 'values' and 'valuables' (in the published translation, 'property'). The witness refers first and foremost to the goods and property stolen from the millions of Jews who were sent to concentration camps, either to be immediately killed, or to be used as slave labourers unto death. But complaint should also be raised against the highest administrative offices of the German Reich that planned the Shoah for simply accepting precedential values. These values, as Hannah Arendt argues in *Eichmann in Jerusalem*, included neither justice nor compassion, but equally neither evil, nor personal power. They included *Recht* only in the sense of following regulations and the flowchart of authority (in German, the *Dienstweg*), tempered with a sense of defending and furthering the German nation. This particular formulation of the paradox comes neither from Weiss himself, nor from one of the distinguished *Dichter* and *Denker* we have been considering in the course of this book. Rather, Weiss here merely cites the exact language of one of the three hundred witnesses who testified at what has come to be known as the Frankfurt Auschwitz trial, which opened on 20 December 1963 and for which verdicts were read on 19 and 20 August 1965.[3]

These second-order observations of law recur with some frequency in Weiss's text, and observe both the 'laws' governing Auschwitz and those governing the Auschwitz trial. To give a few examples: canto six, 'Unterscharführer Stark', ends with defendant Stark explaining how he could murder people without a second thought, because he was told that everything was done according to the law; in canto seven, 'The Black Wall', the presiding judge of the military court that sent prisoners to be shot at the wall is interrogated about the way the trials were conducted; and the very last words of the play are those of the defence attorney invoking the statute of limitations.

Investigation: The Trial

Of the twenty-two defendants at the Frankfurt trial, all of whom had served in the death camp run by the SS where more than a million victims, mostly Jews, had lost their lives, three were acquitted, while the rest received sentences ranging from three years and three months to life imprisonment. These dates represent only the 'eye' of the German legal dealings concerning Auschwitz. The preliminary investigations for the trial (*Vorermittlungen*) had begun at least six years earlier, with efforts on the part of the International Auschwitz Committee in Vienna, the *Zentrale Stelle der Landesjustizverwaltungen* in Ludwigsburg, and the attorney general of the State of Hessen, Fritz Bauer. The result was a 700–page indictment, accompanied by a 300–page history of the camp. Already, then, as in Kafka's novel, it is difficult to pinpoint the actual beginning of the trial, to determine where *Recht* ends and history begins, to determine whether the trial was conducted according to *Rechtsnorm* or *Rechtssatz*, or another kind of *Gesetz* altogether. These writings, at once legal, historical and literary, plus the publicity surrounding the trial itself, were what made the name 'Auschwitz', which before the trial was just

---

3   The official name of the trial was 'Criminal case against Mulka and others' ('*Strafsache gegen Mulka und andere*'). Mulka's name came first because he was the highest-ranking officer in Auschwitz to be indicted. The camp commandant, Rudolf Höss, had been executed after trial in Poland in 1947.

another concentration camp, into one of the chief metonyms for Nazi genocide. (Or, to put it another way, the extensive documentation provided at the trial made it clear that Auschwitz was the leading death camp in terms both of the number of those murdered, and of the rationalization procedures for killing it put into place.)

The Frankfurt Auschwitz trial lasted eighteen months. Three months were devoted to closing arguments. Three hundred and fifty witnesses were heard. The records filled 124 volumes. At least 1400 articles concerning the trial appeared in seventy different newspapers.[4] A number of factors influenced the timing and conditions of the Frankfurt Auschwitz trial. The Nuremberg trials had passed symbolic judgment on the Nazis immediately after the war. Konrad Adenauer's leadership of the fledgling Federal Republic of Germany had emphasized the future rather than the past. The presence of former Nazis in his government could be interpreted as a signal that vigorous prosecution and reckoning with Nazi crimes was not desired. West Germany's uncertain sovereignty also played a role: when complete control over the legal system passed from the Allies to the Germans in 1955, a provision against double jeopardy was made for individuals who had previously been investigated under the occupation. The long absence of some perpetrators from Germany, often in Iron Curtain prison camps, also played a role. The result was that prosecution of war crimes was happenstance, based often on chance recognition of a former camp guard by a former inmate, until the creation of the *Zentrale Stelle für die Landesjustizverwaltungen* in Ludwigsburg in 1958, which represented for the first time a co-operative approach of the *Länder* to prosecuting Nazi crimes. One could see the Frankfurt trial as merely the opening of this office's legal effectiveness. It has investigated well over 100,000 alleged incidents since, albeit with a rate of conviction of under ten per cent.

The mammoth dimension of the Frankfurt trials was due to a wish on the part of Fritz Bauer (1903–1968) to bring together into a single venue the various complaints that had been registered against actors across the Federal Republic. Bauer's Jewish background had caused him to be removed from his judgeship in 1933 and briefly interned by the Nazis, before fleeing to Denmark. From the beginning, Bauer recognized and approved the extra-legal significance of this 'mass trial', and was in the process of planning another against the planners of enforced euthanasia when he died. (It says something about the fragile state of justice in Germany in the 1950s that Bauer is also famous for having given the information on

---

4   Articles collected by David O. Pendas, 'I didn't know what Auschwitz was'.

Adolf Eichmann's whereabouts to Israel's *Mossad* rather than to the German authorities. As a result, Eichmann was tried in Jerusalem rather than in Frankfurt or Bonn.) These trials were part of his general concern with re-educating the German public in an attempt at altering what he regarded as a predisposition in German society to accept totalitarian regimes. According to Mattias Meusch, Bauer saw two different paths to re-education: the direct transmission of historical knowledge; and the use of criminal proceedings against actors of the recent past, 'since from this [latter] medium he hoped to obtain heightened learning through its special effect on the public [*Öffentlichkeitswirkung*] and through its visibility [*Anschaulichkeit*]' (Meusch, *Von der Diktatur zur Demokratie*, 138). '*Anschaulichkeit*' is a particularly interesting word here (though it is not necessarily Bauer's), since it possesses an aesthetic dimension: it indicates what is pleasing to the eye. While he was weaving the various accusations together into a single procedure, Bauer was giving lectures to groups such as the Youth Circle of Rheinland-Pfalz with titles like 'The Roots of Fascist and National Socialist Action'. Near the end of the trial, Bauer even appeared on a television broadcast, talking about the trial and the attitudes of the defendants over a glass of beer with a group of 'ordinary Germans'. There he lamented the fact that not a word of remorse or acknowledgement of guilt had fallen from the defendants' mouths.[5]

Two major English-language studies of the *Auschwitz-Prozess* substantially agree that the entire undertaking was based on an *aporia* that was destined to limit its effectiveness. As opposed to the Nuremberg, Rudolf Höss, and Eichmann trials, Germans were now attempting to bring other Germans to justice for their crimes against humanity. Therefore, they relied on German law, which contained nothing regarding crimes against humanity during the time of the murders, and which also prohibited indictments on ex post facto legislation. Though the massive number of co-defendants and the deliberately spectacular arrangement of the trial were without precedent in German legal history, the trial procedure itself came directly out of a supposedly unbroken chain of legal validity provided by a criminal code that had changed very little since its adoption in 1871, and the functionaries of state-sponsored murder were treated as ordinary murderers or as accomplices to murder: '[T]he court saw the actions of the accused as criminal actions, pure and simple, as German law and precedent mandated. The law dictated what did and did not constitute murder, did and did not constitute perpetration. As legal actors, the members of the court

---

5 This scene is included in the documentary film, *Verdict on Auschwitz*.

were strictly limited in their room for maneuver in interpreting such matters' (David Pendas, *The Frankfurt Auschwitz Trial*, 297). Thus, for example, the standard subjective legal distinction of degree of intent (or lack thereof) was applied, with the predictable result that those defendants who had demonstrated sadistic tendencies (such as Wilhelm Boger, who invented and used his own torture device, the 'Boger swing') received the harshest sentences.[6]

Because article 103 of the West German Basic Law prohibited ex post facto legislation, the defendants could only be tried for crimes committed against law that was supposedly still in force during the Nazi period. It was not possible to introduce concepts not embodied in that law such as genocide, mass murder, hate crime, or the like; thus, the mass murderers of Auschwitz were tried under the framework of ordinary criminal law, including the statute of limitations (whose approaching expiration for felonies committed in the 1940s gave further impetus to the prosecution). The statute of limitations had, in fact, already passed for all but the most serious crime of *Mord*. Proving *Mord* (essentially, first-degree murder) required the establishment of one or more motives, means, or purposes behind the act, which the defendants attempted to counter with the claim that they were simply carrying out orders. Secondly, subjective orientation established the difference between perpetrator (*Täter*) and the less-guilty accomplice (*Gehilfe*). From one perspective, all the defendants were mere accomplices, actors carrying out the wishes of a criminal regime. However, the prosecution was forced into attempts to psychologize the defendants, to read their minds through their testimony, their actions and their conversations with others. The most heavily relied-upon method for doing this was the questioning of witnesses, particularly those who had heard something out of the defendants' mouths. However, the careful interrogation of individual feelings and intentions did not fit the overwhelming machinery of death that was Auschwitz. 'Boger's sadism is privileged, both by the court and the press, over Lucas's reluctant compliance, even though both were functionally interchangeable for the killing apparatus. [...] If Lucas was truly so decent, how could Boger really be that bad?' (David Pendas, '"I didn't know what Auschwitz was"', 440). There is a parallel between this paradox and that of Kafka's *Prozess*, as we observe guilt and innocence become relativized and literally made mobile through different positionings in the machine of *Recht/Unrecht*.

The reduction of the investigation to such issues inhibited its

---

6   Werner Renz examines similar issues in 'Der erste Frankfurter Auschwitz-Prozess'.

pedagogical effectiveness for millions of Germans who had nothing to do with Auschwitz or the Nazi death machine. The vast majority of courtroom trials exhaust themselves in limited, private findings of guilt or innocence. Others, however, take on additional, public meanings. The most extreme form of this is represented by the infamous 'show trials' of the Soviet Union. The most flamboyant and committed of the Frankfurt defence attorneys, Hans Laternser, who had also played a role in the Nuremberg trials, repeatedly referred to the Auschwitz trial as just such a *Schauprozess*. In his formulation, the issue of guilt had already largely been decided, and the trial's main function was the formation of public memory of events.[7]

A further complicating factor was presented by the admission of Friedrich Karl Kaul of the German Democratic Republic as a co-indicter. Kaul ostensibly represented citizens of the DDR (the German abbreviation for the communist East German state) who were victims of Auschwitz, but his real mandate came from the country's Politbüro, which on 19 November 1963 passed a resolution commanding him to make the trial into a 'tribunal against the IG-Farben company' (Annette Rosskopf, 'Zum Leben und Wirken Friedrich Karl Kaul', 186). The term '*Tribunal*', as well as the resolution itself, seems to confirm the show-trial aspect that the defence attorneys complained of. Kaul attempted to fulfil this role with documents, expert testimony and select witnesses from the DDR. However, Chief Judge Hofmeyer diminished these aspects of the trial, because none of the accused had served in Monowitz, where IG-Farben had its operations and where many camp victims had been employed as slave labour. An example of these manoeuvrings concerned the expert testimony (*Gutachten*) of a Professor Jürgen Kucynski of East Berlin, whose purpose was to show that Auschwitz was constructed at the behest of IG-Farben. The defence objected on the grounds of (ideological) prejudice and Kucynski's belonging to the socialist SED party, but Judge Hofmeyer noted that the court should be able to accommodate persons whose basic beliefs differed widely. Judge Hummerich asked Kucynski pointed questions concerning his blatantly Marxist-Leninist intepretations of society:

HUMMERICH: Do you place the Third Reich and the Federal Republic on the same level?
KUCYNSKI: By no means. Not every dictatorship of monopoly capitalism need end in fascism.

---

7   Cf. Laternser's collected speeches for the defence at the trial in *Die andere Seite*.

[HUMMERICH: Stellen Sie das Dritte Reich und die Bundesrepublik auf eine Stufe?
KUCYNSKI: Keineswegs. Nicht jede Monopolherrschaft muß zum Faschismus führen.] (*Frankfurter Neue Presse*, 20 March 1964)

The testimony given by IG-Farben people to the Nuremberg investigation team was later denied during the trial. Hofmeyer ordered it stricken from the record. This game of '*Fort-Da*' typifies the shadowy presence of IG-Farben and the thesis of Auschwitz as 'extreme capitalism' during the trial. Unable to hijack the proceedings as a show trial against capitalism, the representatives of East Germany were forced to be content with the exposing of the court's 'protection' of the industrialists (*Konzernherren*) still active in West Germany.

According to Robert Cohen, the lengthy period that elapsed before the criminals were brought to trial, which made the private matter of determining guilt so difficult, helped formulate its public message with even greater clarity:

> The Auschwitz trial itself, like all trials, collapsed the boundaries between past and present, between deeds and their consequences. The continuities from the Nazi state to West German society of the Adenauer years were a constant subtext in Frankfurt. The trial revealed what had been an open secret all along: that values and attitudes prevalent under Nazism had not suddenly disappeared in 1945, any more than had those who held them. On the one hand, this produced insistent calls for a statute of limitations for war crimes; but it also led to the formation of opposition movements throughout the 1960s. Twenty years after the end of the war, these movements finally forced the debate on Germany's Nazi past into the public discourse. Weiss's play was a key element in this development. (Cohen, 'Political Aesthetics', 62)

Investigation: The Play

At the other end, the post-trial process, there were appeals which lasted until 1969[8] – and there was the play by Weiss, presented simultaneously on fifteen stages in Germany on 19 October 1965. It was also broadcast as a radio play and on television. Ingmar Bergman

---

8 Most of the verdicts were upheld on appeal. The notable exception was Dr Franz Lucas, whose conviction was overturned on the basis that there had been direct testimony in his favour and all incriminating evidence had been hearsay.

directed a version in Swedish. Given the pragmatics of stage presentations, even as documentary drama the play could portray neither the horrors of Auschwitz, nor even the Auschwitz trial with its massive and contradictory discourses. Instead, the oratorio was designed to perform a second-order observation by moving its audience to reflect on the failure of the culprits and the justice system in drawing distinctions: 'The meaning of this play must be that of motivating the audience towards self-conscious [bewussten] thinking and that it questions itself [...] concerning its own behaviours' (Hans Mayer, 'Kann sich die Bühne', 19). Second-order observation, as the name implies, observes how others observe. *The Investigation* investigates both legal investigation and the viewing of performance. 'The first-order observer lives in a world that seems both probable and true [wahr-scheinlich]. By contrast, the second-order observer notices the improbability [Unwahrscheinlichkeit] of first-order observation. A movement of the hand, a sentence spoken – every such act is extremely improbable when considered as a selection among all other possibilities' (Luhmann, *Art as Social System*, 62). For both defendants and witnesses, Auschwitz was a truth; for the observers and theatre audiences not yet familiar with the facts, it was an improbability, an attitude the defence attorneys were obliged to reinforce, for example in constant denials that the defendants personally witnessed or even knew of any murders in the camp. *The Investigation* largely eschews plot and refrains from human drama in order to capture this set of differential relations. The play is set not in Auschwitz, but in the Frankfurt courtroom that observed Auschwitz. The play follows neither the Aristotelian structure of plot, nor the repetitive and diffuse non-structure of the trial testimony. Weiss instead organized his citations into eleven cantos, each based on a particular theme or locus in the camp: Canto One: The Loading Ramp (*Gesang von der Rampe*) deals with the infamous selection process for those arriving at Auschwitz, where those who might become labourers were sent to their barracks and the unfit to immediate execution; Canto Eight: Phenol (*Gesang vom Phenol*) cites testimony on the killing of prisoners through phenol injections, and so forth.

As is the norm in German court proceedings, no official transcript of the Frankfurt trial was taken. The vast majority of witnesses allowed their testimony to be recorded, but these recordings were not available to Weiss, and in fact only became accessible to the general public in the first decade of the twenty-first century.[9] Weiss

---

9   The tape recordings were made only as memory aids for judge and jury, and were supposed to be destroyed after the verdict. They were preserved at the insistence of organizations of Holocaust survivors, and lay forgotten in

added to his own observations of the trial the detailed protocols published in the *Frankfurter Allgemeine Zeitung* as material for the play, so that the oratorio represents neither a depiction of Auschwitz, nor a dramatization of the trial, but rather a single, enormous citation of legal testimony. There was fervent debate, especially at the play's premiere, about Weiss's slanting of the material towards a Marxist interpretation of Auschwitz and of the Federal Republic of Germany, one of the two states to arise from the ashes of the Third Reich, and a government against whom proceedings could not be instituted. Yet Erika Salloch in particular has shown, in minute detail, how carefully and conscientiously Weiss worked from the material he had, including, as noted above, the interventions of the East German representatives at the trial who wished to indict capitalism rather than fascism or the defendants. I agree with Salloch that *The Investigation* is more remarkable for its author's erasing of his own point of view than for any imposition of a Marxist analysis.[10]

Brechtian epic theatre exerted a strong influence on Weiss, but so did the theories of Antonin Artaud and the absurdist plays of Samuel Beckett. These influences came together in the play for which Weiss is best known, *Marat/Sade*, first performed in Berlin in 1964. Weiss's family, originally from Berlin, had spent most of the Nazi period in Sweden. Weiss remarked on Auschwitz that it was meant to be his destination, as a Jew. Life in exile and literary work in two languages no doubt contributed to the detachment, objectivity and subtlety of his treatments of highly political issues, despite Weiss's own deeply rooted leftist leanings (he joined Sweden's Communist party in 1965). Notably, Weiss's last theatrical success, achieved shortly before his death in 1982, was a dramatization of Kafka's *Trial* narrative (*Der neue Prozess*).

Critical readings of Weiss's play have mainly addressed its relationship to the problems of memory and representation of the Shoah. Indeed, the play receives mention in general studies of this topic by Christopher Bigsby, Sidra Dekoven Ezrahi, Lawrence Langer, Alvin H. Rosenfeld and James E. Young. Such problems arose in the course of the trial itself, which had been set in motion in part as a response to German inability to come to terms with its past (a

---

the archives of Hessen until they were subpoenaed for another trial in 1988. Gradually, they have become more accessible and are now available as a DVD-ROM: *Der Auschwitz-Prozess: Tonbandmitschnitte, Protokolle, Dokumente*.

10 As its subtitle indicates, Christoph Weiss's massive *Peter Weiss and* The Investigation *in the Cold War* (»Die Ermittlung« *im Kalten Krieg*) untangles the inevitable perceptions of the play through the lenses of the ideological struggle played out in Germany.

process known in German as *Vergangenheitsbewältigung*) and of the unfinishedness of its legal reckoning with that past. One of the few book-length studies of the trial devotes only two sentences to the play, both of which show inaccuracies:

> Peter Weiss's play, *The Investigation: An Oratorio in 11 Cantos*, presents dialogue taken verbatim from the trial in a form deliberately modeled after Greek tragedy. As important for the history of twentieth-century drama as his earlier avant-garde work, *Marat/Sade*, *The Investigation* is less a history of the Auschwitz Trial than it is a dramatic representation of the tragic character of modernity itself. (Pendas, *The Frankfurt Auschwitz Trial 1963–1965*, 4–5)

'Modeled' presents too strong a parallel between the form of the play (which has no tragic hero or chorus, though the defendants sometimes laugh or applaud as a group) and Greek tragedy per se. Furthermore, Weiss wrote the play more with Dante's *Inferno* in mind (it is divided into *Gesänge* or cantos and structured as a descent into hell) than Greek tragedy. The play is certainly not a history of the trial – it is rather a part of the trial's history. However, it is quite an interpretive leap to say that the play is about modernity in general. In eschewing a central protagonist (very different in this respect from Rolf Hochhuth's 1963 *The Deputy* [*Der Stellvertreter*], which treats similar themes through the fate of conventionally portrayed heroes and villains), Weiss's play implies that the introduction of industrialized killing such as occurred at Auschwitz cannot be captured in the idea of the tragic, nor depicted in the form of tragedies.

Indeed, one is struck by the similarity between the implications of Weiss's play and David Pendas's conclusion that while the Auschwitz trial was valuable for its authoritative determination of the 'facts' of the camp, in terms of making the *Recht/Unrecht* distinction, 'the form of "guilt" that emerged was so strictly delimited and so strongly rooted in individual psychology that the multifaceted complexity of guilt as a social category disappeared; in its rush to discern individual culpability, the trial displaced and eliminated the dimension of collective responsibility' (Pendas, *The Frankfurt Auschwitz Trial 1963–1965*, 304). This conclusion is echoed in the title of Rebecca Wittman's full-length study of the trial, *Beyond Justice*. Wittman rightly places Weiss in a chapter on the trial's reception by the German public. Furthermore, she recognizes the play's function as a second-order observation: 'Some kind of lesson had to be learned from the trial, and since the judgment with its light sentences could not teach it, the task would be left to historians, philosophers, artists, and playwrights. Unfortunately, Weiss' message was not to be carried forward in mainstream depictions of Nazi crime' (Wittman, *Beyond Justice*, 271). Wittman posits here a structural coupling that moves in two directions. Firstly, the Auschwitz trial should teach society a lesson about values. In ST terms, such lessons do not belong to the modern legal subsystem. The decoupling of moral lessons from legal verdicts in, for example, the abstraction and invisibility of punishment or its conversion into 'correction' has been famously analyzed by Michel Foucault in *Discipline and Punish*. There remains, however, a selective structural coupling where certain cases and criminals are deemed to be exemplary for society 'as a whole'. Fritz Bauer did everything he could to make the Frankfurt Auschwitz trial one such example. But conversely, the difficulties, failures and ambiguities of the trial called for a literary supplement that would bring to the legal system values that the latter could not clarify – the old dream of law-and-literature.

Structural Coupling Rechtsbewältigung

While the language of *The Investigation* comes overwhelmingly from the Frankfurt trial, its composition differs substantially from the way a trial proceeds. At a trial with this many defendants and witnesses, the mind can get lost in the huge variety. Weiss cuts down on the number of names, faces and details of circumstance to reduce the size of the cast. In the end, the entire *dramatis personae* of *The Investigation* belong to one of just four categories: judge (*Richter*); counsel (*Ankläger* or *Verteidiger*); defendant (*Angeklagter*); and witness (*Zeuge* or *Zeugin*). The last two monikers are expanded to more than one character through the use of numbers (e.g. *Angeklagter* 5, *Zeuge* 12, etc.) None of the characters bears a personal name, though the defendants can often be inferred by co-ordination with the canto names and witness statements. The judge has the most lines, but is the least memorable character, because his utterances function mainly to incite others to speak. (There are no stage directions to indicate action, meaning that the reader determines 'character' in this play solely through verbal expression.) The counsels, defence and prosecution, have a balanced number of lines and presentations. The prosecution tends to emphasize the role of industry in promoting Auschwitz, while the defence consistently takes a nationalist line that encourages Germany to forget Auschwitz, which happened long ago. The play ends with one such plea:

DEFENDANT #1: Today
                When our nation has worked its way up
                after a devastating war

to a leading position in the world
we ought to concern ourselves
with other things
These recriminations
should have fallen
under the Statute of Limitations
a long time ago
[*loud approbation from the* DEFENDANTS]
(Weiss, *The Investigation*, 296)

[Angeklagter 1: Heute
da unsere Nation sich wieder
zu einer führenden Stellung
emporgearbeitet hat
sollten wir uns mit anderen Dingen befassen
als mit Vorwürfen
die längst als verjährt
angesehen müßten
Laute Zustimmung von Seiten der Angeklagten]
(*Die Ermittlung*, 185–6)

Cantos five and six (Weiss, *The Investigation*, 197–222) are the only ones to carry the names of individuals: Lili Tofler, one of the most heart-rending victims, executed for sending a letter to another inmate; and SS Corporal Stark, a defendant distinguished above all by his young age. Günter Sasse has argued that the techniques of dramatization described above 'deindividualize' the defendants: '*The Investigation* focuses not on individual guilt, but on supra-individual structures of consciousness reflected in structures of language. [... T]he audience is thereby deprived of the possibility of defending itself through reference to the "peculiarity" of the past events or to the anormality of the perpetrators' (Sasse, 'Faktizität und Fiktionalität', 20). An example is the accumulation of sentences with nur ('only') in them, which make the defendants into ends of a chain of command.

Had Weiss been interested in a mimetic treatment of the trial, he might have included bailiffs, reporters, the public, and so forth. He might have started at the trial's beginning (or before the beginning). Instead, the play rearranges the chronology of the citations and begins on the 116th day of the trial, in the middle of an examination. Nor is Weiss concerned with the final verdicts, for several reasons. For one thing, these did not point in a unanimous direction, ranging from acquittal to several years in prison; as noted above, the laws applied to the case made the investigation of intent paramount, and the results of this search varied from defendant to defendant. In a sense, then, concentrating on the verdicts – the focus of interest and turning point in most courtroom dramas, including those by Brecht – would characterize the defendants as individuals, whereas Weiss, in contrast, is concerned with the overall system of social communication in Germany, the state of exception that made murder without intent, remorse, or the assumption of responsibility so easy to carry out. Secondly, his audience was probably better acquainted with the verdicts of the trial than with the information that had been brought to light. Thirdly, the guilty verdicts would have on the audience a cathartic effect that Weiss wanted to avoid. His citation of the trial reduces it to the system of communications that is the law in this case. The reports of Bernd Naumann, for example, which are the most extensive on the trial and which for years substituted the lack of a transcript, are irrelevant to the binary decision *Recht/Unrecht* that the law is constrained to speak. This paring-down is reproduced at the level of diction as well. Weiss is content neither with a language that cites literature, in which case the phrases would differentiate the characters into individuals with names, nor in the bare citation of legal language.

Repetition is used to drive home these points about the trial. Weiss focuses on the moments when the defendants were 'not there', when they refused a morally repugnant task, when they were compelled to participate for the first and only time, when they were ignorant of what was going on a few metres from their position or being carried out by their subordinates. This begins right away, from the first lines of the play, where a witness reveals that he witnessed exactly nothing:

JUDGE:	The witness was stationmaster of the railroad station where the trains arrived How far was the station from the camp
1ST WITNESS:	A mile and a quarter from the old army camp about three miles from the main camp
JUDGE:	Did your work take you into the camp
1ST WITNESS:	No I only had to make sure that the tracks in use were in good condition and that the trains arrived and departed according to schedule
JUDGE:	What condition were the tracks in
1ST WITNESS:	They were in excellent condition
JUDGE:	Were you in charge of

1ST WITNESS:	setting up the train schedules
	No
	I only had to take care of technical measures
	related to scheduling the shuttle traffic
	between the station and the camp
JUDGE:	The record contains scheduling orders
	bearing your signature
1ST WITNESS:	It's possible that in the absence
	of the officer in charge
	I occasionally had to sign one [...]
PROSECUTING ATTORNEY:	You didn't hear anything about conditions in the camp
1ST WITNESS:	There were so many rumours going around
	You never knew what to think
PROSECUTING ATTORNEY:	You heard nothing
	About people being exterminated
1ST WITNESS:	How could anybody believe a thing like that
	(Weiss, *The Investigation*, 119–21)
[RICHTER:	Herr Zeuge
	Sie waren Vorstand des Bahnhofs
	in dem die Transporte einliefen
	Wie weit war der Bahnhof vom Lager entfernt
ZEUGE 12	Kilometer vom alten Kasernenlager
	und etwa 5 Kilometer vom Hauptlager
RICHTER:	Hatten Sie in den Lagern zu tun
ZEUGE 1	Nein
	Ich hatte nur dafür zu sorgen
	dass die Betriebstrecken in Ordnung waren
	und dass die Züge fahrplanmässig
	ein- und ausliefen
RICHTER:	In welchem Zustand waren die Strecken
ZEUGE 1	Es war eine ausgesprochen gut
	ausgestattete Rollbahn
RICHTER:	Wurden die Fahrplananordnungen
	von Ihnen ausgearbeitet
ZEUGE 1	Nein
	Ich hatte nur fahrplantechnische Massnahmen
	im Zusammenhang mit dem Pendelverkehr
	zwischen Bahnhof und Lager durchzuführen
RICHTER:	Dem Gericht liegen Fahrplananordnungen vor
	die von Ihnen unterzeichnet sind
ZEUGE 1	Ich habe das vielleicht einmal

ANKL GER:	vertretungsweise unterschrieben müssen [...] Erfuhren Sie nichts über die Verhälnisse im Lager
ZEUGE 1	Es wurde ja so viel dummes Zeug geredet man wusste doch nie woran man war
ANKL GER:	Hörten Sie nichts über die Vernichtung von Menschen
ZEUGE 1	Wie sollte man sowas schon glauben] (*Die Ermittlung*, 11–13)

Not only does the play deflect any catharsis of decision, it also removes any agonistic confrontation between prosecution and defence, or witness and defendant. There were times during the trial when such confrontations occurred, but Weiss does not take them into the play. One of the few such exchanges occurs between the attorneys when one witness judges the number of Nazi victims to be six million. The defence objects:

COUNSEL FOR THE DEFENCE:	Even though we all feel most deeply for the victims still it is our duty here to counter and oppose all exaggerations and vilification originating from a certain quarter [...]
[The DEFENDANTS laugh nodding in agreement]	
PROSECUTING ATTORNEY:	This is a willful and conscious expression of contempt for those who died in the camp and for those survivors who have appeared here to testify as witnesses The behaviour of the counsel for the defence clearly demonstrates the persistence of that same outlook of which the defendants present were guilty I wish to state this unequivocally and emphatically

COUNSEL FOR THE DEFENCE:	Who is this assistant prosecutor with his unsuitable clothes It is I believe a Middle European custom to appear in court with a closed robe
JUDGE:	The court calls for order (Weiss, *The Investigation*, 293–95)
[VERTEIDIGER:	Selbst wenn wir alle die Opfer aufs tiefste beklagen so ist unsere Aufgabe hier Übertreibungen und von bestimmter Stelle gelenkten Beschmutzungen entgegenzuwirken […]

Die Angeklagten lachen zustimmend

ANKLÄGER:	Das ist eine bewusste und gewollte Missachtung und Kränkung der Toten des Lagers und der Überlebenden die sich bereitgefunden haben hier als Zeugen auszusagen In einem solchen Verhalten der Verteidigung wird offensichtlich die Fortsetzung jener Gesinnung demonstriert die die Angeklagten in diesem Prozess schuldig werden liess Das soll hier mit Nachdruck und mit aller Deutlichkeit festgestellt werden
VERTEIDIGER:	Wer ist denn dieser Nebenkläger mit seiner unpassenden Kleidung Es entspricht mitteleuropäischen Gesellschaftsformen mit geschlossener Robe im Gerichtssaal zu erscheinen
RICHTER:	Wir rufen zur Ordnung] (*Die Ermittlung*, 196–97)

Essentially, the defence calls into question the enormity of the number of deaths overall (which indeed were not technically legally relevant to the charges), the assistant prosecutor then charges the defence with a mindset similar to that of the defendants, and the defence reminds the court that the prosecutor who has just spoken

(Kaul) represents the DDR. The machinery of Nazism is replaced by the automatism of Cold War divisions.

The structure of *The Investigation* thus removes it equally from theatrical tradition, because it cites so heavily and extensively from the trial, and from the legal subsystem because it relativizes the importance of different discourses. Does this positioning between subsystems make the play inaccessible to both, or does it allow it to function all the better as a structural coupling? To begin to answer this question, let us turn to the play's reception.

Beyond Theatricalization

To understand the uniqueness of the structural coupling between trial and theatre piece, let us imagine a Martian ambassador to Germany, who despite its excellent command of German has no familiarity with the German or other humanoid legal systems. Let us suppose further that there is no such thing as theatre on Mars. Martians live thousands of years, so the 180 days of the Frankfurt trial seem to our ambassador, who attends daily, to pass quickly. It is then invited by well-meaning friends to attend the premiere of *Die Ermittlung*, which follows so closely on the conclusion of the trial that it seems almost to be part of it. Seated in the theatre – which doesn't seem to him all that different from the two courtrooms in which the original trials had been held – and watching the drama unfold, the Martian's photographic memory immediately picks up the repetition of testimony exactly as it was given in the trial. But if the trial went by quickly, the play flashes past in the wink of an eye. A lot has been left out. A few things have been put in. The Martian's friends had tried to describe what theatre was all about. For example, to quote from the Borges story where a similar explanation of a theatrical performance is given, 'The persons on this terrace were playing the drum and the lute, save for some fifteen or twenty (with crimson-colored masks) who were praying, singing and conversing. They suffered prison, but no one could see the jail; they traveled on horseback, but no one could see the horse; they fought, but the swords were of reed; they died and then stood up again' (Borges, 'Averroes's Search', 152).

Yet, the Martian watching *Die Ermittlung* experiences the opposite problem: the most important thing seems to be missing, namely the performative force of actual legal verdicts, which is generally not visible to the eye in a real court case.[11] There is little movement or

---

11 As noted in the introductory chapter, Jacques Derrida has questioned exactly this distinction between 'real' and fictional performatives in 'Signature, Event, Context'. Derrida's attempt at upsetting the *prima facie* distinction between real and fictional uses of language is edifying, but in the end

action, no plot to follow, just testimony and legal manoeuvring. It seems to be nothing other than the trial itself, but trimmed down according to an unknown heuristic. Nor is the difference between illocutionary and 'fictional' language-use salient, since no verdict or sentencing is given in the play. Now let us assume that the Martian visits the appeals court where the Frankfurt judgments are being reviewed. This process seems to bear less resemblance to the trial than does the theatre piece, because the testimony plays a muted role, the audience is missing, and the focus is largely on the lengthy text of the judge's ruling, which does not appear in the play. Finally, our Martian consults a dictionary and discovers that the German title of the play, *Die Ermittlung*, indicates a procedure of investigation and interrogation that precedes a trial, which in the case of the Frankfurt trial resulted in a 700-page document, whereas the play is performed after the trial has taken place.[12] What to make of all this?

We do not face the same difficulties as the Martian, because we know in advance that the trial and the play are parts of two separate systems, law and literature, so that even if the language is reproduced exactly from one system to the other, it will incite different observations when used in different contexts – e.g. the difference between performative and literary language noted above. Observers of the play nevertheless noticed that this play did not fit, or fitted only uneasily, within the subsystem of drama.

The reception began even before the play's production. Before writing the play in September or October 1964, Weiss sent his transcripts of the trial to the journal *Kursbuch*, whose *spiritus genii* was the poet Hans Magnus Enzensberger. In a letter of 2 November, Karl Markus Michel returned the manuscript to the author with this declaration:

> The sore point with these notes [*Notizen*] is the question of authenticity, which will undoubtedly be raised, especially regarding the verbal duelling of the lawyers. I would be quite upset were the entire notes [*Aufzeichnungen*] to be called into question because someone is able to prove that a particular statement is not reproduced exactly. [...] I am – despite all the expected objections and precisely in view of such objections – glad, that these notes [*Aufzeichnungen*] will be found in the

---

speech-act theory seems to more closely reflect everyday notions of the distinctive nature of language when used within different subsystems.
12 It is interesting to note as well that the first of a three-part documentary film, *Verdict on Auschwitz*, carries the title *Die Ermittlung*.

first *Kursbuch*. Otherwise, it would have too 'poetic' an effect. (quoted in Christoph Weiss, 1: 97)

The worries about exactitude complement Michel's desire to include something in the journal that would work un- or perhaps counter-poetically. Since the notes became a major basis for the play, we may extrapolate that the latter was to have a similar effect on its theatrical audience, a hypothesis confirmed in some of the reviews discussed below.

Remarkably, a defence lawyer at the actual Frankfurt trial found Weiss's play to be, in a sense, too accurate, and he uncomfortably coupled it with the judicial process. Hans Laternser, mentioned above, was the best known of the defence attorneys, representing three of the accused. Laternser's appearance could be seen as a continuation of his role as a defence counsel at the Nuremberg trials, which he found superior to the Auschwitz trial due to the impartiality of the judges and to the Anglo-Saxon concern for procedure. Along those lines, already in the second paragraph of his memoir of the Frankfurt trial, Laternser pauses to accuse Weiss's play of intervening in the verdict. He makes a powerful claim for the structural coupling between law and literature:

> Amazingly, just after the end of the trial, a theatrical piece appeared. [...] Amazing because in this play the names of the accused are used, and furthermore testimony or arguments of the trial participants are cited [*angeführt*] in a different context than was true of the trial itself. The partially correct, even verbatim quotations – which appear however in the incorrect context – lead to a questionable effect. After all, a legally binding judgment of the trial has not yet been made. It cannot be tolerated, that in our country persons whose guilt has not yet been legally determined should be brought onstage under the rubric 'beasts in human form'. Should the judgment be vacated on appeal and a judge be called to serve on the new bench who has seen this play and been influenced by it, he would be incapable of objectively exercising his duties as a judge. (Laternser, *Die andere Seite*, 11–12)

When Laternser claims that the play was produced before a legally binding decision had been made, he is probably referring to the capacity of the appeals process to overturn the lower court's decision, which it did for one of the defendants, as mentioned above. It is not clear from Laternser's statement whether he himself has seen the play or not. His claims bind *The Investigation* to the law, though perhaps only by making everything a part of the law, as in Kafka. For some reason, the possibility of a judge seeing this play is more compromising than his reading newspaper accounts or books such as Naumann's reports which also, inevitably, place statements into different contexts and connections from the original trial.

As opposed to Laternser's outrage and his certainty that law and literature are continuous with each other, we observe hesitation in the remarks of Siegfried Melchinger, who broadcast his review in the *Westdeutscher Rundfunk* on 13 August 1965. Notice how Melchinger deliberately places Weiss's writing (which has not seen its first performance yet) in a twilight zone between the two systems of *Recht* and *Literatur*: 'This autumn there will be performed on many German stages a play whose theme renders problematic the terminology of this sentence. Is it a "play" ["*Stück*"]? Can it be "performed" [*zur "Aufführung" gebracht werden*]? Can the place it is shown be called a "stage" ["*Bühne*"]? [...] How can it – we must ask – be "theatre"? (quoted in Christoph Weiss, *Auschwitz in der geteilten Welt*, 2: 162). Dieter Hildebrandt makes a similar summary of the play as 'an evening where one cannot utter the nasty statement that "theatre theatricalizes everything"' ('Ein Abend, von dem der böse Satz nicht gesagt werden kann: Das Theater theatert alles ein'). Hildebrandt's judgment denies in the one case of Weiss's play the autonomy and autopoiesis of art, which can take any theme, even the most political, and turn it into just another evening at the theatre. Hildebrandt sees, then, a rest or remainder in the play – the structural coupling itself, perhaps – that does not belong to literature per se. Thirty years after the performances, Klaus Berghahn echoes these same ideas that *The Investigation* exceeds the aesthetic function of theatre: '*The Investigation* is neither a piece of disinterested art nor a drama in the Aristotelian fashion, but a form of tribunal, operative art. [... Weiss's] play truly became an "instrument of political opinion formation", as Weiss had demanded of the documentary theatre, and it influenced in no small part the outcome of the parliamentary debate about the Statue of Limitations for Nazi crimes' (Berghahn, 'Our Auschwitz', 106–8). If Laternser was concerned about the structural coupling of law and literature, Berghahn salutes such coupling in the case of politics and literature. Inasmuch as changes to the statute of limitations directly affect prosecutions, we have an overlap of system that begins to resemble the diagram in my introduction. The statements of Weiss himself and of the critics are thus fairly uniform in their attempt to bring the piece outside the aesthetic realm and make it a second-order observation. There is first of all the recognition that Weiss's play placed Auschwitz, if not in the centre of German consciousness, then at least in a more prominent place than it had occupied until then. In Berghahn's summation, Weiss's documentary drama 'provided an impulse for confronting the Nazi past and for coming to terms with it. [...] In a certain sense Weiss's *Investigation* contributed to a new conscience or to what Adorno called a new categorical imperative: That mankind "should arrange their thoughts and actions so that Auschwitz will not repeat itself, so that nothing similar will happen"' ('Our Auschwitz', 113). In his study of the play, Jürgen Schlunk states that 'the defendants carrying their real names are not to be tried again on stage, but rather serve as symbols for a system which implicated uncounted others who are not called to trial' (Schlunk, 'Auschwitz and Its Function', 20). It is worth contemplating the phrase, 'tried again on stage'. It suggests that it would be possible to do this; that the stage can function as a courtroom, and the audience as the jury. *Die Ermittlung* does not retry the defendants, nor does it focus on procedure the way an appeal would. It does not reproduce or reflect the trial, but conducts a second-order observation of the distinctions drawn by that trial.

For the most part, as Robert Cohen reminds us, the play has been denounced by those defining the canon of the genre of Holocaust literature: 'The attacks of [...] critics on *The Investigation* and its author are startling in their ferocity. In their view Weiss's play was a distortion and exploitation of the Holocaust for ideological reasons; it was artless, lifeless and mechanical and, most disturbingly, it wasn't even about the Jews. It had to be excluded from the canon of the new discourse' (Cohen, 'Political Aesthetics', 44).[13] Nowhere is it stated in the play that the majority of the victims at Auschwitz were Jewish; the only references to Jews are indirect, such as the talk of 'enemies' within the German state, or the appellation of 'Sarah' for a female prisoner. Again, Weiss can be seen as holding to his principle of citation of the trial, since the charges were not for hate crimes or genocide that would call for the identification of an ethnic group or religion, but for individual acts of murder. Yet when we examine one such critique, that of Lawrence Langer, we encounter a language which resembles that of German critics relieved that the subject has not been theatricalized: 'The [play] is singularly undramatic, [...] the chilling evidence in its pages rarely rises above the cold, harsh surface of mere factual truth. [... T]he result is not a new aesthetic distance, but an aesthetic indifference, a failure of the artist's imagination to seduce the spectator into a feeling of complicity with the material of his drama' (Langer, *The Holocaust and the Literary Imagination*, 31). This avoidance of empathy (*Einfühlung*) is a familiar

---

13 For a fuller account of the controversial standing of *The Investigation* as Holocaust literature, see also Marita Meyer, *Eine Ermittlung*.

Brechtian device, and the implication of Langer's judgment is that the standard recourse to aesthetic 'seduction' through empathy would be preferable. However, later German directors agreed that the play's audiences must be made to feel not more sympathetic, but more complicit – and not with the 'material', whatever that is, but with the perpetrators.

Citing a Citation

In 1993 the installation artist Jochen Gerz planned a repetition of Weiss's play, retitled as *Die Wiederholung*. Residents of Bochum, Germany were to read the play and rehearse it, becoming one with their roles. Their experiences were to be filmed and projected on the stage where Gerz's exhibit, EXIT/MATERIALIEN ZUM DACHAU-PROJEKT was installed. The project was not realized in Bochum, but instead revived and brought to fruition in 1996 in Berlin. The idea now was to distribute, on the admission tickets to the performance, lines from the play with numbers to be called out by the actors, provoking the audience member with the corresponding ticket to say the line printed there. Spectators were given lines only of witnesses or defendants. The actors were 'correctors' (*Korrektoren*), who in addition to calling out the numbers also interrupted the readers by urging them to speak louder, and so forth. In 1998, a seminar was held at the Hebbel-Theater, the Volksbühne and the Berliner Ensemble, where 500 potential audience members read passages. Eventually the play was produced in something like the manner described above, with Weiss's text split into three parts, each performed in a separate theatre on a specific day or days from 25 May to 1 June. In the end, the 'actors' spoke not a single word of the playscript. These performances were preceded by a number of radio and television spots, including the mixing of short passages of the play into broadcasts, as though they were advertising jingles. On television, some well-known personalities (e.g. Rita Süssmuth, Volker Schlöndorff) read passages from the play. Newspaper adverts were also run, with the picture of a participant, lines from the play, and a reference to the theatre production.

There are several aspects of Gerz's concept that belong to second-order observation. First, the use of media to promulgate parts of the play among the general citizenry of Berlin constitutes perhaps the most intense and widespread citation of trial testimony – albeit aesthetically shaped by Weiss – in German history. There is a pathway of citation, from legal proceeding to stage production to general public space. Each citation observes the system from which it is extracted. Secondly, the initial title Gerz had given to his project, *The Repetition* (*Die Wiederholung*) applies not only to his adaptation of Weiss, but also to Weiss's play as a reproduction of the trial. In this context, Gerz is more explicit than Weiss about the need for such repetition to complete the work begun by the trial. In Gerz's thinking, this repetition constitutes a necessary reversal of roles. Gerz

> describes the main conception as recycling: all participants in this play abandon their learned [*einstudierten*] behaviours and thus find themselves playing entirely different roles. Gerz wishes to repeat the historical trial against the Auschwitz criminals [*die Täter*] under a nearly inverted rubric: while the trial produces non-guilty [*Unschuldige*] parties, *The Repetition* produces guilty ones [*Schuldige*]. (Christel Weiler, *Die Berliner 'Ermittlung'*, 9)

In referring to the trial producing innocence, the thought is not so much of the defendants as of ordinary German citizens whom the trial 'acquitted' by individualizing the moral culpability of the defendants. In *The Repetition*, on the other hand, the idea of acting and role-playing extends into the courtroom, and out again into daily life. As we have seen above, this is entirely consistent with Weiss's concept of his own play that was neither an aesthetic object nor a mimetic one, but a second-order observation. '*Einstudieren*' is a technical term in acting which refers to learning one's role in a play, but here it refers not just to the actors – who must learn to challenge and to listen rather than to represent and declaim – but to the 'ordinary' citizens who must learn new roles that make them guilty. In a remarkable reversal of Kafka's law, where guilt is omnipresent and inescapable,

> Gerz sees (and not only in the Auschwitz trial) the danger that innocence is produced most of all. In order to avoid this, he wants to (in his words) 'deploy fiction so that it struggles against the disappearance of the audience into their mourning. [...] The audience member is seen as actor, as perpetrator in the theatre, the reader as an informant in the newspaper. Victims are converted into perpetrators, responsible parties. "I was there" (in the theatre) counters "I wasn't there" (on the selection ramp).' (Christoph Rüter, '>>Nach Vollzug<< 1998/2005', 84)

Like a systems theorist, Gerz reduces trial and repetition to processes of distinction, and indeed applies the binary of *Recht/ Unrecht* that grounds the legal system. Gerz's assertion corresponds roughly to historians who have studied the trial, and it points in the direction of subsequent 'truth-and-reconciliation commissions' that have chosen the path of avoiding the *Recht/Unrecht* divide in favour of the co-construction of a narrative of involvement of all parties in historical events. As mentioned earlier, the trial's fatal flaw seemed to have been its use of the German penal code existing at the time the crimes were committed. The relative will to become involved in an entire structure of illegality – a distinction resting on, among other things, the difference between *Täter* and *Gehilfe* – became the basis of guilt.

Weiss's *The Investigation* presents us with one of the most intense structural couplings between law and literature that we have seen, and one where law itself seems to call out for the assistance of literature for help out of the aporias and legal impossibilities it had created for itself. The transfer of information gleaned by judicial inquiry into the system of theatre became a necessary aspect of the investigation. Weiss's intentions as author nearly disappear in the face of the need for law and literature to complement each other in their respective lacks. There are two ways out of the difficulties of the prosecution of crimes committed in the name of a system rather than in contravention of it. One is the path of prosecution by supra-national bodies, such as the International Criminal Court. Schmitt's critique of globalization rehearsed in the last chapter has some validity here; such bodies appear to some as the universalizing of specific national or regional legal concepts. They are composed and imposed the way Captain Delano imposes order on the *San Dominick*. The second path is that examined in this chapter, whereby law calls on other social subsystems to provide the second-order observations it is incapable of. The structural coupling of law in its human rights aspects onto literature shapes new literary genres (e.g. *testimonio*) and reshapes literary criticism.

Conclusion

A system-theory investigation of the relations of law and literature that has guided this study may conceivably yield at least three benefits: (1) the relevant concepts and vocabulary employed (citation, precedent, conjunction, disjunction, autopoiesis, autonomy, structural coupling, and so forth) may provide a useful shorthand for communication about the issues that must inevitably rise in interdisciplinary work of this sort; (2) the focus on system, both in its synchronic and its diachronic aspects, may help us to develop a picture of the relation between law and literature that transcends the treatment of isolated examples and to establish their relation to each other; and (3) the analysis of various conjunctions between German law and literature may furnish study-examples that explain, support, or test the claims of ST. These concluding remarks address mainly this third point, though some of what follows will also have a bearing on the first two.

In an extremely thorough account and critique of Jürgen Habermas's *Between Facts and Norms* (*Faktizität und Geltung*), John McCormick calls one of the book's targets, Niklas Luhmann, 'factually fixated' ('Max Weber and Jürgen Habermas', 306) and 'hyper-empirical' (311). More accurate would be 'facticity fixated', meaning that Luhmann concentrates on existing social systems, their communications and distinctions as empirically verifiable objects of study. As explained in the introduction, ST brackets the black boxes of either individual subjectivity or 'transcendental ego' in favour of empirically verifiable systemic complexity, and is thus unwilling to posit an invisible set of norms or a public sphere guiding societal behaviour and communication.

In my own, non-technical understanding of what constitutes the empirical-factual, however, neither Luhmann nor Habermas is factually fixated. Rather, as stated in chapter 1.2, among the features the two thinkers share is a common ability to theorize on and on for hundreds of pages without providing a single concrete example.

By repeatedly theorizing itself into existence, ST provides a good justification for its own isolation from other theories. Whereas most theories and philosophies achieving vigour in the 1980s and later have been eclectic and synthetic, systems theory remains almost entirely closed upon itself. This is not to say that ST is made out of whole cloth (it synthesizes the thought of Talcott Parsons, Spencer Brown and Umberto Maturana, to name only the three most prominent examples); but whereas other theories depend disseminatively on their citations of other work for their full understanding and their persuasive force, ST is far more autopoietic. To read a major work of ST such as Luhmann's *Law as a Social System* (*Das Recht der Gesellschaft*), for example, is to follow the author's discourse and reasoning, rather than to observe him either synthesizing the work of other theorists, philosophers and sociologists, or arguing against it. Luhmann has indicated ST's affinities with constructivism and deconstruction, and throughout this book I have noted Luhmann's citations of Goethe, Habermas and others. But for the most part, ST has been autopoietically constructed. The dozens of titles on ST that I perused in writing this book mostly engage in yet another explanation of the theory rather than in applying it or supplementing it with examples. The appeal of the theory is due to its high level of abstraction and hence its portability. The high level of generalization achieved by ST constitutes its most powerful weakness. Again, as self-fulfilling prophecy, and somewhat in the manner of structuralism, ST reduces the world's complexity to a few simple operations, performed over and over. This is comforting, but also causes cognitive dissonance as we begin to compare epistemological variety and the chaos of our own minds with systemic simplicity. On the other hand, most of us can agree with ST's main contention – that variety and complexity cause anxiety that systems help reduce. Legal subsystems, for example, in becoming more structured and autonomous do seem to cause people to act in more predictable ways. Furthermore, systems are always described in the abstract; it is very rare to see a full-blown description of a system – to see with one's own eyes, as it were, how it functions autopoietically and what its observations consist of.

What I set out to explore in this book, on the other hand, are a few 'empirical' data. I put 'empirical' in quotes because, for the most part, the data I am interested in belong to a specific order of reality; they are discursive in nature, and I have used the techniques of literary history and criticism to identify and explore them. If I have had any success in this, then what has emerged is a tentative and fragmentary diagram of the discourse networks (*Aufschreibesysteme*) that traverse the systems of law, literature, politics and philosophy in modern Germany and Austria. Each of the following three sections focused on a relatively narrow stretch of years within the continuum of German history. Chapter Two in some sense considered a six-year period from 1804 to 1809, when the Napoleonic incursions into Germany gave both Jacob Grimm and Goethe much to think about.

The next, contrasting period examined was between 1900 – when Germany finally received a single code of laws, the *Bürgerliches Gesetzbuch* – to 1932, when that code, and the constitution that had become a reality in the meantime, were submerged in a state of exception as the country slipped into totalitarian rule. The end of the *Kaiserreich* in Germany and the introduction of a constitution were epochal events, but they were preceded by the gradual development of the 'administered society', ruled by codification, citation and precedent. Comprehensive social welfare had been introduced under Bismarck, expanding immensely the entire realm of administrative law. Analogous developments in Austria provided the apprenticeship for literature's greatest analyst of bureaucracy, Franz Kafka. The development of new media technologies, from cheap mass printing to film and radio, provoked a rash of legislation that increasingly required prolonged political debate. The 'level playing field' created by the Weimar Constitution in 1919 – in terms of abolishing censorship and restrictions on political association, allowing Jews full access to the rights of other German citizens, abolishing the distinction between 'right-handed' and 'left-handed' marriage, and so forth – created a situation in which the subsystems of law, politics and literature could interact with each other more freely than at any previous point in German history, resulting in phenomena such as the *Schund* and *Schmutz* debate, and Borchardt's assumption of the role of attorney for German literature.

My third set of study-examples, Peter Weiss's Auschwitz-trial play and Carl Schmitt's reading of Melville's *Benito Cereno*, engaged a comparative, supra-national dimension of German law and literature that becomes increasingly urgent in the post-war era. Carl Schmitt, whose work on sovereignty and state-of-exception was important for Benjamin in the Weimar period, increasingly turned during the war years (and after his disastrous experiment with Nazism) to exploring the issue of the '*nomos* of the earth' and what the progressive stages of controlling and codifying space meant for the principle of national sovereignty. Schmitt read Melville's *Benito Cereno* as a prophetic allegory for that recodification. Certainly, post-war developments such as the European Union, NATO, the United Nations, and concomitant international agreements and declarations have complicated the notion of nation-state sovereignty central to Schmitt's thinking. The attempt to render justice for Nazi genocide interfaces with Schmitt's problem from a different direction – calling for a supplement to law when it is unable to adjudicate a crime committed in the name of an illegal system. One of those supplements may be precisely a legal order beyond sovereignty; another may be the deliberate coupling of the legal to other subsystems, such as theatre in the case of Peter Weiss.

The number of study-examples I have addressed and, more importantly, their specific literary and mimetic qualities is necessarily limited. Were this book to move instead from Heinrich von Kleist's *Broken Jug* (1808; *Der zerbrochene Krug*) through Gustav Freytag's *Credit and Debit* (1855; *Soll und Haben*) to the Weimar theatre of Hans José Rehfisch and the novels of Hans Fallada to the contemporary law professor-cum-novelist Bernhard Schlink, a rather different outline of subsystems and their structural couplings might emerge. Alternatively, one could lament the absence of one single, exhaustive example – a five- or ten-year slice of time in Weimar Germany, for example, where the structural couplings of *all* relevant social subsystems would be considered. Notable absences from my discussions include journalism, radio, television, and political and legislative discourse, all of which cited and were cited by both literature and law. Lastly, however, no matter how large the number of examples or the comprehensiveness of my grasp of system, there would remain the venerable difference between criticism and theory, or more fundamentally the problem of self-reference. Literary criticism can follow the paths of structural couplings, point to particular texts as precedents and cite their citations, but only theory at the level of abstraction of a Habermas or a Luhmann can truly explain system. Furthermore, if complexity, for example, is one of the fundamental aspects of system to be explained, then it seems rather immune to example. My discussion of the debate between these two sociologists in Chapter 1.2 provided enough abstraction to frame my collection, and in fact uncovered a common theme in this variety of texts that I had not hitherto suspected, and that I will now explain.

There are two ways of viewing Habermas's arguments in favour of the existence of a public sphere. One is that the historical evidence itself argues for the existence of such a sphere. The other is that the sphere is a phantasm created by Grimm-like nostalgia for a supposedly communal life (*Gemeinschaft*) that antedates the differentiation that we call 'society' (*Gesellschaft*). In this utopian vision of a public sphere, all social processes are transparent, there is pure decision rather than parliamentary wrangling, marriages demonstrate love rather than contract, and all citizens return from their day of fishing or cultivating their fig trees to read literature, listen to epic, or attend the festival of tragedy and comedy in the local ampitheatre.

The knowledge and values transmitted through literature (though of course the word 'literature' does not exist in the community's language, since the subsystems are not sufficiently differentiated so as to produce such a concept) directly nurture citizens' thought and activities in all spheres of life. Literary works are treated as precedents and sources of citation in all matters of life, including legal ones. As Jacob Grimm tries so hard to show in various of his writings, law and poetry – and much else – are one.

Such a community would enjoy a definition of justice that is not pulled in different directions and evaluated by different criteria, depending on the particular subsystem in which juridical communication occurs. Today, however, in our factually fixated society, the closed operations of systems warn us about concepts such as 'justice' that appear in the lexica of more than one subsystem. Hence, system theory seems therapeutic for Wai Chee Dimock's understandable confusion about the variety of language games that play with the term: 'Absolute and categoric in philosophy, negotiable and assignable in law, wayward and unsatisfactory in literature, justice, dispensed in different operative theatres, seems to carry different causal circumferences, different modes of evidence, and to yield up different styles of knowledge as well as different descriptive textures of the world' (8). Dimock here names several of the subsystems reviewed in this study, and the possibility of a structural coupling between them, namely justice. Yet communication does not flow easily from one system into another. The rules of mutual citation are constrained. Each subsystem makes use of the sense of justice under its own operative conditions (indeed, Dimock uses the very term, 'operative'). To use Habermas's metaphor, the idea of justice does not present a geometric outline that still retains its semantic shape and performative value when projected onto these various spheres Dimock names.

Readers will have noticed in my above description of the primal public sphere (which goes far beyond what Habermas would argue for as either a possibility or true historical configuration) allusions both to some of the topics treated in this book and also to classical Athens, where Plato introduced one of the first recorded separations of a subsystem, that of philosophy. According to Platonic philosophy, literature (that is, *mousiké*) could no longer provide wisdom (*sofia*) as it had in the past. In the dialogue '*Ion*', each citation the eponymous rhapsode makes from the Homeric corpus is disallowed by Socrates as not conforming to the facts of the matter. Plato's dialogues such as the '*Ion*' and the *Republic* hint that there are some types of knowledge attainable only through literature, for example the special knowledge of inspiration that is not coupled with wisdom.

When I began this study, I thought that I would end up delivering mostly empirical insights into the areas of structural coupling diagrammed in the introduction. The most obvious 'pragmatic' example of this type is the topic of censorship, where we saw legislators acting as arbiters of aesthetics, and writers telling educators and policemen which books should or should not be confiscated at school. But the most visible 'red thread' running through this book turns out to be neither structural coupling per se, nor the 'mirror of justice' idea whereby literature can critique law or supply through mimesis the values that a technical discipline increasingly squeezes out of its own processes. Regarding the former, an appeals court can certainly be said to critique a lower court, but the ST idea of 'second-order observation' is more appropriate, as part of law's autopoiesis or of the general recursive processes of society as a whole. Ideological critique of the nineteenth and early twentieth centuries has been replaced by 'critical theory' as practised by the Frankfurt School and Jürgen Habermas. In order to conform his narrative of *Der Prozess* into this pattern of recursion, Kafka left behind the realm of the novel as a form of realism. The move away from literature as the 'mirror of justice' is related to the *Ausdifferenzierung* of art as an autonomous social subsystem: 'Autonomy, here, does not mean that art can no longer express social, political or other interests, but rather that art will define its own function according to its own standards without relying on non-artistic factors such as morality, economic feasibility, accordance with rules, etc.' (Landgraf, 'Comprehending Romantic Incomprehensibility', 598). If this account of the autonomy of modern artworks is generally true, then the special aspect of works to be sought out for study by law-and-literature scholars should be that they run counter to this trend, as Carl Schmitt wished *Benito Cereno* to do, and as Peter Weiss seems to have accomplished with *The Investigation*. Moreover, the trajectory from novel to Counter-Enlightenment to ideological critique needs at the very least a fourth term: theory. As a new literary genre whose discursive textures are as distinct from philosophy as they are from sociology, theory inherits both the techniques of ideological critique and the nostalgia for the novel as an observation of social processes – an observation of observations. These are combined into a discourse that is portable between a variety of subsystems, as evidenced in Stanley Fish's professorship in law and the appearance of Jacques Derrida's interpretations of Kafka and Benjamin in the pages of law reviews.

Thus, my unexpected discovery concerns not the relationship between writing and law, but the one between writers and their writing. In particular, I believe that the foregoing examples have brought to light the self-consciousness of writers and thinkers about the autonomy of subsystems in modern society, and their attempts to bring about structural couplings through citations. The mutual admiration of the leftist Benjamin and the reactionary Schmitt for each other's work has often been noted with dismay, if not disgust; it rests, I believe, on this common root of searching for structural couplings. The underlying vision of all these authors, it seems to me, goes beyond the mirroring of justice or the critique of law, and certainly beyond the presentation of ethical principles that law cannot express, to the question of how law and literature might (again) work together.

A second unanticipated finding concerns ST's apparent presuppositions, in McCormick's words, 'about systems differentiation that assume its supposedly indefinite continuation into the future' (McCormick, 'Max Weber and Jürgen Habermas', 338). When considered on a discursive basis, such presuppositions may hold true. If, however, when viewing law we set our systemic filters linguistically or geographically, then consolidating or universalizing tendencies can also be observed, for example under the rubrics of the law of European Union (when its rulings trump national laws), of human rights, or of environmental law, to name just a few. Chapter 4.1 read Carl Schmitt's myths of the sea as a primary stage for the coming '*nomos* of the earth' as a theory of this process of dedifferentiation, and it is implicit in Chapter 4.2 on the Frankfurt Auschwitz trials as well, where the crimes of murder committed by a state bureaucracy patently exceeded the capacity of the state to judge them. It seems that the models of ST should become more sensitive to this double directionality of differentiation-universalization, as yet another paradox in its repertoire. At which point it will become incumbent on me to doff my Germanist hat once and for all, and don that of comparative, postcolonial and global studies.

Works Cited

Abbreviations: *Neue Juristische Wochenschrift* = NJW

Primary Works

Allgemeines Landrecht für die preussischen Staaten. 1794. 4 vols. Ed. C. F. Koch. Berlin & Leipzig: Guttentag, 1886.

Benjamin, Walter. *Gesammelte Briefe*. Ed. Christoph Gödde and Henri Lonitz. 5 vols. Frankfurt: Suhrkamp, 1996. Trans. Manfred R. Jacobson and Evelyn M. Jacobson. *The Correspondence of Walter Benjamin 1910–1940*. Chicago: U of Chicago P, 1994.

—. *Gesammelte Schriften*. 7 vols in 14. Eds. Rolf Tiedemann and Hermann Schweppenhäuser. Frankfurt a. M.: Suhrkamp, 1972–89.

—. 'Goethe'. *Gesammelte Schriften* II.2, 705–39. Trans. Rodney Livingstone. 'Goethe'. *Selected Writings Volume 2. 1927–1934*. Ed. Michael W. Jennings, Howard Eiland and Gary Smith. Cambridge, MA: Harvard-Belknap, 1999, 161–93.

—. 'Goethes *Wahlverwandschaften*'. *Gesammelte Schriften* I.1, 123–202. Trans. Stanley Corngold. 'Goethe's *Elective Affinities*'. *Selected Writings Volume 1: 1913–1926*. Ed. Marcus Bullock and Michael W. Jennings. Cambridge, MA: Harvard UP, 1996, 297–360.

—. 'Lebenslauf III'. *Gesammelte Schriften* VI, 217–19. 'Curriculum Vitae (3)'. *Selected Writings Volume 2. 1927–1934*. Ed. Michael W. Jennings, Howard Eiland and Gary Smith. Cambridge, MA: Harvard-Belknap, 1999, 77–8.

—. 'Lebenslauf VI: Curriculum Vitae Dr Walter Benjamin'. *Gesammelte Schriften* VI, 225–8. 'Curriculum Vitae (VI): Dr. Walter Benjamin'. *Selected Writings Volume 4: 1938–1940*. Ed. Howard Eiland and Michael W. Jennings. Cambridge, MA: Harvard UP, 2003, 381–5.

—. 'Schicksal und Charakter'. *Gesammelte Schriften* II.1, 171–9. *Selected Writings Volume 1: 1913–1926*. Ed. Marcus Bullock and Michael W. Jennings. Cambridge, MA: Harvard UP, 1996, 201–6.

—. 'Über das Programm der kommenden Philosophie'. *Gesammelte Schriften* II.1, 157–71. 'On the Program of the Coming Philosophy'. *Selected Writings Volume 1: 1913–1926*. Ed. Marcus Bullock and Michael W. Jennings. Cambridge, MA: Harvard UP, 1996, 100–10.

—. 'Über den Begriff der Geschichte'. *Gesammelte Schriften* 1.2, 691–706. 'On the Concept of History'. *Selected Writings Volume 4: 1938–1940*. Ed. Howard Eiland and Michael W. Jennings. Cambridge, MA: Harvard UP, 2003, 389–400.

—. 'Über Franz Kafka'. *Über Literatur*. Frankfurt: Suhrkamp, 1979, 154–202.
—. *Der Ursprung des deutschen Trauerspiels*. *Gesammelte Schriften* I.1, 203–430. Trans. John Osborne. *The Origin of German Tragic Drama*. London: New Left, 1977.
—. 'Zur Kritik der Gewalt'. 1921. *Gesammelte Schriften* II.1, 179–203. Trans. Edmund Jephcott. 'Critique of Violence'. *Selected Writings Volume 1: 1913–1926*. Ed. Marcus Bullock and Michael W. Jennings. Cambridge, MA: Harvard UP, 1996, 236–52.
Borchardt, Rudolf. 'Die Aufgaben der Zeit gegenüber der Literatur'. *Reden*. Ed. Marie-Luise Borchardt. Stuttgart: Klett-Cotta, 1955, 345–96.
—. *Briefe 1931–1935*. Ed. Gerhard Schuster. Munich & Vienna: Tenschert, 1996.
—. *Deutsche Literatur im Kampfe um ihr Recht*. Munich: Georg Müller, 1932.
Bourdieu, Pierre. 'Censorship and the Imposition of Form'. *Language and Symbolic Power*. Trans. Gino Raymond and Matthew Adamson. Cambridge, MA: Harvard UP, 1991, 137–59.
—. *Distinction: A Social Critique of the Judgment of Taste*. Trans. Richard Nice. Cambridge, MA: Harvard UP, 1984.
—. *Les règles de l'art*. Paris: Seuil, 1992. Trans. Susan Emanuel. *The Rules of Art: Genesis and Structure of the Literary Field*. Cambridge, UK: Polity, 1996.
—. *Pascalian Meditations*. Trans. Richard Nice. Stanford: Stanford UP, 2000.
Bourdieu, Pierre, and Loïc J. Wacquant. *An Invitation to Reflexive Sociology*. Chicago: U of Chicago P, 1992.
Goethe, Johann Wolfgang von. *Amtliche Schriften*. Ed. Willy Flachland and Helma Dahl. 3 vols. Weimar: Böhlau, 1950–72.
—. *Gespräche mit Eckermann in den letzten Jahren seines Lebens*. *Sämtliche Werke*. Ed. Heinz Schlaffer. Munich: Hanser, 1986.
—. *Die Wahlverwandtschaften*. 1809. *Goethes Werke*. Weimar: Böhlau, 1892. 20: 1–416.
Grimm, Jacob. *Deutsche Rechtsalterthümer*. 1828. 2nd ed. Göttingen: Dietrich, 1854.
—. *Kleinere Schriften*. 8 vols. Ed. K. Müllenhoff. Hildesheim: Friedrich Olms, 1965.
—. 'Von der Poesie im Recht'. *Kleinere Schriften* 6: 152–91.
Vorlesung über deutsche Literaturgeschichte. Ed. Matthias Janssen. Kassel & Berlin: Brüder Grimm-Gesellschaft, 2005.
—. 'Das Wort des Besitzes'. *Kleinere Schriften* 1: 113–44.
Grimm, Jacob, and Wilhelm Grimm. *Briefe an Savigny*. Ed. Wilhelm Schoof and Ingeborg Schnack. Berlin: Erich Schmidt, 1953.
Habermas, Jürgen. *Faktizität und Geltung. Beiträge zur Diskurstheorie des Rechtsund des demokratischen Rechtsstaats*. Frankfurt am Main: Suhrkamp, 1992. Trans. William Rehg. *Between Facts and Norms. Contributions to a Discourse Theory of Law and Democracy*. Cambridge, MA: MIT Press, 1996.
—. 'Law and Morality'. *The Habermas Reader*. Ed. William Outhwaite. Cambridge: Polity, 1996, 203–13.
—. *The Inclusion of the Other: Studies in Political Theory*. Eds. Ciaran P. Cronin and Pablo de Greiff. Cambridge, MA: MIT P, 1998.
—. *Der philosophische Diskurs der Moderne. Zwölf Vorlesungen*. Frankfurt am Main: Suhrkamp, 1985. Trans. Frederick Lawrence. *The Philosophical Discourse of Modernity*. Cambridge: MIT P, 1987.
—. *Strukturwandel der Öffentlichkeit. Untersuchungen zu einer Kategorie der bürgerlichen Gesellschaft*. 2nd ed. Frankfurt am Main: Suhrkamp, 1990. Trans.

Thomas Burger and Frederick Lawrence, *Structural Transformations of the Public Sphere: An Inquiry into a Category of Bourgeois Society*. Cambridge: MIT Press, 1989.
—. 'Wie ist Legitimität durch Legalität möglich?' *Kritische Justiz* 20 (1987): 1–16.
—, and Niklas Luhmann. *Theorie der Gesellschaft oder Sozialtechnologie – Was leistet die Systemforschung?* Frankfurt am Main: Suhrkamp, 1971.
Kafka, Franz. *Amtliche Schriften*. Ed. Klaus Hermsdorf and Benno Wagner. Frankfurt am Main: Fischer, 2004. Trans. Eric Patton and Ruth Hein. *The Office Writings*. Eds. Stanley Corngold, Jack Greenberg and Benno Wagner. Princeton: Princeton UP, 2009.
—. *The Complete Stories*. Ed. Nahum H. Glazer. New York: Schocken. 1968.
—. *Der Prozess*. Berlin: Fischer, 1960. Trans. Breon Mitchell. *The Trial*. New York: Schocken Books, 1998.
—. *Sämtliche Erzählungen*. Frankfurt am Main: Fischer. 1975.
—. *Der Verschollene*. Ed. Jost Schillemeit. 2 vols. Frankfurt am Main: Fischer, 1983. Trans. Michael Hofmann. *Amerika (The Man Who Disappeared)*. New York: New Directions, 2002.
Kant, Immanuel. 'Metaphysische Anfangsgründe der Rechtslehre'. *Gesammelte Schriften*. 29 vols. Berlin: Königlich Preussischen Akademie der Wissenschaften, 1900–1983. 20: 445–67.
—. *Rechtslehre*. 1797. Ed. Hermann Klenner. Berlin: Akademie-Verlag, 1988.
Luhmann, Niklas. 'Ausdifferenzierung der Kunst'. *Art & Language & Luhmann*. Vienna: Passagen, 1997, 133–48.
—. *Ausdifferenzierung des Rechts: Beiträge zur Rechtssoziologie und Rechtstheorie*. Frankfurt am Main: Suhrkamp, 1981.
—. 'Autopoiesis of Social Systems'. *Essays on Self-Reference*. 1–20.
—. 'The Cognitive Program of Constructivism and the Reality that Remains Unknown'. Luhmann, *Theories*, 128–52.
—. *Essays on Self-Reference*. New York: Columbia UP, 1990.
—. *Die Gesellschaft der Gesellschaft*. 2 vols. Frankfurt am Main: Suhrkamp, 1997.
—. *Die Kunst der Gesellschaft*. Frankfurt a. M.: Suhrkamp, 1995. *Art as a Social System*. Trans. Eva M. Knodt. Stanford: Standford UP, 2000.
—. *Liebe als Passion. Zur Codierung von Intimität*. Frankfurt a. M.: Suhrkamp, 1982. Trans. Jeremy Gaines and Doris L. Jones. *Love as Passion: The Codification of Intimacy*. Cambridge, UK: Polity P, 1986.
—. 'Operational Closure and Structural Coupling: The Differentiation of the Legal System'. *Cardozo Law Review* 13.5 (March 1992): 1419–41.
—. *Das Recht der Gesellschaft*. Frankfurt am Main: Suhrkamp, 1993. Trans. Klaus A. Ziegert. *Law as a Social System*. Oxford: Oxford UP, 2004.
—. 'Society, Meaning, Religion — Based on Self-Reference'. *Essays on Self-Reference*. New York: Columbia UP, 1990, 147.
—. *Theories of Distinction: Redescribing the Descriptions of Modernity*. Stanford: Stanford UP, 2002.
—. 'Work of Art and Self-Reproduction'. *Essays on Self-Reference*. 191–214.
Mann, Thomas. 'Über Rudolf Borchardt'. 1926. *Thomas Mann Miszellen*. Frankfurt am Main: Fischer, 1968, 92–4.
Melville, Herman. *Benito Cereno*. 1854. *The Piazza Tales and Other Prose Pieces 1839–1860*. Ed. Harrison Hayford et al. Evanston and Chicago, IL: Northwestern University Press, 1987, 47–117.
Richter, Werner. 'Der Fall Borchardt'. *Berliner Tageblatt* 62. 6 February 1932. Morning edition.

—. *Die literarische Diktatur der deutschnationalen Handlungsgehilfen*. Berlin: Berliner Tageblatt, 1931.
Savigny, Friedrich Carl von. *Juristische Methodenlehre. Nach der Ausarbeitung von Jacob Grimm*. Ed. Gerhard Wesenberg. Stuttgart: Koehler, 1951.
—. *The Vocation of Our Age for Legislation and Jurisprudence*. Trans. Abraham Hayward. 1831. Rpt. New York: Arno Press, 1975.
Schmitt, Carl. *Briefwechsel mit einem seiner Schüler*. Ed. Armin Mohler, Irmgard Huhn and Piet Tommissen. Berlin: Akademie Verlag, 1995.
—. *Die Diktatur. Von den Anfängen des modernen Souveränitätsgedankens bis zum proletarischen Klassenkampf*. Munich & Leipzig: Duncker & Humblot, 1921.
—. *Ernst Jünger-Carl Schmitt, Briefe 1930–1983*. Stuttgart: Klett-Cotta, 1999.
—. *Ex captivitate salus*. Cologne: Greven, 1950.
—. *Glossarium: Aufzeichnungen der Jahre 1947–1951*. Berlin: Duncker & Humblot, 1991.
—. *Hamlet oder Hekuba. Der Einbruch der Zeit in das Spiel*. Stuttgart: Klett, 1956.
—. *Jawohl, der Schmitt. Zehn Briefe aus Plettenberg*. Berlin: Support Edition, 1988.
—. *Land und Meer. Eine Weltgeschichtliche Betrachtung*. 1954. Stuttgart: Klett-Cotta, 1993.
—. *Der Leviathan in der Staatslehre des Thomas Hobbes. Sinn und Fehlschlag eines politischen Symbols*. Hamburg: Hanseatischer Verlag, 1938.
—. *Nomos der Erde im Völkerrecht der Jus Publicum Europaeum*. Berlin: Duncker & Humblot, 1950. Trans. G. L. Ulmen. *The Nomos of the Earth in the International Law of the Jus Publicum Europaeum*. New York, NY: Telos P, 2003.
—. *Politische Theologie. Vier Kapitel zur Lehre von der Souveränitat*. Berlin: Duncker & Humblot, 1934.
—. *Staat, Großraum, Nomos. Arbeiten aus den Jahren 1916–1969*. Berlin: Duncker & Humblot, 1995.
—. *Theodor Däublers »Nordlicht«. Drei Studien über die Elemente, den Geist und die Aktualität des Werkes* [1916]. Berlin: Duncker & Humblot, 1991.
—. *Theory of the Partisan: Intemediate Commentary on the Concept of the Political*. Trans. G. L. Ulmen. New York: Telos, 2007.
—. *Verfassungslehre*. Munich & Leipzig: Duncker & Humblot, 1928.
Unruh, Fritz von. 'Der Gedenktag der Weimarer Verfassung'. *Die Hilfe: Zeitschrift für Politik, Wirtschaft und geistige Bewegung* 32 (1926): 303–4.
Weiss, Peter. *Die Ermittlung. Werke in Sechs Bänden. Dramen 2*. Ed. Gunilla Palmsiterna-Weiss. Frankurt am Main: Suhrkamp, 1991. Trans. Jon Swan, Ulu Grosbard and Robert Cohen. *The Investigation. Marat/Sade, The Investigation, and The Shadow of the Body of the Coachman*. German Library, 92. New York: Continuum, 2004, 117–298.
—. *Notizbücher 1960–1971*. Frankfurt am Main: Suhrkamp, 1982.

Criticism, Theory, and Legal Literature

25 Jahre Georg Müller Verlag. Munich: Georg Müller, 1928.
175 Jahre DVA. Die DVA von 1831 bis 2006. Munich: DVA, 2006.
Abraham, Ulf. 'Mose "Vor dem Gesetz": Eine unbekannte Vorlage zu Kafkas Türhüterlegende'. *Deutsche Vierteljahrsschrift für Literatur und Geisteswissenschaft* 57 (1983), 636–50.
Adorno, Theodor W. 'Die Beschworene Sprache. Zur Lyrik Rudolf Borchardts'. *Noten zur Literatur IV*. Frankfurt am Main: Suhrkamp, 1974, 63–89. Trans.

Shierry Weber Nicholsen. 'Charmed Language: On the Poetry of Rudolf Borchardt'. *Notes to Literature*. Ed. Rolf Tiedemann. New York: Columbia UP, 1992, 193–210.

—. 'Notes on Kafka'. *Prisms*. Trans. Samuel and Shierry Weber. London: Neville Spearman, 1967, 243–71.

Adorno, Theodor W., and Max Horkheimer. *Dialektik der Aufklärung. Philosophische Fragmente*. Frankfurt am Main: Suhrkamp, 1969.

Agamben, Giorgio. *Homo Sacer: Sovereign Power and Bare Life*. Trans. Daniel Heller-Roazen. Stanford UP, 1998.

—. *Stato di Eccezione*. Turin: Bollati Boringheri, 2003. Trans. Kevin Attell. *State of Exception*. Chicago: U of Chicago P, 2005.

Andriopoulos, Stefan. *Possessed: Hypnotic Crimes, Corporate Fiction, and the Invention of Cinema*. Chicago: U of Chicago P, 2008.

Arendt, Hannah. *Eichmann in Jerusalem: A Report on the Banality of Evil*. Rev. ed. New York: Viking, 1964.

Assmann, Aleida, and Jan Assmann. 'Kanon und Zensur', 7–27. *Kanon und Zensur. Beiträge Zur Archäologie der Literarischen Kommunikation*. Munich: W. Fink, 1987.

Aulich, Reinhard. 'Elemente einer Functionalen Differenzierung der literarischen Zensur'. *'Unmoralisch an sich ...'. Zensur im 18. und 19. Jahrhundert*. Ed. Herbert G. Göpfert and Erdmann Weyrauch. Weisbaden: Otto Harrassowitz, 1988, 177–230.

Baxter, Hugh. 'Autopoiesis and the "Relative Autonomy" of Law'. *Cardozo Law Review* 19.6 (July 1998): 1987–2090.

Beerbaum, Alfred W. *Rudolf Borchardt: A Biographical and Bibliographical Study*. New York: New York UP, 1952.

Beissner, Friedrich. *Der Erzähler Franz Kafka*. Stuttgart: Kohlhammer, 1952.

Berghahn, Klaus L. '"Our Auschwitz": Peter Weiss's *The Investigation* Thirty Years Later'. *Rethinking Peter Weiss*. Eds. Jost Hermand and Marc Silberman. *German Life and Civilization* 32. New York: Peter Lang, 2000, 93–119.

Bersier, Gabrielle. 'Der Fall der deutschen Bastille. Goethe und die Epochenschwelle von 1806'. *Recherches Germaniques* 20 (1990): 49–78.

Bigsby, Christopher. 'Peter Weiss: The Investigation'. *Remembering and Imagining the Holocaust: The Chain of Memory*. Cambridge: Cambridge UP, 2006, 149–75.

Binder, Guyora, and Robert Weisberg. *Literary Criticisms of Law*. Princeton: Princeton UP, 2000.

Binder, Helmut. *'Der Prozess'. Kafka. Kommentar zu den Romanen, Rezensionen, Aphorismen, und zum Brief an den Vater*. Munich: Winkler, 1976, 160–261.

Birnbaum, Antonia. *Bonheur Justice Walter Benjamin. Le détour grec*. Paris: Payot, 2008.

Bishop, Will. 'The Marriage Translation and the Contexts of Common Life From the Pacs to Benjamin and Beyond'. *diacritics* 35.4: 59–80.

Bloch, Ernst. *Natturrecht und menschliche Würde*. Frankfurt am Main: Suhrkamp, 1961. *Natural Law and Human Dignity*. Trans. Dennis J. Schmidt. Cambridge, MA: MIT Press, 1986.

Bockius, Fritz. *Die strafrechtliche Bedeutung der internationalen Verträge über das Urheberrecht an Werken der Literatur und Kunst*. Berlin: Carl Heymanns, 1910.

Borges, Jorge Luis. 'Averroës's Search'. Trans. James E. Irby. *Labyrinths*. New York: New Directions, 1964, 148–55.

Bosch, Annette van den. 'Museums: Constructing a Public Culture in the Global Age'. *Museums and their Communities*. Ed. Sheila Watson. New York: Routledge, 2007, 501–9.
Bosse, Heinrich. *Autorschaft ist Werkherrschaft. Über die Entstehung des Urheberrechts aus dem Geist der Goethezeit*. Paderborn: Ferdinand Schöningh, 1981.
Boyle, Nicholas. 'Goethe, *Die Wahlverwandtschaften*'. In *Landmarks in the German Novel (1)*. Ed. Peter Hutchinson. Oxford: Peter Lang, 2007, 49–66.
Breuer, Dieter. *Geschichte Der Literarischen Zensur in Deutschland*. Heidelberg: Quelle & Meyer, 1982.
Brooks, Peter. *Reading for the Plot: Design and Intention in Narrative*. Cambridge, MA: Harvard UP, 1984.
—. *Troubling Confessions: Speaking Guilt in Law and Literature*. Chicago: U of Chicago P, 2000.
Brooks, Peter, and Paul Gerwitz, eds. *Law's Stories*. New Haven: Yale UP, 1996.
Brown, Edward D. *The International Law of the Sea*. Aldershot: Dartmouth Publishing, 1994.
Bruchner, Gisela. 'Rudolf Borchardt und der Buchhandel. Ein Beitrag zur Situation des deutschen Buchhandels in den letzten Jahren der Weimarer Republic'. *Archiv für Geschichte des Buchwesens* 14 (1973/74): 286–347.
Buber, Martin. *Schuld und Schuldgefühle*. Heidelberg: L. Schneider. 1957.
Caldwell, Peter. *Popular Sovereignty and the Crisis of German Constitutional Law: The Theory and Practice of Weimar Constitutionalism*. Durham, NC: Duke UP, 1997.
Cohen, Mark R. *Under Crescent and Cross: The Jews in the Middle Ages*. Princeton: Princeton UP, 1995.
Cohen, Robert. 'The Political Aesthetics of Holocaust Literature: Peter Weiss's *The Investigation* and Its Critics'. *History and Memory* 10.2 (1998): 43–67.
Conklin, William E. *Hegel's Laws: The Legitimacy of a Modern Legal Order*. Stanford: Stanford UP, 2008.
Connery, Christopher L. 'Ideologies of Land and Sea: Alfred Thayer Mahan, Carl Schmitt, and the Shaping of Global Myth Elements'. *boundary 2* 28.2 (2001): 173–201.
Crosby, Margaret Barber. *The Making of a German Constitution: A Slow Revolution*. Oxford & New York: Berg, 2008.
Daly, Glyn. 'Radical(ly) Political Economy: Luhmann, Postmarxism and Globalization'. *Review of International Political Economy* 11:1 (2004): 1–32.
Dalzell, Frederick. 'Dreamworking Amistad'. *New England Quarterly* 71.1 (1998): 173–201.
de Boor, Hans Otto. *Vom Wesen des Urheberrechts*. Marburg: Elwert, 1933.
Deggau, Hans-Georg. *Die Aporien der Rechtslehre Kants*. Stuttgart: Friedrich Frommann, 1983.
Delano, Amasa. *A Narrative of Voyages and Travels, in the Northern and Southern Hemispheres*. Boston: 1817.
Deleuze, Gilles, and Felix Guattari. *Kafka: Pour une littérature mineure*. Paris: Minuit, 1975. Trans. Dana Polan. *Kafka: Toward a Minor Literature*. Theory and History of Literature, Vol. 30. Minneapolis: U of Minnesota P, 1986.
Derrida, Jacques. 'Devant la loi'. *Kafka and the Critical Performance: Centenary Readings*. Trans. Avitall Ronell. Ed. Alan Udoff. Bloomington: Indiana, 1987, 128–49.

—. 'Force of Law: The "Mystical Foundation of Authority"'. Trans. Mary Quaintance. *Acts of Religion*. By Jacques Derrida. Ed. Gil Anidjar. New York: Routledge, 2002, 230–298.

—. 'Signature, Event, Context'. Trans. Alan Bass. *A Derrida Reader: Between the Blinds*. Ed. Peggy Kamuf. NY: Columbia UP, 1991, 82–111.

Deuber-Mankowsky, Astrid. *Der frühe Walter Benjamin und Hermann Cohen. Jüdische Werte, Kritische Philosophie, vergängliche Erfahrung*. Berlin: Vorwerk, 2000.

Diederichsen, Uwe. '*Die Wahlverwandtschaften* als Werk des Juristen Goethe'. *NJW* 57.9 (2004): 537–44.

Dilcher, Gerhard. 'Jacob Grimm als Jurist'. *200 Jahre Brüder Grimm. Dokumente ihres Lebens und Wirkens*. Ed. Dieter Hennig and Bernhard Lauer. Kassel: Weber & Weidemeyer, 1986, 25–41.

Dimock, Wai Chee. *Residues of Justice: Literature, Law, Philosophy*. Berkeley: U of California P, 1996.

Dolan, Kieran. *A Critical Introduction to Law and Literature*. Cambridge: Cambridge UP, 2007.

Dubber, Markus Dirk. 'The German Jury and the Metaphysical *Volk*. From Romantic Idealism to Nazi Ideology'. *American Journal of Comparative Law* 43.2 (Spring 1995): 227–71.

Dyck, Joachim. 'Ästhetischer Hochverrat: Johannes R. Becher'. Kogel, 171–87.

Emmel, Hildegard. *Das Gericht in der deutschen Literatur des 20. Jahrhunderts*. Bern & Munich: Francke, 1963.

Ezrahi, Sidra DeKoven. *By Words Alone: The Holocaust in Literature*. Chicago: U of Chicago P, 1980.

Faber, Richard. '"Benito Cereno" oder die Entmythologisierung Euro-Americas. Zur Kritik Carl Schmitts und seiner Schule'. *Kultursoziologie: Symptom des Zeitgeistes?* Ed. Richard Faber. Würzburg: Königshausen & Neumann, 1989, 68–83.

Fabio, Udo di. 'Luhmann im Recht – Die juristische Rezeption soziologischer Beobachtung'. In *Niklas Lumanns Denken. Interdisziplinäre Einflüsse und Wirkungen*. Ed. Helga Fripp-Hagelstange. Constance: UVK, 2000, 139–55.

Fehr, Hans. *Das Recht in der Dichtung*. Bern: Francke Verlag, 1933.

Fenves, Peter. *The Messianic Reduction: Walter Benjamin and the Shape of Time*. Stanford: Stanford UP, 2011.

Fichte, Johann Gottlieb. *Grundlage des Naturrechts*. Werke. 6 vols. Leipzig: Félix Meiner, 1911. 2: 1–389.

Figal, Günter. 'Recht und Moral als Handlungsspielräume'. *Zeitschrift für philosophische Forschung* 36.3 (1982): 361–77.

Fish, Stanley. *Doing What Comes Naturally: Change, Rhetoric, and Practice of Theory in Literary and Legal Studies*. Durham: Duke UP, 1989.

Franklin, H. Bruce. 'Slavery and Empire: "Benito Cereno"'. *Melville's Evermoving Dawn*. Ed. John Bryant and Robert Milder. Kent, OH: Kent State UP, 1997, 147–61.

Fraser, Andrew. 'A Marx for the Managerial Revolution: Habermas on Law and Democracy'. *Journal of Law and Society* 28.3 (2001): 361–83.

Freeman, Michael, and Andrew D. E. Lewis, eds. *Law and Literature*. Current Legal Issues, Vol. 2. Oxford: Oxford UP, 1999.

Friedländer, Max. *Rechtsanwälte und Anwaltsprobleme in der schönen Literatur*. Essen: Juristischer Fachbuchverlag, 1979.

Gailus, Andreas. *Passions of the Sign: Revolution in Language in Kant, Goethe, and Kleist*. Baltimore, MD: Johns Hopkins UP, 2006.

Geertz, Clifford. 'Thick Description: Toward an Interpretive Theory of Culture'. *The Interpretation of Cultures*. New York: Basic Books, 2003, 3–32.

Gellert, Christian Fürchtegott. *Moralische Vorlesungen. Gesammelte Schriften Band 6*. Berlin: de Gruyter, 1992.

'Germany'. *Censorship: A World Encyclopedia*. 3 vols. London: Fitzroy Dearborn, 2001. 2: 918–34.

Ginschel, Gunhild. *Der junge Jacob Grimm 1805–1819*. 2nd ed. Stuttgart: S. Hirzel, 1989.

Giono, Jean. *Pour saluer Melville*. Paris: Nouvelle Revue Française, 1943.

Göpfert, Herbert. '"Die Aufgaben der Zeit gegenüber der Literatur". Rudolf Borchardt und der Buchhandel'. *Das Buch in der dynamischen Gesellschaft. Festschrift für Wolfgang Strauss zum 60 Geburtstag*. Tier: Spee-Verlag, 1970, 123–31.

Gray, Jefferson M. Review of *Franz Kafka: The Office Writings*. Federal Lawyer 56 (Oct. 2009): 52–4.

Greenberg, Jack. 'Wraparound: From Kafka to Kafkaesque'. *The Office Writings*. Ed. Stanley Corngold, Jack Greenberg and Benno Wagner. Princeton: Princeton UP, 2009, 355–72.

Groh, Ruth. *Arbeit an der Heillosigkeit der Welt*. Frankfurt am Main: Suhrkamp, 1998.

Gross, Raphael. *Carl Schmitt and the Jews: The 'Jewish Question', the Holocaust, and German Legal Theory*. Madison: U of Wisconsin P, 2007.

Grundmann, Günter, Michael Strich, and Werner Richey. *Rechtssprichwörter*. Hanau: Werner Dausien, 1984.

Hamel, Iris. *Völkischer Verband und nationale Gewerkschaft. Der Deutschnationale Handlungsgehilfen-Verband 1893–1933*. Frankfurt am Main: Europäische Verlagsanstalt, 1967.

Hannover, Heinrich, and Elisabeth Hannover-Drück. 'Justiz gegen Literatur und Kunst'. *Politische Justiz 1918–1933*. Bornheim-Merten: Lamuv, 1987, 238–62.

Hanssen, Beatrice. *Critique of Violence: Between Poststructuralism and Critical Theory*. NY: Routledge, 2000.

Harder, Hans-Bernd, and Ekkehard Kaufman. *Die Brüder Grimm in ihrer amtlichen und politischen Tätigkeit*. Kassel: Weber & Weidemeyer, 1985.

Harrison, Paul R. 'Luhmann and the Theory of Social Systems'. *Reconstructing Theory: Gadamer, Habermas, Luhmann*. Ed. David Roberts. Melbourne: Melbourne UP, 1995, 65–90.

Haupt, Jürgen. 'Schmutz und Schund. Heinrich Mann und der Niedergang der Weimarer Republik'. *L'80. Demokratie und Sozialismus* 16 (Dec. 1980): 125–40.

Haverkamp, Anselm. 'Ein unabwerfbarer Schatten: Gewalt und Trauer in Benjamins Kritik der Gewalt'. *Gewalt und Gerechtigkeit. Derrida – Benjamin*. Ed. Anselm Haverkamp. Frankfurt am Main: Suhrkamp, 1994, 162–84.

Heald, Paul J., ed. *Literature and Legal Problem Solving: Law and Literature as Ethical Discourse*. Durham, NC: Carolina Academic P, 1998.

Hegel, G. W. F. *Grundlinien der Philosophie des Rechts*. Berlin: Akademie Verlag, 1981. Trans. T. M. Knox. *Hegel's Philosophy of Right*. Oxford: Oxford University Press, 1967.

Henel, Insgeborg. 'Die Türhüterlegende und ihre Bedeutung fur Kafka's Prozeß'. *Deutsche Vierteljahresschrift für Literatur und Geistesgeschichte* 37 (1963): 50–70.

Hermsdorf, Klaus, and Bruno Wagner. Introduction. Kafka, *Amtliche Schriften*, 1–83.

Hett, Benjamin Carter. 'Hans Litten and the Politics of Criminal Law in the Weimar Republic'. *Modern Histories of Crime and Punishment*. Ed. Markus D. Dubber and Lindsay Farmer. Stanford: Stanford UP, 2007, 175–97.

Hildebrandt, Dieter. 'Ohne Applaus. Picators Inszenierung der "Ermittlung"'. *Frankfurter Allgemeine Zeitung*, Feuilleton, 21 October 1965, n.p.

Höcherl, Robert. 'Dr. jur. Franz Kafka (1883–1924)'. *NJW* 1995, Heft 13: 829–35.

Hofmann, Gert, ed. *Figures of Law: Studies in the Interference of Law and Literature*. Tübingen & Basel: A. Francke, 2007.

Hofstadter, Douglas R. *Gödel, Escher, Bach: An Eternal Golden Braid*. New York: Basic, 1979.

Hornung, Bernd R. 'Luhmann's Legal and Political Sociology'. King and Thornhill, 187–216.

Houben, H. H. *Verbotene Literatur von der klassischen Zeit bis zur Gegenwart*. 2 vols. Berlin: Rowohlt, 1924.

Hume, David. 'Of the Standard of Taste'. 1757. *The Norton Anthology of Theory and Criticism*. Ed. Vincent B. Leitch. New York: Norton, 2001, 486–99.

Hutchinson, Allan, ed. *Critical Legal Studies*. Totowa, NJ: Rowman & Littlefield, 1986.

Jacobson, Arthur J. 'Habermas and Luhmann in the American Legal Tradition'. *Rechtshistorisches Journal* 14 (1995): 3–12.

Jacobson, Arthur J., and Bernhard Schlink. *Weimar: A Jurisprudence of Crisis*. Berkeley: U of California P, 2000.

Jaffe, Adrian. *The Process of Kafka's Trial*. Lansing, MI: Michigan State UP, 1967.

Jäger, Georg. 'Der Kampf gegen Schmutz und Schund. Die Reaktion der Gebildeten auf die Unterhaltungsindustrie'. *Archiv für Geschichte des Buchwesens* 31 (1988): 163–91.

Janouch, Gustav. *Gespräche mit Kafka*. Berlin: Fischer, 1951.

Jones, Howard. *Mutiny on the Amistad*. New York: Oxford UP, 1987.

Jünger, Ernst. *Auf den Marmorklippen*. Hamburg: Hanseatische Verlagsanstalt, 1939.

Kamir, Orit. 'Judgment by Film: Socio-Legal Functions of *Rashomon*'. *Yale Journal of Law and the Humanities* 12.1 (Winter 2000): 39–88.

Kanzog, Klaus. 'Zensur'. *Reallexikon der deutschen Literaturgeschichte, Band III P-Z*. Berlin: de Gruyter, 1984, 891–4.

—. *Literatur und Wandel im Rechtsdenken*. Stuttgart: Scharr, 1993.

Kastner, Klaus. *Literatur und Wandel im Rechtsdenken*. Stuttgart: Boorberg, 1993.

Kauffmann, Kai. *Rudolf Borchardt und 'Der Untergang der deutschen Nation'*. Tübingen: Niemeyer, 2003.

Kambas, Chryssoula. 'Walter Benjamin liest Georges Sorel: "Réflexions sur la violence"'. *Aber ein Sturm weht vom Paradiese her. Texte zu Walter Benjamin*. Ed. Michael Opitz and Erdmut Wizisla. Leipzig: Reclam, 1992.

Kauffmann, Kai. 'Rudolf Borchardts und Walter Benjamins Berliner Kindheiten um 1900'. *Zeitschrift für Germanistik* 8 (1998): 375–87.

Kelsen, Hans. *Reine Rechtslehre. Einleitung in die rechtswissenschaftliche Problematik*. 1934. Aalen: Sicentia, 1985. Trans. Max Knight. *Pure Theory of Law*. Berkeley: U of California P, 1967.

Kesting, Marianne. 'Begegnungen mit Carl Schmitt'. *Schmittiana 4 1994.* Ed. Piet Tommissen. Berlin: Duncker & Humblot, 1994, 98–112.
—. '"Benito Cereno" und seine Interpretationen'. *Benito Cereno.* By Herman Melville. 2nd ed. Ed. Marianne Kesting. Frankfurt am Main: Insel, 1983, 141–54.
Kiefner, Hans. 'Der Einfluss Kants auf Theorie und Praxis des Zivilrechts im 19. Jahrhundert'. *Ideal wird, was Natur war*, 59–82.
—. 'Ideal wird, was Natur war'. *Ideal wird, was Natur war*, 137–44.
—. *Ideal wird, was Natur war. Abhandlungen zur Privatrechtsgeschichte des späten 18. Und des 19. Jahrhunderts.* Goldbach: Keip, 1997.
Kilian, Michael, ed. *Dichter, Denker und der Staat : Essays zu einer Beziehung ganz eigener Art.* Tübingen: Attempto, 1993.
King, Michael. 'What's the Use of Luhmann's Theory?' King and Thornhill eds, 37–52.
King, Michael, and Chris Thornhill. *Niklas Luhmann's Theory of Politics and Law.* London: Palgrave-MacMillan, 2003.
King, Michael, and Chris Thornhill, eds. *Luhmann on Law and Politics: Critical Appraisals and Applications.* Oxford and Portland, OR: Hart, 2006.
Klenner, Hermann. 'Als Recht und Poesie aus einem Bette aufzustehen schienen. Juristische Rückblicke auf die Geburtswehen der Germanistik'. Impulse 10. Eds Walter Dietze and Werner Schubert. Berlin & Weimar: Aufbau Verlag, 1987, 168–85.
Klickovic, Sava. '"Benito Cereno": Ein moderner Mythos'. Barion 2: 265–73.
Kluge, Alexander. 'Film and the Public Sphere'. Trans. Thomas Y. Levin and Miriam Hansen. *New German Critique* 24–5 (Fall-Winter 1981): 206–20.
Knothe, Hans-Georg. '"Umfunktionierte" Klassiker-Aufführungen ohne Hinweis — vertragsgemäße Theaterleistung?' *NJW* 37 (1984): 1070–9.
Koch, Hans-Albrecht, Gabriela Rovagni, and Bernd H. Oppermann, eds. *Grenzfrevel. Rechtskultur und literarische Kultur.* Bonn: Bouvier, 1998.
Kodat, Catherine G. 'Saving Private Property: Steven Spielberg's American Dreamworks'. *Representations* 71 (Summer 2000): 77–105.
Koepnick, Lutz. *Walter Benjamin and the Aesthetics of Power.* Lincoln: U of Nebraska P, 1999.
Kogel, Jörg-Dieter, ed. *Schriftsteller vor Gericht.* Frankfurt am Main: Suhrkamp, 1996.
Koivisto Julia, and Esa Valiverronen. 'The Resurgence of Critical Theories of the Public Sphere'. *Journal of Communication Inquiry* 20.2 (Fall 1996): 18–36.
Kolbenheyer, Ernst Guido. *Paracelsus. Romantrilogie.* Heusenstamm: Orion-Heimreiter, 1964; rept. 1979.
Kord, Susanne. 'The Curtain Never Rises: Femininity and Theater Censorship in Eighteenth- and Nineteenth-Century Germany'. *German Quarterly* 70.4 (Fall 1997): 358–75.
Koselleck, Reinhart. *Preussen zwischen Reform und Revolution. Allgemeines Landrecht, Verwaltung und soziale Bewegung von 1791 bis 1848.* Stuttgart: Klett-Cotta, 1967.
Kraus, Wolfgang. 'Schuld und Sinnfrage in Kafkas *Prozeß*'. *Franz Kafka Symposium 1983.* Ed. Wilhelm Emrich and Bernd Goldmann. Die Mainzer Reihe no.62. Mainz: Hase & Koehler, 1985, 201–14.
Ladeur, Karl-Heinz, and Tobias Gostomzyk. 'Mephisto Reloaded: Zu den Bücherverboten der Jahre 2003/2004 und der Notwendigkeit, die

Kunstfreiheit auf eine Risikobetrachtung umzustellen'. *NJW* 58.9 (2005): 566–9.
Lamond, Grant. 'Do Precedents Create Rules?' *Legal Theory* 11.1 (March 2005): 1–26.
Landgraf, Edgar. 'Comprehending Romantic Incomprehensibility. A Systems-Theoretical Perspective on Early German Romanticism'. *MLN* 121 (2006): 592–616.
Lane, Richard J. *Reading Walter Benjamin: Writing Through the Catastrophe.* Manchester & New York: Manchester UP, 2005.
Langer, Lawrence L. *The Holocaust and the Literary Imagination.* New Haven: Yale UP, 1975.
Laternser, Hans. *Die andere Seite im Auschwitz-Prozess 1963/65. Reden eines Verteidigers.* Stuttgart: Seewald, 1966.
Leisching, Peter. 'Rechtshistorische Parallelen zu Immanuel Kants Ehelehre'. *Bruno Primetshofer zum 60. Geburtstag.* Ed. Josef Lenzenweger et al. Vienna : Verlag des Verbandes der Wissenschaftlichen Gesellschaften Oesterreichs, 1989, 106–29.
Lethen, Helmut. 'Der Habitus der Sachlichkeit in der Weimarer Republik'. *Hansers Sozialgeschichte der deutschen Literatur vom 16. Jahrhundert bis zur Gegenwart.* Vol. 8. Ed. Bernhard Weyergraf. Munich: Hanser, 1995, 371–445.
Lévi-Strauss, Claude. 'The Structural Study of Myth'. *The Structuralists From Marx to Lévi-Strauss.* Ed. Richard and Fernade DeGeorge. Garden City. NY: Doubleday-Anchor, 1972, 169–94.
Lindenau, Herbert. 'Zur ersten grundsätzlich wichtigen Entscheidung der Oberprüfstelle über den Begriff der Schundschrift'. *Deutsche-Juristen-Zeitung* 33 (1928): 511–12.
Linder, Jutta. *'Falsche Tendenzen'; Der Staatsdiener Goethe und der Dichter.* Soveria Manelli (Catanzaro): Rubbetino, 2001.
Lindner, Burkhardt. 'Goethes *Wahlverwandtschaften* und die Kritik der mythischen Verfassung der bürgerlichen Gesellschaft', in *Goethes Walhverwandtschaften: Kritische Modelle und Diskursanalysen zum Mythos Literatur.* Ed. Norbert W. Bolz. Hildesheim: Gerstenberg, 1981, 23–44.
Der literarische Hochverrat von Johannes R. Becher. Berlin: MOPR-Verlag, 1928.
Litowitz, Douglas. 'Max Weber and Franz Kafka: A Shared Vision of Modern Law'. *Journal of Law, Culture, and the Humanities* 7.1 (2011): 48–65.
Llewellyn, Karl N. *The Case Law System in America.* Trans. Michael Ansaldi. Ed. Paul Gewirtz. Chicago: U of Chicago P, 1989.
Llewellyn, Karl N., and E. Adamson Hoebel. *The Cheyenne Way : Conflict and Case Law in Primitive Jurisprudence.* Norman, OK : Oklahoma UP, 1941.
Lotze, Dieter P. 'Eine alltägliche Verwirrung? Zur Struktur und Interpretation von Kafkas *Prozeß*'. *Franz Kafka. Eine Aufsatzsammlung nach einem Symposium in Philadelphia.* Ed. Maria Luise Caputo Mayer. Berlin: Agora, 1978, 37–45.
Lüderssen, Klaus. 'Die Juristen und die schöne Literatur — Stufen der Rezeption'. *NJW* 50.17 (1997): 1106–11.
Margolitch, David. 'Performance as Force for Change: The Case of Billie Holiday and "Strange Fruit"'. *Cardozo Studies in Law and Literature* 11.1 (Summer 1999): 108.
Mayer, Hans, and Peter Weiss. 'Kann sich die Bühne eine Auschwitz-Dokumentation leisten? Peter Weiss im Gespräch mit Hans Mayer (October 1965). *Peter-Weiss-Jahrbuch* 4 (1995): 8–30.

McClintock, Scott. 'The Penal Colony: Inscription of the Subject in Literature and Law, and Detainees as Legal Non-Persons at Camp X-Ray'. *Comparative Literature Studies* 41.1 (2004): 153–67.

McCole, John. *Walter Benjamin and the Antinomies of Tradition*. Ithaca: Cornell UP, 1993.

McCormick, John P. 'The Dilemmas of Dictatorship: Carl Schmitt and Constitutional Emergency Powers'. Dyzenhaus, 217–51.

—. 'Max Weber and Jürgen Habermas: The Sociology and Philosophy of Law During Crises of the State'. *Yale Journal of Law and the Humanities* 9 (1997): 297–344.

Mermall, Thomas. Introduction. *La rebelión de las masas*. By José Ortega y Gassett. Madrid: Clásicos Castalia, 1998, 7–83.

Merton, Robert. *Social Theory and Social Structure*. Rev. ed. Glencoe, IL: Free Press, 1957.

Meusch, Matthias. *Von der Diktatur zur Demokratie. Fritz Bauer und die Aufarbeitung der NS-Verbrechen in Hessen 1956–1968*. Wiesbaden: Historische Kommission für Nassau, 2001.

Meyer, Andreas. 'Die Verlagsfusion Langen-Müller. Zur Buchmarkt- und Kulturpolitik des DHV in der Endphase der Weimarer Republik'. *Archiv für Geschichte des Buchwesens* 32 (1989): 1–273.

Mitchell, Robert. *Sympathy and the State in the Romantic Era: Systems, State Finance, and the Shadows of Futurity*. New York: Routledge, 2007.

Mitteis, Heinrich. 'Recht und Dichtung'. *Die Rechtsidee in der Geschichte*. Weimar: Böhlau, 1957, 681–97.

Moenkemeyer, Heinz. 'RBs Lessing-Essay (1929) und der Kampf um die Weimarer Republik'. *Views and Review of Modern German Literature: Festschrift for Adolf D. Klarmann*. Ed. Karl S. Weimar. Munich: Delp, 1974, 133–47.

Mölk, Ulrich, ed. *Literatur und Recht: Literarische Rechtsfälle von der Antike bis in die Gegenwart*. Göttingen: Wallstein, 1996.

Müller, Jan-Werner. 'Myth, Law and Order: Schmitt and Benjamin Read Reflections on Violence'. *History of European Ideas* 29 (2003): 459–73.

Müller-Dietz, Heinz. *Grenzüberschreitungen: Beiträge zur Beziehung zwischen Literatur und Recht*. Baden-Baden: Nomos Verlagsgesellschaft, 1990.

Müller-Sievers, Helmut. *Self-Generation: Biology, Philosophy, and Literature around 1800*. Stanford: Stanford UP, 1997.

Nägele, Rainer. 'Public Voice and Private Voice: Freud, Habermas, and the Dialectic of Enlightenment'. *Reading After Freud: Essays on Goethe, Hölderlin, Habermas, Nietzsche, Brecht, Celan, and Freud*. New York: Columbia UP, 1987.

Neaman, Elliot Y. *A Dubious Past: Ernst Jünger and the Politics of Literature after Nazism*. Berkeley: U of California P, 1999.

Negt, Oskar, and Alexnder Kluge. *Public Sphere and Experience: Toward an Analysis of the Bourgeois and Proletarian Public Sphere*. Trans. Peter Labanyi, Jamie Owen Daniel, and Assenka Oksiloff. Minneapolis: U of Minnesota P, 1993.

Nixon, Nicola. 'Men and Coats: or, the Politics of the Dandiacal Body in Melville's "Benito Cereno"'. *PMLA* 114.3 (May 1999): 359–72.

Noack, Paul. *Carl Schmitt. Eine Biografie*. Berlin: Propyläen, 1993.

Nörr, Dieter. *Savignys philosophische Lehrjahre: Ein Versuch*. Frakfurt am Main: Klostermann, 1993.

Nussbaum, Martha C. *Poetic Justice: The Literary Imagination and Public Life*. Boston: Beacon P, 1995.

Nussberger, Angelika. 'Wer zitiert wen? – Zur Funktion von Zitaten bei der Herausbildung gemeineuropäischen Verfassungsrechts'. *Juristenzeitung* 61.15–16 (2006): 763–70.

Oborniker, Alfred. 'Kunst-Verfolgung,' *Die Justiz* 1.2 (December 1925): 203–15.

Osterkamp, Ernst. '"Verschmelzung der kritischen und der dichterischen Sphäre". Das Engagement deutscher Dichter im Konflikt um die Munckernachfolge 1926/27 und seine wissenschaftsgeschichtliche Bedeutung'. *Jahrbuch der deutschen Schillergesellschaft* 33 (1989): 348–69.

Pan, David. 'Against Biopolitics: Walter Benjamin, Carl Schmitt, and Giorgio Agamben on Political Sovereignty and Symbolic Order'. *German Quarterly* 82.1 (Winter 2009): 42–62.

—. 'Political Aesthetics: Carl Schmitt as Hamlet'. *Telos* 72 (Summer 1987): 353–9.

Pausch, Afons, and Jutta Pausch. *Goethes Juristenlaufbahn. Rechtsstudent, Advokat, Staatsdiener*. Cologne: Otto Schmidt, 1996.

Pawel, Ernst. *The Nightmare of Reason: A Life of Franz Kafka*. New York: Farrar, 1984.

Pencak, William. *The Conflict of Law and Justice in the Icelandic Sagas*. Amsterdam: Rodopi, 1995.

Pendas, David O. *The Frankfurt Auschwitz Trial 1963–1965: Genocide, History, and the Limits of the Law*. Cambridge, UK: Cambridge UP, 2006.

—. '"I didn't know what Auschwitz was": The Frankfurt Auschwitz Trial and the German Press, 1963–65'. *Yale Journal of Law and Humanities* 12.2 (Summer 2000): 397–446.

Peters, H. F. 'Ernst Jünger's Concern with E. A. Poe'. *Comparative Literature* 10.2 (Spring 1958): 144–9.

Peters, Julie Stone. 'Law, Literature, and the Vanishing Real: On the Future of an Interdisciplinary Illusion'. *PMLA* 120.2 (2005): 442–53.

Petersen, Klaus. 'Censorship and the Campaign against Foreign Influences in Film and Theater during the Weimar Republic'. *Zensur und Kultur/Censorship and Culture*, Eds. John A. McCarthy and Werner von der Ohe. Tübingen: Niemeyer, 1995, 149–58.

—. *Literatur und Justiz in der Weimarer Republik*. Stuttgart: Metzler, 1988.

—. *Zensur in der Weimarer Republik*. Stuttgart: Metzler, 1995.

Phelan, Anthony. *Reading Heinrich Heine*. Cambridge: Cambridge UP, 2007.

Poe, Edgar Allen. 'A Descent into the Maelström'. *The Science Fiction of Edgar Allen Poe*. Ed. Harold Beaver. Harmondsworth, UK: Penguin, 1976, 72–88.

Politzer, Heinz. *'Der Prozess* Against The Court'. *Franz Kafka: Parable und Paradox*. Ithaca: Cornell UP, 1962, 163–217.

—. 'Rudolf Borchardt: Poet of Assimilation,' *Commentary* 9 (1950): 57–65.

Poscher, Rolf. 'Verfassungsfeiern in verfassungsfeindlicher Zeit'. *Der Verfassungstag*. Ed. Rolf Poscher. Baden-Baden: Nomos, 1999, 11–50.

Posner, Richard. 'Kafka: The Writer as Lawyer'. *Columbia Law Review* 110 (Jan. 2010): 207–14.

—. *Law and Literature*. Third ed. Cambridge: Harvard UP, 2009.

Protokolle der von der hohen deutschen Bundesversammlung durch Beschluß vom 16.Juli 1863 einberufenen Commission zur Ausarbeitung des entwurfes eines für sämmtliche deutsche Bundesstaaten gemeinsamen Gesetzes zum Schutze des Urheberrechts. Frankfurt am Main: Bundesdruckerei, 1864.

Quaritsch, Helmut. *Positionen und Begriffe Carl Schmitts*. Berlin: Duncker & Humblot, 1989.
Rabel, Gabriele. *Goethe und Kant*. 2 vols. Vienna: Selbstverlag, 1927.
Rasch, William. *Niklas Luhmann's Modernity: The Paradoxes of Differentiation*. Stanford: Stanford UP, 2000.
—. *Sovereignty and its Discontents: On the Primacy of Conflict and the Structure of the Political*. London: Birkbeck Law Press, 2004.
Rasehorn, Theo. *Justizkritik in der Weimarer Republik: Das Beispiel der Zeitschrift 'Die Justiz'*. Frankfurt am Main & New York: Campus, 1985.
Rathenau, Ernst. *Das Buch als Rechtsobjekt*. Greifswald: Hans Adler, 1919.
Reichsjustizministerium. *Entwurf eines Gesetztes über das Urheberrecht an Werken der Literatur, der Kunst und der Photographie, mit Begründung*. Berlin: Walter de Gruyter, 1932.
Reijen, Willem van. 'Die Allegorisierung des Bürgertums in Benjamins Ursprung des deutschen Trauerspiels'. *Global Benjamin*. 3 vols. Ed. Klaus Garber and Ludger Rehm. Munich: Fink, 1992, 1:657–69.
Renz, Werner. 'Der erste Frankfurter Auschwitz-Prozess. Völkermord als Strafsache'. *1999: Zeitschrift für Sozialgeschichte des 20. und 21. Jahrhunderts* 15 (2000): 11–48.
Reschke, Nils. *'Zeit der Umwendung'. Lektüren der Revolution in Goethes Roman*. Freiburg im Breisgau: Rombach, 2006.
Richards, Donald Ray. *The German Bestseller in the 20th Century. A Complete Bibliography and Analysis 1915–1940*. Bern: Herbert Lang, 1968.
Ridder, Helmut K. 'Bermerkungen eines Juristen zum Zensurproblem'. *Zensur und Selbstzensur in der Literatur*. Ed. Peter Brockmeier and Gerhard R. Kaiser. Würzburg: Königshausen & Neumann, 1996, 5–24.
Rieder, Bernd. *Die Zensurbegriffe des Art. 118 Abs. 2 der Weimarer Reichsverfassung und des Art. 5 Abs. 1 Satz 3 des Bonner Grundgesetzes*. Berlin: Duncker & Humblot, 1970.
Roberts, David. 'Paradoxie der Literatur als Form'. Baecker, 22–4.
Roberts, Patricia. 'Habermas, *Philosophes*, and Puritans: Rationality and Exclusion in the Dialectical Public Sphere'. *Rhetoric Society Quarterly* 26.1 (Winter 1996): 47–68.
Robertson, Ritchie. *Kafka: Judaism, Politics, and Literature*. Oxford: Clarendon P, 1985.
Rosenfeld, Alvin H. *A Double Dying: Reflections on Holocaust Literature*. Bloomington: Indiana UP, 1980.
Rosskopf, Annette. 'Zum Leben und Wirken Friedrich Karl Kaul'. *Neue Justiz* 55.4 (2001): 186.
Rüdesheim, Hans 'Aus den Dunkelkammern'. *Die Justiz* 7.1 (1931): 13–32.
Rudolf Borchardt. Special issue of *Text + Kritik*. Ed. Heinz Ludwig Arnold and Gerhart Schuster. Munich: Boorberg, 2007.
Rüter, Christoph. '"Nach Vollzug" 1998/2005'. Weiler, 84–8.
Safranski, Rüdiger. *Martin Heidegger: Between Good and Evil*. Trans. Ewald Osers. Cambridge, MA: Harvard UP, 1998.
Salloch, Erika. *Peter Weiss' Die Ermittlung. Zur Struktur des Dokumtartheaters*. Frankfurt am Main: Athenäum, 1972.
Salzwedel, Johannes. 'Gellert und die *Wahlverwandschaften*'. *Euphorion* 83.3 (1989): 297–308.
Sasse, Günter. 'Faktizität und Fiktionalität: Literaturtheoretische Überlegungen am Beispiel des Dokumentartheaters'. *Wirkendes Wort* 36.1 (Jan.-Feb. 1986): 15–26.

Schierloh, Nicolaus. *Die Beleidigung in den §§185, 186, 187 RStGB und die Wahrnehmung berechtigter Interessen mit besonderer Berücksichtigung der Presse*. Breslau: Schletter, 1925.

Schlick, Werner. *Goethe's* Die Wahlverwandtschaften: *A Middle-Class Critique of Aesthetic Aristocratism*. Heidelberg: C. Winter, 2000.

Schlunk, Jürgen E. 'Auschwitz and Its Function in Peter Weiss' Search for Identity'. *German Studies Review* 10.1 (Feb. 1987): 11–30.

Schmidhäuser, Eberhard. 'Kafkas "Der Prozeß". Ein Versuch aus der Sicht des Juristen'. In *Literatur und Recht: Literarische Rechtsfälle von der Antike bis in die Gegenwart*. Ed. Ulrich Mölk. Göttingen: Wallstein, 1996, 341–55.

Schmidt, Siegfried J. *Die Selbstorganisation des Sozialsystems Literatur im 18. Jahrhundert*. Frankfurt am Main: Suhrkamp, 1989.

Schmidt-Wiegand, Ruth. *Jacob Grimm und das genetische Prinzip in Rechtswissenschft und Philologie*. Marburg: Hitzeroth, 1987.

Schneider, Peter. *Ausnahmezustand und Norm. Eine Studie zur Rechtslehre von Carl Schmitt*. Stuttgart: Deutsche Verlags-Anstalt, 1957.

—. *'Ein einzig Volk von Brüdern': Recht und Staat in der Literatur*. Frankfurt am Main: Athenäum, 1987.

Schoeps, Hans-Joachim. 'Theologische Motive in der Dichtung Franz Kafkas'. *Die Neue Rundschau* 42.1 (1951): 21–37.

Schudson, Michael. 'Was There Ever a Public Sphere?' *Habermas and the Public Sphere*. Ed. Craig Calhoun. Cambridge, MA: MIT P, 1992, 143–63.

Schultze, Ernst. *Die Schundliteratur. Ihr Wesen, Ihre Folgen, Ihre Bekämpfung*. Halle: Verlag der Buchhandlung des Waisenhauses, 1911.

—. 'Selbstmord und Schundliteratur'. *Hamburger Zeitschrift für Wohnungskultur* 14 (May 1909): 107.

—. 'Schundliteratur früher und jetzt'. *Beiträge zur gesitig-sittlichen Kenntnis unserer Zeit*. Berlin: Kohlhammer, 1913, 91–108.

Schumann, Karl. *Das Gesetz zur Bewahrung der Jugend vor Schund- und Schmutzschriften vom 18.12.1926. Eine staatsrechtliche Betrachtung*. Borna-Leipzig: Noske, 1929.

Schütz, Anton. 'Thinking the Law With and Against Luhmann, Legendre, Agamben'. *Law and Critique* 11.2 (2000): 107–36.

Schwab, Dieter. 'Jena und die Entdeckung der romantischen Ehe'. *Zeitschrift für Neuere Rechtsgeschichte* 27.3–4 (2007): 177–88.

Schwab, George. *The Challenge of the Exception*. 2nd ed. New York: Greenwood Press, 1989.

Schwan, Werner. *Goethes* Wahlverwandtschaften: *Das nicht erreichte Soziale*. Munich: Wilhelm Fink, 1983.

Schwanitz, Dietrich. *Systemtheorie und Literatur: Ein neues Paradigma*. Opladen: Westdeutscher Verlag, 1990.

Schwarz, Gotthart. 'Berliner Tageblatt, Berlin (1872–1939)'. *Deutsche Zeitungen des 17. Bis 20. Jahrhunderts*. Ed. Heinz-Dietrich Fischer. Pullach: Verlag Dokumentation, 1972.

Schwartz, Peter J. *After Jena: Goethe's* Elective Affinities *and the End of the Old Regime*. Lewisburg: Bucknell UP, 2010.

—. '"An Unpublished Essay by Goethe?" Staatssachen. Ueber mündliche deutsche Rechtspflege in Deutschland'. *The Germanic Review* 73.2 (Spring 1998): 107–31.

Seifert, Jürgen. 'Theoretiker der Gegenrevolution: Carl Schmitt'. *Die juristische Aufarbeitung des Unrechts-Staats*. Ed. Thomas Blanke et al. Baden-Baden: Nomos, 1998, 363–72.

Sereni, Angelo Piero. 'The Code and the Case Law'. Bernard Schwartz, 55–79.
Shershow, Scott Cutler. 'Myth and Nihilism in the Discourse of Globalization'. *The New Centennial Review* 1.1 (2001): 257–82.
Siemann, Wolfram. 'Von der offenen zur mittelbaren Kontrolle'. *'Unmoralisch an sich…'. Zensur im 18. und 19. Jahrhundert.* Ed. Herbert G. Göpfert and Erdmann Weyrauch. Weisbaden: Otto Harrassowitz, 1988, 293–308.
Simmel, Georg. *Kant und Goethe: Zur Geschichte der Modernen Weltanschauung.* Leipzig: Kurt Wolff, 1924.
Slaughter, Joseph R. *Human Rights, Inc.: The World Novel, Narrative Form, and International Law.* New York: Fordham UP, 2007.
Springman, Luke. 'Poisoned Hearts, Diseased Minds, and American Pimps: The Language of Censorship in the "Schund und Schmutz" Debates'. *German Quarterly* 68 (1995): 408–29.
Stapel, Wilhelm. *Die Fictionen der Weimarer Verfassung. Versuch einer Unterscheidung der formalen und der funktionalen Demokratie.* Hamburg/Berlin/Leipzig: Hanseatische Verlagsanstalt, 1924.
Sternberg, Theodor. *Die Selektionsidee in Strafrecht und Ethik.* Berlin: Puttkammer & Mühlbrecht, 1911.
Stolleis, Michael. *Geschichte des öffentlichen Rechts in Deutschland.* 3 vols. Munich: Beck, 1988–99.
Storim, Mirjam. *Aesthetik im Umbruch. Zur Funktion der 'Rede über Kunst' um 1900 am Beispiel der Debatte um Schmutz und Schund.* Tübingen: Niemeyer, 2002.
—. '"Einer, der besser ist, als sein Ruf". Kolportageroman und Kolportagebuchhandel um 1900 und die Haltung der Buchbranche'. Maase and Kaschuba, 252–89.
Stringfellow, Frank. 'Kafka's Trial: Between the Republik and Psychoanalysis'. *Cardozo Studies in Law and Literature* 7.1 (Spring/Summer 1995): 173–205.
Strippel, Jutta. 'Zum Verhältnis von deutscher Rechtsgeschichte und deutscher Philologie'. *Germanistik und deutsche Nation 1806–1848. Zur Konstitution bürgerlichen Bewisstseins.* Ed. Jörg Jochen Müller. Stuttgart: Metzler, 2000, 113–66.
Sundquist, Eric. *To Wake the Nations: Race in the Making of American Literature.* Cambridge: Harvard UP, 1993.
Sussman, Henry. 'The Court as Text: Inversion, Supplanting, and Derangement in Kafka's *Der Prozess*'. *PMLA* 92 (1977): 41–55.
Tacitus. *History.* Trans. Alfred John Church and William Jackson Broadrib. *Tacitus.* New York: Modern Library, 1942, 419–552.
Tanner, Tony. *Adultery in the Novel: Contract and Transgression.* Baltimore: Johns Hopkins UP, 1979.
Tantillo, Astrida Orle. *Goethe's* Elective Affinities *and the Critics.* Rochester, NY: Camden House, 2001.
Teubner, Gunther. 'Breaking Frames: The Global Interplay of Legal and Social Systems'. *American Journal of Comparative Law* 45 (Winter 1997): 149–69.
—. *Law as an Autopoietic System.* Oxford: Oxford UP, 1993.
Tierno Galván, Enrique. 'Benito Cereno oder der Mythos Europas'. *Barion* 2: 354–6.
Toews, John Edward. *Becoming Historical: Cultural Reformation and Public Memory in Early Nineteenth-Century Berlin.* New York: Cambridge UP, 2004.
Ufeld, Ulrich. 'Carl Schmitt und Ernst Jünger. Positionen und Begriffe im Lichte der Korrespondenz'. *NJW* 54 (2001): 565–71.

Uyttersprot, Herman '*Der Prozess*: Its Structure'. *Franz Kafka Today*. Ed Angel Flores and Homer Swander Madison: U of Wissonsin P, 1958, 127–44.

Verdict on Auschwitz: The Frankfurt Auschwitz Trial 1963–1965. Dir. Rolf Bickel and Dietrich Wagner. New York: First Run, 2007.

Vesting, Thomas. 'Die permanente Revolution: Carl Schmitt und das Ende der Epoche der Staatlichkeit'. *Metamorphosen des Politischen*. Ed. Andreas Göbel, Dirk van Laak, and Ingeborg Villinger. Berlin: Akademie, 1995, 191–202.

Vitofranceschi, Giuseppe de. 'L'istituto del matrimonio secondo Emmanuele Kant'. *Sophia* (Podova) 38.3–4 (1970): 244–55.

Vonessen, Hedwig. 'Friedrich Karl von Savigny und Jakob Grimm'. Ph.D. diss. Ludwig-Maximilians-Universität Munich. Cologne: Höricke, 1958.

Vorländer, Karl. *Kant, Schiller, Goethe*. Leipzig: Verlag der Dürr'schen Buchhandlung, 1907.

Wachler, Dietrich. 'Mensch und Apparat bei Kafka. Versuch einer soziologischen Interpretation'. *Sprache im Technischen Zeitalter* 78 (June 1981): 142–57.

Walzel, Oskar. 'Goethes *Wahlverwandtschaften* im Rahmen ihrer Zeit'. *Goethes Roman* Die Wahlverwandtschaften. Ed. Ewald Rösch. Darmstadt: Wissenschaftliche Buchgesellschaft, 1975, 35–64.

Weigel, Sigrid. 'Der Märtyrer und der Souverän: Szenarien eines modernen Trauerspiels, gelesen mit Walter Benjamin und Carl Schmitt'. Witte and Ponzi, 94–106.

—. *Walter Benjamin.Die Kreatur, Das Heilige, Die Bilder*. Fischer: Frankfurt am Main, 2008.

Weiler, Christel, ed. *Die Berliner 'Ermittlung' von Jochen Gerz und Esther Shalev-Gerz*. Eggersdorf: Tastomat, 2005.

Weisberg, Richard. *Poethics, And Other Strategies of Law and Literature*. New York: Columbia UP, 1992.

Weisberg, Robert. 'The Law-Literature Enterprise'. *Yale Journal of Law and Humanities* 1 (1989): 1–67.

Weisberg, Robert, and Guyora Binder. *Literary Criticisms of Law*. Princeton: Princeton UP, 2000.

Weiss, Christoph. *Auschwitz in der geteilten Welt: Peter Weiss und »Die Ermittlung« im Kalten Krieg*, 2 vols. St. Ingbert: Röhrig, 2000.

West, Robin. 'Authority, Autonomy, and Choice: The Role of Consent in the Moral and Political Visions of Franz Kafka and Richard Posner'. *Harvard Law Review* 99.2 (Dec. 1985): 384–428.

White, James Boyd. *Justice as Translation: An Essay in Cultural and Legal Criticism*. Chicago: U of Chicago P, 1990.

Whitman, James Q. *The Legacy of Roman Law in the German Romantic Era*. Princeton: Princeton UP, 1990.

Williams, Raymond. *Keywords: A Vocabulary of Culture and Society*. Rev. ed. Oxford: Oxford UP, 1985.

Witteveen, Willem J. 'The Hidden Truth of Autopoiesis'. Freeman & Lewis, 645–65.

Wittmann, Rebecca. *Beyond Justice: The Auschwitz Trial*. Cambridge, MA: Harvard UP, 2005.

Wohlhäupter, Eugen. *Dichterjuristen*. Ed. H.G. Seifert. Tübingen : J. C. B. Mohr, 1953–57.

Wolin, Richard. *Walter Benjamin: An Aesthetic of Redemption*. New York: Columbia UP, 1982.

Young, James E. *Writing and Rewriting the Holocaust: Narrative and the Consequences of Interpretation*. Bloomington, IN: Indiana UP, 1988.

Ziegler, Vickie. *Trial by Fire and Battle in Medieval German Literature*. Rochester: Camden House, 2004.

Ziolkowski, Theodore. *The Mirror of Justice : Literary Reflections of Legal Crises*. Princeton: Princeton University Press, 1997.

Žižek, Slavoj. *The Ticklish Subject: The Absent Centre of Political Ontology*. London: Verso, 1999.

—. 'Why Does the Law Need an Obscene Supplement?' *Law and the Postmodern Mind: Essays on Psychoanalysis and Jurisprudence*. Eds. Peter Goodrich and David Gray Carlson. Ann Arbor: U of Michigan P, 1998, 75–97.

Index

Page numbers in italics refer to discussion in footnotes

9/11 attacks 43, *107*, 132

Abraham, Ulf 106
administrative law 17, 93, 100–1
Adorno, Theodor 90, 162, 169, 188, 194, 238
   Dialectic of Enlightenment 194
adultery 67–9, 74–5, 80–3, 113, 116, 126
aesthetic(s) 3, 25, 37, 74, 77, 141–2, 144–6, 154–8, 169, 190, 195, 214, 221, 237–40, 247
   autonomy 30, 216–17
   Bourdieu on 157–8
   Carl Schmitt on 131–2, 192–3, 214
   censorship and 141–2, 144–6, 154–8
   Kantian 77
   legal use of 3, 247
   political 224
Agamben, Giorgio 107, 120–1, 133
Allgemeines Landrecht (Prussia) 18, 46, 50–1, 76–7, 211
   compared with French Academy 56
   goal of 81
   laws on marriage and family 76
ALR. *See Allgemeines Landrecht*
Alverdes, Paul 181

American Constitution 115
Amistad (court trial) *207*
Amistad (film) 207
Andriopoulos, Stefan 91
anomie 21, 121
anthropology 44, 124, 164
antipositivism. *See* positivism
anti-Semitism 160, 168, 188, *196*
apartheid 91
Archiv für Sozialwissenschaft und Soizalpolitik 120
Arendt, Hannah 35, 218
Aristotle 27, 154, 199
Arnim, Achim von 56
Arnim, Bettine von 53
art 7–8, 22–7, 36–7, 53, 56
Artaud, Antonin 226
Assmann, Aleida 140–1
Assmann, Jan 140–1
Athens 246
Aulich, Reinhard 143–4
Austen, Jane 21, 69
Austin, J. L. 14, *93*
Austria,16, 70, 101, 139, 244
Austrian Constitution 19, 133
Austrian Law 90–3
   Criminal Code 92

Baroque 128–30, 137, 213
Bartels, Adolf 167
Barthes, Roland 121
Basel 16
Basic Law 35, 222

Battleship Potemkin (film) 143
Bauer, Felice *105*
Bauer, Fritz 219–21, 228
Baum, Vicky 182
Bavaria 160, 176
Baxter, Hugh 13, 26
Beaumarchais 72
Becher, Johannes 186, 187
Beckett, Samuel 226
Beebee, John *90*
Beethoven 85
Beleidigung (libel) 184
Benjamin, Walter 2, 21, 37, 63, 70–1, 78, 83–5, 90, 105–7, 111–37, 169, 179, 189, 190, 192, 194, *210*, 244, 247–8
    'Goethes *Wahlverwandtschaften*' 64, 70, 74, 84, 85, 112, 116–18, 120, 127, 135
    Lebenslauf 113, 169
    on experience *116*
    on fate, *see* fate, in Benjamin
    on Rudolf Borchardt 162
    Paralipomena to 'Über den Begriff der Geschichte' *1*
    redemptive criticism *113*, 116, 128
    'Schicksal und Charakter' 125
    'Über das Programm der kommenden Philosophie' 116
    'Über den Begriff der Geschichte' *113*
    Ursprung des Trauerspiels 112, 113, 128–30
    'Zur Kritik der Gewalt' 107, 112–13, 116, 119, 133, 192
Benton, Lauren 191
Berghahn, Klaus 237
Bergman, Ingmar 224
Berlin 5, 53, 62, *105*, 131, 145, 156, 168, *179*, 195, 226, 239
    Academy of the Arts 175
    Benjamin in 114, 169
    Borchardt in 168, 169
    East 223
    as capital of Germany 111
    Prüfstelle of 153, 154, 159–60
    University of 49
Berliner Tageblatt 159, 163, 165–6, 176–7, 181, 183–5, 188
Bersier, Gabrielle 70–1
Bertram, Ernst *169*
Big Other 98–9
Bigsby, Christopher 226
Binder, Guyora 5–6
biopolitics 107
Birnbaum, Antonia *128*
Bishop, Will 68
Bismarck 46–244
blasphemy 144, 148, 159
Bleak House 17
Bloch, Ernst 77–8
Boccaccio 75
Bochum 239
Bodin, Jean 208
Bodmer, Johann Jakob 62
Boger, Wilhelm 222
Bohemia 70, 88, 176
Bonn 131, 221
Borchardt, Rudolf 139, 161–90, *197*, 244
    Aufgaben der Zeit gegenüber der Literatur 170
    Deutsche Literatur im Kampfe um ihr Recht 163–89
    reactions to 179
    hoffnungslose Geschlecht, Das 170, 174
    libel trial 164, 182–5
    on Lessing 172
    on publishing crisis 171
    reactions to libel trial 179, 185–6
    Schriften 174
    Vereinigung durch den Feind hindurch 170
    Villa 169

Borges, Jorge Luis 234
Börne, Ludwig *171*
Börsenblatt für den deutschen Buchhandel 172
Bosch, Annette van den 43
Bourdieu, Pierre 3, 22, 102–3, 142, 157–8, 164
  on deferral 102
Boyle, Nicholas 71
Brandt, Willy 33
Brecht, Bertolt 159, 180, 217, 230, 239
  gute Mensch von Szechwan, Der 217
  Kaukasische Kreidekreis, Der 39, 217
Bremen 170, 173, *175*, 181
Bremer Presse 174
Brentano, Clemens 53
Brentano, Kunigunda 49
Breuer, Dieter 144
Brockhaus 174
Brod, Max *89*, 104
Brooks, Peter 4, 7, 69
Brown, Edward 211
Brown, Spencer 23, 243
Bruchner, Gisela 171–2
Buber, Martin 90
Buchhändler Börsenverein 174
Budapest 175
Bundespressegesetz of 1854, 144
Bundesprüfstelle für jugendgefährdende Medien 161
bureaucracy 86, 88, 90, 92, 98, 99, 244, 248
Bürgerliches Gesetzbuch 244
Bürgerrechte 70
Burke, Edmund 200

Caldwell, Peter 115, *135*
Campbell v. Wood (court case) *11*
canonization 138–40, 150, 161
Cardozo Studies in Law and Literature 4

Cartesian subject 22
catharsis 232
Catholic church 84, 139
censorship 3, 5, 11, 32, 112, 138–50, 154, *156*, 158, 161, *188*, 189, *197*, 244, 247 *See Zensur*
Cervantes, Miguel de 102
cinema 150
citation 48, 51, 94, 192–3, 200, 202, 225–6, 229, 238, 239, 242–8
  and precedent 2, 7–16
  as communication 31, 230
  as second-order observation 216–41
  as structural coupling 2–21
  by law 30, 66, 115, 194, 214
  by literature 92, 107, 112, 173, 216–17
  gone wrong 61
  of *Recht/Unrecht* 69
  self- 108, 194
civil rights 70, 100, 187
Classicism 155, 160
club-law 124, 189–90
Code Napoléon 46–7, 56, 64, 70, 71, 73, 214
codification 3, 9, 50, 57, 64, 65, 66, 81, 244
Cohen, Hermann 115, 133
Cohen, Mark *187*
Cohen, Robert 224, 238
Cohn, Emil 182
Columbus, Christopher 213
Commentary 189
compromise 136–7
Concepción 208
Congress of Vienna 53
conjunction 1, 2, 4, 5, 8, 12, 19, 48, 52, 58, 68, 159, 160, 164, 242
Conklin, William *80*
Connery, Christopher 209
Conservative Revolution 168
copyright 3, 32, 139, 140, 143, 146–8

Coster, Charles de 167
Cotta publisher 174
court trial 10, 14, 17, 35, 102–6, 109, 182–8, 198, 217–44 244
  theatrical representation 226
Crosby, Margaret 115
Curtius, Ernst Robert 173

Daly, Glyn 13–14
Dante 168–9, 227
Das eiserne Kreuz 154
Das Leben der Anderen (film) 43
Das Zigeunerkind oder die Geheimnisse eines Fürstenhauses 154
Däubler, Theodor 131, 175, 193
DDR, see German Democratic Republic
de Boor, Hans 147
death penalty 66, 122, 125
Deggau, Hans-George *119*
Deleuze, Gilles 99, 101
democracy 172–3, 213
  and law 41
  and public sphere 38, 42
  deliberative 34, 131
  Weimar 111–14, 122, 168, 195
Denmark 220
Derrida, Jacques 4, 14, 34, 107, 112, 123, 234, 247
Deuber-Mankowsky, Astrid *115*
Deutsche Juristen-Zeitung 156
Deutsche Verlags-Anstalt 178
Deutsche Volkspartei 154
Deutscher Bund 148
Deutsches Filminstitut 156
Deutschnationaler Handlungsgehilfen-Verband (German National Association of Booksellers' Employees 163, 166–8, 173–4, 176–8, 181, 184–6, 188
Dickens, Charles 17

dictatorship 130, 133, 172, 173, 223
Dictionnaire de l'Académie Française 56
Diederichsen, Uwe 67, 82
Dilcher, Gerhard 49, 61
Dimock, Wai Chee 246
disjunction 1, 3, 12, 17, 19, 21, 47, 48, 67, 75, 125, 242
divorce 46, 73, 75, 80–3
Döblin, Alfred 175
Dolan, Kieran 12
Dostoevsky, Fyodor 4, 160
Dubber, Markus *44*
Durkheim, Émile 121
Dworkin, Ronald *13*
Dyck, Joachim *145*
Dylan, Bob 86, 87

East Germany, *see* German Democratic Republic
Eça de Queiroz 69
Eckermann, Johnn Peter 77
education 76, 159, 160
ehelich/unehelich (married unmarried) 65
Eichmann in Jerusalem 218
Eichmann, Adolf 221
Einstein, Carl 148–9, 159
Eisenstein, Sergei 143
Elem, Theo 99
Emmel, Hildegard 17
empathy 238, 239
Engels, Friedrich 26
England
  as Germany's foe 210
  as sea power 210
  parliamentary system 115
Enzensberger, Hans Magnus 235
Epko von Repko 56, *57*
Erlangen *172*
Ernst August, King of Hannover 53
Ernst, Paul 165, 175

Index   271

European law 10
European Union 214, 244, 248
Ezrahi, Sidra 226

Fabio, Udo di *24*
Fallada, Hans 245
fascism 101, 166, 201, 223, 226
fate 72, 91, 129, 137, 189, 227
  in Benjamin 112–13, 118, 120,
    123–7, 129–30
  in Kant 118
  in Schmitt 199–202
  in the *Wahlverwandtschaften* 66,
    67, 68, 75, 122, 126
Faustbuch 8
Federal Republic of Germany 21,
  35, 138, 141, 160, 161, *170*, 220,
  223, 226
Fehr, Hans 5
Fenves, Peter 117–18
Feuchtwanger, Lion 159, 182
Fichte, Johann 33, 44, *79*
Fidelio 85
Figal, Günter 127
Fish, Stanley 4, *13*, 23, 247
Fontane, Theodor 69
Foucault, Michel 228
France 37, 46, 73, 80, 170, 185
  role in globalization 212
Frankfurt am Main 48, 64
Frankfurt Auschwitz trial 93,
  219–27, 228, 248
  description of 220
  difficulties of 222
Frankfurter Allgemeine Zeitung
  176, 217, 226
Fraser, Andrew 34
Frederick the Great (of Prussia)
  81
French Constitution 115
French Revolution 44, 50, 58, 66,
  74, 75, 80, 84, 85, 130, 200
Freud, Sigmund 4, 134
Freytag, Gustav 167, 245

Soll und Haben 245
Friedländer, Max 6
functionalism 33, 34, 42

Gailus, Andreas 75
Gandhi, Mohandas 170
Gans, Abraham 52
Geertz, Clifford 164
Gellert, Christian
  Moralische Vorlesungen 84
George, Stefan *116*
German constitution 49–51,
  110–15
German Constitutional Court 10
German Democratic Republic 43,
  139, 160, 187, 216, 223–4, 226,
  234
German law
  early 47, 54, 59, 60, 61, 78, 122
  formation of 16, 17
Gessler, Otto 167
Gestapo 91
Gewirtz, Paul 7
Ginschel, Gunhild *47*
globalization 192, 193, 208–13,
  241
Gödel, Kurt *99*
Goethe, August von 66
Goethe, Johann Wolfgang von 2,
  8, 9, 16, 17, 21, 23, 24, 35, 55, 56,
  64–86, 112–37, 159, 172–5, 181,
  214, 243–4
  Amtliche Schriften 65, 86,
    88–90
  and Kant 76, 65
  Faust 65–6
  Gespräche mit Eckermann 77
  Leiden des Jungen Werther, Die
    65, 74
  Die Wahlverwandtschaften
    (novel) 64–85, 112, 117, 118,
    120, 127, 135
    reception of 84
  Wahlverwandtschaften, Die

64–85, 112, 117, 120, 127, 135, 214
Wilhelm Meisters Lehrjahre 44
Xenien 173
Göpfert, Herbert 164, *172*
Göschen press 174
Gostomzyk, Tobias *141*
Gotthelf, Jeremias 167
Göttingen 49, 51, 52–3, 77
Grass, Günter 11
Gray, Jefferson *86*
Great Depression 114
Greenberg, Jack 12
Greenwich line 212
Grimm, Hans 167
Grimm, Jacob 1, 2, 21, 26, 35, 42–66, 90, 121, 123, 127, 189–90, 244–6
  biography 52–3
  Deutsche Rechtsalterthümer 2, 48
  Deutsches Wörterbuch 35, 56, 153, 155
  friendship with Savigny 62
  Hausmärchen 1, 47
  theory of poetic law 54
  'Von der Poesie im Recht' 55, 59
  'Wort des Besitzes' 47–8, 61–2
Grimm, Wilhelm 2, 47, 52–3
Groh, Ruth 202
Gross, Hans 87, 92
Gross, Otto 88
Gross, Raphael *210*
Gründgens, Gustav 141
Grundgesetz (Basic Law) 35
Grundmann, Günter 123
Guantánamo 91
Guattari, Félix 99, 101
Günderrode, Caroline von 53
Gundolf, Friedrich 116, *169*

Habermas, Jürgen 15–16, 21–4, 32–42, 45, 100, 101, 173, 242, 243, 245, 246, 247, 248
  debate with Luhmann 32–4
  Faktizität und Geltung 16, 36, 39, 242
  Strukturwandel der Öffentlichkeit 34–7
habeus corpus 107
habitus 13, 48, 164
Halem, G. A. von 170
Hamburg 145, 167
Hamburg auf den Barrikaden 145
Hamel, Iris 167, 168, 188
Hamlet 90, 192
Hamsun, Knut 167
Hanseaten-Verlag 174
Hanseatische Verlagsanstalt 163, *197*
Hansen, Niels *179*
Hanssen, Beatrice 122
Harder, Hans-Bernd *47*
Haringer, Jakob 182
Harrison, Paul 33
Haupt, Gunther 179
Haverkamp, Anselm 122
Heald, Paul 27–8
Hegel, Georg Friedrich Wilhelm 44, 51, 52, 80, 135
  Grundlinien der Philosophie des Rechts 80
Heilbronn 183
Heine, Heinrich *171*
Heinle, Wolfgang *127*
Herder, Johann Gottfried 44
Hermsdorf, Klaus 90
Hesse-Darmstadt 46
Hessen 53, 219, *226*
Hett, Benjamin 135
Hildebrandt, Dieter 237
Hitler, Adolf 188, 196, 197
Hobbes, Thomas 208
Höcherl, Robert 86
Hochhuth, Rolf 227
Hoebel, E. A. 124
Hoffmann, E. T. A. 2, 5
Hofmann, Gert 6

Index 273

Hofmannsthal, Hugo von 168, 175
Hofstadter, Douglas 86, 96–7, 99, 108
Hölderlin, Friedrich von 53
Holiday, Billie 11
Hollering, Franz 186, 187
Holmes, Oliver Wendell 27, 44
Holocaust 7, 21, 91, 202, 216, 225, 226, 238
Holy Roman Empire 16
Holy Roman Empire *(Heiliges Römisches Reich)* 66
Homer 4, 57
Horkheimer, Max 194
Hornung, Bernd 32
Höss, Rudolf 2*19*, 221
Houben, H. H. *149*
Hugenberg, Alfred 166, 176
Hugo, Gustav 49, 77
Hume, David 158
Hutchinson, Allan 4
Hyperion (novel) 53

IG-Farben 223–4
Inherit the Wind 217
intellectual property 71, 146, 148, 177
International Auschwitz Committee in Vienna 219
intertextuality 13
Italy 77, 168, 169, 170, 179, 185

Jacob, Heinrich 159
Jacobi, Heinrich *44*
Jacobson, Arthur 34, 115
Jaffe, Adrian *100*
Janouch, Gustav 88–9
Jean Paul 56
Jérôme, King of Westphalia 46, 52
Jerusalem 106, 221
Johst, Hanns 180
Joyce, James 169, 170
Jung, Edgar *186*

Jungbuchhändlerrundbriefe 172
Jungenstreiche 154
Jünger, Ernst 132, 167, 192–7, 199, 201, 202, 203, 205, 209, 210
 Auf den Marmorklippen 197
 friendship with Carl Schmitt 195
 jus publicum Europaeum 191, 203, 206, 208, 211, 214
Justinian 49, 50, *57*

Kaduk, Oswald 217
Kafka, Franz 2, 4, 8, 12, 13, 21, 65, 86–109, *130*, 131, 194, 219, 222, 226, 237, 240, 244, 247
 Amtliche Schriften 65, 86, 88, 89, 90
 'Beim Bau der chinesischen Mauer' 89
 'In der Strafkolonie' *87*
 'Jäger Gracchus, Der' 8
 Prozess, Der 21, 86–109, 247
 recursivity in 95
 Schloss, Das 87, 96
 'Urteil, Das' 88
 Verschollene, Der 89, 95
 'Verwandlung, Die' 88
 'Vor dem Gesetz' 91, 98, 104
Kaiser, Georg 11
Kambas, Chryssoula *121*
Kamir, Orit 11–12
Kant, Immanuel 15, 21, 33, 38, 44, 51, 64, 69, 74–5, 113, 155. *See also* neo-Kantianism
 Benjamin on 115–20, 122, 124, 125
 'Beantwortung der Frage Was ist Aufklärung?' 35
 Ding an sich 60
 Ethikvorlesung 118
 Influence on Goethe 76–7
 Kritik der Urteilskraft 30
 on marriage 69, 76–9, 83, 84, 128, 135, 137

Rechtslehre, Die 65, 76, 78, 118, *119*, 133
    Streit der Fakultäten 77
Kanzog, Klaus 140
Kastner, Klaus 6, 18
Kauffmann, Kai *169*
Kaul, Friedrich 223, 234
Keller, Gottfried 167
Kelsen, Hans 15, 19, 77, 94, 95, 133–5
    normative theory of law 95
    Reine Rechtslehre 134
Kern, Fritz *122*, *123*
Kerr, Alfred 177
KGB 91
Kiefner, Hans 53, 77
Kierkegaard, Søren 132
Kilian, Michael 17
Kilpper, Gustav 178–9, 182–3, 186
King, Michael 42
kitsch 154, 156, 196
Kläber, Kurt 151
Kladderadatsch 115
Kleist, Heinrich von 2, 19, 167, 245
    zerbrochene Krug, Der 19, 245
Klickovic, Sava 203, 205, 206
Kluge, Alexander 37, 38
Knothe, Hans-Georg 147
Koch, Hans-Albrecht 6
Koepnick, Lutz 130
Kogel, Jörg-Dieter 5, 11
Koivisto, Julia 37
Kolbenheyer, Guido 165, 167, 175
Königsberg 168
Kord, Susanne 140, 144
Koselleck, Reinhart 50, *81*
KPD (German Communist Party) 157
Kraus Karl 169, *171*
Kraus, Wolfgang 90
Krause, Karl 163, 165, 166, 168, 175, 176, 177, 183, 184, 185

Kuhlmann, Quirinus 11
Kursbuch 235, 236

La Fontaine, Jean de 10
La Roche, Sophie von 73
Lacan, Jacques 98
Ladeur, Karl-Heinz *141*
Lagerlöf, Selma 167
Lahn (river) 62
Landes, Joan 37
Lane, Richard *116*
Langer, Lawrence 226, 238–9
Laternser, Hans 223, 236–7
Law and Literature 4
law of the sea 211
Law, Culture, and the Humanities 4
Lawrence, Jerome 217
Lazarillo de Tormes 8
Lee, Robert 217
legal proverbs 47, 123
Legal Realism 27
Leibrecht, Otto 183, 186
Leipzig 159
Leisching, Peter 119
Lene und Lotte 154
Lenin, Vladimir 170
Lessing, Gotthold 172
Lethen, Helmut 115
Lévi-Strauss, Claude 95
Lindenau, Herbert 156
Linder, Jutta *66*
Lindner, Burkhardt 120
Literarische Welt 166
literary treason 145, 160, 187
Litowitz, Douglas 92
Llewellyn, Karl 26, 124
Lucas, Franz 222, *224*
Lucinde 85
Ludwigsburg 219–20
Luhmann, Niklas 3, 21, 23–43, 75, 96, 100, 102, *121*, 141, 158, 164, 225, 242–3, 245
    and Bourdieu 102–3
    and Kafka 87

debate with Habermas 32–4
influences on 23, *109*, 243
Liebe als Passion 71
on art 8
on law 15–16, 100, 124
on marriage 71–2
on the novel 96
on religion 99
reception in US 34
on recursivity 93–4
Luther, Martin 51
Lyotard, Jean-Francois 35, 37

Machiavelli 200
MacKinnon, Catharine 4
Madrid 204
Mahan, Alfred 211
Mahrholz, Werner 159
Mann, Klaus 141
Mann, Thomas 8, 159, 165, *166*, 169, 176
  Betrachtungen eines Unpolitischen 165
  Doktor Faustus 8
  Lotte in Weimar 8
Marburg 45, 48–9, 52, 62–3
Margolitch, David 11
marriage 7, 46, 65–85, 97, 113, 116–20, 122, 124–7, 130, 134, 135, 137, 187, 214, 244, 245
  in Christian thought 119
  in France 72
  in relation to the state 117
  libertine views of 76, 83
  philosophy of 76
Marriage of Figaro 72
Marschner, Robert *88*
martyr 129, 130, 202, 213
Marx, Karl 2, 23, 26, 34, 158
Marxism 115, 155, 169, 226
  Theory derived from 12, 27, 70, 223, 226
Maturana, Humberto 23, *109*, 243
Matz, Elsa 154

Mayer, Elizabeth *64*
Mayer, Hans 217, 225
McClintock, Scott 91, 93
McCole, John 116
McCormick, John 133, 242, 248
Meeropol, Abel 11
Melchinger, Siegfried 237
Melville, Herman 21, 192, 193, 195–201, 203–7, 208–9, 212, 213, 244
  Benito Cereno 21, 191–210, 213, 241, 244, 247
    basis in fact 208
    Kesting's reading of 206–7
    Schmitt's reading of, *see* Schmitt, Carl
    Tierno Galván's reading of 203–5, 213
    compared with Poe 199–200
  Moby-Dick 196, 209
  view of Spain and Europe 201
Mephisto 141
Merton, Robert 121
Meusch, Mattias 221
Michel, Karl 235
Michelet, Jules 209
mimesis 3, 9, 19, 55, 217, 229, 240, 245, 247
Minnesänger 56
Mitchell, Robert 20
Mitteis, Heinrich 147–8
Modernism 92
Moenkemeyer, Heinz 172
Mohler, Arnim 193, *200, 201, 206*
Mölk, Ulrich 6
monarchy 122
Moretti, Franco 23
Mörike, Eduard 167
Moritz Graf von Sachsen 76
mourning-play. *See Trauerspiel*
Mozart, Wolfgang 85
Mulka, Robert *219*
Müller, Jan-Werner 121
Müller-Dietz, Heinz 6

Müller-Langen (publisher) 163, 166, 170, 185, 186
Müller-Sievers, Helmut 72
Münchener Neueste Nachrichten 180
Münchner Post 183, 185
Muncker, Franz 169
Munich 159, 163, 165, 166, 167, *169*, 172, 173, 175, 176, 177, 183, 185, 190
municipal law 205, 208, 211, 212, 214
Musenalmanach 173
Musil, Robert
   Mann ohne Eigenschaften, Der 20
myth 74, 111, 194, 197
   Benjamin on 116, 119–21, 123, 125–7
   and law 21, 112–13
   of Europe 202
   Schmitt on 131–3, 202, 203, 205, 213–15
   Siegfried 111
   structural study of 95

Nadler, Josef *169*
Nägele, Rainer 37–9
Napoleon Bonaparte 46, 47, 50, 66, 70, 130
Napoleonic Code 46, 50, 66, 70
National Socialism 114, 131, 135, 139, 159–60, 167–9, 175, 177, 180, 195, 196, *197*, 201, 202, 203, 203, 205, 216, 220, 222–4, 226, 228, 232, 237–8, 244–5
nation-state 132, 191, 244
NATO 244
natural law 13, 41, 45, 54–6, 63, 77, 93, 119, 122, 194, 205
Naturalism 171
Naumann, Bernd 217, 230, 237
Neaman, Elliot *196*
Negt, Oskar 38

neo-Kantianism 77, 115, 120, 122, 131, 133, 135
Neue Deutsche Beiträge 116
Neue Juristische Wochenschrift 86
Neue Rundschau 87
New Objectivity 170
Nibelungenlied (epic poem) 57, 147
Nick Carter 153–4
Nietzsche, Friedrich 8, 46, 135
Niobe, myth of 123–6
Nixon, Nicola *206*
nomos (custom, law) 121, 191, 209, 212
normative law 94, 134–5
Nörr, Dieter 44
Nuremberg 131, *179*
Nuremberg Trials 220, 221–4, 236
Nussberger, Angelika 10

Oborniker, Alfred 145
Odyssey 57, 196
Öffentlichkeit 17, 22–3, 32, 34–40, 42–3, 45, 48, 84, 173, 187, 242, 245–6. See also Habermas, Jürgen
   and court trials 221
   vs. structural coupling 35
ordinary language 36, 37, 39, 45
Ortega y Gassett, José 161, 200
   Rebelión de las masas, La 203
Osterkamp, Ernst *169*
Ovid 123

Palatinate 46
Palm, Johann 172
Pan, David 119, 131
Paris 45, 52, 58, 169
Parsons, Talcott 243
Parzifal 155
Pausch 65
Pawel, Ernst 88
Pencak, William 5
Pendas, David *220*, 222, 227
Pérez Galdós, Benito 69
Perthes press 174

Peters, H. F. 196
Peters, Julie 6
Petersen, Klaus 139, 140, *143*, 144, 154, 156, 157
Petrarch 8
Petzet, Wolfgang *188*
Pezold, Gustav 163, 165, 174, 182–6
Phelan, Anthony *171*
photography 129
Pierce, Charles 28
piracy 198, 206, 208, 210
Plato 30, 128, 246
Plaut v. Spendthrift Farm Inc. (court case) 12
Pocci, Franz *175*
Poe, Edgar Allen 193–200
  'A Descent Into the Maelström' 195, 198
  Narrative of Arthur Gordon Pym 195
  'Pit and the Pendulum' 198
Poland *219*
Polenz, Wilhelm von 167
Politzer, Heinz 106, 109, 189
Polybius 200
Portugal 131
Poscher, Rolf 111
positive law 41, 50, 118, 122, *123*, 124–5
positivism 15, 17, 133, 194
  vs. antipositivism 135
Posner, Richard 4, 66, *86*, 93
postmodernism 22
poststructuralism 7, [15] ?
Prague 87, 88, 103
precedent 2, 4, 12–13, 19, 42, 90, 96, 107, 116, 119, 123, 145, *172*, 192, 242, 244–6
  and system 30–1, 94, 107
  historical whole as 48, 58, 115
  in law 7–10, 16, 18, 54, 78, 109, 138, 194, 198, 221
  Luhmann on 8

Preuss, Hugo 115, 136, 187
Pringsheim, Katja 165–6
Privatruhe (domestic peace) 84
Proust, Marcel 169, 170
Prüfstelle (examining board) 154, 156, 159, 160
Prussia 18, 45, 46, 49, 50–1, 53, 56, 65, 70, 76, 141, 148, 175, 188, 196
public sphere. See *Öffentlichkeit*

Quaritsch, Helmut *131*

Raabe, Wilhelm 167
Rabel, Gabriele 77
radio 129, 160, 224, 239, 244, 245
Rang, Florens 128
Rasch, William 27, 28, 41, 134, 214
Rashomon (film) 11, 13, 30
Rathenau, Ernst 146–7
Recht/Unrecht (legal/illegal) 24–5, 39, 65, 69, 82, 83, 91, 95, 163, 177, 217–18, 222, 227, 230, 240–1
Rechtsstaat (rule of law) 92, 100–1
recursivity 93
  narrative 94, 95
Rehfisch, Hans 159, 160, 245
Reichsgericht 145
Reichskammergericht 16, 65
Reijen, Willem van 128–9
Reinhardt, Stephen 11
Reinhold, Karl Leonhard 77
Reissner, Larissa 145, 151
religion 1, 15, 26, 40, 45, 72, 83, 85, 99, 106, 111, 115, 157, 238
  and bureaucracy 98
  and conflict 208
  pagan 112
Remarque, Erich 182
repetition 59, 124, 230, 234, 239–40
Reschke, Nils 80
Reynolds, Thomas 154
Rhein (river) 60
Rheinland-Pfalz 221

Rhenan Prussia 46
Richards, Donald 175
Richter, Werner 147, 163, 166, 177–8, 184–8, 228
Ridder, Helmut 138, 142
Rieder, Bernd 150
Riegl, Alois 113
Rights of Man 56
Rivarol, Antoine de 200
Roberts, Patricia 37
Robertson, Richie 104, 106
Roman. *See* novel
Roman law 16–17, 45–6, 48–9, 52, 54–5, 57, 65, 79, 133
Roman society 200
Romanticism 20, 42, 79, 80, 111, 116, 209, 247
Rosenfeld, Alvin 226
Rousseau, Jean-Jacques 4
  Julie 73
Rowohlt press 174
Rüdesheim, Hans 150
Rüter, Christoph 240
Ryle, Gilbert *164*

Sachsenspiegel (compilation of laws) 16, 56, *57*
Safranski, Rüdiger 132
Salamanca 204
Salloch, Erika 226
Salzwedel 76, 84, 85
Sasse, Günter 229
Savigny, Carl Friedrich von 1, 16, 21, 44–63, 80
  Das Recht des Besitzes 49
  Vom Beruf unseres Zeitalters 55
  Vom Beruf unsrer Zeit für Gesetzgebung und Rechtswissenschaft 53
Saxony 16, 51
Schäfer, Wilhelm 167, 175
  Thirteen Books of the German Soul 175

Schälicke (publisher) 151
Scheffel, Viktor von 167
Schelling, Friedrich 33
Scherer, Wilhelm 171
Schierloh, Nicolaus 184
Schiller, Friedrich 2, *44*, 65, 77, 138–9, 141, 147, 154, 155, *166*, 172, 173
  Don Carlos 154
  Maria Stuart 154
  Räuber, Die 139, 147
  Xenien 173
Schlaf, Johannes 175
Schlegel, Friedrich *44*, 85
Schlick, Werner 74
schlimme Botschaft, Die 148
Schlink, Bernhard 2, 115, 245
Schlöndorff, Volker 239
Schmidhäuser, Eberhard 92
Schmidt, Siegfried 11, 19, 20, 50
Schmidt-Wiegand, Ruth 47
Schmitt, Carl 21, 107, 111, 113–14, 119, 120–1, 130–7, 191–215, 241, 244, 245, 247, 248. *See also* myth
  anti-Semitism of 210
  Begriff des Politischen 196
  Buribunken 131
  Die Diktatur 130, 133
  early years 130
  Hamlet interpretation 192
  Land und Meer 209, 210, 211
  Leviathan 201
  on globalization 211
  Politische Theologie 113, 130, 132, 133, 192, 194
  reading of *Benito Cereno* 194, 204
  Theorie des Partisanen 206
Schneider, Peter 5, 133
Schoeps, Hans-Joachim 90
Scholem, Gershom 115
Schönlank, Bruno 159–60
Schröder, Rudolf 168
Schudson, Michael 37

Schultze, Ernst 153, 159
Schumann, Karl 154–5
Schund (pulp fiction) 2, 138, 139, 141, 144, 147, 149–61, 166, 244
  1926 law against 153
  definition 153
Schwab, George 133
Schwanitz, Dieter 20, 28
Schwanitz, Dietrich 20
Schwartz, Peter 65, 66, 70, *71*
Schwarz, Gotthart 177
Schwindel. Gefühle 8
Sebald, W. G. 8
Seeger, Ernst 156
Seligsohn, Rita *127*
Sereni, Angelo *9*
Siegfried (myth) 111
Silesia 70
Simmel, Georg *77*
Sinn 29, 33, 47, 54, 69, 104
situation 194–201
Slaughter, Joseph 4–5
slavery 78, 206, 207, 210, 213
Sonnleithner, Joseph 85
Sorel, Georges 120–1
sovereignty 70, 119, 120, 130, 132, 133, 134, 137, 244
  in Schmitt 191–3, 195, 203, 205, 208, 211–12, 214, 220
Spain 131
  role in globalization 213
SPD (German Socialist Party) 167
speech acts 14, 93, *235*
  performatives 14, 234
Speidel, Ludwig 171
Spengler, Oswald 161
Spielberg, Steven 207
Springman, Luke 161
Stapel, Wilhelm 165, 167, 168
state of exception 13, 91, 98, 230, 244
  feudal 66, 70
  in Agamben 107
  in Benjamin 119–22, 128–33

  in Schmitt 113–14, 121, 192, 194
  United States v. Amistad 209
Stellvertreter, Der 227
Sternberg, Theodor 150–1
Sternheim, Carl 176, 182
stimmig / nicht stimmig (pleasing/ unpleasing) *25*, 30
Stolleis, Michael 100–1
Storim, Mirjam 144–5, 151
Story, Joseph 209
'Strange Fruit' (song) 11, 13, 30
Strasbourg (Strassburg) 64, 130
Strauss, Emil 175–6
Strindberg, August 167
Strippel, Jutta *47*
structural coupling 5, *11*, 13, 31–2, 41, 42, 48, *66*, 69, 71, 75, 93, 112, 139, 145, 149, *157*, 164, 212, 214, 217, 228, 234, 236, 237, 241, 242, 245–8
  diagram of 16
  of law and literature 2–3, 9, 16–19
  Oeffentlichkeit as 35, 36
Sundquist, Eric 207
Sussman, Henry 102, 105, 106
Süssmuth, Rita 239
Switzerland 53, 114
system 1, 2
  Ausdifferenzierung 8, 12, 21, 25, 26, 31, 40, 45, 61, 74, 124, 193, 214, 247
  autonomy of 7–8, 13, 22, 23, 26, 27, 28, 29, 30, 31, 32, 34, 41, 72, 77, 131–2, 141, 158, 194, 214, 237, 242, 247, 248
  autopoiesis of 9, 10, 13–14, 19, 20, 23, 27–32, 40, 45, 49, 61, 72, 87, 96, 108, 141, 142, 143, 194, 237, 242, 243, 247
  biological 12, 23, 29, *109*
  canonizing. *See* canonization
  communication in 9, 10, 11, 13,

15, 22–32, 34, 37, 39, 45, 47, 75, 99, 119, *147*, *189*, 230, 246
  distinction 3, 8, 9, 14, 20, 24, 25, 26, 28, 30, 31, 39, 41, 56, 62, 63, 65, 68, 69, 75, 94, 95, 96, 113, 122, 124, 139, 140, 141, 155, 157, 158, 217, 218, 222, 227, 234, 240, 241, 244
  economy 30, 32
  environment and 2, 3, 8, 25, 26, 29, 30, 31, 37, 69, *100*, 121, 158
  examples of 3
  observation 8, 10, 19, 25, 26, 28, 30, 34, 69, 77, 82, 87, 96, 100, 102, 124, 139, 140, 147, 182, 196, 217, 218, 225, 227, 235–41, 243, 247
    second-order 217, 225
  psychic 3, 25, 26, 28, 31, 134, 170, 188
  self-reflexivity of 29, 121
  vs. field 22
  vs. subsystem 3
  system theory 2, 4, 8–10, 12, 13, 15, 19–23, 25, 27, 28, 31, 32, 33, 36–7, 40, 45, 65, 67, 87, 94, 102, 121, 158, 193–4, 214, 228, 242–3, 247–8
    reactions to 21, 32–4

Tacitus 167, 200–1
Tanner, Tony 67–8
Tantillo, Astrida 74
Terrorism 205
testimonio 43, 241
Teubner, Gunther 15, 23, 30
The Last of the Mohicans 154
The New Robinson Crusoe 154
The Thousand and One Nights 97
thick description 13, 164, 188
Thoma, Ludwig 176
Thornhill, Chris 42
Thucydides 200

Tierno Galván, Enrique 203–5, 213
Till Eulenspiegel 167
Tillich, Paul 132
Tocqueville, Alexis de 200
Toews, John 47, 53
Tolstoy, Leo 69
Tönnies, Ferdinand 2
Tordesillas line 212
translation 28
Trauerspiel 114, 128–30, 132, *210*
Treaty of Westphalia 191
tyrant 128, 129, 130, 137, 197, 202

Uexküll, Jakob von *109*
Ufeld, Ulrich 195
United Nations 211, 213, 244
United States 4, 192, 193, 207, 213, 214
  role in globalization 211
Unruh, Fritz von 110–11, 115

Valiverronen, Esa 37
Vergangenheitsbewältigung 227
Verne, Jules 151
Versailles 111–12
Vesting, Thomas 214
Vico, Giambattista 2
Vienna 53–171, 175, 219
Villiers de l'Isle Adam, Auguste 197
violence 61, 98, 102, 107, 111, 115, 116, 119–27, 132, 133, 134, 136, 189, 190, 194, 198, 205
  divine 111, 119, 123, 126, 127, 133
Vitofranceschi 79
Volksgeist 42, 44, 45, 111, 115, 122, 189
Volksgeist (spirit of the people) 5, 44, 46, 48, 53, 58, 135, 152
Vonessen, Hedwig 46, 47
Vorländer, Karl 77
Voss, Johann 57

Vossische Zeitung 152, 160, 181
Vulpius, Christiane 66, 70

Wachler, Dietrich 99
Wacquant, Loic 22
Wagner, Bruno 90
Wallace, Edgar 170
Walzel, Oskar 74–5
Wanda von Brannburg 145, 153
Weber, Max 2, 3, 23, 87, 91–2, 99, 131, 142, 242, 248
Weber, Samuel *130*
Wedekind, Frank 167, 175, 176
Weigl, Sigrid *130*
Weiler, Christel 240
Weimar (city) 64
Weimar Republic 3, 5, 64–6, 70, 110–25, 133, 135–7, 138, 140, 142, 143, 144, 145, 146, 148–51, 155, 159–61, 162, 164, 165, *167*, 168–70, 172, 173, 175, 186, 187, 189, 195, 203, 244, 245
  Constitution 110, 112–14, 187
    Article 118, 149
    Article 218, 170
  democracy in, *see* democracy, Weimar
Weisberg, Robert 5, 6
Weiss, Christoph 226, 236–7
Weiss, Peter 2, 9, 14, 21, 93, 216–45
  Ermittlung, Die 2, 21, 216, 218, 226, 231, 234–5, 238, 247
    adaptation of 239
    reception of 227, 235
    influences on 226
    Marat/Sade 226–7
Wellmann, Franz 181

Weltfremdheit (alienation) 154–6
West, Robin 93
Wetzlar 16, 65
White, James Boyd 28, 40
Whitman, James 17
Widmann, Josef 171
Williams, Raymond *31*
Winnig, August 168
Witteveen, Willem 30
Wittman, Rebecca 227–8
Wohlhäupter, Eugen 5
Wolfenstein, Alfred 182
Wolff, Friedrich 182
Wolff, Theodor 177
Wolin, Richard *112*
World War I 101, 114, 127, 131, 153, 160, *181*, 195
World War II 21, 114, 192, 193, 210, 211
Württemberg 139

Yale Journal of Law and the Humanities 6
Young, James 226

Zauberflöte, Die 85
Zeitschrift für geschichtliche Rechtswissenschaft 49, 55, 58
Zeitstück 151–2
Zensur 138–42, 144, 149–50, 154
Zentrale Stelle für die Landesjustizverwaltungen 219–20
Ziegler, Vickie 5
Zimmer, Dieter 216–17
Ziolkowski, Theodore 5, 13, 17, 21, 92, 93
Žižek, Slavoj 22, 98, 99, 101
Zuckmayer, Carl 182
Zweig, Arnold 159, 160

www.ingramcontent.com/pod-product-compliance
Lightning Source LLC
Chambersburg PA
CBHW050323020526
44117CB00031B/1651